Racket Sports Collectibles

Robert T. Everitt

Schiffer Publishing Ltd

4880 Lower Valley Road, Atglen, PA 19310 USA

Dedication

To Mom and Dad

Library of Congress Cataloging-in-Publication Data

Everitt, Robert T., 1956-
Racket sports collectibles/by Robert T. Everitt.
p. cm.
ISBN 0-7643-1647-8
1. Racket games—Collectibles. I. Title.
GV990.3.E94 2002
796.34—dc21
2002009768

Designed by John P. Cheek
Cover design by Bruce M. Waters
Type set in University Roman Bd BT/Aldine 721 BT

ISBN: 0-7643-1647-8
Printed in China
1 2 3 4

Published by Schiffer Publishing Ltd.
4880 Lower Valley Road
Atglen, PA 19310
Phone: (610) 593-1777; Fax: (610) 593-2002
E-mail: Schifferbk@aol.com
Please visit our web site catalog at
www.schifferbooks.com
We are always looking for people to write books on new and related subjects. If you have an idea for a book please contact us at the above address.

This book may be purchased from the publisher.
Include $3.95 for shipping.
Please try your bookstore first.
You may write for a free catalog.

In Europe, Schiffer books are distributed by
Bushwood Books
6 Marksbury Ave.
Kew Gardens
Surrey TW9 4JF England
Phone: 44 (0) 20 8392-8585; Fax: 44 (0) 20 8392-9876
E-mail: Bushwd@aol.com
Free postage in the U.K., Europe; air mail at cost.

Contents

Acknowledgments

It has been a very challenging task to organise the writing and collation of this book. All the rackets, prints, trophies, and other items have been selected, packed, carried, and delivered to other rooms, studios and clubs, and then transported back again. They've been measured, weighed, assessed, counted, photographed, described, identified, positioned, and coded.

Needless to say, I would have never completed all this on my own, and have very special friends and family members who have given their time, judgement, patience, and guidance, especially when I was discouraged or tired. An extra special mention must go to my Mother and Father (Joan and Tom Everitt). They have helped me in every conceivable respect. They have been through everything from travelling around the country with me to discovering rare items at antique fairs. They have carried, fetched, listened, and sympathised, and have supplied innumerable cups of tea and meals during the endless hours when I have been busy at the computer. (We have worn away our shoes and carpets!)

Thanks to Graham Jebb and Janet Ward for spurring me on and showing so much interest; Judy and Graham Marsh for proof reading, commenting, and keeping me encouraged whenever I met them; Cheers to Andrew Inskip for donating some of the items featured; William Andrews, Hayley Bennett, Cees de Bondt, Brendan Casey, Alan Chalmers, Bob Fuller, Heiner Gillmeister, Margaret Gilmour, Gerald Gurney, Mary Herian, Leslie Hinson (former Bussey employee), Chuck Hoey, Guy Litherland, Bill Marshall, Mike Price, John Mullock, Frank Phelps, Ellen & Geoff Roberts, Peter Schiffer, Manfred Schotten, Peter Sneddon, William Stephens of The Queen's Club, Fiona Taylor, and the Committee of Bilston Lawn Tennis Club for allowing me to photograph items on their courts.

My appreciation goes to David Peters and his staff at the 'Photographic Studio' in Wolverhampton, and especially ace photographer - Sallie Magnante, Bilston Public Library, Wolverhampton Public Library, Birmingham Public Library, The Kenneth Ritchie Wimbledon Library, and to any other people I have forgotten, who know they have helped in some way, to them my heartfelt thanks and apologies.

A big hello to all my friends at Bilston Lawn Tennis Club, who have never given the merest hint of boredom or even apathy, and have always been supportive — even when I had dwelt on the latest trauma or success. (I'm sure they thought I would never finish.)

Many thanks to Bob Holland (Secretary of Edgbaston Archery Lawn Tennis Club) who gave me permission to photograph many of the items in this book at the Archery club courts, wonderfully prepared by Bob Cooper (Groundsman).

Finally I would like to express my sincerest gratitude to Barry and Dianne Ordish, who have very kindly donated many significant items from their extensive and outstanding collection. They have stood by me throughout this book's preparation. It would be much diminished without their generous help, valuable input, and sincere friendship.

Introduction

The games and sports that we play are numerous and varied, but if we wrote a list of the sports which we think are truly international, it wouldn't be a very long one. Very few sports have captured the imagination of the world's population. It is said that the most popular sport in England is fishing. (The true enthusiast could rightly claim that it is an art form). It is enjoyed by millions all over the world; it's also an activity that has gone on for thousands of years and it has recently seen a 'collecting boom'. I have no valuable knowledge to pass on to the collector of fishing memorabilia, but it's obvious that the amount of equipment that has been devised over the years for the dedicated fisherman is considerable. Rods, reels, split reed creels, lures, floats, flies, and books about how to use them all are numerous. The names of Hardy's of Alnwick, Farlow of London, and Samuel Allcock have been passed down into fishing folklore. An added bonus to collectors is that craftsmen have created most of the items.

Television and the internet have become very pervasive forms of communication all over the world. Coverage of major sporting events is 'big business'. Essentially, fishing is a solitary sport, not a spectator one; this can't be said of Association Football or 'Soccer' as it's otherwise known. For many years football has been unable to establish a strong and lasting foothold in the United States; it has been constantly challenged by the massive interest in the traditional sports of baseball, basketball, and American Football. On the other hand, the American game has always failed to equal the international appeal of Association Football; even the English game has seen the World Cup hosted in the United States. Nevertheless, collectibles associated with all four are frantically sought after and contested for at auctions, where even the catalogues are now considered as worthy collectibles.

The Essential Criteria

It appears that the most popular sporting collectible has certain criteria to meet. For example it must have an undeniable heritage; thousands of people must play it; it should have lots of media coverage and promotion; and the limited availability of associated memorabilia. Golf, for instance, is huge, in every respect. It has a long and fascinating history, which can be traced back hundreds of years to at least the fifteenth century. Rules and equipment have changed steadily over that time, and millions of people have come to know, love, and participate in it. Tournaments from around the world can be watched on satellite television twenty-four hours a day and it has been written about and supplied with equipment by manufacturers and writers for hundreds of years. The game of lawn tennis meets all these criteria too; present day players are 'superstars' and a huge international following automatically encourages some interest in the history of the game.

The Subject of This Book

This book contains many examples from the huge range of racket sport collectibles that can be found, including those which vary between the sublime and the ridiculous. Mainly it concerns itself with lawn tennis collectibles, their history, and how some of them have found their place in the history of the game. When I was about seventeen years old I started to play tennis with my father at nearby park, and I was encouraged to join my local club. I became a coach, and then, intrigued by the history of a game I loved so much, I became a collector. While I was searching for interesting items to extend my collection, it became obvious that my game did not come into being totally of its own accord. There has always been evidence that all kinds of 'bat and ball' games had an influence upon its development. Consequently, I never did find a convincing reason why I should collect items associated with only one game, and this is why this book contains items that are associated with so many different ones.

A cursory glance at a list of racket sports shows how difficult it is to untangle the filigree of historical associations between them all. There has been Real Tennis (Court Tennis in the USA, Royal Tennis in Australia) Fives, Bat Fives, (The game of) Racquets, Battledore and Shuttlecock, Field Tennis, Badminton, Pallone, Table Tennis, Table Badminton, Padder Tennis, Squash, Trapball, Hurling, and Club Ball, to name just a few.

The subject of this book can be defined more accurately; it limits itself to those games in which a racket (strung) or bat (without strings) is used to hit a projectile (usually a ball or a shuttlecock) over a net or a mark, into a court. Battledore and shuttlecock is so closely related to badminton, I will regard them as one.

Lawn tennis was my first love and, because the modern game is only just over 125 years old, with a fairly neatly recorded playing history, I felt that the whole of its past lay before me (or behind me!) waiting to be discovered.

Another reason for my passion is that although the playing history of the game is fairly well documented, the history of people who made their fortunes providing equipment is certainly not. This fact alone can give a discerning collector a demanding and sometimes a very rewarding challenge. It's quite understandable then, that on the whole, racket sports collectors have researched the history of lawn tennis manufacturers, their employees and equipment. Primarily, this is a reference book for collectors and dealers. The majority of the items are from England, but there are many pieces from other countries and I'm sure the emphasis would be different if I had lived in any other country. Luckily, lawn tennis passed its formative years here, although its popularity meant that the history of the game in all other countries is very closely related. If you have an item needing further investigation, identification, or confirmation, then I hope you will find this book useful. I have described items as accurately as I can, and where I don't know, I have made an educated guess. I do not claim that all my comments or opinions are watertight, and would welcome any suggestions, should the publication run to a second edition. The notes and comments often relate to any information that I have discovered regarding an item's past or related history. The prices are simply a guide as to how I think an item might sell at auction, if it's in prime condition, two or more people require it, and the wind is in the right direction! At the very least they can give you some idea of how items can be compared to each other.

Some Useful Advice

When I first started collecting, about twenty years ago, prices for lawn tennis collectibles were quite low. I remember visiting Newark antiques fair, in Nottinghamshire, England, and I came home with about a dozen good quality early tennis rackets. Not one of them cost more than £25 ($37.50) and a good testament to their quality is the fact that I still have most of them. In those days, rackets commonly known as 'fishtails' were quite easily found, and those which cost around £8-10 ($12-15) are now realising £150 ($225) or more at auctions. To be honest, when I visit antiques fairs I expect to see or find very little, but there's always a chance of meeting someone who has that 'special' item either packed away at the back of the stall, or at home. If a dealer shows any indication that there's a possibility he or she may have 'something somewhere' then follow up on this contact. In fact, leaving a list of your collecting interests with someone is quite a successful way of finding items; every now and then a telephone call comes with news of an item 'you might be interested in'. Before you realise it, you have brought together half a dozen collectibles, and you have become a racket sports collector.

The First Collector

It's probably impossible to find out who the first racket sports collector was. He or she gathered together informed selections and in doing so decided that together they had a value. They may not necessarily have had a monetary value, but it could have been that they were a very good cross-section, so they were valuable in their uniqueness. It could have been that the collector valued these items for their aesthetic appeal. Let's imagine that a particularly successful player formed the very first collection. His possessions had a personal value, when they were passed on to relatives they had a nostalgic value too, and finally when these items fall into the hands of 'the trade' they have a monetary value to the trader and a historic one to the collector.

How then did all these racket games begin? The evidence is that all of them began as a pastime, a simple form of entertainment, until someone decided to formulate some basic rules.

At this point I think it would be useful to relate some basic history of the sports and games featured in this book, as well as informing the reader of some of the items which it might be possible to find associated with this history. If you are new to 'racket sports collectibles', and are totally unaware of the heritage behind them, this will be of benefit to you.

An Historical Background

Real Tennis

Otherwise known as 'Court Tennis' in America and 'Royal Tennis' in Australasia, the game was simply known as 'Tennis' until 1874 when it became necessary to distinguish it from 'Lawn Tennis'. Diligent research has discovered that the game was identified by the word 'Tennis' in England as early as 1396, in Italy between 1367 and 1370, and the United States about 1640. France can hold a justifiable claim to have entertained the game earlier than this; however, we would then have to consider more than the word 'tennis', but also include the analysis of origins and linguistics. The game is now played on an indoor court approximately ninety-six feet long by thirty-two feet wide, the players employing such obstacles as the 'penthouse', 'grill', 'tambour', and a net in the centre of the court. From the very beginning, the size of a court has not always been arbitrary.

The prime difference between playing Real Tennis and its younger cousin, Lawn Tennis, is that the boundaries formed by the walls and other obstacles of an indoor court can be employed by the player to his or her advantage, by playing the ball off them. In lawn tennis, there are no targets other than the area of the court that one's opponent defends. Lawn tennis can be played indoors too, but the target remains the same as it does on an outside court.

Real Tennis rackets of the late nineteenth century are still sometimes indistinguishable from lawn tennis models, because they resemble each other so closely. They will both have a sturdy wooden frame, are asymmetrical, and have thick square handles, sometimes covered in a continual band of calfskin. The names attributed to them can sometimes give a guide to their purpose.

Barcellon and Brouaye 'Real Tennis' rackets have been known to turn up at auction houses, but usually command premium reserve prices. A note of caution is that Brouaye also provided lawn tennis rackets for early suppliers of boxed lawn tennis sets. Facilities for the game are now few and far between; insufficient courts are available in a small number of countries, although there has been a resurgence of interest in the last few years.

Table Tennis

There has been much conjecture on the subject of how and where the game began. It is very likely that it developed as a necessary indoor alternative to the outdoor game of lawn tennis in the late nineteenth century, when rain made play impossible. 'Lawn tennis on a dining-room table' had become very popular by 1900, one might even say that it had become a 'craze'. Over a dozen books had been written about it, and various boxed sets were soon available. The introduction of celluloid balls (c.1900) meant that valuable household items were no longer in danger of being destroyed by the use of India-rubber balls, or some other impromptu substitute. Very recently I found a hand written poem on a small piece of writing paper, which was tucked inside a copy of *Ping-Pong, The Game and How to Play It* (1902) by Arnold Parker. The piece is entitled: 'A Ping Pong Song' and is attributed to R. H. Titherington, who wrote for *Argosy Magazine* during this period. Two of the verses relate how the game was regarded:

> Ping out the old, pong in the new, - Ping, merry balls, across the table; Shatter as much as you are able, of china, glass, and ormulu. Ping in the craziest fad of all; And while the eggshell spheroid flies, Set tumult, dust, and shouting rise, In every household's dining hall!

Despite a sudden down turn in popularity, various amendments to the rules, and a new enthusiasm which has endured since the 1930s, table tennis has become a truly International Sport.

Badminton, Battledore, and Shuttlecock

In Joseph Strutt's, *The Sports and Pastimes of the People of England* (1801), a sub-heading entitled 'Shuttlecock' shows an early engraving of two boys hitting a shuttlecock up in the air with hard wooden bats. Described as a 'boyish sport of long standing' the game certainly wasn't reserved for younger people. Later, the book refers to some early evidence: 'It appears to have been a fashionable pastime among grown persons in the reign of James I.' In the *Two Maids of Moreclacke*, a comedy printed in 1609, it is said, 'to play at shuttlecock methinks is the game now.' The invention of such a game would certainly not have required much imagination; two pieces of flat wood and a piece of cork with feathers forced into it would have been quite sufficient. There are certainly quite a few illustrations and paintings showing battledores and shuttlecocks from throughout the eighteenth and nineteenth centuries. More importantly, there have been several battledores sold at auction recently which have recorded on them the number of 'hits' attributed to a player or a team pair. By 1872 players were hitting over a net and into a garden court, rather than just keeping the shuttlecock up in the air. The first rules were drawn up in India one year later and when the weather began to play more of a part in games than the players, it was brought indoors. Several more alterations to rules took place and in 1899 London had held the first 'All-England' Championships. By 1901 the game had its own set of rules, a rectangular court, and a governing association.

Racquets

The game is played against a wall and not over a net, but certainly has its own qualities, skills, and nuances. It takes place in an enclosed walled court, which is about sixty feet long by thirty feet wide. Its origins are much speculated about but there is ample evidence in writings to show that in England the game was very popular at many small town inns and areas of recreation in the late eighteenth century. The game was very popular at the debtors' prisons too, and a painting by Thomas Rowlandson in 1807 shows such a game in progress at the Fleet Prison. Later in the nineteenth century, public schools and gentlemen's clubs had adopted it. The officers of military garrisons had spread the game around the world, and at one time India had as many as seventy outdoor courts. The game continues to be played at schools and a few select establishments, but is not widely known.

Squash Rackets

Squash Rackets is an enclosed four wall court game, very similar to its older cousin Racquets, but on a much smaller court. It is believed to have originated at Harrow Public School where, awaiting their time to play racquets, boys played with a small soft ball in a more confined area called the 'corner'. By 1900 owners were building 'Squash Courts' at country homes, university colleges, and gentlemen's clubs. The Squash Rackets court (which is thirty-two feet by twenty-one feet) is said to have been based upon the small court area at Rugby School where boys also used to play the game of Fives, (a glove and ball game). The game is enjoyed in courts all over the world.

Lawn Tennis

It wasn't until the early 1880s that the game really 'found its feet' after being treated with scorn and regarded merely as a 'pastime'. Quite a few people had posted their claim as 'inventors' when Major Walter Clopton Wingfield became the first to commercialise a boxed set in 1874 (with its unusual name of Sphairistike) but they were all too late. His original court was sixty feet long, twenty-one feet wide at the net, and thirty feet wide at the baselines. The service was delivered into the court from a diamond shape marked on the ground; this was on one side of the court only.

Wingfield's ideas may not have endured in any major respect (many alterations to his original rules quickly followed) but they paved the way for a much more popular outdoor game, which could be played by both sexes. In 1877 the first Wimbledon Lawn Tennis Championships were played on a rectangular court measuring seventy-eight feet by twenty-seven feet, and the game was being well received in many countries of the world.

Chapter 1.

Books, Trade Catalogues, Programmes, Newspapers, and Magazines

Some of the very earliest references to racket sport games can be found in ancient books. At first they were literal in form, then as hand drawn observations or hand cut wood block illustrations, and later, steel engravings. Sports historians continue to speculate upon ancient writings, objects, and carvings, which might prove to be very early evidence of a nation's pastimes. It wasn't until these records could be printed in large numbers on a truly transportable medium that the collector had any real chance of acquiring an item of early racket sports history. Fine historically based books have been published which list many of the literary records of past centuries. If you would like to read about the history of racket sports, I recommend any of the following books: Heiner Gillmeister's *Tennis A Cultural History*, Malcolm D. Whitman's *Tennis Origins and Mysteries*, Gianni Clerici's *Tennis*, L. St. J. Butler and P. J. Wordie's *The Royal Game* (which has a chapter with specific regard to *The Books of Hours*) and Robert Henderson's *Ball Bat and Bishop*. You will find a more extensive reference to them in the pages of this book.

Classic Books

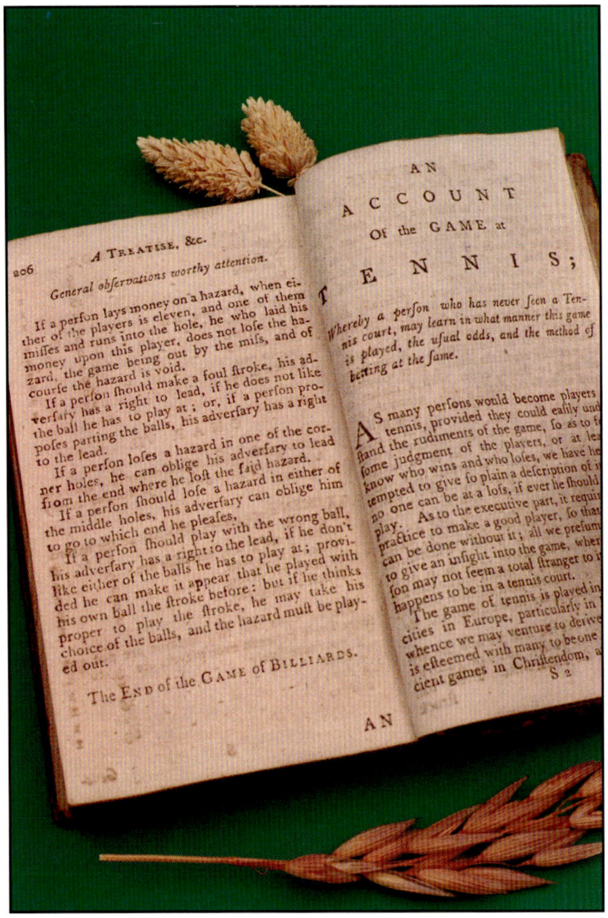

Fig. 1.1. ***Hoyle's Games***[1]
Hoyle's Games Improved - Edmond Hoyle, by James Beaufort Esq.,London, Printed for Osborne and Griffin; and H. Mozley, Gainsborough 1788, 216pp., 142 x 86mm., hard (calf covered) covers. On page 207 there's chapter of ten pages, dedicated to the game of (Royal) Tennis. £150-200 ($225-300)

The condition of a book means everything to the discerning collector and belies the saying that 'you should never judge a book by its cover'. The condition of those covers and all the pages inside them can make all the difference between an acquisition and a liability. You see, some publications, usually recent ones, are printed in such large quantities that the possibility of finding a sound, untarnished copy with a perfect dust jacket are quite high. Whereas older books were sometimes printed in very small runs and dust covers quickly disintegrated.

Naturally, those tennis books which were printed in the nineteenth century or earlier are much more difficult to locate than more recent publications, and if you do happen to find an edition of *'The Laws of Lawn Tennis and Badminton'* (1876) by Henry Jones, condition is less of a consideration than the state of a book printed in the twentieth century. Acquire a poor copy of an early book first, hoping to upgrade it later, but give your find some serious thought before leaving it behind because you may never find another!There are books which both collectors and dealers agree are 'classics', or those which are so difficult to find that they are an extremely valuable asset when one does. More often than not, these books tend to be early rules or coaching books, or those that were printed in very small numbers. Look for authors who have a special relevance to the history of the game, especially those who are associated with particular time frames, such as the years when playing rules were unresolved, tournaments began, or when clubs or associations were first formed.

Annuals such as Ayres, The Field Calendar, Dunlop, or Lowe's are very helpful in this respect as these facts were often written about in small articles, and then there are often biographies of players and officials or tournament records included too. History books are invaluable, although you should never take them all as being totally accurate. Often, historical accounts have literally been copied from an earlier publication, which was also inaccurate. Always investigate an early 'Book of Games', those which pre-date the introduction of lawn tennis (1874); they often have interesting information and illustrations associated with Shuttlecock and Battledore, Real Tennis, or the game of Racquets.

Fig. 1.2. ***The Everyday Book***
The Everyday Book, Vols.1 & 2 - William Hone, for William Hone by Hunt and Clarke, London 1826, 860pp.,(approx), 210 x 134 mm., hard covers. 'The Every-Day Book; or, Everlasting Calendar of Popular Amusements, Sports, Pastimes, Ceremonies, Manners, Customs, and Events, Incident to each of the Three Hundred and Sixty-Five Days, in Past and Present Times; forming a Complete History of the Year, Months, & Seasons, and a Perpetual Key to The Almanack'. With articles on hand ball, hand tennis, fives-play and ball-play customs at Copenhagen House. £100-150 ($150-225)

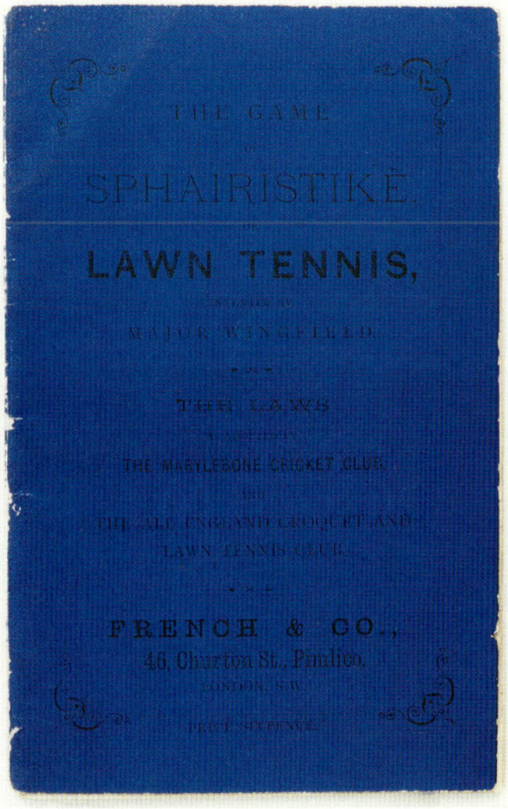

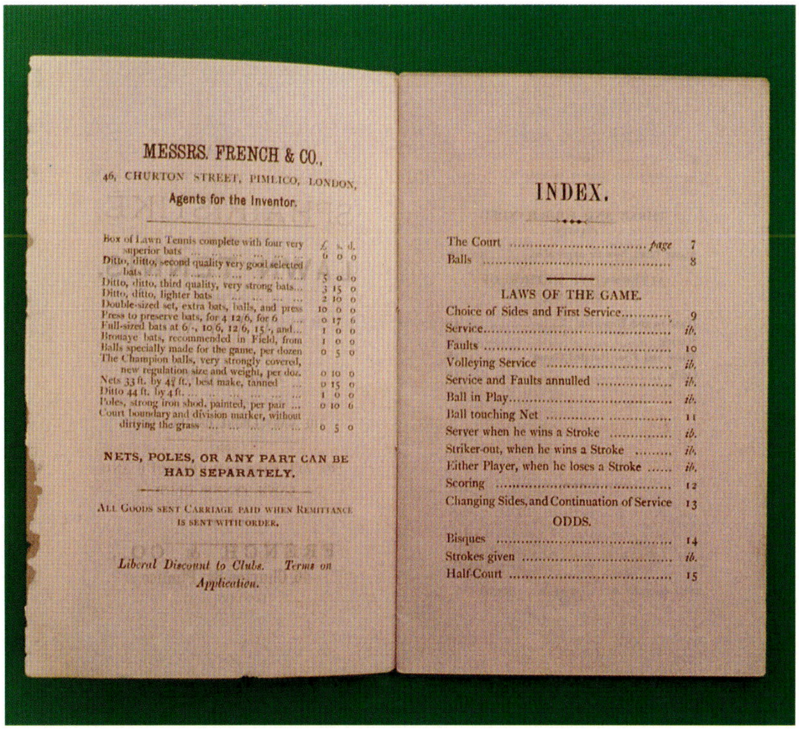

Fig. 1.3. ***The Game of Sphairistike***[2]
The Game of Sphairistike or Lawn Tennis invented by Major Wingfield. The laws as adopted by The Marylebone Cricket Club and The All England Croquet and Lawn Tennis Club - French and Co., London, 1878. 19pp., (plus advertisements) 158 x 101mm., soft covers. This is an extremely rare booklet, unlisted in Forster's tennis bibliography of 1897 and unknown at either The British Library or The Kenneth Ritchie Library Wimbledon. £1500-2500 ($2250-3750)

Fig. 1.4. ***Lawn Tennis***[3] , Shown below left
Lawn Tennis - Jasper Smythe, George Routledge, London, n.d. (c. 1878) 83pp., 167 x 107mm., hard covers. The decorative cover, which appears multi-coloured, is in fact quite cleverly printed in a combination of three colours. The publishers do not hold a copy of this publication and couldn't help with the original publication date. The rules contained within are totally consistent with the rules as published by the M. C. C. in May 1875. 'In the Marylebone rules, where the court is 26 yards long (78 ft.) and ten yards wide (30 ft.) at the base lines, the net is five feet high at the posts, and four feet high at the centre.' £750-1000 ($1000-1500)

Fig. 1.5. ***The Games of Lawn Tennis and Badminton***[4]
The Games of Lawn Tennis and Badminton - Henry Jones 'Cavendish', 3rd Edition, Thomas De La Rue, London 1880, 30pp., 168 x 106mm., hard covers. This book is a delightful example, from a series of nine editions dating from 1876-90, all of them written by Henry Jones. This copy has beautiful red and gold floral printed end papers. Only the first five editions (the edition of 1883 being the fifth) covered the game of badminton too. £500-750 ($750-1000)

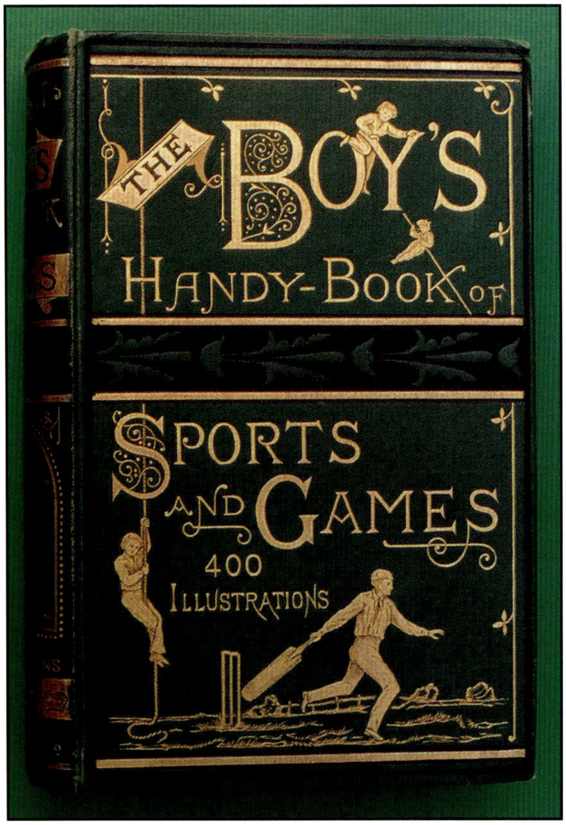

Fig. 1.6. ***The Boys Handy-Book of Sports and Games***
The Boys Handy-Book of Sports and Games - Ward, Lock & Tyler, Paternoster Row, London, c. 1880, 374pp., 192 x 134mm., hard covers. A wonderfully decorated book, which contains articles on Tennis, Rackets, as well as Battledore and Shuttlecock. Curiously, there's an illustration of the game of 'Long Tennis' but no mention of the game in the text. Despite the date, lawn tennis is not featured either. £100-150 ($150-225)

Fig. 1.7. ***Edgbastonia***[5]
Edgbastonia, Vol.1 (May to December) – 'Conducted by Eliezer Edwards', E. Edwards, Birmingham, 1881, 144pp., 211 x 136mm., quarter bound hard covers. A bound volume (by Frederick Grew) containing the first eight issues of *Edgbastonia a Monthly Local Magazine*. On p.126 of the December copy (No.8), begins an eight-page article: 'The Late Major Gem. Edgbastonian Origin of Lawn Tennis.' It describes Gem's eventful life and includes a reprint of the laws of 'Lawn Tennis or Pelota; Laws of the Game, as played by the Leamington Club.'(c. 1872). £350-450 ($475-675)

Fig. 1.8. ***The Book of Brighton***[6]
The Book of Brighton (as it was and as it is) - Charles H. Ross - 'Judy' Office, 99 Shoe Lane, London, 1881, 118pp., 213 x 137mm., hard covers. A little, curiously entertaining guide to the town of Brighton (and its environs) with many amusing drawings. The author writes: 'I can hardly tell what my book is supposed to be...'

Bound together with this book is a copy of, ***Sports Spiced and Pastimes Peppered*** (in a Pungent, Aromatic, yet Emollient Manner) - Greendragon and Dandelion, 'Judy' Office, 99 Shoe Lane, London, 1884, 120pp., 213 x 137mm., hard covers. An amusing observation (in a Victorian manner) of contemporary sports and pastimes. There are chapters on Rackets, Fives, Battledore and Shuttlecock, and 'Tennis and Lawn Tennis.' The book includes nine wonderful little illustrations of subjects such as 'The aim', 'The idiot who faces hand-in', and 'The duffer', as well as a full-page drawing devoted to 'Lawn Tennis – Crushing'. £250-300 ($375-450)

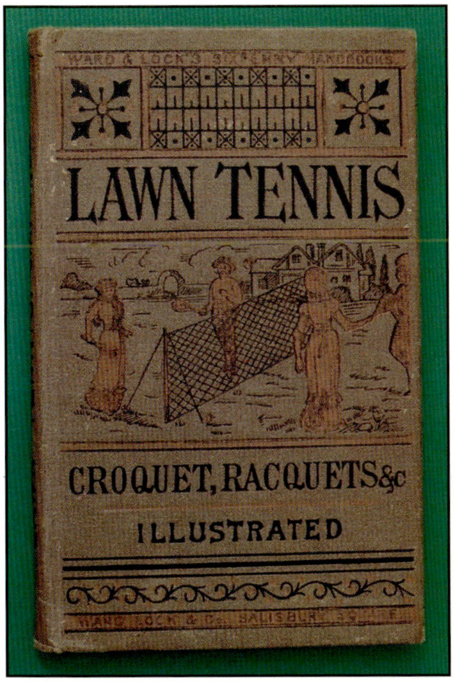

Fig. 1.9. ***Lawn Tennis, Badminton, Croquet, Troco, Racquets***[7]
Lawn Tennis, Badminton, Croquet, Troco, Racquets - Ward, Lock and Co. London, n.d. c. 1882, 88pp., 154 x 100mm., hard covers. A delightful little book which looks at the history, the implements, setting out the ground, and the rules of each game. The book examines other games, including Fives, Pallone, Nurr and Spell, Bowling, Hurling, and Balloon Ball. £850-1000 ($1300-1500)

Fig. 1.10. ***The Tiny Lawn Tennis Club***
The Tiny Lawn Tennis Club – 'M. A. C.', E. P. Dutton and Co., 39 West Twenty-Third Street, New York, 1882, 30pp. 220 x 180mm., hard covers. A delightful children's book of 30 pages written in 1882 by 'M. A. C.' It is full of pretty coloured illustrations with charming poems and rhymes. For example: 'The Lost Ball' – 'Harry and Mable have lost their ball – Oh where, and oh where can it be? Is it hidden among the grasses tall, or lodged in the bow of a tree?' It is an extremely rare book. £850-1000 ($1300-1500)

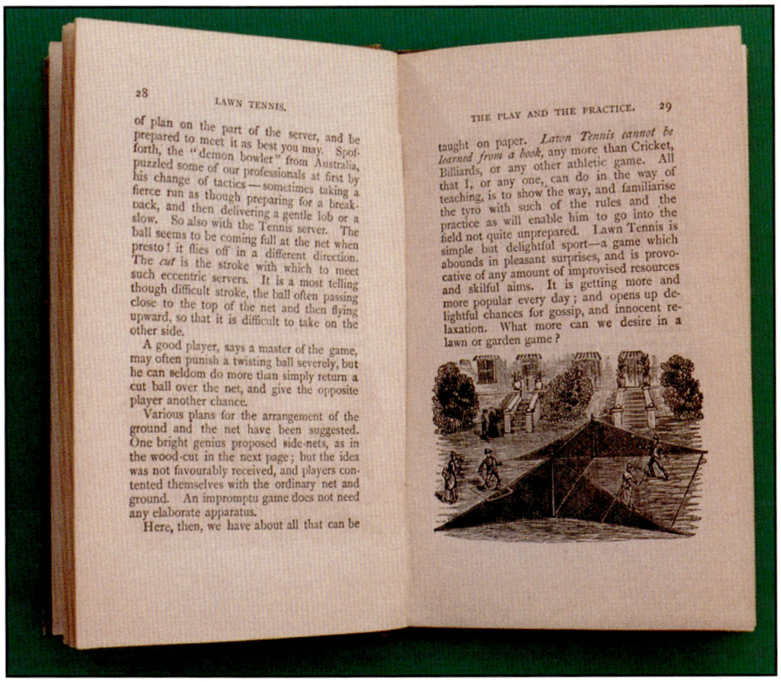

28 LAWN TENNIS.

of plan on the part of the server, and be prepared to meet it as best you may. Spofforth, the "demon bowler" from Australia, puzzled some of our professionals at first by his change of tactics—sometimes taking a fierce run as though preparing for a break-back, and then delivering a gentle lob or a slow. So also with the Tennis server. The ball seems to be coming full at the net when presto! it flies off in a different direction. The *cut* is the stroke with which to meet such eccentric servers. It is a most telling though difficult stroke, the ball often passing close to the top of the net and then flying upward, so that it is difficult to take on the other side.

A good player, says a master of the game, may often punish a twisting ball severely, but he can seldom do more than simply return a cut ball over the net, and give the opposite player another chance.

Various plans for the arrangement of the ground and the net have been suggested. One bright genius proposed side-nets, as in the wood-cut in the next page; but the idea was not favourably received, and players contented themselves with the ordinary net and ground. An impromptu game does not need any elaborate apparatus.

Here, then, we have about all that can be

THE PLAY AND THE PRACTICE. 29

taught on paper. *Lawn Tennis cannot be learned from a book*, any more than Cricket, Billiards, or any other athletic game. All that I, or any one, can do in the way of teaching, is to show the way, and familiarise the tyro with such of the rules and the practice as will enable him to go into the field not quite unprepared. Lawn Tennis is simple but delightful sport—a game which abounds in pleasant surprises, and is provocative of any amount of improvised resources and skilful aims. It is getting more and more popular every day; and opens up delightful chances for gossip, and innocent relaxation. What more can we desire in a lawn or garden game?

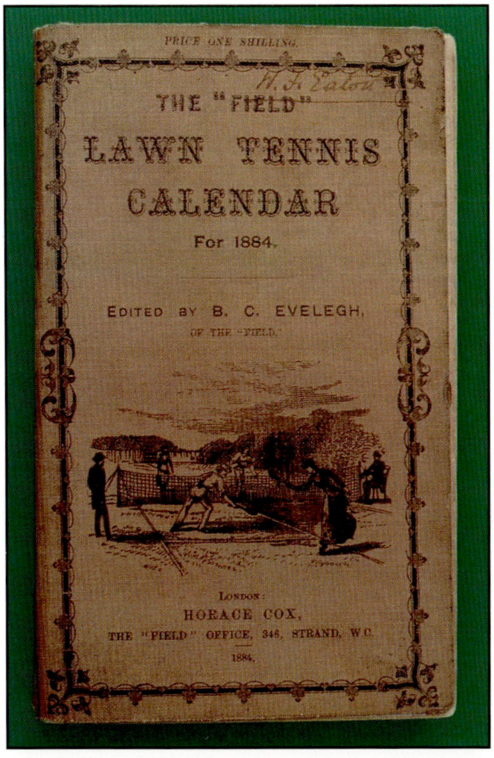

Fig. 1.11. ***The 'Field' Lawn Tennis Calendar***[8]
The 'Field' Lawn Tennis Calendar for 1884 - edited by B. C. Eveleigh, Horace Cox, The *"Field"* Office, London, 1884, 354pp., 166 x 102mm., card covers. 'A synopsis of the laws of lawn tennis; revised list of secretaries and their addresses; summary of the season, 1883; on the making of tennis lawns and cinder and gravel courts; with full reports of all tournaments and club matches of the season 1883.' It contains six full-page advertisements and has an owner's signature of 'Rev. W. F. Eaton' on the front cover and inside covers. £350-400 ($525-600)

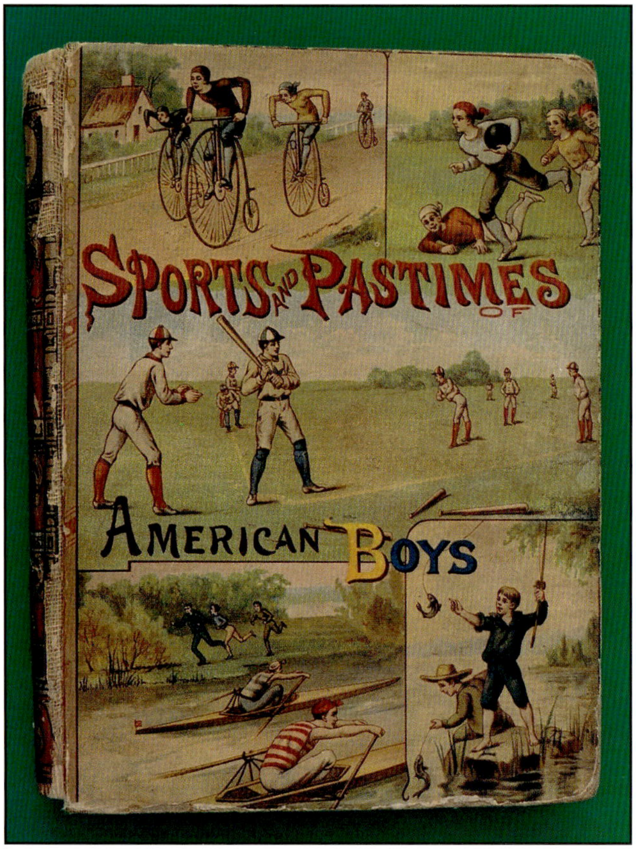

Above:
Fig. 1.12. ***Sports and Pastimes of American Boys***
Sports and Pastimes of American Boys - George Routledge and Sons, 9 Lafayette Place, New York, 1884, 303pp., 223 x 164mm., hard covers. A thirteen-page chapter on lawn tennis covers equipment, how to play, and the rules. A fine engraving shows a game being played on an 'hour-glass' shaped court. The games of Rackets, Battledore and Shuttlecock, and Badminton, which is described as 'a weak variation of lawn tennis' are also covered. Peck and Snyder equipment is strongly recommended and the company may well have been a sponsor of this book. £300-350 ($450-525)

Top right:
Fig. 1.13. ***Modern English Sports, Their Use and Their Abuse***[9]
Modern English Sports, Their Use and Their Abuse - Frederick Gale, large paper edition, number 15 of 100, Sampson Low, Marston, Searle & Rivington, London 1885, 201pp., 216 x 140mm., hard covers with vellum covering. With chapters on field sports and others, interest focuses mainly on Chapter 11 which concentrates (quite light-heartedly) on 'Lawn Tennis, Tennis Racquets, and Golf.' In Gale's opinion tennis is 'more enjoyable when there is a conspicuous absence of chicken salad, champagne cup, garden-party dresses, and the fashionable parapherna-lia.' £250-350 ($375-525)

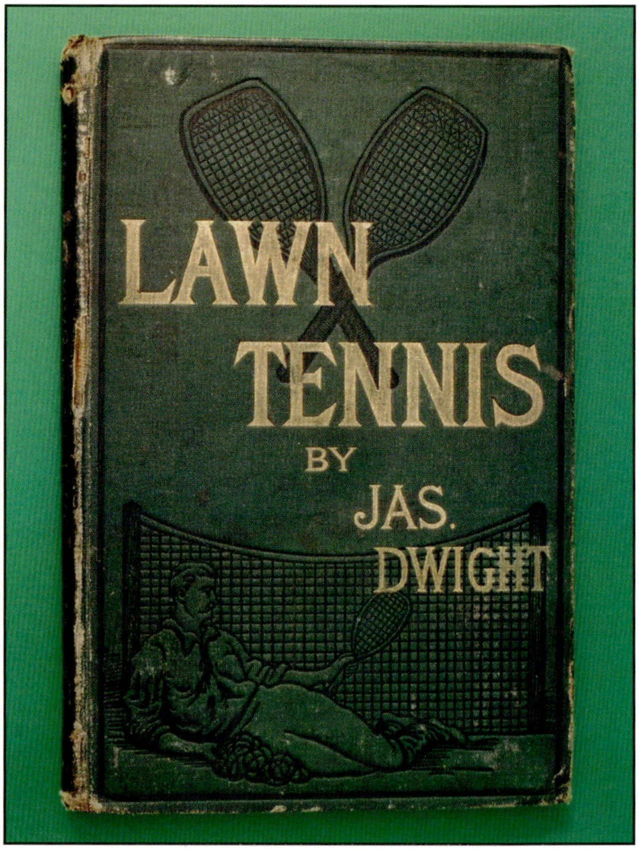

Right:
Fig. 1.14. ***Lawn Tennis***[10]
Lawn Tennis - James Dwight, The *'Pastime'* Office, London, 1886, 94pp., 193 x 128mm., hard covers. Essentially, this is the first American lawn tennis coaching book to be published. Dwight observed that: 'Young players seem to take pleasure in selecting the most extraordinary rackets in a shop. Let me strongly advise them to avoid all unusual handles, heads, or methods of stringing. All these eccentricities are useless at the best.' The final chapter lists the 'Results of Championship matches and Principal Open Competitions' and at either end of the book, amongst others, there are early full-page advertisements for Slazengers, Ayres, Deverell Bros., and Wright & Ditson lawn tennis requisites. £250-350 ($375-525)

Fig. 1.15. ***Tennis, Rackets, Fives***
The All England Series - Tennis, Rackets, Fives - Julian Marshall, Major J. Spens, J. Arnan Tait, George Bell & Sons, London, 1890, 104pp., 171 x 117mm., hard covers. This is a difficult coaching manual to find, which also takes a look at the history of each game. There are three full-page advertisements for Ayres, Prosser, and Gradidge's equipment. £300-350 ($450-525)

Fig. 1.17. ***The Boy's Modern Playmate***
The Boy's Modern Playmate, Rev'd. J. G. Wood - Frederick Warne and Co. London and New York, 1891, 816pp., 209 x 146mm., hard covers. A huge 'New Edition' reference compendium for children covering all types of sports and games, including: 'Cricket, and other Grand Ball Games' as well as Tennis, Battledore and Shuttlecock, and Rackets. £50-75 ($75-100)

Fig. 1.16. ***Lawn Tennis, Rackets, Fives***[11]
Lawn Tennis, Rackets, Fives - Heathcote and Others, The Badminton Library of Sports and Pastimes, The Duke of Beaufort and Alfred E.T.Watson, 1st edition, Longmans, Green, and Co., London, 1890, 484pp., 197 x 140mm., quarter bound special binding with hard covers. One of many editions concerning games, pastimes, and field sports published by the Badminton Library from 1890 onwards. £250-350 ($375-525)

Lawn Tennis, Rackets, Fives - Heathcote and Others, The Badminton Library of Sports and Pastimes, The Duke of Beaufort and Alfred E.T.Watson, 2nd edition, Longmans, Green, and Co., London, 1891, 484pp., 187 x 134mm., quarter bound special binding with hard covers and marbled end papers. Profusely illustrated with fine plates and woodcuts. £200-250 ($300-375)

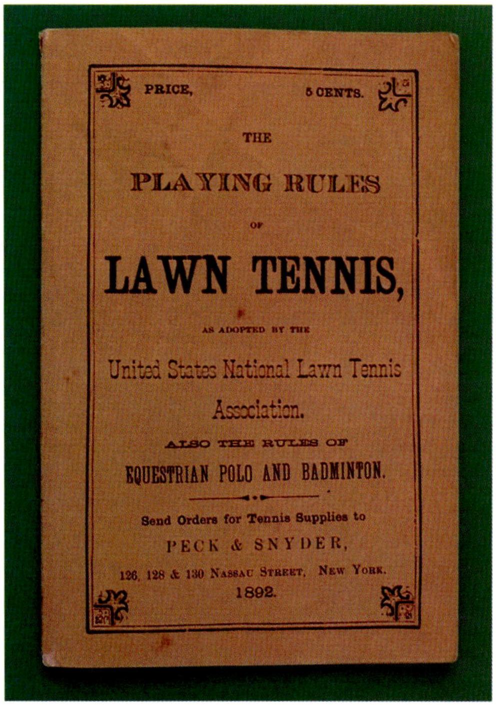

Fig. 1.18. ***The Playing Rules of Lawn Tennis***[12]
The Playing Rules of Lawn Tennis as adopted by the United States National Lawn Tennis Association - Peck & Snyder, 1892. 32pp., 144 x 98mm., soft covers. A classic, invaluable little book, packed with information about the game in 1892. Containing eight pages on the 'Laws of Lawn Tennis' and notes upon the 'United States Lawn Tennis Association Constitution', 'By-Laws' and 'Rules for Umpires'. There are also six pages which cover the 'Laws of Badminton - as adopted by the Bath Badminton Club, Bath, England. 1889-90' followed by three pages of the 'Rules of the Westchester Polo Club, revised May 22nd, 1889.' £200-250 ($300-375)

Fig. 1.20. ***Sportspiele im Frein, Lawn Tennis***
Sportspiele im Frein, Lawn Tennis – Waarenhaus Hermann Tietz, Germany, 1899, 228pp., 200 x 134mm., hard covers. A wonderful little book, written in German, which discloses much early information concerning the development of the game in European countries. There's also an entrance form for the tennis tournament at Hamburg and a foldout handicap form listing various players' handicaps during the 1898 tournament. £175-250 ($250-375)

Fig. 1.19. ***Lawn Tennis***[13]
Lawn Tennis - Wilfred Baddeley, 1st edition, Routledge & Sons Ltd., (The "Oval" Series of Games) London 1895, 158pp., 181 x 123mm., soft covers. And the 3rd edition, London 1903, 173pp. 187 x 125mm., hard covers. This book is basically a coaching manual, but does cover historical details including, 'The Lawn Tennis Association and its' formation', 'The Development of Play', and 'The Spread of Lawn Tennis'. £175-250 ($250-375)

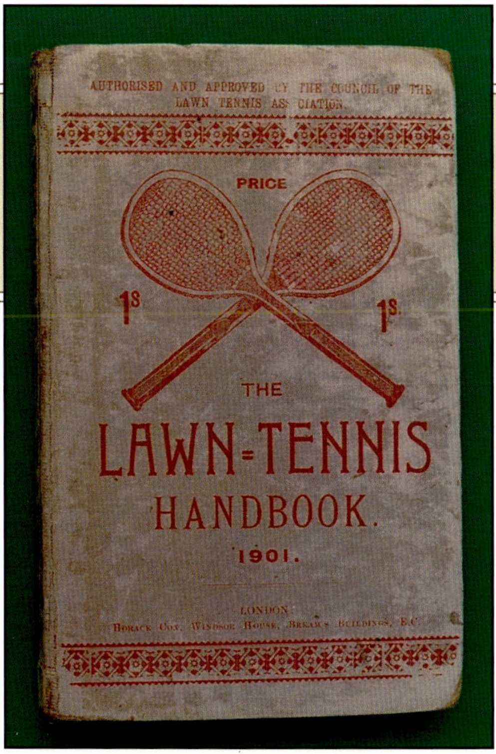

Fig. 1.21. ***The Lawn Tennis Handbook***
The Lawn Tennis Handbook 1901, Horace Cox, *'The Field'* Office, London, 1901, 186pp., 166 x 107mm., hard covers. A small but very informative volume, basically forming a collection of all matters connected with the English Lawn Tennis Association. Contents include: Council Members; Clubs; Laws; Regulations; Competitions; Prize-winners, and Addresses of Secretaries. £175-250 ($250-375)

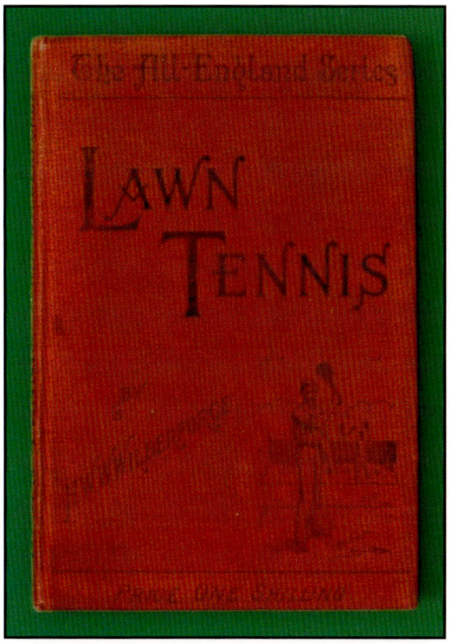

Fig. 1.23. ***Lawn Tennis***[14]
Lawn Tennis - H.W.W.Wilberforce, 6th? edition, George Bell & Sons, London, 1901, 78pp., 170 x 118mm., hard covers. A coaching book which also covers the history of the game and how, by 1901, the game had developed. There are eleven 'action' photographs of Herbert Lawford and Arthur Gore, all taken at the old 'Worple Road' Wimbledon grounds, and eleven full page advertisements for sports and games manufacturers. The 1st edition of this book was printed in 1889. Other editions were published in 1891, '92, '95, '97, 1904, 1911, and 1915. £100-200 ($150-300)

Fig. 1.22. ***The Book of Sport***
The Book of Sport - James Patten, J. F. Taylor & Co., New York, 1901, 411pp., 362 x 272mm., Edition De-Luxe (number 525 of 1500 limited copies), hard covers. An extremely heavy book! As well as covering such sports as Polo, Golf, Hunting, and many others, it also features extensive coverage of the racket sports, personalities, and clubs to be found on the East Coast of America around 1900. They extend to over 100 pages and include over 100 delightful drawings and photographs of American racket sport stars and dignitaries. £250-350 ($375-525)

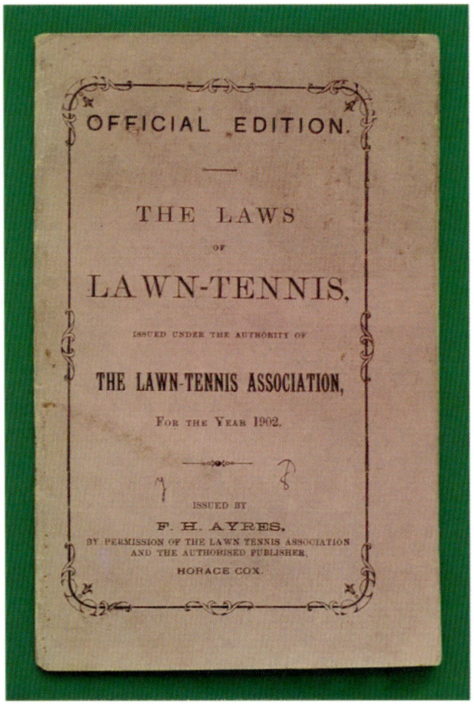

Fig. 1.24. ***The Laws of Lawn Tennis***[15]
The Laws of Lawn Tennis, for the Year 1902, (Official Edition), F. H. Ayres, (by permission of the Lawn Tennis Association and the authorised publisher, Horace Cox), 16pp., (plus advertisements), 159 x 104mm., soft card covers. A self-promotional exercise by F. H. Ayres, which in hindsight appears to have backfired a little. Alongside the advertisements for their rackets and croquet sets, on the back cover one can be found which expounds the virtues of their 'Championship' lawn tennis ball. It includes a copy of a testimonial from the secretary of the All England Lawn Tennis and Croquet Club, following the meeting in the previous year, in which the praises of their special ball was well and truly sung! It is well known that from 1902 and for the last 100 years, only Slazenger lawn tennis balls have been used. £125-175 ($200-235)

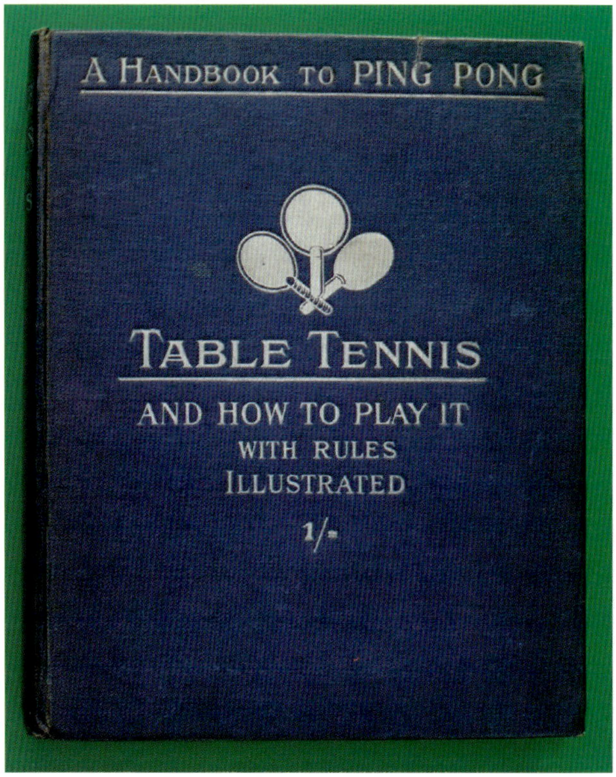

Fig. 1.25. ***A Handbook to Ping Pong***
A Handbook to Ping Pong. Table Tennis and how to play it, with rules, illustrated - M. J. G. Ritchie and Walter Harrison, C. Arthur Pearson Ltd., London, 1902, 116pp., 159 x 126mm., hard covers. A wonderful little coaching book, which also examines the history of the game. It contains six full-page advertisements for equipment manufacturers. Six illustrations are included. £25-35 ($40-50)

Fig. 1.26. ***Ping-Pong, the game of Parlour Tennis and how to play it***
Ping-Pong, the game of Parlour Tennis and how to play it - Arnold Parker, R. F. Fenno & Co., New York, 1902, 113pp., 177 x 118mm., hard covers. A rare, wonderful little book with chapters on the history, implements, grips, how to run tournaments, and the laws of the game. Illustrated with 39 hand drawn diagrams. This copy came with a hand written poem entitled: 'A Ping Pong Song' by R. H. Titherington, a regular contributor to the *Argosy* magazine. £25-35 ($40-50)

Fig. 1.27. ***The Laws of Ping-Pong***
The Laws of Ping-Pong, (Official Edition), Authorised by The Ping-Pong Association, J. Jaques & Son Ltd., and Hamley Bros., Ltd., London, n.d., c. 1902, 20pp., 183 x 120mm., paperback. Includes information on 'The Rules of the Association'; the Challenge Cup; Ping-Pong rackets; laws of Ping-Pong; and Jacques equipment. £100-150 ($150-225)

Ping-Pong or Gossima
Ping-Pong or Gossima, (Standard Edition), Rules and Directions, J. Jacques & Son Ltd., and Hamley Bros., London, n. d. (c. 1902) 12pp., 169 x 110mm., paperback. 'With Directions for the Arrangement and Conduct of Matches and Tournaments.' £50-75 (£75-100)

Fig. 1.28. ***Lawn Tennis at Home and Abroad***
Lawn Tennis at Home and Abroad – A. Wallis Myers (editor), George Newnes Limited, Southampton Street, Strand, W. C. London, 1903, 328pp., 222 x 142mm., hardback. A marvellous book which gives the reader a 'tour' of many of the prominent European tournament venues, while touching upon others farther afield. It contains over 150 photographs, many of which are unique to this book. £100-150 ($150-225)

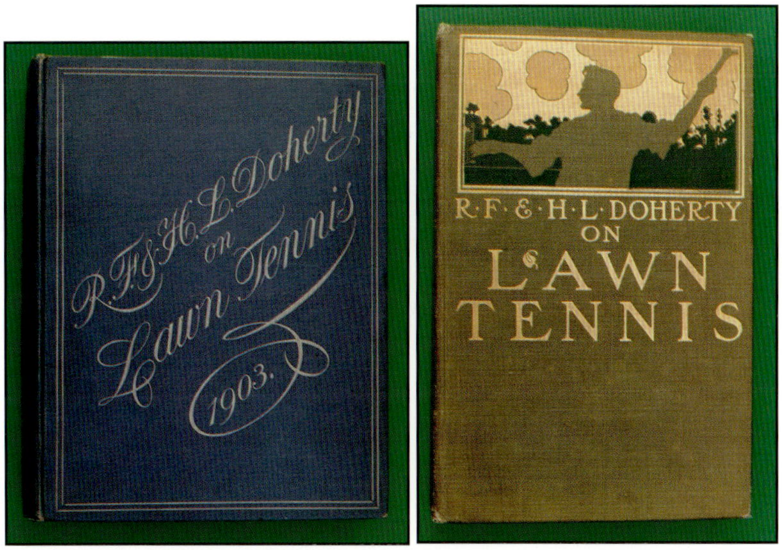

Fig. 1.29. ***R. F. & H. L. Doherty on Lawn Tennis***[16]
R. F. & H. L. Doherty on Lawn Tennis, (English large paper edition), 'Lawn Tennis', London, 1903, 146pp., 218 x 174mm., hard covers, & (the American edition), The Baker & Taylor Company, New York, August 1903, 233pp., 198 x 132mm., hard covers. Despite the fact that the English edition contained less pages, (the typesetting was a different size and style) there is little to choose between them. There are two extra photographs of more relevance to the home market in the American edition. It is noticeable that in the English version, (unlike its American cousin) photographs of 'her Imperial Highness The Grand Duchess Anastasie of Mecklenburg-Schwerin' (to whom the book was dedicated) and a posed studio photograph of the brothers, are real photographs which have been glued onto the page. Their photograph is stamped in the bottom right hand corner 'under copyright to the London Stereographic Company.' These beautiful books are very sought after and very difficult to find in good condition. They must also be one of the earliest examples of how an item was specifically redesigned and marketed to meet the demands of different cultural styles. £150-250 ($225-375)

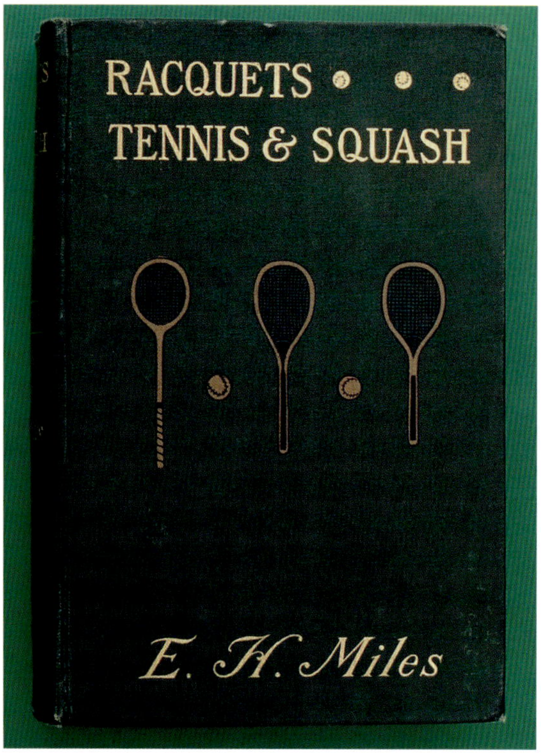

Fig. 1.30. ***Racquets, Tennis, and Squash***
Racquets, Tennis, and Squash - Eustace Miles, M. A., D. Appleton and Company, New York, January 1903, 336pp., 192 x 126mm., hard covers. This book contains a thorough examination of how to play three different games and a look back at their histories. Containing many photographs and diagrams. £85-150 ($130-225)

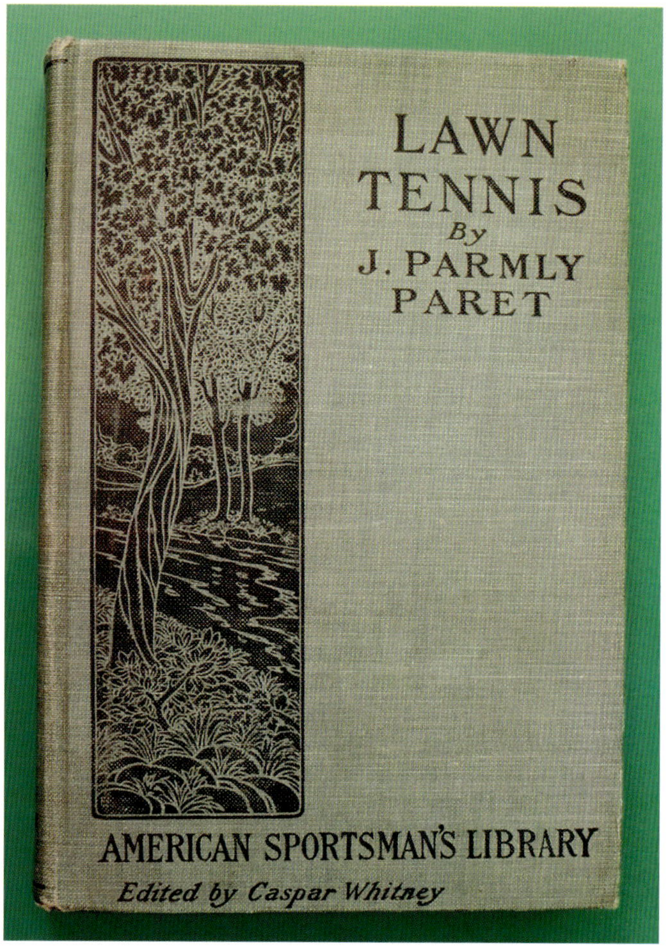

Fig. 1.31. ***Lawn Tennis, It's Past, Present, and Future***
Lawn Tennis, Its Past, Present, and Future - J. Parmly Paret, The MacMillan Company, New York, October 1904, 419pp., 204 x 141mm., hard covers. A fascinating book which examines the history of the game, methods of play, the physiological side of the game, laws, tennis terms, and even includes a very informative bibliography. A chapter by William Harvey Maddren on Lacrosse is included too. £125-175 ($200-250)

Opposing page, bottom:
Fig. 1.32. ***Modern Lawn Tennis***
Modern Lawn Tennis - P. A. Vaile, 1st edition, William Heinemann, London, 1904, 224pp., 188 x 124mm., hard covers. A typical coaching manual of its day. £50-75 ($75-100)

On the Court and Off
On the Court and Off - Anthony F. Wilding, 1st edition, Methuen & Co. Ltd., London, 1912, 273pp., 196 x 129mm., hard covers. Signed in ink: 'with the author's compliments, April 27th. 1912.' Reminiscences and friendly advice from Wilding, edited by A. W. Myers. The book contains 58 photographs. £50-75 ($75-100)

Everybody's Lawn Tennis Book
Everybody's Lawn Tennis Book - E. E. M., Review copy, W. Collins & Sons, & Co. Ltd., London, 7th June 1923, 234pp., 226 x 151mm., hard covers. An unusual edition in that the writer is anonymous. Some 35 amusing little silhouette style drawings by Robert Spence illustrate the text. A coaching book, which uses the styles and mannerisms of famous players to demonstrate the text. A difficult book to find. £50-75 ($75-100)

The Lawn Tennis Masters Unveiled
The Lawn Tennis Masters Unveiled - B. H. Liddell Hart, 1st edition, J. W. Arrowsmith Ltd., London, May 1926, 264pp., 189 x 125mm., hard covers. The book examines styles of play of 20 Gentlemen and Lady players of the day, with a photograph of each and every one of them. £40-60 ($60-90)

Tennis in Baltimore
Tennis in Baltimore - Frank G. Roberts, 1st edition, Dulany-Vernay Co., Baltimore, 1928, 241pp., 195 x 136mm., hard covers. Another extremely difficult edition to track down, containing masses of information about tennis in the city of Baltimore since municipal tennis was played in parks and at the famous Baltimore Cricket Club. Containing seven photographs. £85-135 ($130-200)

Great Lawn Tennis
Great Lawn Tennis, Pen Pictures of Famous Matches - A. Wallis Myers, 1st edition, Cassell and Company Ltd., 1937, 223pp., 190 x 127mm., hard covers. The title says it all, reports on epic lawn tennis matches from the era, from Anthony Wilding through to Perry and Budge. Containing nine photographs. £40-60 ($60-90)

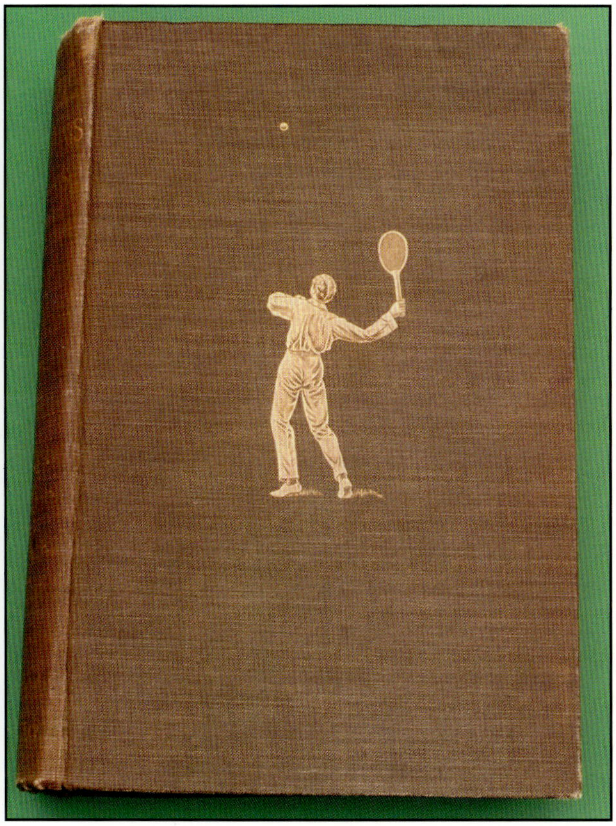

Fig. 1.33. ***Great Lawn Tennis Players, Their Methods Illustrated***[17]
Great Lawn Tennis Players, Their Methods Illustrated - George W. Beldham and P. A. Vaile, Macmillan and Co. Ltd., London, 1905, 403pp., 227 x 159mm., hard covers. A huge, profusely illustrated coaching manual with over 130 photographs of contemporary players. £100-150 ($150-225)

Fig. 1.34. ***The Complete Lawn Tennis Player***[18]
The Complete Lawn Tennis Player - A. Wallis Myers, 1st edition, Methuen & Co., London, 1908, 333pp., 225 x 142mm., hard covers. A huge, superbly informative tome which covers all areas and topics associated with the game in its early life. Over 80 photographs. £85-150 ($125-225)

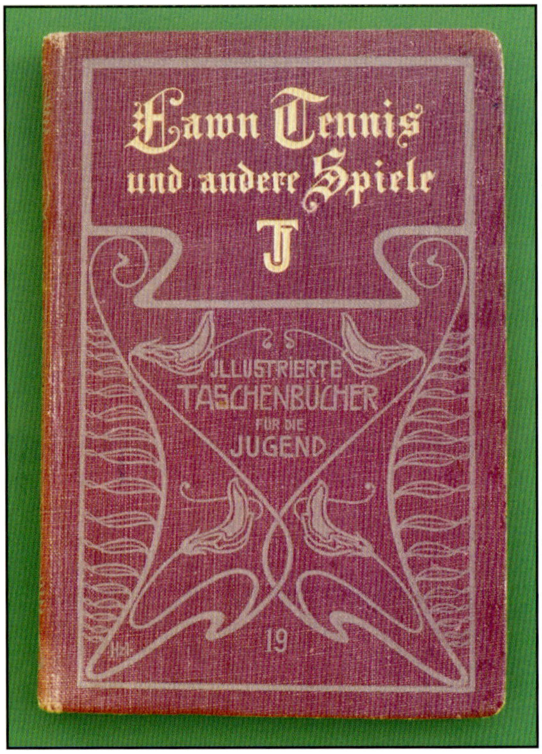

Fig. 1.35. ***Lawn Tennis und andere Spiele***
Lawn Tennis und andere Spiele – P. Heineken, (Taschenbucher illustriertet fur die Jugend) Stuttgart, 1910, 155 x 108mm., 118pp., hard covers. A lovely little book which, quite apart from looking at the history of lawn tennis and its implements, also examines Croquet, Hockey, Ice-Hockey, Golf, Association Football, and Rugby Football. £75-125 ($100-200)

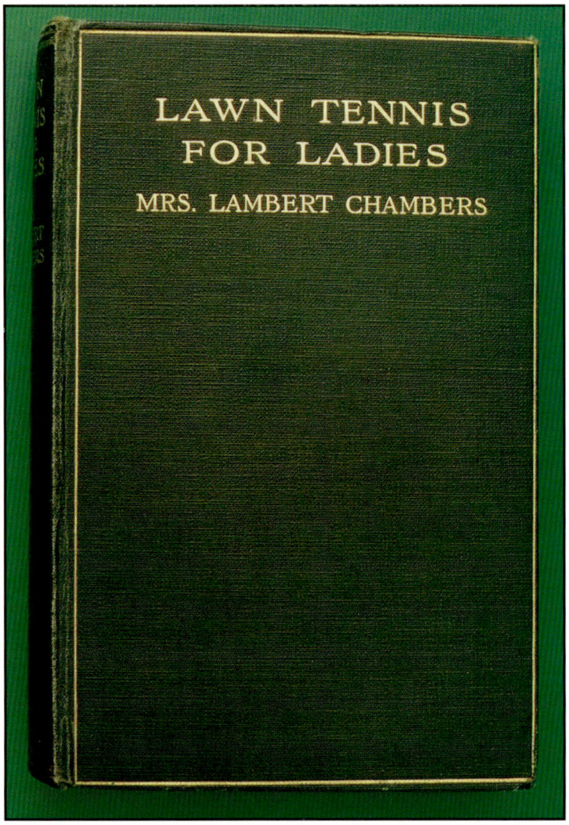

Fig. 1.37. ***Lawn Tennis for Ladies***
Lawn Tennis for Ladies - Mrs. Lambert Chambers, 1st edition, Methuen & Co., Ltd., London, 1910, 135pp., 197 x 129mm., hard covers. Mainly a coaching book, but not too technical (unlike so many others of the day). Two interesting chapters on 'Personal Reminiscences' and 'My Most Memorable Match' provide a much more personal insight. The book contains 23 photographs. £50-75 ($75-100)

Fig. 1.36. ***Text Book of Lawn Tennis***
Text Book of Lawn Tennis - M. J. G. Ritchie, 3rd edition, Ewart, Seymour & Co. Ltd., London, n.d., c. 1910, 80pp., 180 x 120mm., board covers. This is a small coaching manual. £25-45 ($40-70)

Fig. 1.38. ***The Encyclopaedia of Sport & Games***
The Encyclopaedia of Sport & Games in Four Volumes, - The Earl of Suffolk and Berkshire (editor), new and enlarged edition, William Heinemann, London, 1911, over 1600pp., 273 x 183mm., hard covers. Articles on most racket and ball sports except for Table Tennis. Over 500 illustrations. £40-75 ($60-100)

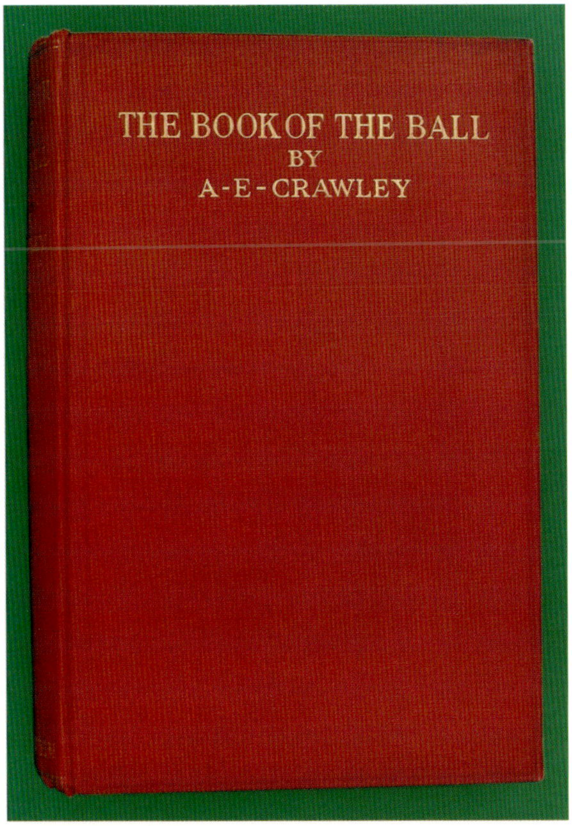

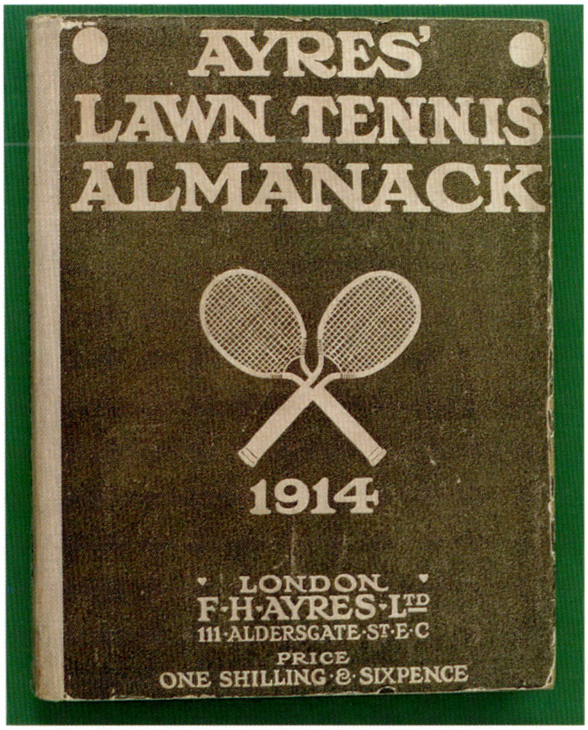

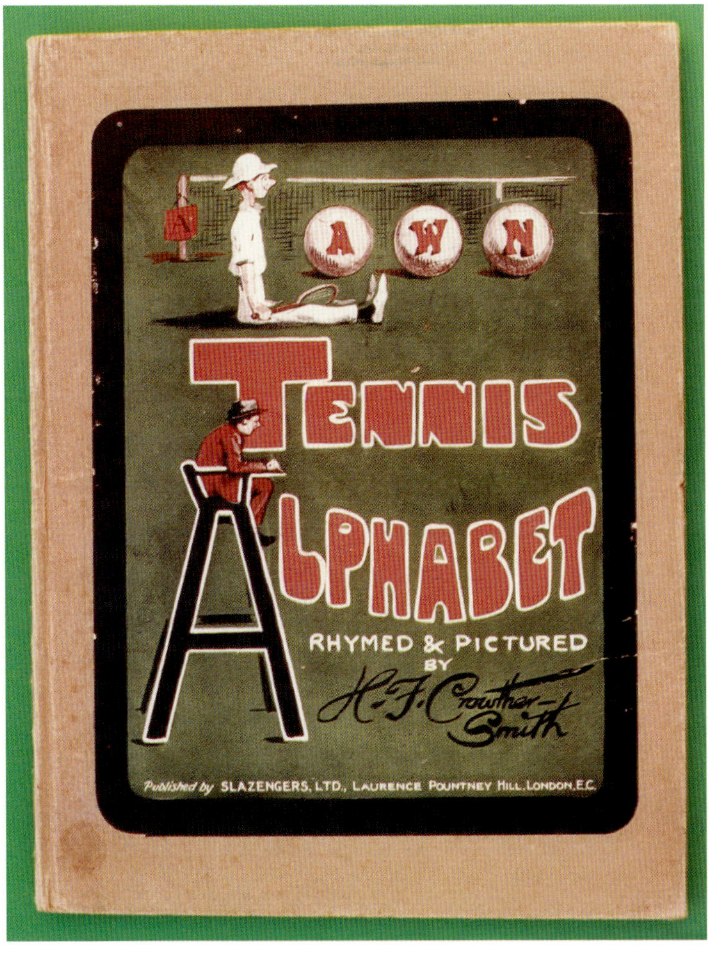

Top left:
Fig. 1.39. ***The Book of The Ball***[19]
The Book of The Ball - A. E. Crawley, 1st edition, Metheun & Co. Ltd., London, 1913, 220pp., 195 x 133mm., hard covers. A difficult book to locate, with a chapter on 'Some Principles of Ball Games', featuring (Real) Tennis, and Lawn Tennis. £75-125 ($100-200)

Left:
Fig. 1.40. ***A Lawn Tennis Alphabet***
A Lawn Tennis Alphabet – H. F. Crowther Smith, Slazengers Ltd., Laurence Pountney Hill, London, E. C., 1914, 36pp., 250 x 190mm., hard covers. As the title indicates each of the coloured illustrations are the author's drawings. Each of them is accompanied by a rhyme on a letter of the alphabet. For instance 'V for the vigorous volleys which oust and vanquish the various victims of Doust' or 'J for the jestre the Cantab, Hope Crisp; it may be far fetched, but still I hope crisp'. This excellent book provides amusement for all followers of Lawn Tennis. Includes twenty-six coloured plates and five pages of advertisements. £650-750 ($1000-1200)

Above:
Fig. 1.41. ***Ayres Lawn Tennis Almanac***
Ayres Lawn Tennis Almanac 1914, - Edited by A. Wallis Myers, (7th year of issue) F. H. Ayres Ltd., London, 1914, 560pp., 163 x 130mm., hard board covers. A wonderfully informative time capsule, which reviews a year in lawn tennis before the Great War. Filled to the gunnels with information concerning tournaments, players, and equipment. The book contains over 30 photographs. £85-150 ($135-225)

Fig. 1.42. ***Tennis for All***
Tennis for All, Simple and Comprehensive Instructions - A. M. Lethbridge, Universal Publications Ltd., London, n.d. (c. 1914), 90pp., 165 x 104mm., soft covers. A small wartime coaching manual printed completely on pink paper. Illustrated with several line drawings. £15-20 ($20-30)

Fig. 1.44. ***Lawn Tennis***
Lawn Tennis - M. J. G. Ritchie, Athletic Publications, London, n.d., c. 1915, 88pp., 186 x 125mm., card covers. A coaching manual, illustrated with photographs of the author in action. This book is almost identical in content to the edition *Text Book of Lawn Tennis* by the same author. £30-50 ($45-75)

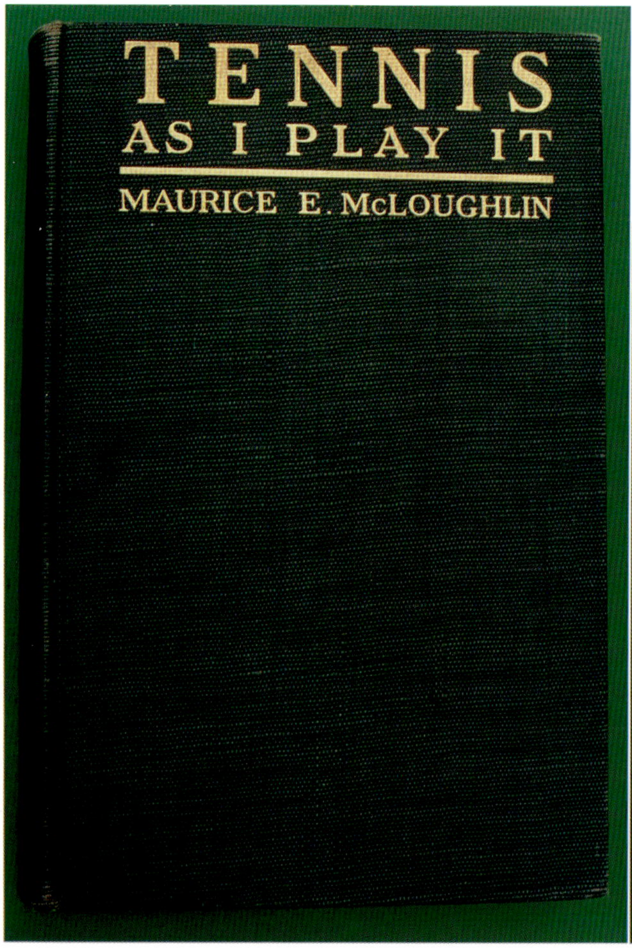

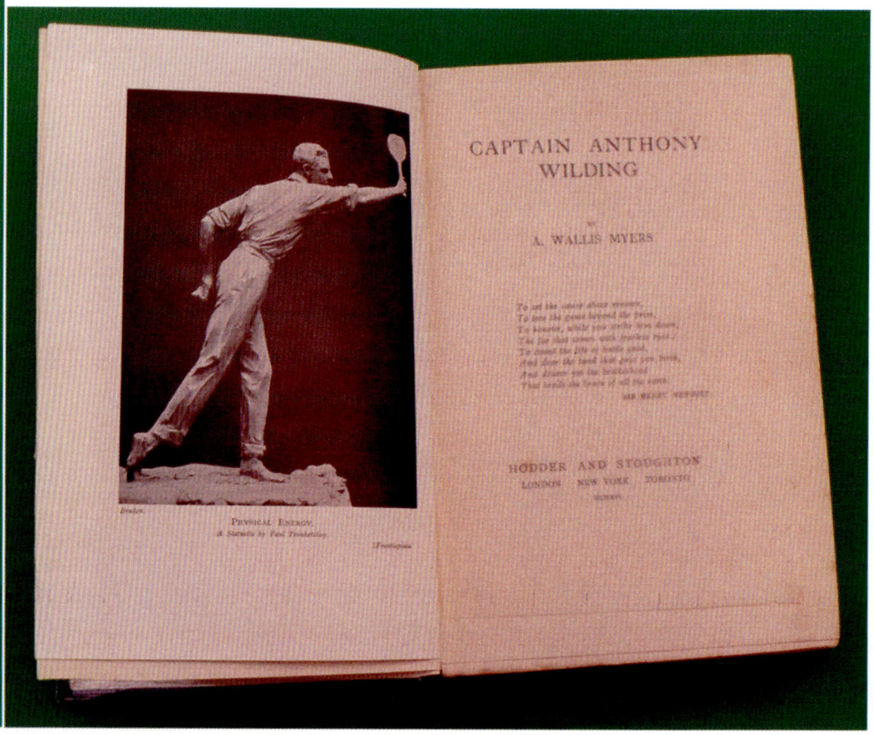

Fig. 1.43. ***Tennis as I Play it***
Tennis as I Play it - Maurice E. McLoughlin, 1st edition, George H. Doran Co., New York, 1915, 347pp., 235 x 155mm., hard covers. A pleasing coaching book, interspersed with observations and tips from the author. Ten photographs. £75-100 ($100-150)

Fig. 1.45. ***Captain Anthony Wilding***
Captain Anthony Wilding - A. Wallis Myers, 1st edition, Hodder & Stoughton, London, 1916, 306pp., 205 x 138mm., hard covers. A fascinating insight into the life of Anthony Wilding, and a review of lawn tennis in New Zealand. Containing 36 photographs. £40-60 ($60-90)

Fig. 1.46. ***Among the Sportsmen***
Among the Sportsman, Tom Webster of the *Daily Mail* - Published at Carmelite House, London, 1920, 96pp., 184 x 246mm., paperback. This is a book containing wonderful cartoons of sporting characters, it also includes six pages with observations upon 'The Lawn Tennis Championships, Wimbledon, 1919' showing caricatures of players like Patterson, Kingscote, Lenglen, and Brookes. These books were stapled at the spine and are very fragile. £50-75 ($75-100)

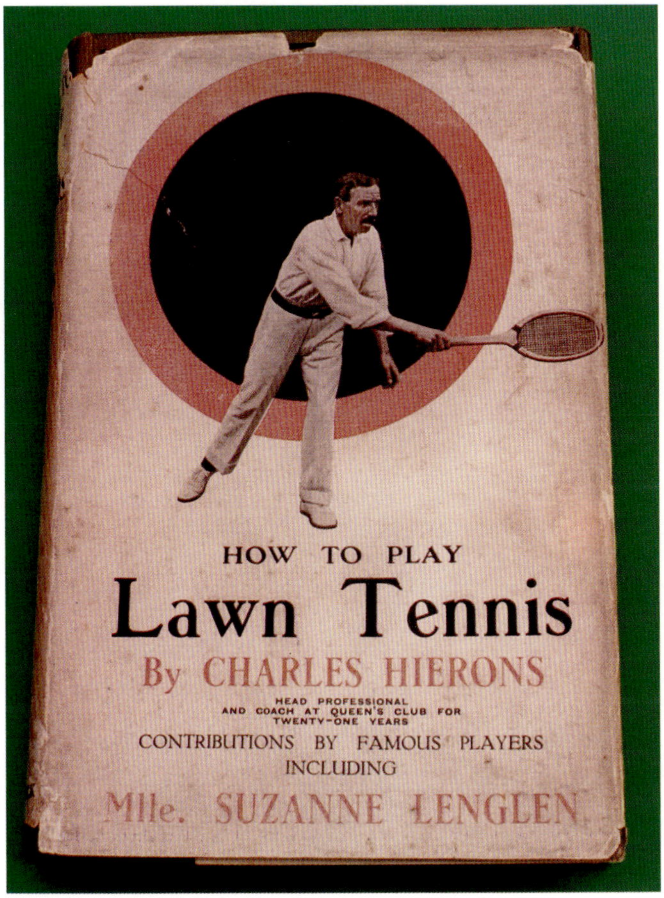

Fig. 1.47. ***How to Learn Lawn Tennis***
How to Learn Lawn Tennis, A Simple, Instructive Treatise - Charles Hierons, revised and enlarged edition, Ward, Lock & Co., Ltd., n.d., c. 1920?, 190pp., 191 x 125mm., hard covers. A coaching manual, which includes literary contributions from famous contemporary players. Illustrated with 31 photographs. This copy is in a rare dust cover, but more commonly it is found in either red, grey, blue, or green decorated boards. £30-50 ($45-75)

Fig. 1.48. ***The Art of Lawn Tennis***
The Art of Lawn Tennis - William T. Tilden, 3rd edition, Methuen & Co. Ltd., London, 1921, 163pp., 196 x 128mm., hard covers. Mainly a coaching manual but it also includes useful advice and observations on famous contemporary players. Containing 30 photographs. £30-50 ($45-75)

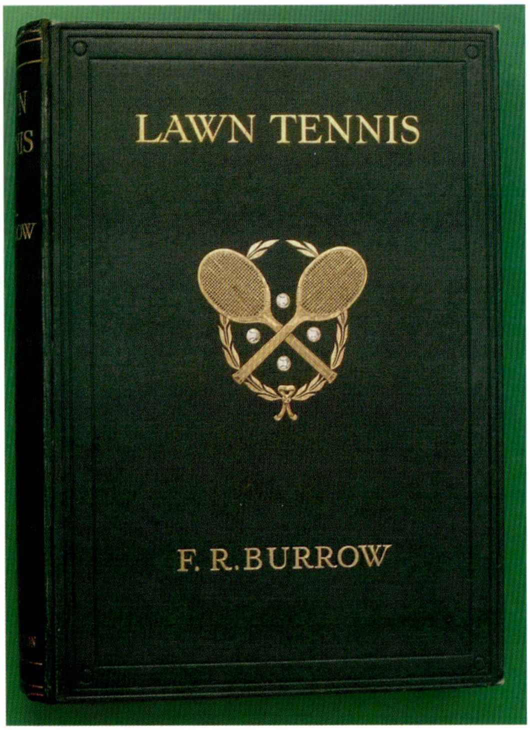

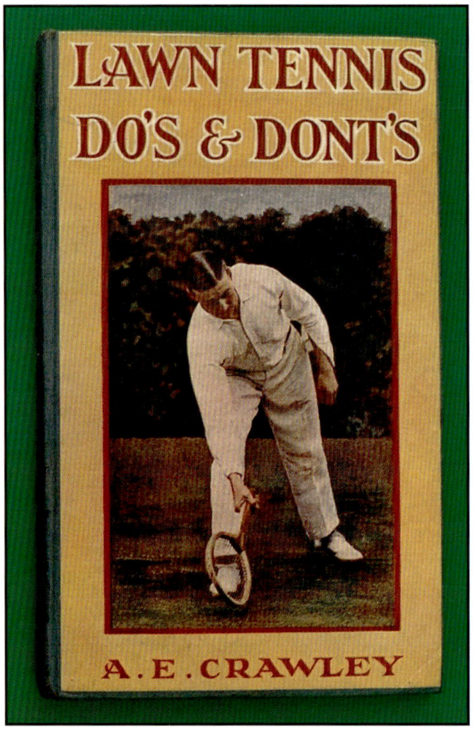

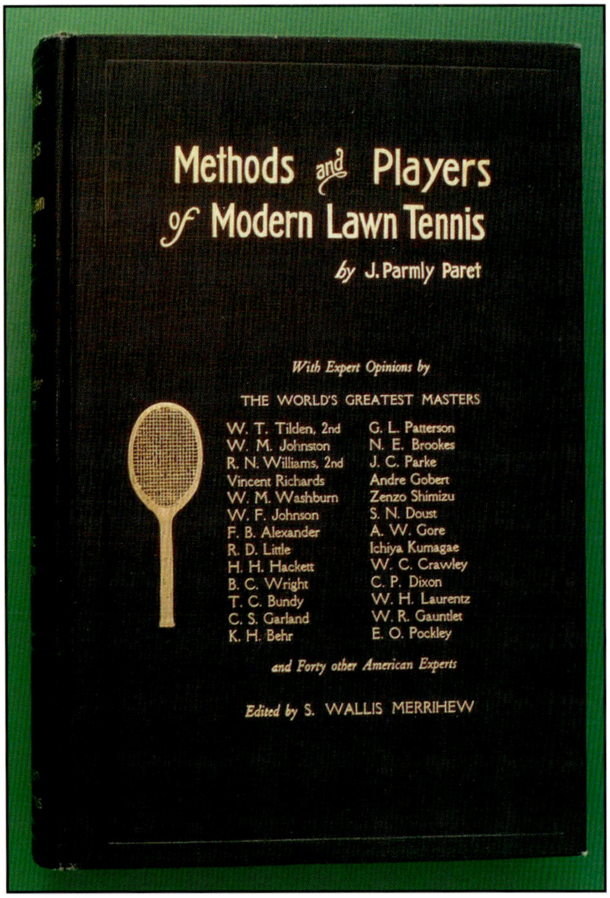

Top left:
Fig. 1.49. ***Lawn Tennis, The World Game of To-day***[20]
Lawn Tennis, The World Game of To-day - F. R. Burrow, 1st edition, Hodder & Stoughton, London, 1922, 271pp., 236 x 170mm., hard covers. Essentially a coaching book which, in the first chapter, takes a retrospective look at the few newspapers and publications which paid any attention to the new game of lawn tennis. He wrote: 'In 1896 a rival to *Pastime* appeared in *Lawn Tennis*, but the new paper only lived through that one season. (I wonder if there is anyone except myself who possesses a complete file of it? Probably not.)' The book also has over 50 action photographs of the players of the day. £75-125 ($100-200)

Left:
Fig. 1.50. ***Methods and Players of Modern Lawn Tennis***[21]
Methods and Players of Modern Lawn Tennis - J. Parmly Paret, 2nd American edition, American Lawn Tennis, New York, August 1st, 1922, 399pp., 238 x 160mm., hard covers with a very early dust-cover. On the inside front cover there's a small adhesive label by A. H. Esch & Co. Ltd., Stationers of Edmonton, Alberta. A handsome coaching book with detailed contents pages and an unusual chapter entitled: 'New Opinions of the World's Experts.' It contains over 60 photographs of famous players 'in action'. £75-125 ($100-200)

Top center:
Fig. 1.51. ***Lawn Tennis Do's & Don'ts***
Lawn Tennis Do's & Don'ts - A. E. Crawley, 1st edition, Methuen & Co. Ltd., London, 1922, 51pp., 174 x 107mm., hard covers. An attractive little coaching manual, with an unusually early, full colour photograph of the author pasted onto the front cover. £35-45 ($50-70)

Top right:
Fig. 1.52. ***Lawn Tennis***
Lawn Tennis - A. E. Crawley, 1st edition, Methuen & Co. Ltd., London, 1922, 112pp., 176 x 109mm., hard covers. A basic coaching manual with eight photographs and an extremely rare dust cover, with an interesting little chapter entitled 'Training and Health'. Under the sub-heading 'Material other than Rackets' the author recommends that tennis bags should be: '...deep enough to hold four rackets with presses, two tennis suits and a dress suit.' It contains eight (posed) photographs of the author, (not attired in his dress suit!). £30-50 ($45-75)

Fig. 1.53. ***Fifty Years of Sport***
Fifty Years of Sport at Oxford, Cambridge and the Great Public Schools, volume 2 (Oxford & Cambridge in two volumes) - A. C. M. Croombe (editor) Walter Southwood & Co., Ltd., 1913, 325pp., 325 x 250mm., hard covers. A huge book, which includes chapters on the games of rackets, real tennis, and 30 pages on lawn tennis, all played at or between the two universities. Also contains a useful biographical section and contains many photographs of early players. £85-125 ($130-200)

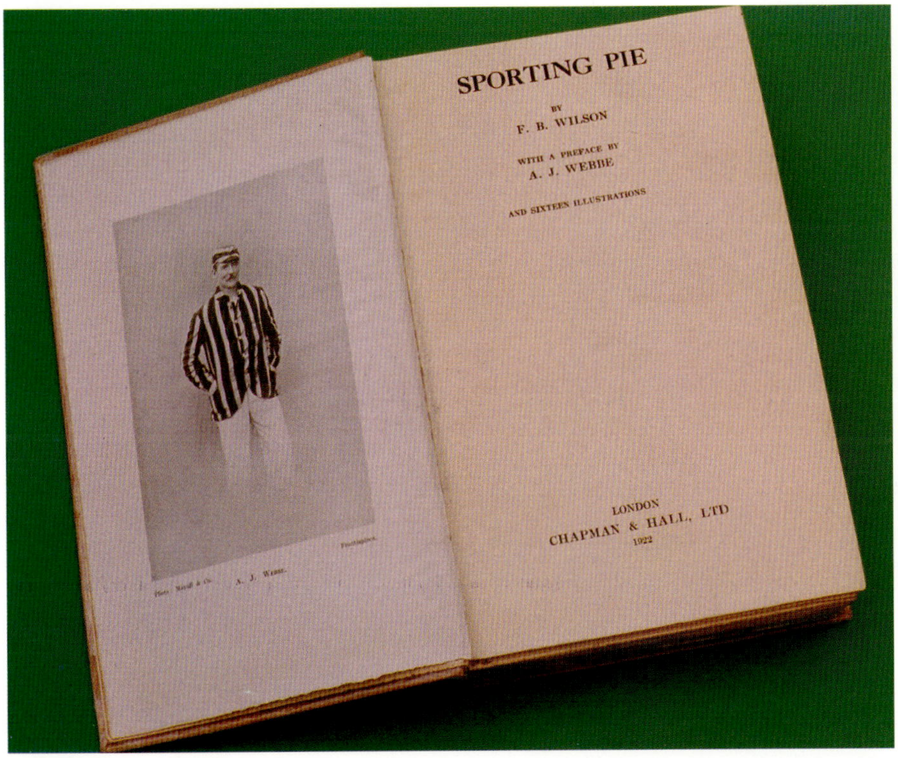

Fig. 1.54. ***Sporting Pie***
Sporting Pie - F. B. Wilson, 1st edition, Chapman & Hall, London, 1922, 287pp., 225 x 142mm., hard covers. Primarily concerning Wilson's cricketing life at Harrow school, this book also takes a look at the game of Racquets, Ping-Pong, Fives, and racket and ball games at Queen's Club. Contains 16 photographs. £25-35 ($40-55)

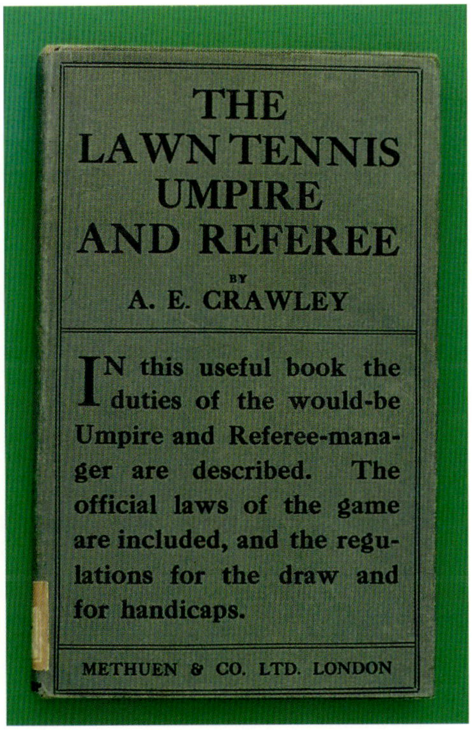

Fig. 1.55. ***The Lawn Tennis Umpire & Referee***
The Lawn Tennis Umpire & Referee, What he must know and what he must do, - A. E. Crawley, 1st edition, Methuen & Co., London, 1923, 63pp., 172 x 109mm., hard covers. An unusual little book which covers rules, scoring, handicapping and foot-faults, among many other topics. An interesting chapter concerns itself with 'The Origin of Lawn Tennis Scoring.' The book is contained in a rare, perfect dust cover. £25-35 ($40-50)

Top left:
Fig. 1.56. ***Forty Years of First-Class Lawn Tennis***[22]
Forty Years of First-Class Lawn Tennis - G. W. Hillyard R. N., 1st American edition, American Lawn Tennis, New York, 1924, 260pp., 226 x 149mm. Hillyard looks back at his tennis career and the game as it developed from the very earliest days. The book contains 24 photographs. £75-100 ($100-150)

Bottom left:
Fig. 1.57. ***Lawn Tennis Made Easy***
Lawn Tennis Made Easy, A Handbook for Juniors, Beginners & Others - Sir F. Gordon Lowe, Bart., Hutchinson & Co. Ltd., London, ?, 124pp., 177 x 112mm., paperback. A small coaching book, which includes a list of the names and addresses of contemporary professional coaches. It contains eight photographs. £30-50 ($45-75)

Top right:
Fig. 1.58. ***Concerning Lawn Tennis and Badminton***[23]
Concerning Lawn Tennis and Badminton, The Birmal Book - The Birmal Racket Dept. Smethwick, Staffs., 1925, 128pp., 190 x 127mm., card covers. A wonderful little book which examines the qualities needed to play the game successfully and relates them to the advantages of using their revolutionary new aluminium racket, the 'Birmal'. Consequently, there are several full page advertisements concerning the 'Birmal' racket, especially related to its construction. £50-75 ($75-100)

Bottom right:
Fig. 1.59. ***Lawn Tennis, The Game of Nations***
Lawn Tennis, The Game of Nations - Suzanne Lenglen, 1st edition, George G. Harrap & Co. Ltd., London, 1925, 127pp., 187 x 127mm., hard covers. A fairly standard coaching manual, written by a far from standard lawn tennis player. Includes eight interesting photographs of the author in action. In a rare dust cover. £40-60 ($60-90)

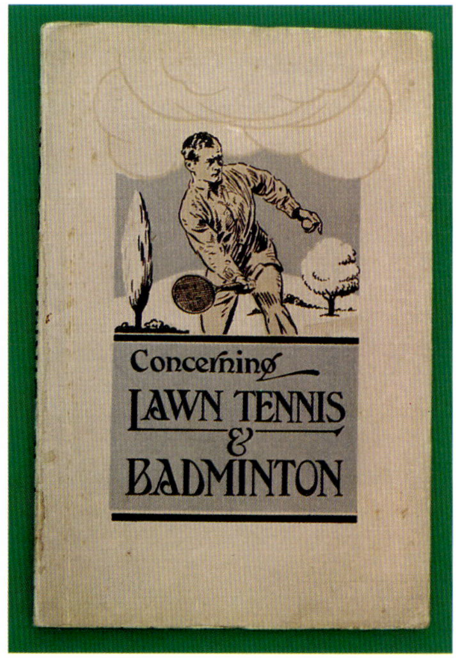

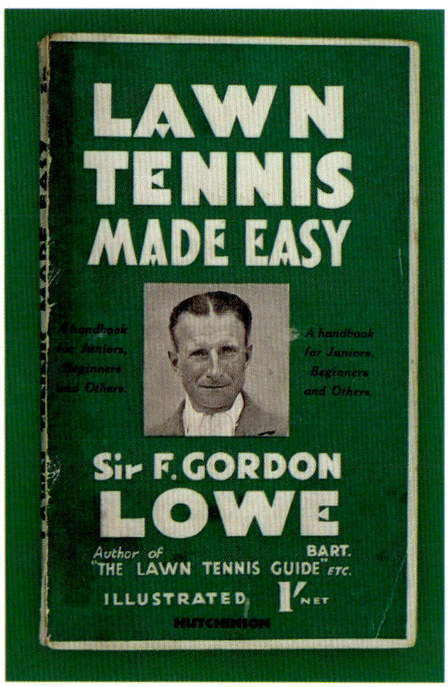

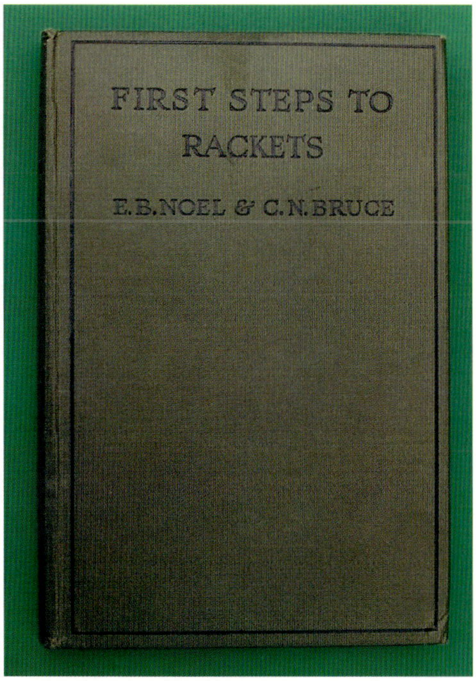

Fig. 1.60. ***First Steps to Rackets***
First Steps to Rackets - E. B. Noel & C. N. Bruce, Mills and Boon, Ltd., London, 1926, 136pp., 190 x 128mm., hard covers. A fine coaching manual with a historical section and championship listings. Includes 13 photographic plates provided by 'Messrs. Pathe Freres Cinema, Ltd. ... thus enabling readers to see illustrations of Rackets taken by the Cinematograph and Slow Motion Camera for the first time.' £75-125 ($100-200)

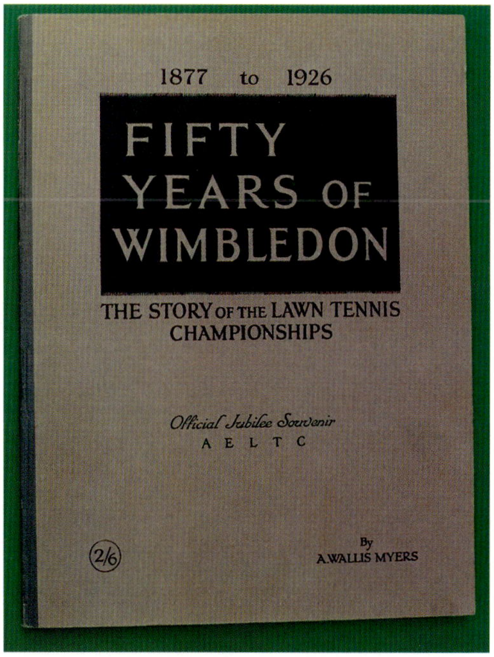

Fig. 1.62. ***Fifty Years of Wimbledon***
Fifty Years of Wimbledon, The Story of the Lawn Tennis Championships – A. Wallis Myers, C. B. E., *"The Field"* London, 1926, 96pp., 277 x 213mm., board covers. An illustrated history of the championships and the results, from the first tournament in 1877 up until 1925. This book was sold as the 'Official Jubilee Souvenir' at the 1926 Championships. It cost 2/6d. and a more expensive 'de-luxe' version with leather covers was also available. £125-150 ($200-225)

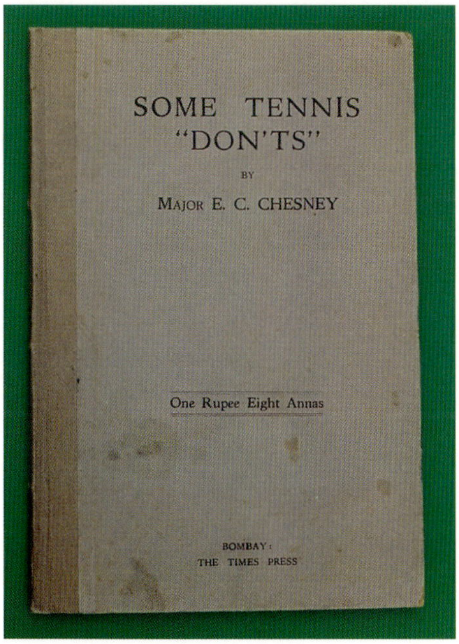

Fig. 1.61. ***Some Tennis "Don'ts"***
Some Tennis "Don'ts" - Major E. C. Chesney, The Times Press, Bombay, n.d., c. 1926, 45pp., 181 x 122mm., board covers. A coaching manual with 50 annotated paragraphs on what *not* to do when playing tennis. £20-30 ($30-45)

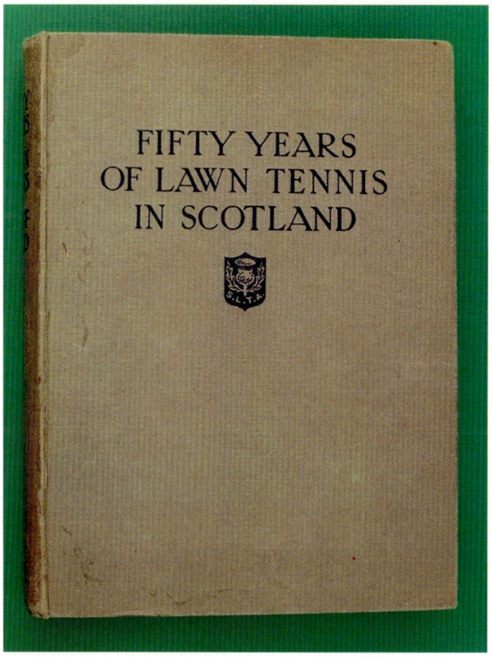

Fig. 1.63. ***Fifty Years of Lawn Tennis in Scotland***
Fifty Years of Lawn Tennis in Scotland - A. Wallis MacGregor, 1st edition, The Scottish Lawn Tennis Association, Edinburgh, 1927, 287pp., 252 x 188mm., hard covers. A large and wonderful book, which examines the development of the game in Scotland from 1874. Printed with over 150 photographs, the majority of which (as far as I know) are not printed in any other publication. £150-200 ($225-300)

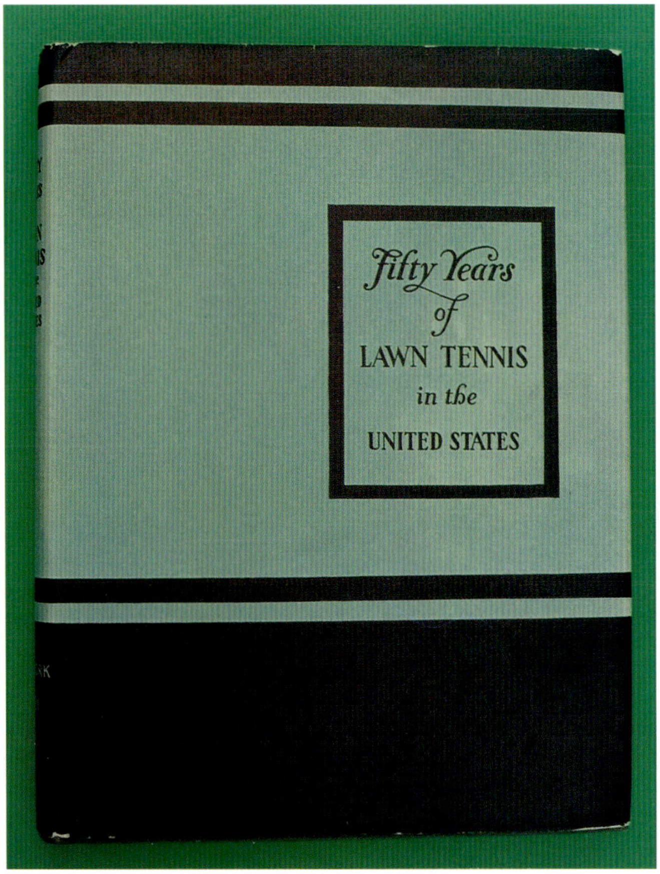

Fig. 1.64. ***Fifty Years of Lawn Tennis in the United States***
Fifty Years of Lawn Tennis in the United States – United States Lawn Tennis Association, New York, 1931, 256pp., 259 x 196mm., hard covers, with dust wrapper and glassine covers, limited edition of 3,000 copies. A very pleasant book, which was produced to celebrate the Golden Jubilee of the U. S. Lawn Tennis Association. It covers book covers the history of the game in America and how it had developed by 1931. Contains over 60 photographs. £125-150 (£185-225)

Fig. 1.66. ***The World's Tennis Stars and How to Play the Game***
The World's Tennis Stars and How to Play the Game - Pat O'Hara Wood, 2nd enlarged edition, The Imperial Press, Melbourne, 1927, 137pp., 190 x 128mm., hard covers. A very difficult book to find. It is basically a coaching book, but includes in its pages 29 photographs and small biographies of the world's leading players at the time. £75-125 ($100-185)

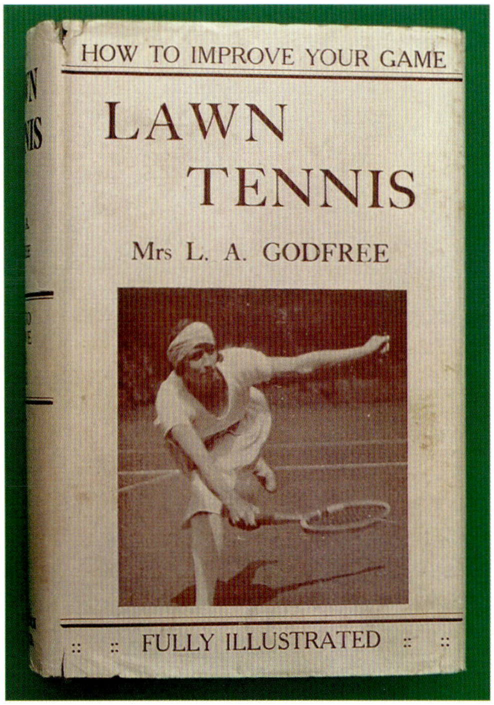

Fig. 1.65. ***Lawn Tennis How to Improve Your Game***
Lawn Tennis How to Improve Your Game - Mrs. L. A. Godfree, Ward, Lock & Co., Ltd., London, 1927, 250pp., 190 x 125mm., hard covers. Thoughts and advice on strokes, equipment, and tactics from the former Wimbledon Ladies Singles champion. It has a rare dust cover. £50-75 ($75-100)

Fig. 1.67. ***Lawn Tennis for Match Players***
Lawn Tennis for Match Players - W. T. Tilden, 2nd edition revised, Methuen & Co. Ltd., London, 1928, 48pp., 171 x 109mm., hard covers. A small book devoted to sound advice from one of the masters of the game. Contains ten photographs of famous players in action. It has a rare dust-cover, considering that it is over 70 years old. £35-50 ($50-75)

Fig. 1.68. ***Squash Rackets***
Squash Rackets - Charles R. Read, 1st edition, William Heinemann Ltd., London, 1929, 153pp., 219 x 140mm., hard covers. A coaching book, with chapters on the history and development of the game too. Contains nineteen photographs. £20-40 ($30-60)

Fig. 1.69. ***Rackets in India***
Rackets in India - Col. A. R. Winsloe, The Times of India Press, Bombay, 1930, 98pp., 192 x 130mm., hard covers. A fascinating little book, which examines the history and development of Rackets in India. Topics include: the preservation of the racket and ball, the metal bat, Indian markers, major Indian championship results, and the electric lighting of courts. A special note should be made concerning the inclusion of three folded vellum sheets, which can be found in a pocket inside the back cover. These are printed with drawings of a 'Map showing racket courts, Design of reinforced concrete door, and Plan of electric lighting of racket court.' Accompanying this book is a signed letter from the late (Lord) Colin Cowdrey (17 August 1976) thanking a gentleman for lending the book to him. £100-150 ($150-225)

Fig. 1.70. ***Rackets, Squash Rackets, Tennis, Fives and Badminton***
Rackets, Squash Rackets, Tennis, Fives and Badminton - Lord Aberdare & Others, The Lonsdale Library volume XVI, 1st edition, Seeley Service & Co. Ltd., London, 1930, 328pp., 218 x 144mm., quarter bound hard covers. A huge coaching manual, which examines the history of ball games too. Containing one hundred and fifteen photographs. It boasts marbled end papers and a ribbon bookmark. £100-150 ($150-225)

Top:
Fig. 1.71 ***Squash Rackets***
Squash Rackets – Edward Snell & Major T. Moss (in consultation with J. E. Tomkinson), 1st edition, Seeley Service & Co., Ltd., London, 1932, 32pp., 222 x 142mm., hard covers. The contents of the book are taken from *Rackets, Squash Rackets, Tennis Fives & Badminton* by Lord Aberdare (editor), 1930. A coaching manual, with many plates and hand-drawn diagrams. £10-15 ($15-22.50)

Eton & Rugby Fives
Eton & Rugby Fives, A complete handbook of practical advice, instruction and rules – David Egerton & John Armitage, Seeley Service & Co. Ltd., London, 1932, 96pp., 222 x 142mm., hard covers. Again, the contents are extracted from Lord Aberdare's book of 1930. A coaching book on how the two games are played. It contains 19 plates. £10-15 ($15-22.50)

Center:
Fig. 1.72. ***Memory's Parade***[24]
Memory's Parade - Arthur Wallis Myers C. B. E., Methuen & Co. Ltd., London, 1932, 211pp., 228 x 143mm., hard covers. Myers looks back fondly at his life, tennis, and journalistic careers. This copy is signed with a dedication by Jean Borotra (one of the four French tennis 'musketeers'), and by Myers too. Also included is a calling card for: 'Mr. & Mrs. A. Wallis Myers, The Misses Wallis Myers, Berrow Epsom.' £25-35 ($40-55)

My Story
My Story - Fred J. Perry, 1st edition, Hutchinson & Co. Ltd., London, 1935?, 317pp., 237 x 157mm., hard covers. Perry looks back at his tennis career up to 1934. £100-175 ($150-250)

Off the Racket[25]
Off the Racket, Tennis Highlights and Lowdowns - Phillip B. Hawk, 1st edition, American Lawn Tennis, New York, 1937, 391pp., 233 x 156mm., hard covers. A huge but amusing book concerning world tennis, with a personal slant on events and personalities. Wallis Merrihew introduces the book: 'By his own admission the purpose of the author of this work has been to entertain and amuse rather than to advise and instruct.' Merrihew ends the chapter with: 'It is tinctured with Rabelaisianisms, being full of humour and intensely human.' It contains over 50 illustrations including many delightful cartoons by Blythe Wilson. A fictional results sheet entitled: 'First Open Championship of the World' is often missing from this book. This volume came from the Christian Literature Society, Tokyo. £30-50 ($45-75)

Bottom:
Fig. 1.73. ***Lowes Lawn Tennis Annual***[26]
Lowes Lawn Tennis Annual and Compendium for 1933 - Sir F. Gordon Lowe, Eyre & Spottiswoode, London, 1933, 547pp., 188 x 129mm., hard covers. A magnificent book filled with illuminating facts and figures concerning contemporary lawn tennis events and players. £30-50 ($45-75)

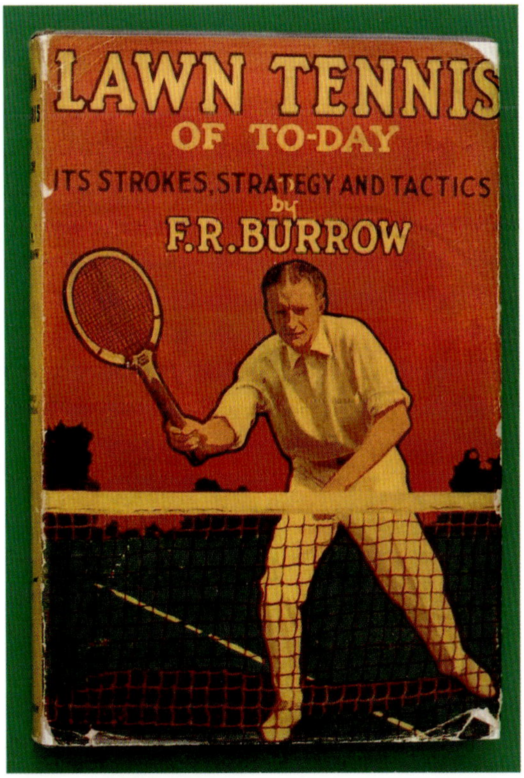

Fig. 1.74. ***Lawn Tennis of To-day***
Lawn Tennis of To-day, its strokes, strategy, and tactics – F. R. Burrow, New and Revised (3rd) Edition, C. Arthur Pearson Ltd., London, 1933, 124pp., 185 x 124mm., hard covers. A standard coaching manual, which has a rare and attractively designed dust cover. £35-55 ($50-80)

Fig. 1.76. ***Perry Wins***
Perry Wins, Expert advice for all on Lawn Tennis - Fred J. Perry, Hutchinson & Co. Ltd., London, 1935, 156pp., 181 x 119mm., stiff board covers. It takes a retrospective look at the life of: 'England's 1st International Tennis Champion for 25 years.' Because of its fragile construction, this book is very difficult to find in good condition. It contains 27 photographs. £30-40 ($45-60)

Fig. 1.75. ***Wimbledon's Who's Who and Tennis Celebrities***
Wimbledon's Who's Who and Tennis Celebrities - Ed. J. Burrow & Co. Ltd., Dunlop Rubber Co., Ltd., 1st edition, London, 1934, 154pp., 202 x 128mm., soft covers. This is mainly a (very informative) biographical reference to many contemporary lawn tennis players. £30-45 ($45-70)

Fig. 1.77. ***British Sports and Sportsmen***
British Sports and Sportsmen, athletic sports, tennis, rackets and other ball games - Number 857 of a limited edition of 1000 copies, Sports & Sportsmen Ltd., London, c. 1931, 421pp., 385 x 270mm., hard covers. A large and impressive book, concerning itself with all kinds of sports ranging from the Olympic Games through to the Grasmere and Highland Sports. There are chapters on real tennis, lawn tennis, rackets and squash rackets, fives and badminton. It contains nine photogravures of eminent sportsmen and over 125 other photographs. With marbled end papers, this book was one of a whole series of similarly bound limited edition copies, and this particular copy was from the personal library of J. D. P. Wheatley, a 1930s British Davis Cup Player. £175-275 ($250-400)

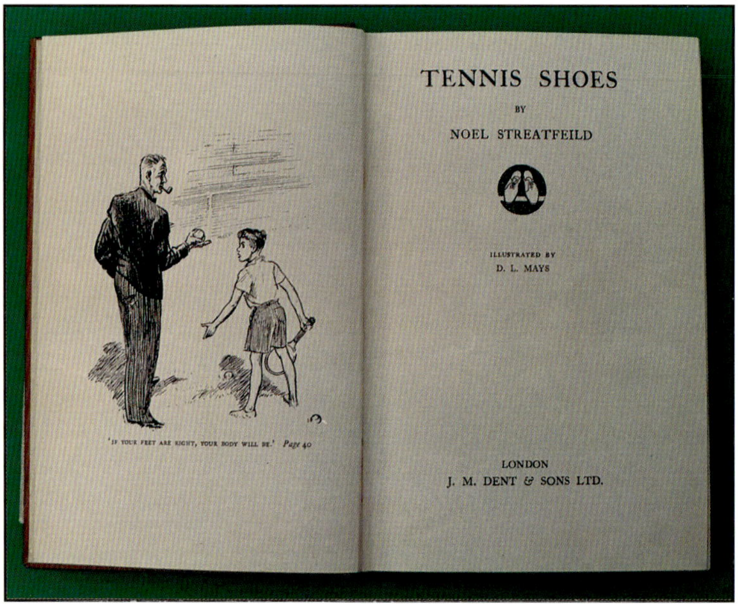

Fig. 1.78. ***Tennis Shoes***
Tennis Shoes - Noel Streatfield, 1st edition, J. M. Dent & Sons Ltd., London, 1937, 227pp., 201 x 134mm., hard covers. A pleasing tennis novel, with illustrations by D. L. Mays. £30-50 ($45-75)

Fig. 1.80. ***The Art of the Tennis Racket-Maker and of Tennis***[27]
The Art of the Tennis Racket-Maker and of Tennis - M. de Garsault, 1st English translation, (Number three of two hundred copies) privately printed by Raven Printers Ltd., Great Britain, 1938, 45pp. + 5 plates, 257 x 189mm., hard covers. This is a very special book. The first one hundred and fifty copies only were numbered and were reserved for Members of The Royal Tennis Court. This copy is dedicated to: 'E. Latham with best wishes Revelstoke, June 16 1938'. 'Emille' Latham was the son of Peter Latham, the former World Real Tennis Champion. The book is signed by the club secretary, Christopher Gabriel. £300-500 ($450-750)

Fig. 1.79. ***The Squash Rackets Annual***
The Squash Rackets Annual - Hubert Winterbotham (edit.), Eyre & Spottiswoode, London, 1937-38, 230pp., 208 x 141mm., hard vellum covered covers. A superbly informative, detailed annual, which tells you all you would need to know about the world of squash rackets, just before the Second World War. £30-50 ($45-75)

Fig. 1.81. **"Service"**
"Service" booklet from Slazengers Ltd., issues for 1938, 1939, and 1947 (all 36pp.), 176 x 113mm., paperback. The 1938 issue explains the reason for its publication: 'In this little booklet you will find details of Lawn Tennis events in the coming season; records of the game and tennis personalities of the past and present; useful information about equipment, and many other items of interest, all of which perhaps may remind you that, for over half a century, the name of Slazengers has been synonymous with Lawn Tennis and good "Service" in the fullest sense of the word.' This edition has an interesting four page article on how a racket is made. The 1939 copy has details on: 'The (historic) Development of 'Court' and 'Lawn' Tennis.' The post-war edition concentrates on advice from Dan Maskell. £10-15 ($15-22.50)

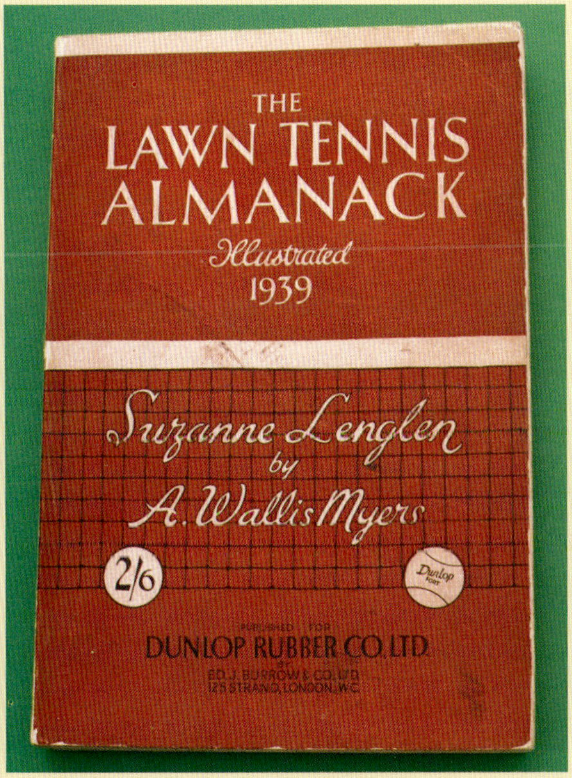

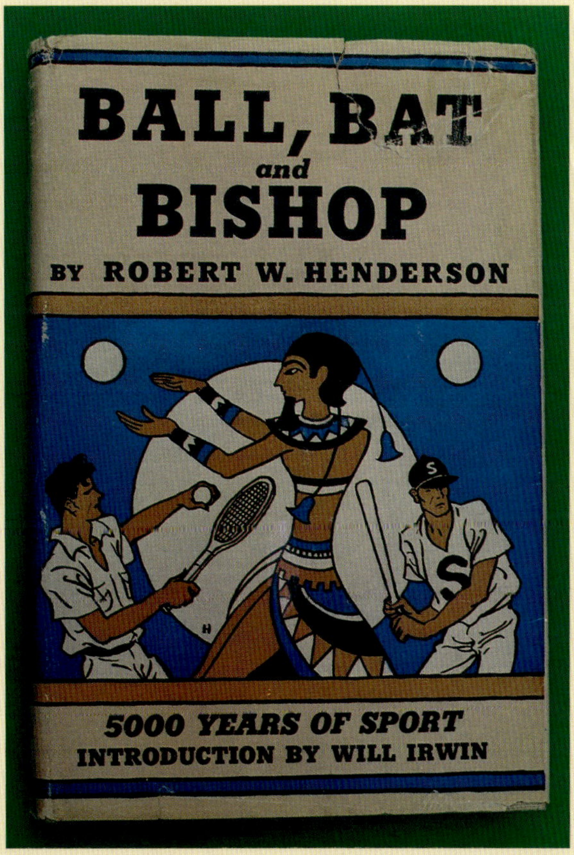

Top left:
Fig. 1.82. ***The Lawn Tennis Almanac***
The Lawn Tennis Almanac - A. Wallis Myers (edit.), Ed. J. Burrows & Co. Ltd., for Dunlop Rubber Co. Ltd., 1939, 428pp.,183 x 123mm., card covers. A wonderfully researched book covering British, European, and world tournaments and their records. It contains 31 photographs and also dedicates the opening chapter to the life of the late Suzanne Lenglen, who had passed away during the Wimbledon Championships, just one year before. £30-60 ($45-90)

Bottom left:
Fig. 1.83. ***Table Tennis***
Table Tennis, A guide for beginners & enthusiasts – Eric Hyde, W. Foulsham & Co. Ltd., London, n.d., c. 1941, 92pp., 114 x 103mm., paperback. A very small coaching manual with a rare and fragile dust cover. Containing eight photographs. 'This book was first published just after a vital change in the rules of the game, namely, the lowering of the net from 6 3/4ins. to 6ins.' £10-15 ($15-22.50)

Top right:
Fig. 1.84. ***Cradle of Lawn Tennis***
Cradle of Lawn Tennis, The Story of Warwickshire and Its Clubs - Ronald Lerry, 1st edition, Stanford & Mann Ltd., Birmingham, December 1946, 142pp., 226 x 146mm., hard covers. 'This book not only gives a history of club and county life, rich in incident, but throws a remarkable new light on the origin of the game itself.' It also includes a pocket history of all the clubs in Warwickshire up until 1947. Susan Partridge signed it on the dust cover and on an inside page. £25-45 ($40-70)

Bottom right:
Fig. 1.85. ***Ball, Bat and Bishop***
Ball, Bat and Bishop, the origin of ball games – Robert W. Henderson, 1st edition, Rockport Press, Inc., New York, 1947, 220pp., 234 x 156mm., hard covers. Primarily a history of Baseball, with the origins of other bat and ball games (including tennis and racquets) somewhere in the middle. This book was originally published in a rather incongruously designed dust cover, which is quite difficult to find. Personally I'd rather see it without one! This copy has a signed dedication by Henderson. £150-250 ($225-375)

Fig. 1.86. ***That Badminton Racket***
That Badminton Racket - Betty Uber, Hutchinson's Library of Sports and Pastimes, London, n.d., c. 1950, 122pp., 216 x 138mm., hard covers. An autobiographical book which also covers the history of badminton and coaching tips too. This book is particularly special in that it is signed by over 75 players of the day, including the author. £35-50 ($50-75)

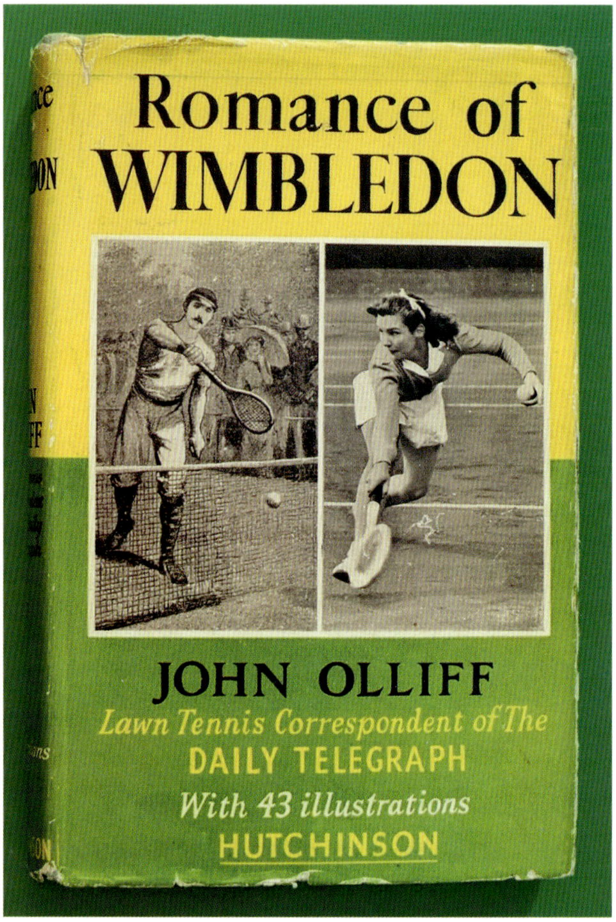

Fig. 1.88. ***The Romance of Wimbledon***
The Romance of Wimbledon - John Olliff, Hutchinson & Co. Ltd., 1st edition, London, 1949, 183pp., 220 x141mm., hard covers. Basically, a history of Wimbledon up until the late 1940s. 43 photographs. £20-25 ($30-40)

Fig. 1.87. ***The International Lawn Tennis Club of Great Britain***
The International Lawn Tennis Club of Great Britain, Silver Jubilee (1924 - 1949), 1st edition, Tonbridge, 1949, 127pp., 190 x 123mm., hard covers. Arthur Wallis Myers was the founder of the club, and the book traces its history over the first 25 years. £20-30 ($30-45)

Fig. 1.89. ***Tennis A-Z***
Tennis A-Z, How to Play Better Tennis - William T. Tilden, Victor Gollancz Ltd., London, 1950, 192pp., 204 x 136mm., hard covers. 'Tilden not only plays a great game of tennis, he can also teach it. He knows as much about theory, tactics, technique and winning psychology as anyone who ever swung a racket. All that he knows about the art and science of playing tennis is in the 20 chapters of this book. Reading it is like taking 20 personal lessons from The Old Master.' Now I wouldn't quite go that far! Quite an 'in-depth' coaching manual illustrated with drawings by Frederick E. Banbery. £20-35 ($30-50)

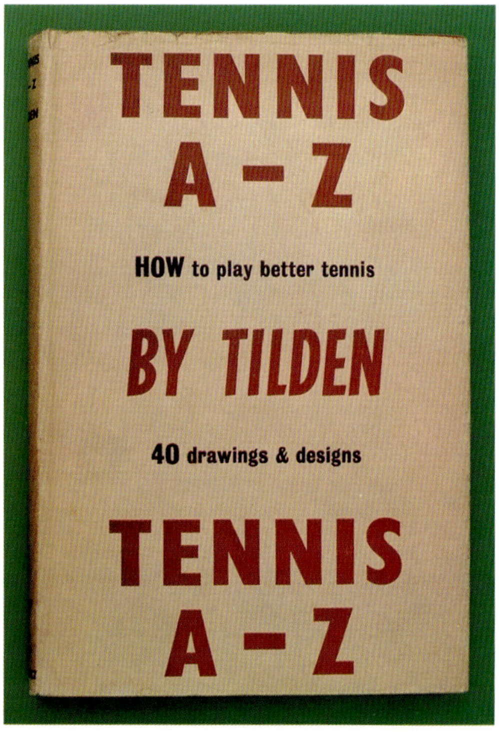

Fig. 1.90. ***Dunlop Lawn Tennis Almanack***
Dunlop Lawn Tennis Almanack - G. P. Hughes editor, Ed. J. Burrow & Co. Ltd., London, for Dunlop Sports Co. Ltd., editions for 1951, 1953, 1955, 1956, 1957, 1958. Containing between 320 and 400pp., 184 x 121mm., soft covers. A very informative annual concentrating upon the game in England, but containing international results and news too. The book has many advertisements and photographs. £20-25 ($30-40)

Fig. 1.92. ***The Hurlingham Club***
The Hurlingham Club (1869-1953) - Capt. Taprell Dorling, The Hurlingham Club, London, 1954, 69pp., 210 x 142mm., hard covers. The history and development of this sporting club ever since it was established in 1869 for the purpose of pigeon shooting! The club first became acquainted with the game of lawn tennis in 1877 when the committee decided to give a silver tennis racket '...to be played for by members on the lawn racket ground...' £10-15 ($15-22.50)

Fig. 1.91. ***British Sports Past & Present, Lawn Tennis***
British Sports Past & Present, Lawn Tennis - Brigadier J. G. Smyth, 1st edition, B. T. Batsford, London, 1953, 240pp., 223 x 143mm., hard covers. A history of lawn tennis. This book has an attractive full colour cover, which is often missing or severely damaged. 54 photographs. £15-25 ($22.50-40)

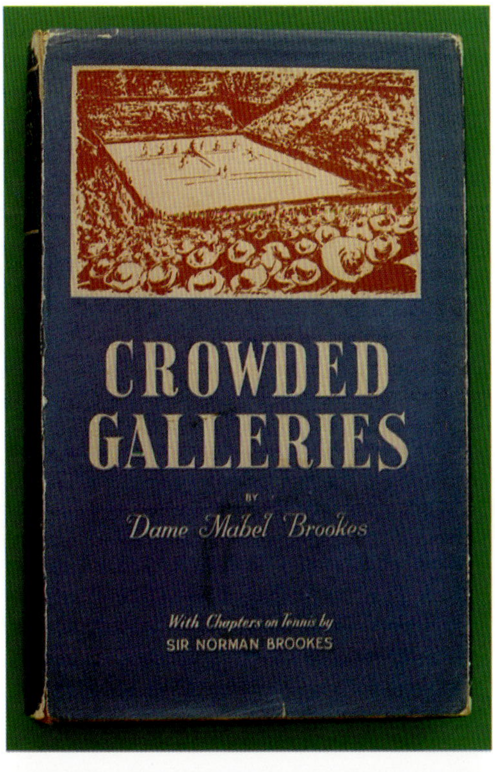

Fig. 1.93. ***Crowded Galleries***
Crowded Galleries - Dame Mabel Brookes, 1st edition, William Heinemann Ltd., London, 1956, 324pp., 221 x 143mm., hard covers. This book records the life of Norman Brookes, the Australian Wimbledon Champion, as well as their life together in later years. £15-25 ($22.50-40)

Left:
Fig. 1.94. ***Budge on Tennis***
Budge on Tennis - Donald Budge, Hamilton & Co. (Stafford), Ltd., London, published as a Panther Book, 1957, 160pp., 179 x 114mm., paperback. 'An outstanding champion and a real sportsman tells in this book how he became one of the world's greatest tennis players.' The book contains 64 action photographs of Budge demonstrating how all the shots should be played. Jarrolds (London) Ltd. first published it in June 1939 and four reprints were to follow. £10-15 ($15-22.50)

Bottom left:
Fig. 1.95. ***The Centre Court Story***
The Centre Court Story - Maurice Brady, W. Foulsham & Co. Ltd., London, 1957, 227pp., 222 x 144mm., hard covers. A history of The All-England Club and its most prominent players, mainly since its time at the new location. £15-25 ($22.50-40)

Below:
Fig. 1.96. ***The B. P. Yearbook of Lawn Tennis***
The B. P. Yearbook of Lawn Tennis - Lance Tingay & John Barrett, Clipper Press, London, 1970, 288pp., 199 x 132mm., hard covers. 'This 1970 INTERNATIONAL EDITION covers these events (Laver's 2nd Grand Slam & Ann Jones' Wimbledon) in depth and brings the crowded events of 1969 into sharp focus through the pens of some of the world's leading tennis journalists.' £15-25 ($22.50-40)

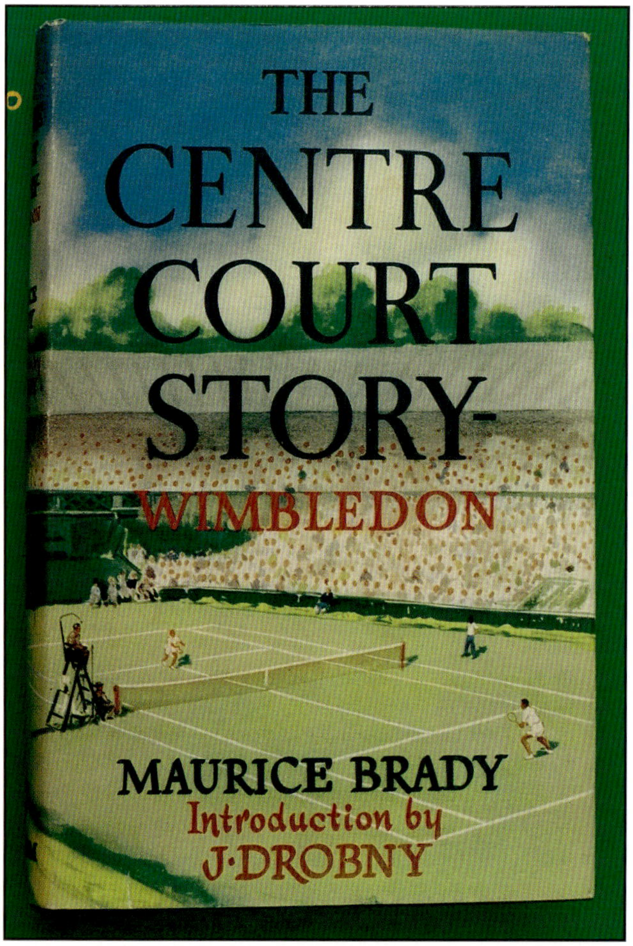

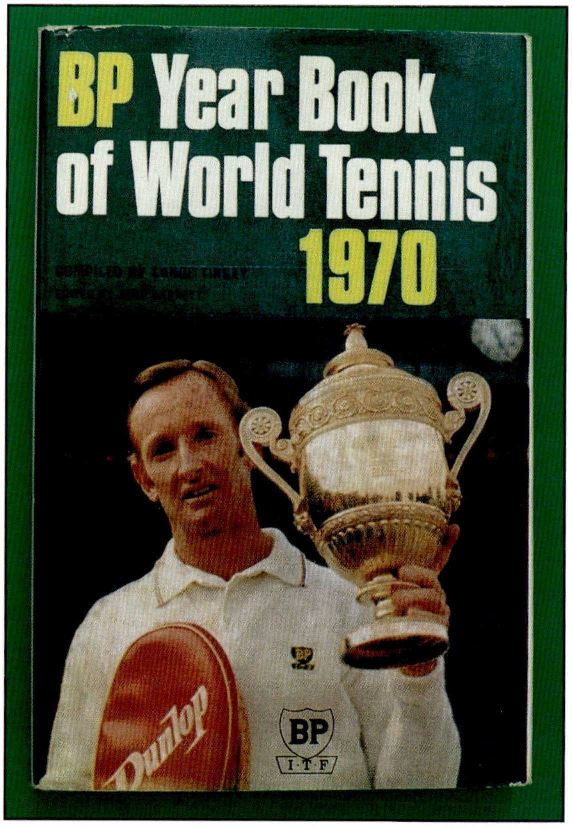

Fig. 1.97. ***The Lawn Tennis Year***
The Lawn Tennis Year - Sidney Moorhouse (editor), Pelham Books Ltd., London, 1971, 143pp., 223 x 141mm., hard covers. An interesting review of the lawn tennis world in 1970. Although the American, European, and Australian seasons are covered, the book concentrates on Great Britain. Chapters on 'The Scottish Scene' the Midlands and Northern and Southern regions provide an informative insight into 'grass-roots' tennis. Containing 16 photographs. £15-25 ($22.50-40)

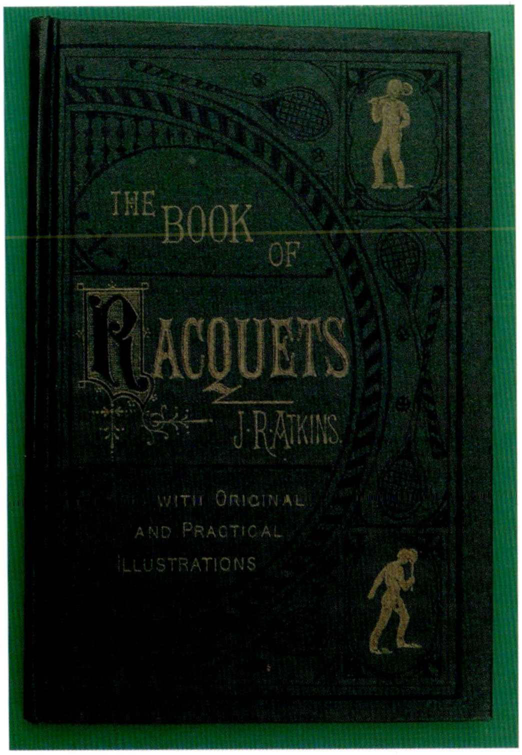

Fig. 1.99. ***The Book of Racquets***
The Book of Racquets, a practical guide to the game and its history, and to The Different Courts in which it is played. - J. R. Atkins, number 228 of a limited number edition of 250 copies, Raquetier Productions Ltd., 1981 reprint of 1873? 1st edition, 108pp., 190 x 130mm., hard covers. A detailed publication, which provides a lot of useful information about the game. The original is extremely difficult to find. Over 25 woodcut illustrations. £40-75 ($60-100)

Fig. 1.98. ***The Fireside Book of Tennis***
The Fireside Book of Tennis, A complete history of the game and its great players and matches - Allison Danzig & Peter Scwed, 1972, 1043pp., 237 x 161mm., hard covers. A truly enormous volume, which primarily looks back at the great matches and events from tennis history. Containing 75 photographs. £20-30 (30-45)

Fig. 1.100. ***The Lawn Tennis Association Official Handbook***
The Lawn Tennis Association Official Handbook - The Lawn Tennis Association, London, editions for 1939, 1973, and 1983, pages vary between 320 and 520pp., approx. 164 x 103mm., paperback. Prior to the publication of the 'Tennis Great Britain' range, this publication stood as a guide to the Association and British tennis. Each copy contains a good many advertisements by companies which were suppliers to the game in one capacity or another. £10-20 ($15-30)

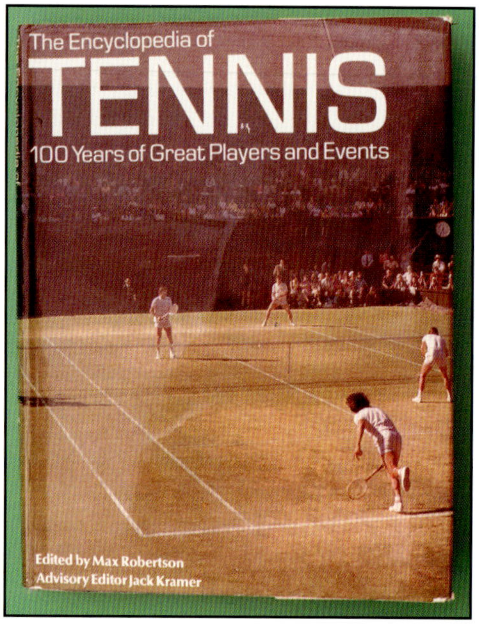

Fig. 1.101. ***The Encyclopaedia of Tennis***
The Encyclopaedia of Tennis, 100 Years of Great Players and Events - Max Robertson (editor), The Viking Press Inc., New York, 1974., 392pp., 285 x 220mm., hard covers. A large book which explores the origins of the game right through to 1974. Many photographs and a good A-Z section too. £20-25 ($30-40)

Fig. 1.102. ***Tennis***
Tennis - Gianni Clerici, 1st edition, Octopus Books Ltd., London, 1976, 335pp., 308 x 245mm., hard covers. A huge, informative book about the history and development of lawn tennis and other racket and ball games. Containing hundreds of photographs, this book is very prone to damage due to its size. £30-60 ($45-90)

Fig. 1.103. ***100 years of Wimbledon***
100 years of Wimbledon - Lance Tingay, Guinness Superlatives Ltd., Enfield, 1977, 256pp., 302 x 215mm., hard covers. An interesting book, with a fine biographical section. This book also provides a list of all the names of the semi-finalists at Wimbledon (in all the main competitions). There's also a fine double-page photograph of a selection of very old lawn tennis rackets (including a sphairistike racket) from the Wimbledon Museum collection. The book contains lots of photographs. £15-20 ($22.50-30)

Fig. 1.104. ***100 Years of The Wimbledon Tennis Championships***
100 Years of The Wimbledon Tennis Championships - James Medlcott, The Hamlyn Publishing Group Ltd., London, 1977, 93pp., 286 x 218mm., hard covers. An 'easy to read' book based upon exactly what the title says it is! It contains many photographs. £15-25 ($22.50-40)

Fig. 1.105. ***The Annals of Tennis***
The Annals of Tennis - Julian Marshall, a 1973 reprint of the original 1878 edition. 226pp., 253 x 192mm., hard decorative covers. Commonly regarded as *the* reference manual on the game of Real or Royal Tennis, with numerous illustrations and a very comprehensive index. £100-175 ($150-225)

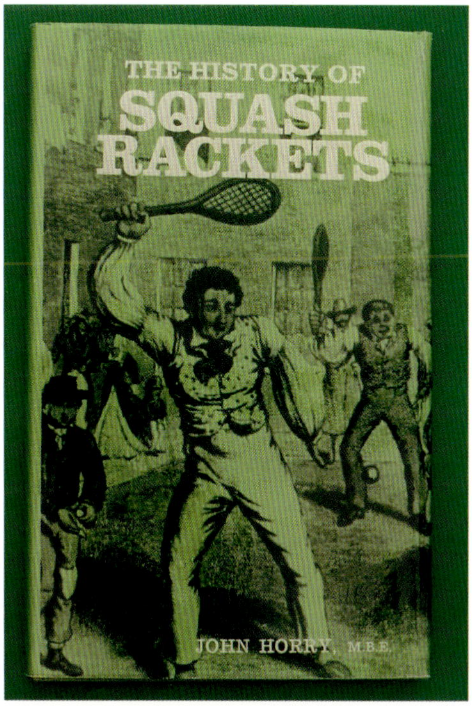

Fig. 1.107. ***The History of Squash Rackets***
The History of Squash Rackets - John Horry, M. B. E., 1st edition, A. C. M. Webb (Publishing) Co. Ltd., England, 1979, 183pp., 218 x 137mm., hard covers. Everything you would wish to know about the game. The book contains 14 photographs. £10-15 ($15-22.50)

Fig. 1.106. ***The Concise Dictionary of Tennis***
The Concise Dictionary of Tennis - Martin Hedges, Bison Books, London, 1978, 278pp., 262 x 199mm., hard covers. This book takes us neatly through the alphabet while concentrating upon the primary tennis topics. Occasionally the reader is given snippets of information which are quite difficult to find anywhere else. For example, there is paragraph about Harold S. Barlow, F. S. Stoker, and lawn tennis in Wales. Containing many photographs. £15-20 ($22.50-30)

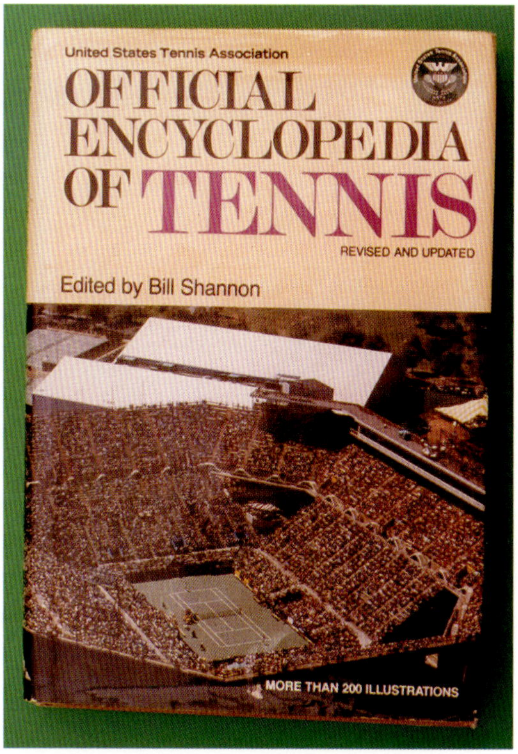

Fig. 1.108. ***Official Encyclopaedia of Tennis***
Official Encyclopaedia of Tennis, United States Tennis Association - Edited by Bill Shannon with the staff of the U S T A, revised and updated, Harper & Row, Publishers, New York, 1979, 497pp., 266 x 185mm., hard covers. It has seven chapters full of facts and statistics, chiefly about the American game and contains a large number of photographs. £15-25 ($22.50-40)

Fig. 1.109. ***The Tennis Players***
The Tennis Players, from pagan rites to strawberries and cream - Tom Todd, 1st edition, Vallency Press (F. H. Books Ltd.), Guernsey, 1979, 240pp., 283 x 220mm., hard covers. A superbly researched and presented book. It contains many images and much information that I have never seen before. Filled with illustrations and photographs, and limited to 500 copies. £350-450 ($475-675)

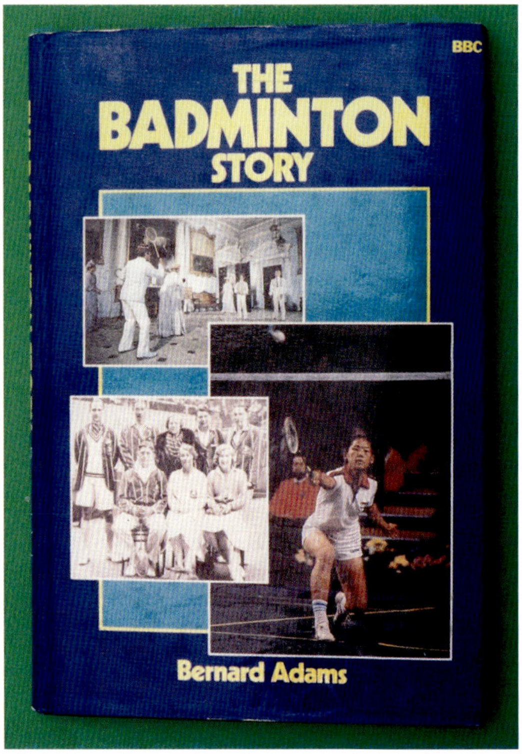

Fig. 1.111. ***The Badminton Story***
The Badminton Story - Bernard Adams, 1st edition, BBC, London, 1980, 144pp., 238 x 159mm., hard covers. '...the first, fully illustrated account of how the game developed from the 'hit-and-scream' of Victorian times to the modern world game.' A book about everything associated with badminton, including many photographs of early equipment and players. £10-15 ($15-22.50)

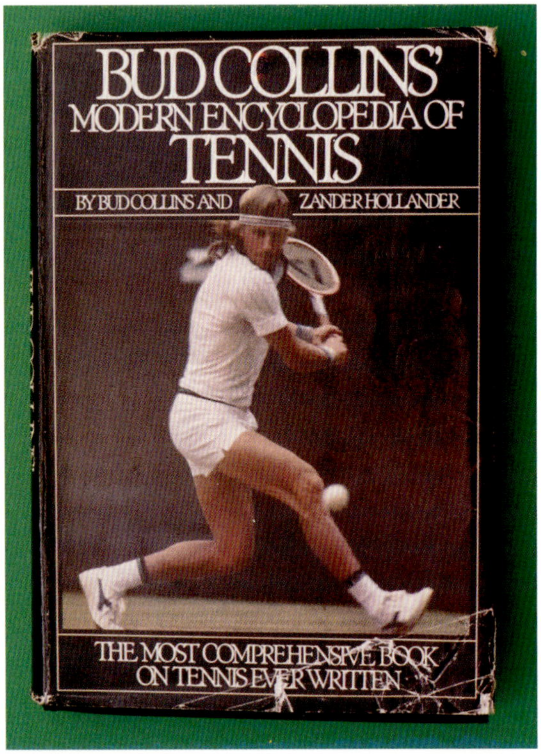

Fig. 1.110. ***Bud Collins' Modern Encyclopaedia of Tennis***
Bud Collins' Modern Encyclopaedia of Tennis - Edited by Bud Collins and Zander Hollander, Doubleday & Company, Inc., New York, 1980, 389pp., 265 x 185mm., hard covers. A large illustrated, informative book with ten chapters dedicated to all manners of facts and figures. £15-25 ($22.50-40)

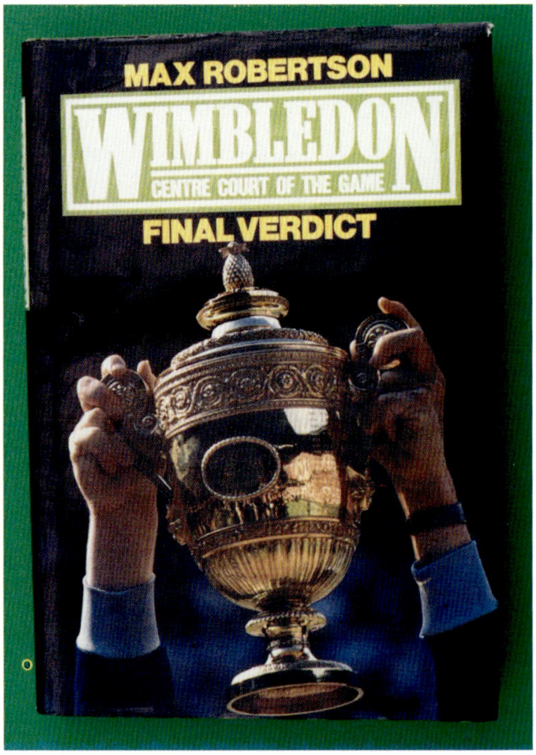

Fig. 1.112. ***Wimbledon Centre Court of The Game***
Wimbledon Centre Court of The Game, Final Verdict - Max Robertson, 3rd edition, BBC Books, London, 1981, 500pp., 254 x 177mm., hard covers. The story of the Wimbledon Championships from the first year in 1877. Filled with photographs. £15-20 ($22.50-30)

Fig. 1.113. ***Wimbledon of the North***
Wimbledon of the North, 100 Years at the Northern - David Allaby, E. J. Morten, Manchester, 1981, 183pp., 228 x 142mm., hard covers. A history of the 'Northern' tournament since its inception in 1880. £15-25 ($22.50-40)

Fig. 1.115. ***The Renee Richards Story***
The Renee Richards Story, Second Serve - Renee Richards with Richard Ames, Stein and Day, New York, 1983, 373pp., 236 x 158mm., hard covers. The story of how, following a sex change operation, a man named Richard H. Raskind became tennis playing Renee Richards. The book also includes a letter to Vanessa Redgrave (who played Richards in a feature film) from Linda Yellen of Chrysalis-Yellen Productions, Inc., New York: 'Dear V: The excitement has started already. I can't wait to be working with you again, While the script is being written, I thought you'd like to look at the book - and yes I knew you were a great tennis player!' Contains 35 photographs. £40-50 ($60-75)

Fig. 1.114. ***The Wimbledon Lawn Tennis Museum***
The Wimbledon Lawn Tennis Museum – Valerie Warren, Leonard Lawrance, 1982, 28pp., 203 x 212mm., paperback. A guided tour through the Wimbledon Museum with the aid of many photographs and diagrams. £10-15 ($15-22.50)

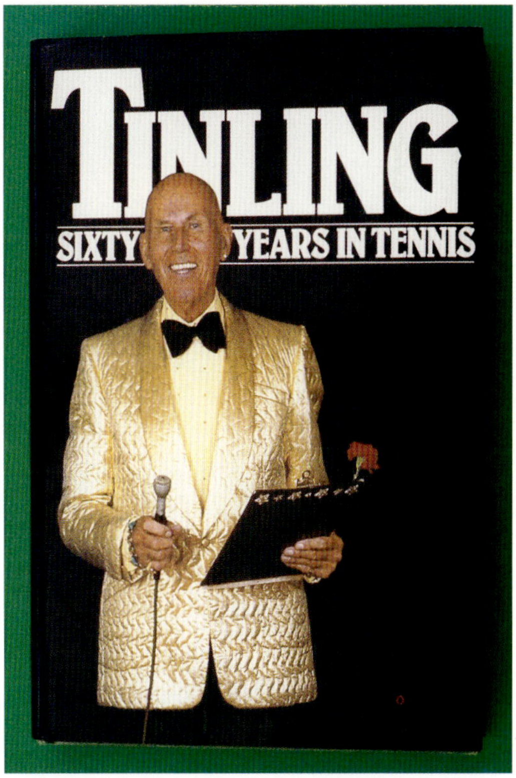

Fig. 1.116. ***Tinling Sixty Years of Tennis***
Tinling Sixty Years of Tennis - Ted Tinling, Sidgwick & Jackson, London, 1983, 222pp., 240 x 160mm., hard covers. A very entertaining autobiographical volume recalling Tinling's memories of people and events in the tennis world. Illustrated with over 30 photographs. £15-20 ($22.50-30)

Fig. 1.117. ***Tennis, Squash and Badminton Bygones***
Tennis, Squash and Badminton Bygones - Gerald N. Gurney, Shire Publications Ltd., Aylesbury, 1984, 32pp., 210 x 147mm., paperback. A fine little booklet, which introduces racket sports collecting as a hobby. Containing over 60 photographs and diagrams. £5-10 ($7.50-15)

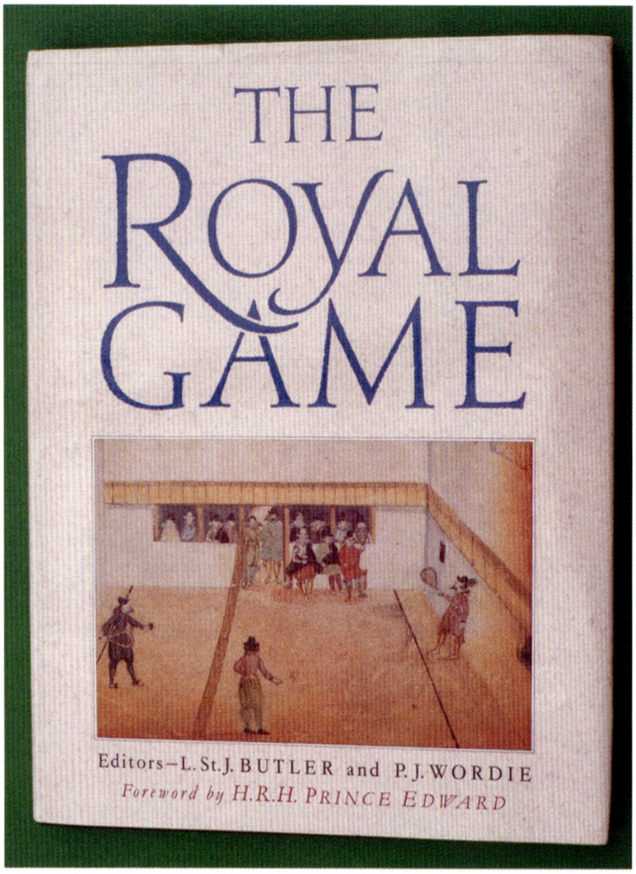

Fig. 1.119. ***The Royal Game***
The Royal Game – Editors – L. St. J. Butler and P. J. Wordie, Falkland Palace Real Tennis Club, Stirling, 1989, 144pp., 252 x 194mm., hard covers. 'This collection of pieces on real tennis celebrates the 450th Anniversary of the oldest surviving tennis court in the world, the Royal tennis court at Falkland Palace in Fife.' The book contains many photographs and drawings. £20-25 ($30-40)

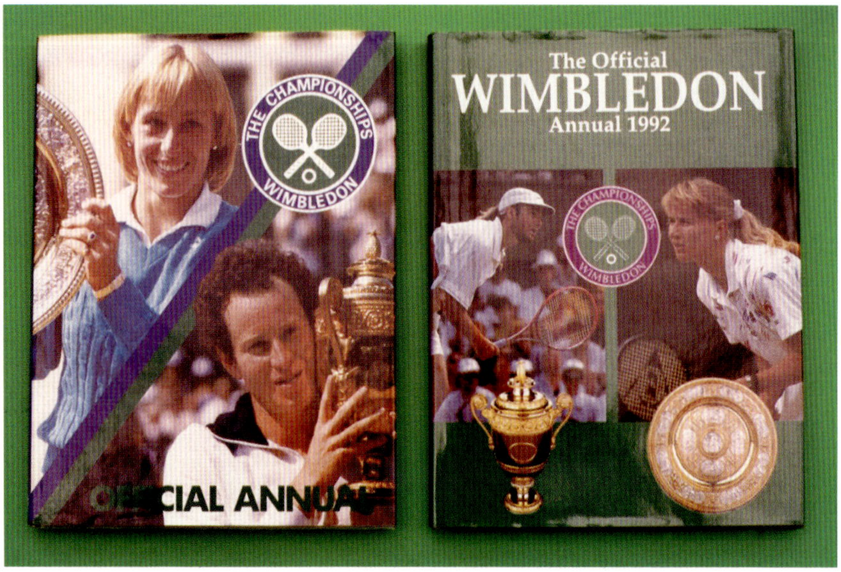

Fig. 1.118. ***The Championships Wimbledon, Official Annual***
The Championships Wimbledon, Official Annual - John Parsons, Pavilion Books Ltd, London, 1984, 160pp., 282 x 214mm., hard covers. A 'blow by blow' (I couldn't resist using that phrase!) account of the championships during the 'tennis fortnight' in Britain. It contains many outstanding photographs by Tommy Hindley and other very accomplished photographers. £40-60 ($60-90)

The Official Wimbledon Annual, 1992
The Official Wimbledon Annual, 1992 - John Parsons, Chapmans Publishers, London, 1992, 156pp., 280 x 216mm., hard covers. A superbly produced book, which continues the 'series' of offical Wimbledon annuals. Unlike its predecessor, this copy is printed in full-colour throughout. Wonderful photographs by Bob Martin, Chris Cole, and Gary M. Prior. £15-25 ($20-35)

Fig. 1.120. ***Game, Set and Glory***
Game, Set and Glory, A History of the Australian Tennis Championships - Bruce Matthews, 1st edition, The Five Mile Press, Victoria, 1985, 138pp., 287 x 217mm., hard covers. A book which guides us through the history of the national championships, from day one until 1985. It contains many photographs. £10-15 ($15-22.50)

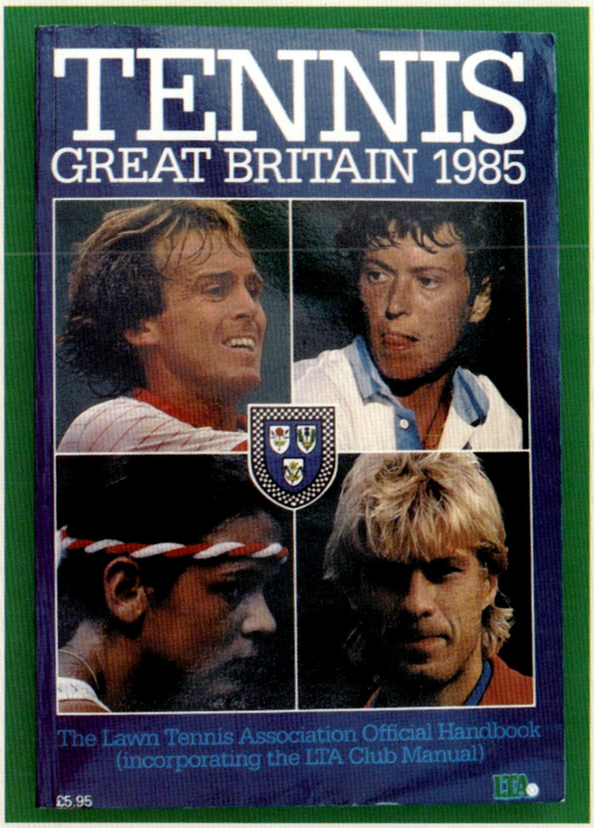

Fig. 1.121. ***Tennis Great Britain***
Tennis Great Britain, The Lawn Tennis Association Official Handbook (incorporating the LTA Club Manual) - David Irvine (editor), The Lawn Tennis Association, London, copies for 1985, '86, and '87, between 360 and 460pp., 218 x 148mm., soft covers. These handbooks covered everything associated with the game in Great Britain, from ranking lists to tournaments regulations for club matches. In each copy there follows a section entitled 'The Lawn Tennis Association Club Manual' running to some 50 or so pages, which concerns itself with advice on the establishment and funding of private clubs. Each volume has many photographs of players and clubs. £10-20 ($15-30)

Fig. 1.123. ***100 Wimbledon Championships***
100 Wimbledon Championships, a celebration - John Barrett, Willow Books, William Collins Sons & Co. Ltd., London, 1986, 287pp., 281 x 223mm., hard covers. A wonderful, well-presented and well researched book. Of particular interest and use is a chapter dedicated to the: 'Full results of the gentlemen's and ladies' singles, plus finals of all other events.' However, the fact that it lacks an index always seems to be a frustration. Full of photographs. £20-30 ($30-45)

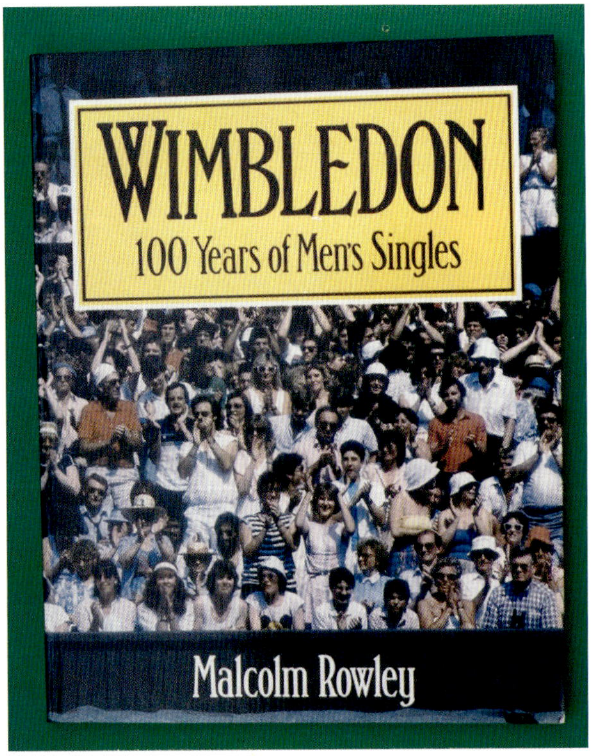

Fig. 1.122. ***Wimbledon, 100 Years of Men's Singles***
Wimbledon, 100 Years of Men's Singles - Malcolm Rowley, Sidgwick & Jackson Ltd., London, 1986, 120pp., 275 x 218mm., paperback. An unusual book in that it looks back at all the finals by using contemporary magazine and newspaper reports. Profusely illustrated. £12-15 ($18-22.50)

Fig. 1.124. ***The Queen's Club Story 1886-1986***
The Queen's Club Story 1886-1986 - Roy McKelvie, Stanley Paul & Co., Ltd., London, 1986, 306pp., 265 x 208mm., hard covers. A history of this fine old club including chapters on real tennis, rackets, lawn tennis, and squash. Filled with illustrations and drawings. £15-25 ($22.50-40)

Fig. 1.126. ***The Seeds of Lawn Tennis***
The Seeds of Lawn Tennis, Royal Leamington Spa - W. G. Gibbons, Jones-Sands Publishing, Coventry, 1986, 52pp., 210 x 148mm., paperback. A fascinating little booklet based upon the lives and exploits of Harry Gem and his friends, when they experimented with early games of lawn tennis. Containing many photographs. £5-10 ($7.50-15)

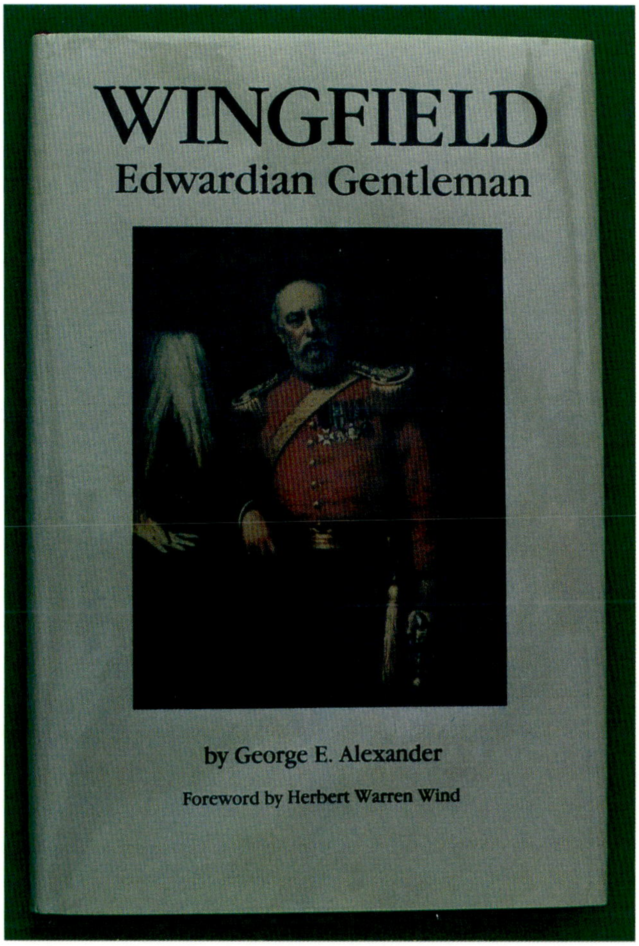

Fig. 1.125. ***Wingfield, Edwardian Gentleman***
Wingfield, Edwardian Gentleman - George E. Alexander, 1st edition, Peter E. Randall, Portsmouth, NH, 1986, 313pp., 236 x 156mm., hard covers. Examines the history of the Wingfield family and how Walter Clopton came to be associated with the game of lawn tennis. It contains many illustrations. Signed by the author. £40-60 ($60-90)

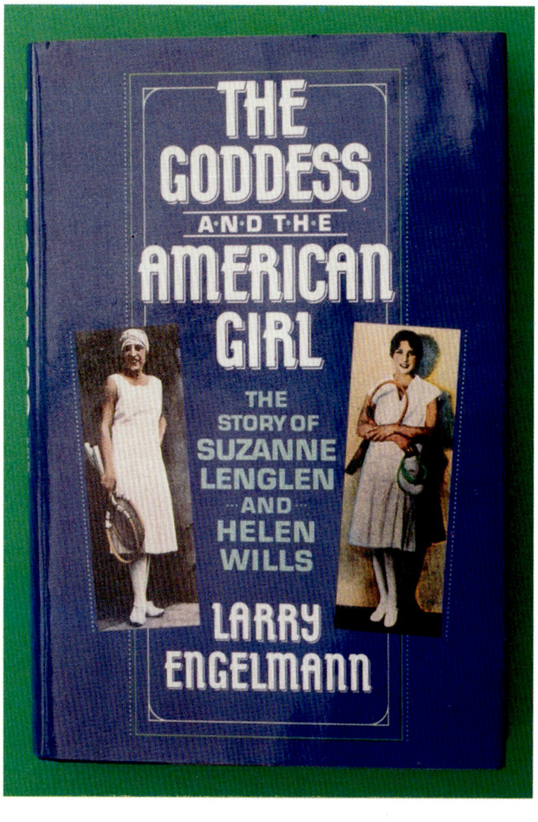

Fig. 1.127. ***The Goddess and the American Girl***
The Goddess and the American Girl, The Story of Suzanne Lenglen and Helen Wills - Larry Engelmann, Oxford University Press, New York and Oxford, 1988, 464pp., 240 x 163mm., hard covers. Engelmann compares the parallel lives of two of the finest lady players of all time, who met on the tennis court on only one occasion in 1926. Contains 33 photographs. £15-20 ($22-30)

Fig. 1.128. ***Table Tennis, The Early Years***
Table Tennis, The Early Years - Gerald N. Gurney, The International Table Tennis Federation, St. Leonards-on-Sea, n.d., c. 1990, 36pp., 297 x 210mm., paperback. An informative 'journey' through the history and development of the tabletop game. Containing 52 photographs and drawings. £10-15 ($15-20)

Fig. 1.130. ***The Art of Tennis***
The Art of Tennis, 1874-1940 - Gary H. Schwartz, 1st edition November 1990, Wood River Publishing, California, 1990, 171pp., 279 x 210mm., paperback. A fine collection of 'tennis' images from magazine covers, illustrations, postcards, and advertising. Hundreds of photographs. £20-25 ($30-40)

Fig. 1.129. ***Le Tennis et L'object***
Le Tennis et L'object - Francois Valleriaux, L'Alberon, Societe Presence du Livre, Thonon-les-Bains, 1990, 95pp., 263 x 214mm., hard covers. A collection of lawn tennis artefacts, and collectibles. Many photographs. £25-30 ($40-45)

Fig. 1.131. ***A History of Tennis***
A History of Tennis - E. B. Noel and J. O. M. Clark, Gerald Duckworth & Co. Ltd., London, 1991, 587pp., 285 x 194mm., hard covers. This book was first printed as 2 volumes in 1924 by Oxford University Press and is regarded as one of the premier 'histories' of Real Tennis. It contains over 100 photographs and diagrams and a good biography (up until 1924) too. £50-70 ($75-105)

Fig. 1.132. ***Tennis & Oxford***
Tennis & Oxford - Jeremy Potter, 1st edition, Oxford Unicorn Press, Oxford, 1994, 152pp., 240 x 160mm., hard covers. A wonderful little book, which relates the history of real tennis in Oxford since 1450. Of particular interest to collectors is Chapter Six 'Courts, Inns and Theatres' in which an illustrated article examines the three kinds of Tradesmen's tokens which can still be found. £20-25 ($30-40)

Fig. 1.134. ***Tennis in Scotland***
Tennis in Scotland, 100 Years of the Scottish Lawn Tennis Association 1895-1995 - George Robertson, 1st edition, The Scottish Lawn Tennis Association, Edinburgh, 1995, 317pp., 252 x 194mm., hard covers. Published to mark the Association's centenary, it chronicles the events and personalities involved throughout its history. Over 100 photographs. £15-20 ($20-30)

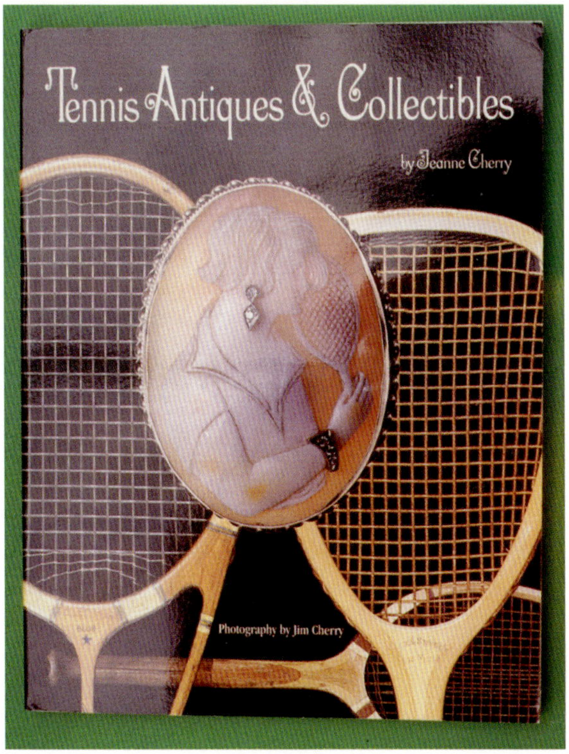

Fig. 1.133. ***Tennis Antiques & Collectibles***
Tennis Antiques & Collectibles – Jeanne Cherry, Amaryllis Press, Santa Monica, 1995, 200pp., 279 x 215mm., paperback. An entertaining book which takes us through almost every conceivable kind of collectible, which is associated with lawn tennis. Profusely illustrated and well researched. Signed by the author. £30-50 ($45-75)

Fig. 1.135. ***Sporting Gentlemen***
Sporting Gentlemen, Men's Tennis from the Age of Honour to the Cult of the Superstar - E. Digby Baltzell, 1st edition, The Free Press, New York, 1995, 420pp., 242 x 162mm., hard covers. A well researched historical analysis, with an American slant. 34 photographs. £15-20 ($20-30)

Fig. 1.137. ***Tennis in Robin Hood's County***
Tennis in Robin Hood's County - Andy Lusis, 1st edition (signed), self published, Nottingham, 1998, 136pp., 209 x 147mm., soft covers. An amazingly detailed book based upon the development of lawn tennis in Nottinghamshire. Information concerning the establishment and sometimes the termination of all the clubs for which Lusis could find evidence. Historically, a very informative little book. £15-20 ($20-30)

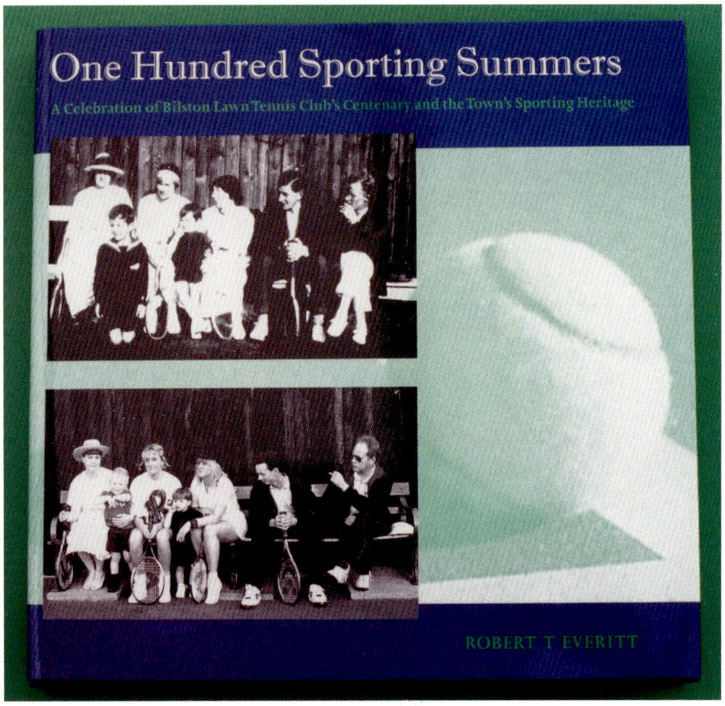

Fig. 1.136. ***One Hundred Sporting Summers***
One Hundred Sporting Summers, A Celebration of Bilston Lawn Tennis Club's Centenary and the Town's Sporting Heritage - Robert T. Everitt, George Street Press, Stafford, 1995, 186pp., 208 x 214mm., hard covers. In essence a club history book, it examines the town's records for evidence of the games of fives, rackets, and lawn tennis, as well as celebrating 100 years of the town's lawn tennis club. Containing many photographs, and limited to 500 copies. £15-20 ($20-30)

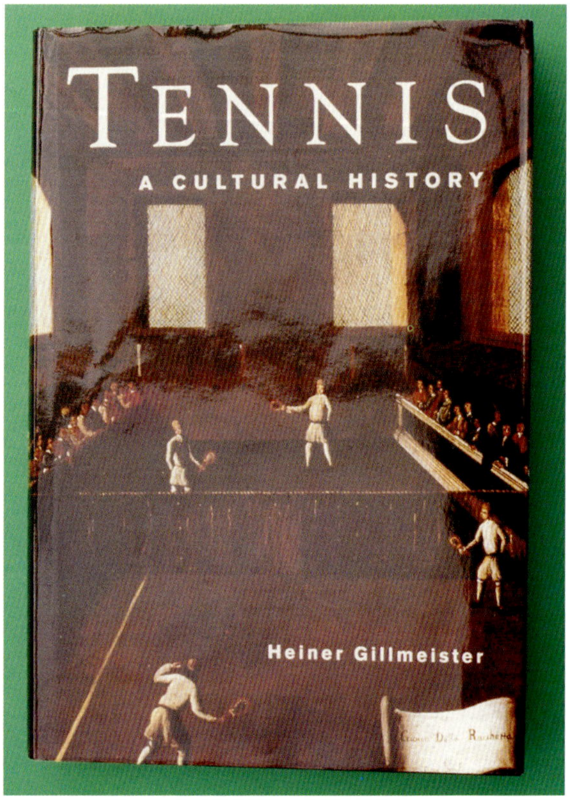

Fig. 1.138. ***Tennis a Cultural History***
Tennis a Cultural History - Heiner Gillmeister, Leicester University Press, London and Washington, 1997, 452pp., 251 x 171mm., hard covers. A huge, superbly researched volume, with an extensive index and notes. It contains masses of information concerning the origins, history, and development of the game. A particularly special chapter examines the birth of the game in Germany. Containing numerous full colour plates and black and white photographs. £45-75 ($70-100)

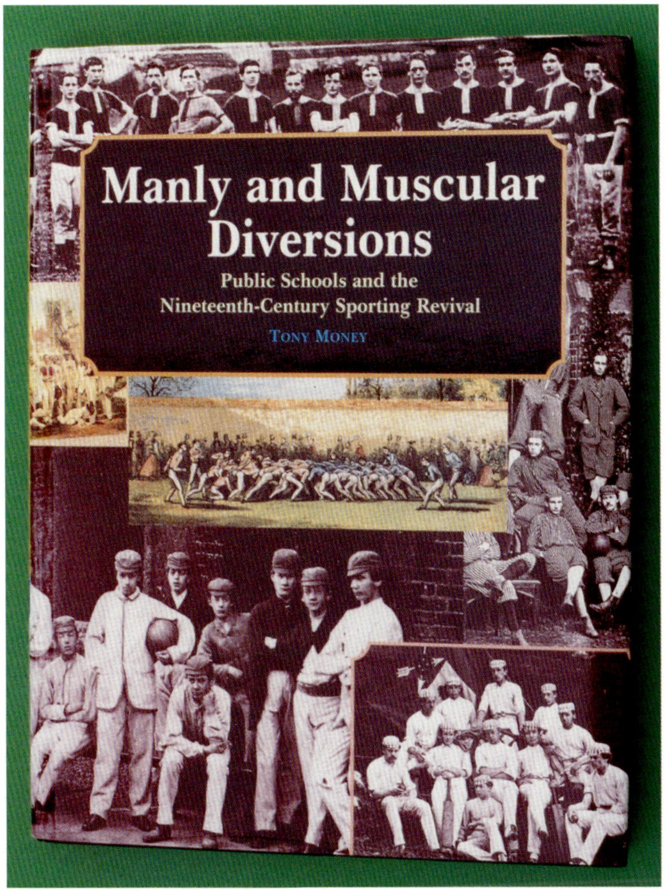

Fig. 1.139. ***Manly and Muscular Diversions***[28]
Manly and Muscular Diversions, Public Schools and the Nineteenth Century Sporting Revival - Tony Money, Gerald Duckworth & Co. Ltd., London, 1997, 191pp., 252 x 194mm., hard covers. Contains a chapter on the game of Fives and includes information on Tennis, Rackets, and Real Tennis too. The book comes with 92 illustrations. £20-30 ($30-45)

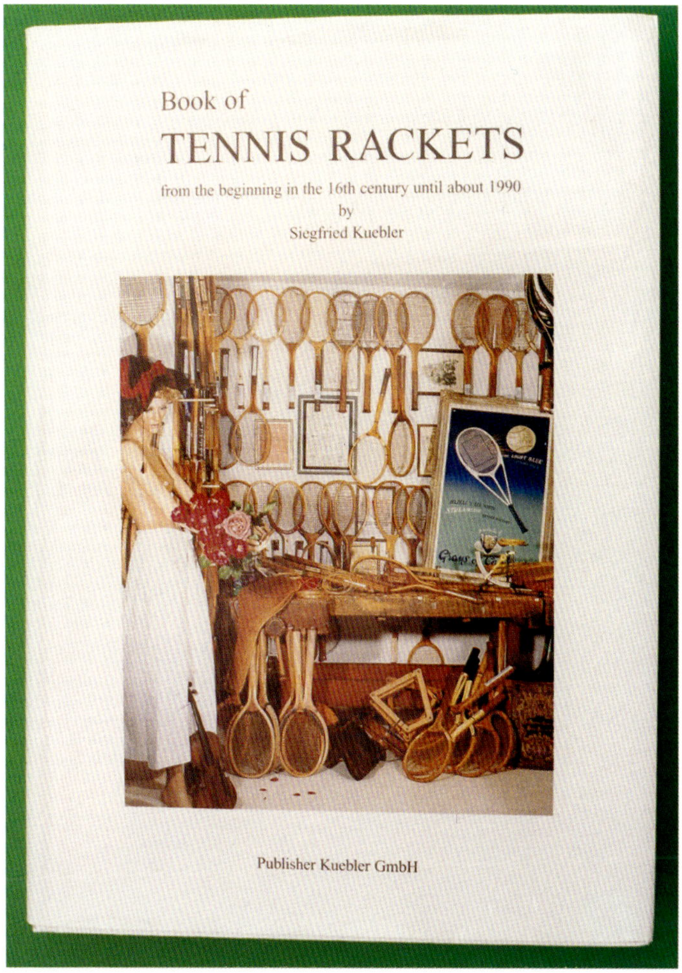

Fig. 1.141. ***Book of Tennis Rackets***
Book of Tennis Rackets, from the beginning in the 16th century until about 1990 – Siegfried Kuebler, Kuebler GmbH, D-78224 Singen, Germany, 1990, 635pp., 303 x 216mm., hard covers. A huge, extremely useful book, which is packed with information and photographs concerning racket manufacturers and their implements. If you have a racket that is not described in this book, Siegfried wants to know about it! £40-60 ($60-90)

Fig. 1.140. ***Tennis, Nostalgia, Playing the Game***
Tennis, Nostalgia, Playing the Game - Christopher Dunkley, - Open Door Ltd., Lincolnshire, 1998, 192pp., 221 x 223mm., (folder size) hard covers. An unusual publication, in as much as it consists of two identically sized books, which neatly slide into a hard board container which fastens with a green ribbon. The first book, *Nostalgia*, features tennis history and some of the equipment and memorabilia associated with it. The second, *Playing the Game*, covers strokes, tactics, coaching, and training. A pleasing book with many full colour photographs. £20-30 ($30-45)

Programmes & Trade Catalogues

A programme can be a curious piece of ephemeral history. If, for instance, it's a first day copy, it will inform you of the competitions which are to come, all the competitors, who they will play, the prizes, the committee, and sometimes much more. If, however, you own a programme from the last day of the same tournament, or even a 'completed programme' (one in which all the results have been printed), it is a retrospective look at all the events in the days preceding it. In essence, it becomes a time capsule of the whole tournament. This is why programmes from the latter days of a tournament, rather than from the beginning are much more sought after by collectors.

Obviously, those which cover famous tournaments are very desirable, but to be quite candid, any programme printed before 1920 is very difficult to find and those which are pre-1900 will be the most coveted and are truly desirable items. This is because in those early days most 'programmes' were regarded simply as a guide for the day. They were often very fragile too, commonly just a few pages long, and, unless they were of particular personal interest, were discarded and soon forgotten. The programmes that survive will certainly relate to a tennis world that is different to the one we know today. It's always a good tip to have a look through the draw sheet; if there's a 'famous name' there, his or her name adds a different dimension to the item, even though it could be from a fairly unknown provincial tournament. It could have been that it was one of their first tournaments; on the other hand it could be at the end of their tennis careers, a celebrity name saying goodbye to the beloved game.

As always the condition of the item is important, but it's not the end of the world if the staples have rusted away, providing that they don't adversely affect the remainder of the programme. Some papers are very high in chalk content and, unless they have always been kept in dry conditions, have a tendency to absorb water from the air which, together with damp and light, can ruin the condition of paper. As with books, or for that matter any printed item, if you find an autograph, of perhaps an official or a player, it will add value and uniqueness to the programme. (In the early years, some of the referees were as much a celebrity as the players.)

Trade Catalogues

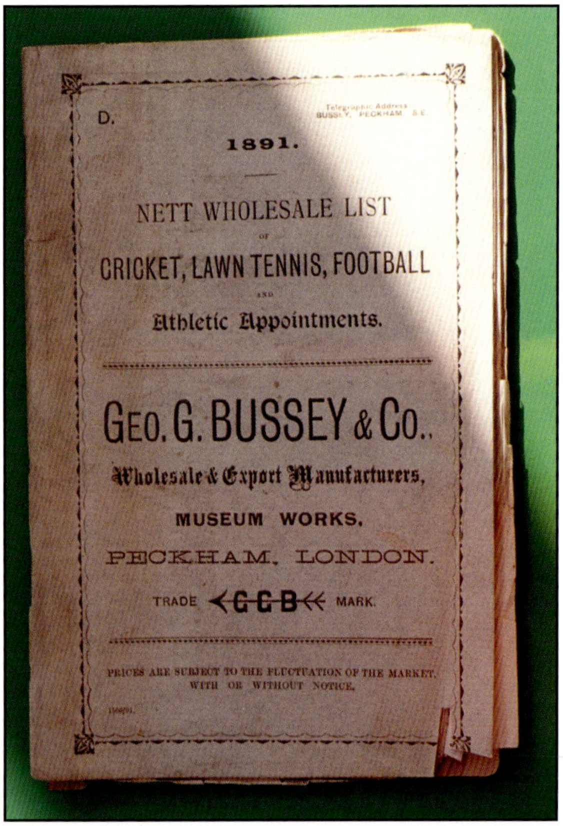

Fig. 1.142. **Geo G. Bussey, 1891**[29]
Nett Wholesale List of Cricket, Lawn tennis, Football and Athletic Appointments. Geo G. Bussey & Co. Wholesale & Export Manufacturers, Museum Works, Peckham, London, 1891, 64pp., 212 x 138mm., paperback. A fragile, but fascinating insight into the requisites supplied by Victorian sports manufacturers in London. Ten pages are devoted to lawn tennis, and the products covered range from rackets to lawn tennis belts and 'portable courts' (consisting of a set of tapes punched with a number of eyelet-holes for use when marking the lawn is objectionable'). Fourteen rackets are featured, notable ones being; The 'Sandringham' racket, with a 'barrel' shaped handle (Extra Close Strung, 120/- per doz.); The Lunn's Patent Ventilated Holdfast-Handle Racket (168/- per doz.); and (at the same price) the Nightingale's Patent Racket, the 'Smasher' which clearly shows diagonal stringing. The catalogue also features prices for badminton, fives, and raquets items. A rather curious inclusion is a listing for the 'New Patent Game of 'Poko.' A small printer's note at the bottom of the cover suggests that there were originally 1500 printed copies of this catalogue. £125-175 ($200-250)

Fig. 1.143. **Buchanan Ltd., c. 1895**
Illustrated Price List, Buchanan Ltd., 215, Piccadilly, London.W., n.d., c. 1895, 48pp., 238 x 182mm., paperback. A fine, well illustrated catalogue featuring badminton, fives; tennis; bat, trap, and ball; drum battledores; racquets; lawn tennis goods; squash racquets, and shuttlecocks. Of particular interest was the availability of the 'Horace Bayly bat' with special tight stringing, which cost 21/-. Other rackets listed were: 'The Buchanan'; 'The Burlington'; 'The Duplex'; and 'The Imperial'. £100-150 ($150-225)

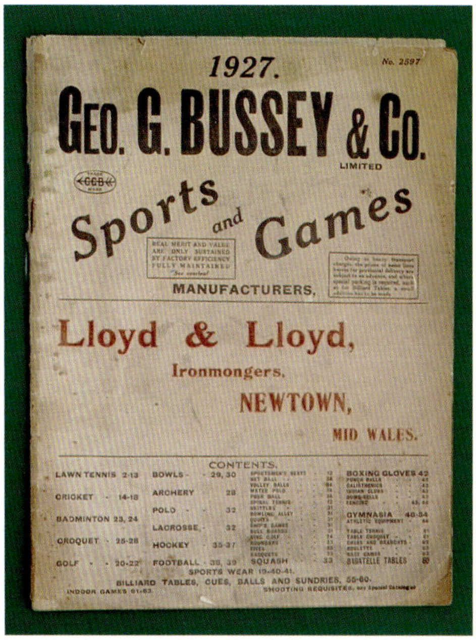

Fig. 1.145. **Geo.G.Bussey, 1927**
Geo.G.Bussey & Co. Ltd., Sports and Games Manufacturers, February 1927, 63pp., 280 x 217mm., paperback. This catalogue was issued from Lloyd and Lloyd Ironmongers, Newtown, Wales. There are eleven pages dedicated to lawn tennis equipment, badminton has two pages, and sports like fives and racquets and squash have only one each. Bussey's 'premier' racket was the 'Demon Driver 1'. It had the characteristic 'Wave-shaped profile' wedge, inlaid cork handle, and each racket was individually numbered on the side, for easy reference. This, including an airtight cover and press, would cost the tennis enthusiast 65/-. 'Demon Driver' squash and badminton rackets were also made. £100-150 ($150-225)

Fig. 1.144. **Piggott Bros., c. 1895**
Piggott Bros. & Co., Manufacturers, 57, 58 & 59 Bishopsgate St., London, n.d., c. 1895, 314pp., 217 x 142mm., hard covers. Piggott's described themselves as: 'Manufacturers of Marquees and Tents, for Sporting, Travelling, Engineering, Surveying, & Prospecting, also Artistic Designs of Tents for Garden Grounds and Lawns.' There are numerous advertisements for badminton, fives, and lawn tennis. Of particular interest is a 'Polished Walnut or Mahogany Tennis Bat Stand' which could be purchased for 21/6. £100-150 ($150-225)

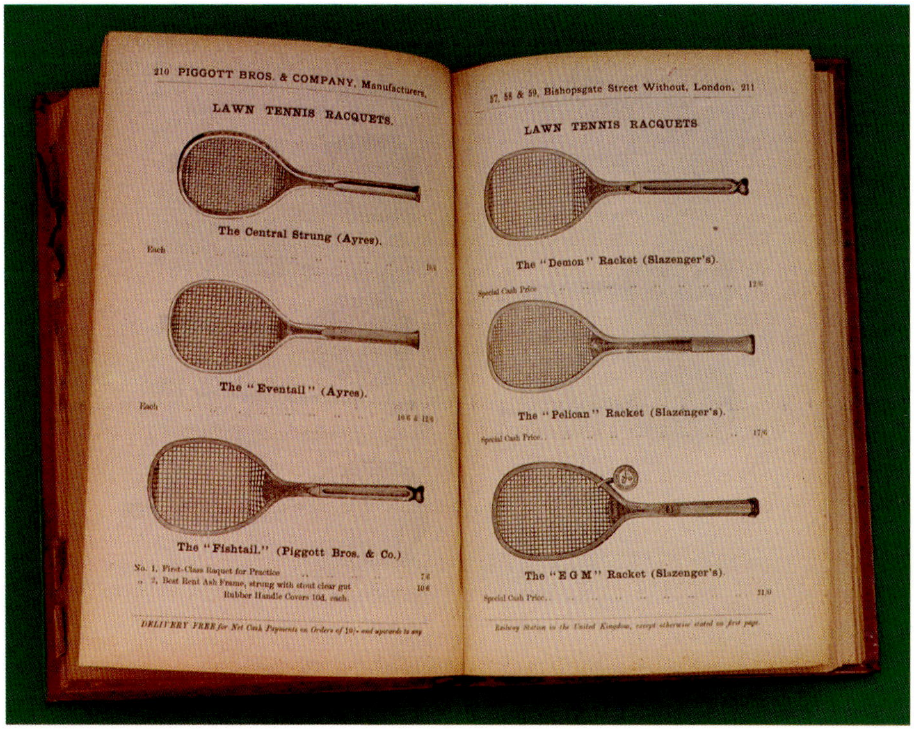

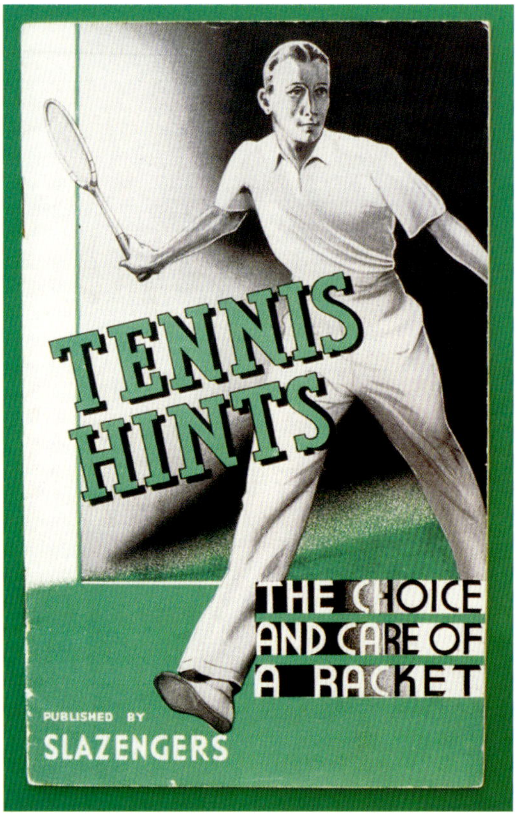

Fig. 1.146. **Slazengers Ltd., 1934**
Tennis Hints, The Choice and Care of a Racket, Slazengers Ltd., 1934., 16pp., 221 x 140mm., paperback. 'A flag-waving exercise' from Slazengers, with a contribution from Dan Maskell. Eight different models of tennis racket are featured; The 'Queen's' Tournament Model 69/6; The 'Victory' 32/6; The 'Doherty' 60/-; The 'Special Demon' 45/-; The 'Meteor' 42/-; The 'Pall Mall' 37/6; The 'Cheltenham' 30/-; The 'Eclipse' 25/-. A page is also devoted to The 'Slazenger' Ball 14/6 per dozen, and The Slazenger 'Demon' Ball at 11/6 per dozen. £25-35 ($40-50)

Fig. 1.147. **Wilson 1987**
Wilson 1987 Tennis & Squash Catalogue, Made to Win, 32pp., 210 x 147mm., paperback. It contains articles on the season's equipment, including tennis rackets, tennis balls, squash rackets, tennis shoes, and sports bags. £10-15 ($15-25)

Provincial Tournament Programmes

Fig. 1.148. **Buxton Tennis Tournament, 1884**
A very rare programme, from the Buxton Tournament in 1884. 10pp., 280 x 210mm., paperback. The booklet is subtitled 'The song of the Tournament, As told by Hiawatha to his children' (after Longfellow) written by W. French and illustrated by W. Pigot. It is very amusing and topical, referring to various participants and officials. i.e. 'Browne', 'Deykin', 'Taylor', 'Grinstead', 'Henry Malings' (Racket Maker), etc. The book is very rare. £650-750 ($1000-1200)

Fig. 1.149. **The Nottinghamshire Lawn Tennis Tournament, 1891** The Nottinghamshire Lawn Tennis Tournament 1891, 12pp., 220 x 141mm., Played at The Castle Cricket Ground, Nottingham, England, Arthur Johnson, Printer, Nottingham. The first annual Nottingham tournament was held at the Trent Bridge Cricket Ground in 1887. From 1889-93 it was held at the Castle Cricket Ground, with B. C. Evelegh as Referee and Handicapper. For those collectors who concentrate their efforts on attaining engraved trophies and prizes for their collections, this programme is quite enlightening. Here is a list of just a few of the prizes awarded: Fish Carvers and Crumb Scoop, value £3.3s; Electro-plate Toddy Stand, value £12.12s; Electro-plate Punch Bowl, value £5.5s., presented by His Grace the Duke of Portland; and Four Electro-plate Salts in Case, value £2.2s. Gerald Goodwin, a Newark Lawn Tennis Club member and Nottinghamshire County player, originally owned the programme. £175-200 ($250-300)

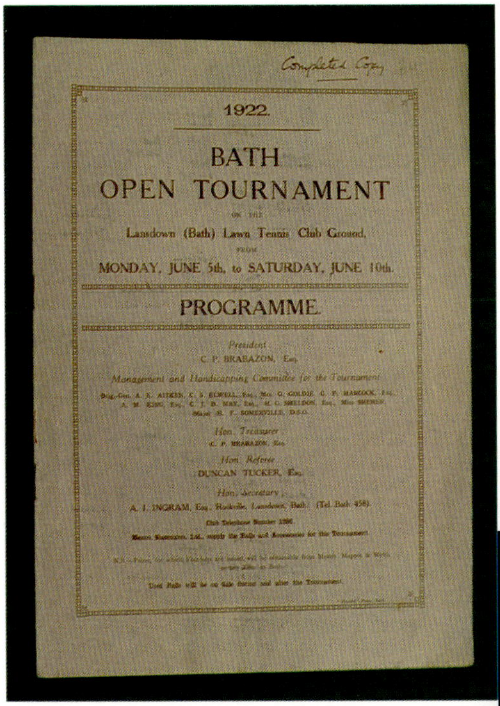

Fig. 1.150. **The Bath Open Tournament, 1922** Bath Open Tournament 1922, 12pp., self covers printed black throughout, 319 x 227mm., 'Herald' Press, Bath. $20-30 ($30-45)

Fig. 1.151. **The Lammas and Walpole Parks, 1927-46**
The Lammas and Walpole Parks Lawn Tennis Association, Open Lawn Tennis Tournaments, 1927-46, Earlier copies have 4pp., later copies are 8pp., approx. 204 x 128mm. Single colour printing throughout. £4-6 ($6-9)

Fig. 1.152. **The Roehampton Club, 1929**
Roehampton Club, 5th Annual Reception of Overseas Lawn Tennis Players 1929, 4pp., 208 x 124mm., Single colour. Produced in conjunction with the International Lawn Tennis Club of Great Britain. £5-7 ($7-10)

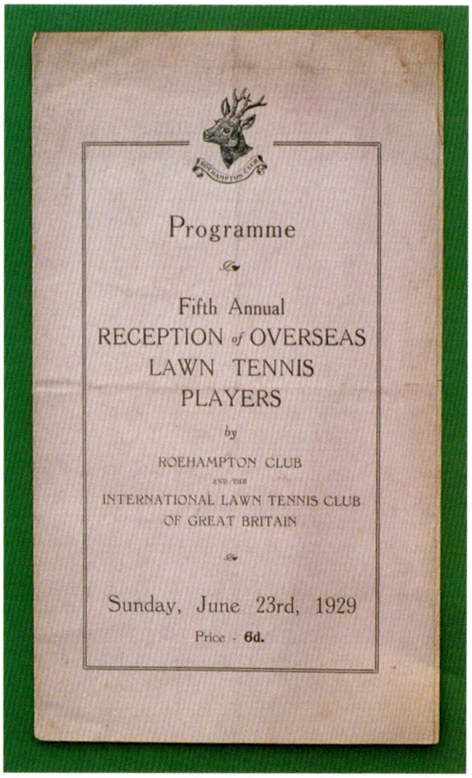

Fig. 1.154. **The Championships of London, 1951**
The Championships of London on Grass, The Queen's Club, London, 1951, (Festival of Britain Year), 30pp., 300 x 237mm., two colour cover, single colour throughout. £10-20 ($15-30)

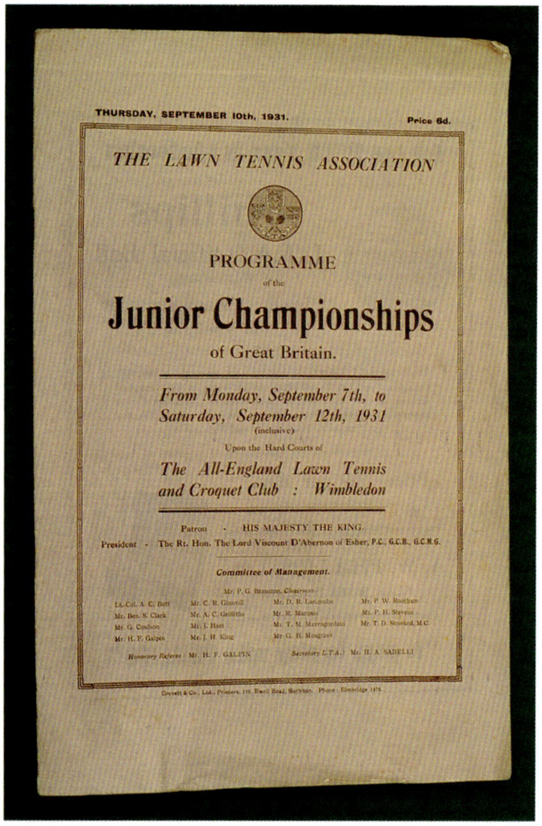

Fig. 1.153. **The Junior Championships of Great Britain, 1931**
Programme for The Junior Championships of Great Britain 1931, self cover, 16pp., single colour throughout. £7-10 ($10-15)

Fig. 1.155. **Coronation Year Match, 1953**
Coronation Year Match Programme 1953, 4pp., 173 x 127mm., The All England Club v. Queen's Club & International L. T. Club of Great Britain at Wimbledon. £15-20 ($20-30)

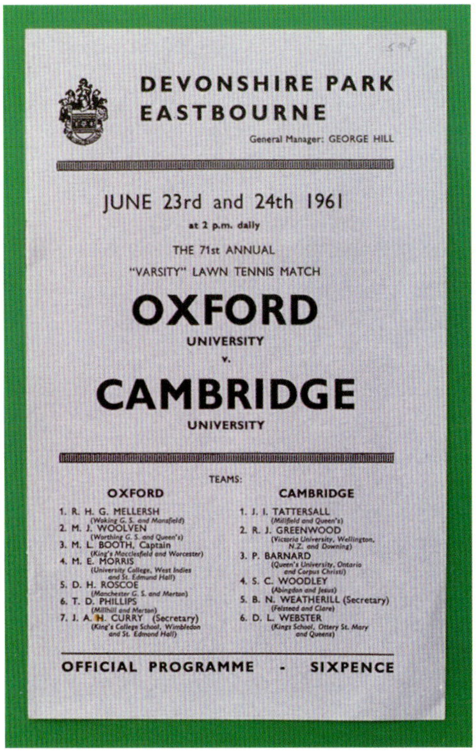

Fig. 1.156. **Annual Varsity Match, 1961**
Devonshire Park, The 71st Annual 'Varsity' Lawn Tennis Match, 1961, 8pp., 202 x 126mm., single colour. Sussex Printers Ltd., Eastbourne. £4-6 ($6-10)

Fig. 1.157. **The Hard Court Championships, 1964**
The Hard Court Championships of Great Britain 1964, 40pp., 278 x 217mm., three colour cover. Played at West Hants. L. T. C. Bournemouth. £10-15 ($15-25)

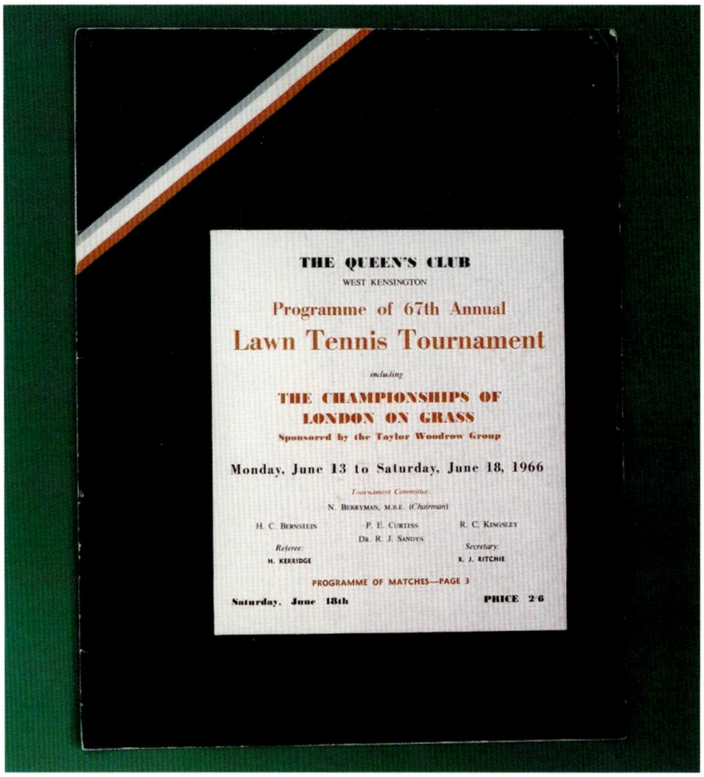

Fig. 1.158. **Queen's Club, 1966**
Queen's Club, 67th Annual Lawn Tennis Tournament 1966, 20pp., 298 x 234mm., three colour cover. Black printing throughout. £10-15 ($15-25)

Fig. 1.159. **The Dewar Cup 1968**
The Dewar Cup 1968, 12pp., 287 x 226mm., black throughout. Played at The Crystal Palace National Recreation Centre, England. £5-10 ($8-15)

Fig. 1.160. **The Stella Artois, 1979**
The Stella Artois Grass Court Championships 1979, 42pp., 279 x 210mm., full colour throughout. Played at The Queen's Club, London, England. £5-10 ($8-15)

Fig. 1.162. **The Pilkington Glass Championships, 1990**
The Pilkington Glass Ladies Championships 1990, 56pp., 297 x 210mm. Full Colour. Played at Devonshire Park, Eastbourne. Complete with separate draw sheet. £7-10 ($10-15)

Fig. 1.161. **The Stella Artois, 1983**
The Stella Artois Grass Court Championships 1983, 8pp., 279 x 210mm., full colour cover. Played at The Queen's Club, London, England. £5-10 ($8-15)

Fig. 1.163. **The DFS Classic, 1998**
The D F S Classic Ladies International 1998, 40pp., 297 x 210mm., full colour. With draw sheet. Played at Edgbaston Priory Club, Birmingham, England. £7-10 ($10-15)

Davis Cup Programmes

Fig. 1.164. **Great Britain v. Germany, 1928**
The Davis Cup, 1928, Great Britain v. Germany, 16pp., 246 x 136mm., soft covers, printed black throughout. Played at Edgbaston Cricket & Lawn Tennis Club, Birmingham, England. Stanford & Underwood Ltd., Birmingham. £150-200 ($225-300)

Fig. 1.165. **Great Britain v. Australia, 1933**
The Davis Cup, 1933, Great Britain v. Australia, 4pp., 229 x 178mm., card covers. Final of European Zone. £150-200 ($225-300)

Fig. 1.166. **Great Britain 1934-37**
The Davis Cup, 1934 -37, Great Britain v. U.S.A. & Australia, 12pp., 247 x 177mm., two colour cover, black print throughout. £150-200 each ($225-300)

Fig. 1.167. **France v. Italy, 1949**
The Davis Cup, 1949, France v. Italy, 16pp., 211 x 135mm., soft covers, green print throughout. Played at Stade Roland Garros, Paris, France. £20-30 ($30-45)

Fig. 1.169. **Great Britain v. France, 1958**
The Davis Cup, 1958, Great Britain v. France, 12pp., 216 x 140mm., two colour cover, blue throughout. Played at The Northern Lawn Tennis Club, Manchester. £10-20 ($15-30)

Fig. 1.168. **Great Britain v. Chile, 1956**
The Davis Cup, 1956, Great Britain v. Chile, 4pp., 235 x 155mm., card covers. Two-colour front cover, blue printing throughout the programme. Played at Bristol Lawn Tennis Club, England. £10-20 ($15-30)

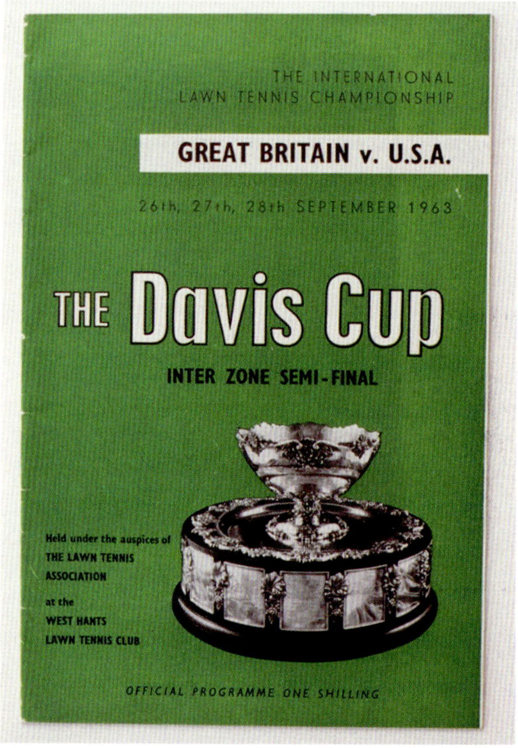

Fig. 1.170. **Great Britain v. U.S.A., 1963**
The Davis Cup, 1963, Great Britain v. U.S.A. - Inter Zone Semi-Final, 20pp., 210 x 140mm. Played at The West Hampshire Lawn Tennis Club, England. £10-12 ($15-18)

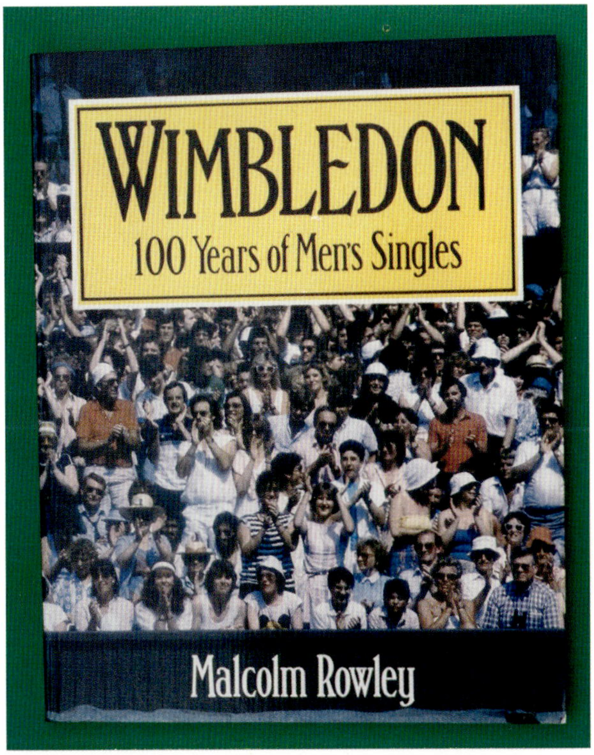

Fig. 1.122. ***Wimbledon, 100 Years of Men's Singles***
Wimbledon, 100 Years of Men's Singles - Malcolm Rowley, Sidgwick & Jackson Ltd., London, 1986, 120pp., 275 x 218mm., paperback. An unusual book in that it looks back at all the finals by using contemporary magazine and newspaper reports. Profusely illustrated. £12-15 ($18-22.50)

Fig. 1.123. ***100 Wimbledon Championships***
100 Wimbledon Championships, a celebration - John Barrett, Willow Books, William Collins Sons & Co. Ltd., London, 1986, 287pp., 281 x 223mm., hard covers. A wonderful, well-presented and well researched book. Of particular interest and use is a chapter dedicated to the: 'Full results of the gentlemen's and ladies' singles, plus finals of all other events.' However, the fact that it lacks an index always seems to be a frustration. Full of photographs. £20-30 ($30-45)

Fig. 1.124. ***The Queen's Club Story 1886-1986***
The Queen's Club Story 1886-1986 - Roy McKelvie, Stanley Paul & Co., Ltd., London, 1986, 306pp., 265 x 208mm., hard covers. A history of this fine old club including chapters on real tennis, rackets, lawn tennis, and squash. Filled with illustrations and drawings. £15-25 ($22.50-40)

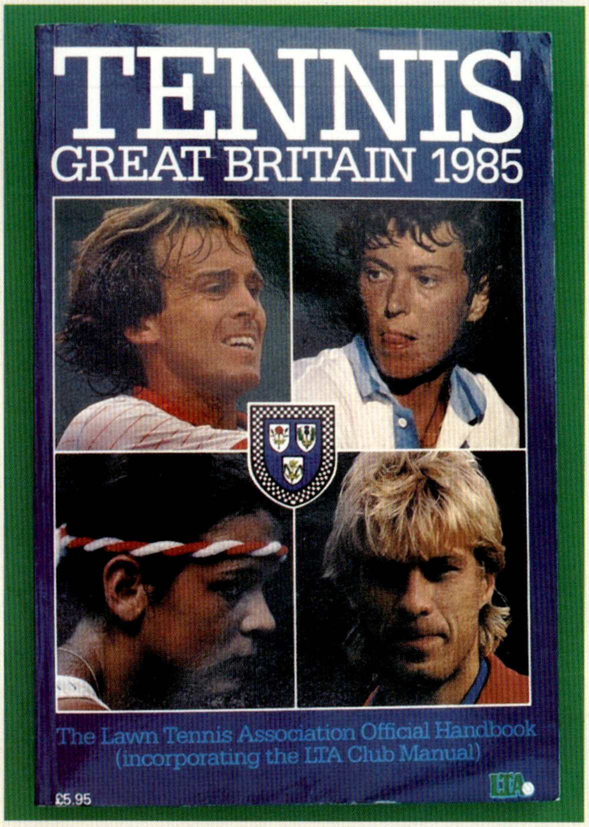

Fig. 1.121. ***Tennis Great Britain***
Tennis Great Britain, The Lawn Tennis Association Official Handbook (incorporating the LTA Club Manual) - David Irvine (editor), The Lawn Tennis Association, London, copies for 1985, '86, and '87, between 360 and 460pp., 218 x 148mm., soft covers. These handbooks covered everything associated with the game in Great Britain, from ranking lists to tournaments regulations for club matches. In each copy there follows a section entitled 'The Lawn Tennis Association Club Manual' running to some 50 or so pages, which concerns itself with advice on the establishment and funding of private clubs. Each volume has many photographs of players and clubs. £10-20 ($15-30)

Fig. 1.171. **Great Britain v. Spain, 1986**
The Davis Cup, 1986, Great Britain v. Spain, World Group First Round, 32pp., 210 x 148mm., full colour card covers. £7-10 ($10-15)

Fig. 1.173. **G B v U S A, 1999**
G B v U S A The Davis Cup Programme 1999, 48pp., 335 x 240mm., gloss laminated covers, full colour throughout. Event Merchandising Ltd. £10-12 ($15-18)

Fig. 1.172. **United States v. Australia, 1999**
100 Years of The Davis Cup United States v. Australia 1999, 136pp., 276 x 211mm., full colour. Played at Longwood Cricket Club, Boston, U.S.A. £10-15 ($15-25)

Professional Tournament Programmes

Fig. 1.174. **Professional Indoor Lawn Tennis, 1953 & 1956**
International Professional Indoor Lawn Tennis, 1953 & 1956, 8pp. & 12pp., 240 x 183mm., the 1953 copy, marked 'GUEST COPY', includes a menu sheet and an invitation to Mr. and Mrs. H. Garton Ash to attend 'Sir Arthur Elvin's Party'. The 1956 copy is signed by Frank Sedgman & Richard 'Pancho' Gonzales. Both events played at The Empire Pool, Wembley, England. £20-30 ($30-45)

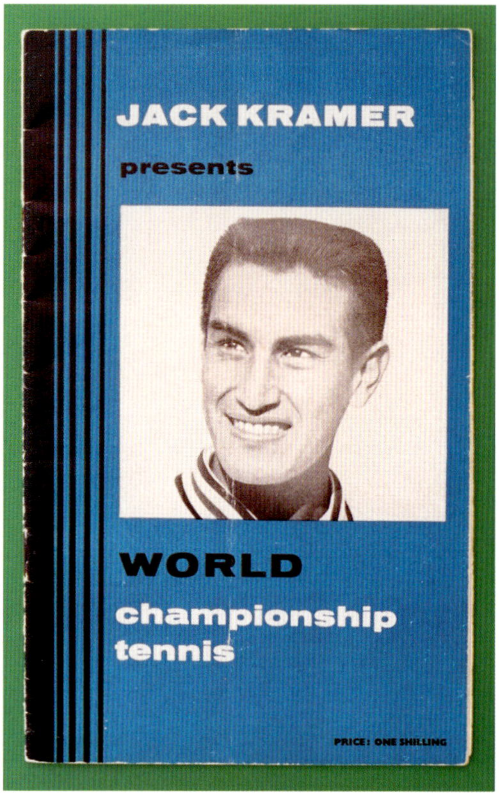

Fig. 1.175. **World Championship Tennis, 1960**
Jack Kramer presents World Championship Tennis, 1960, 28pp., 215 x 133mm., two colour cover. With a typewritten order of play, Maxwell, Love & Co. Ltd., London SE1. £10-15 ($15-25)

Fig. 1.176. **World Series Tennis, 1963**
The First World Series Tennis Championship, 1963, 32pp., 240 x 171mm., full colour cover, blue print throughout the programme. £7-10 ($10-15)

Fig. 1.177. **Devonshire Park 1963**
Devonshire Park Professional Exhibition Match 1963, 4pp., 205 x 131mm., single colour. Sussex Printers Ltd., Eastbourne. £5-10 ($7-15)

Wightman Cup Programmes

Fig. 1.178. **The Wightman Cup, 1932**
Wightman Cup 1932, 4pp., 203 x 127mm., card. Great Britain v. United States played at Wimbledon. Unwin Brothers Ltd., London and Woking. £100-150 ($150-225)

Fig. 1.179. **The Wightman Cup Souvenir, 1932**
Souvenir Programme of The Wightman Cup 1932, 4pp., 238 x 157mm., card. Played at Wimbledon. £20-40 ($30-60)

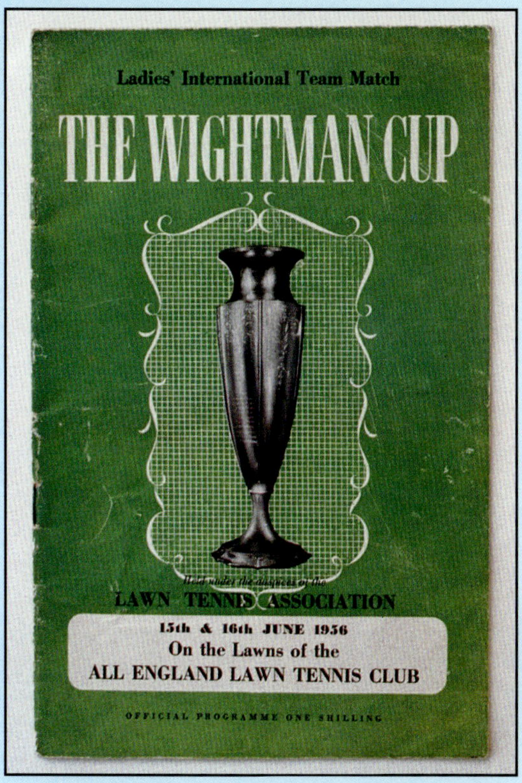

Fig. 1.180. **The Wightman Cup, 1956**
The Wightman Cup 1956, 16pp., 215 x 139mm., soft covers. Played at Wimbledon. Two colour covers and printed black throughout. £10-15 ($15-25)

National Tournament Programmes

Fig. 1.181. **The South African Championship, 1896**
The South African Championship Meeting 1896, 8pp., (plus a four page outer cover), 194 x 129mm., soft covers. This extremely rare completed programme, relates the events at the sixth annual meeting at the Port Elizabeth Club. This club (in the Eastern Province) was formed in 1882 and became the major centre for tennis in South Africa. In *The Encyclopaedia of Tennis* (1974), Max Robertson takes up the story: 'In 1891 the Port Elizabeth L. T. C. assumed the functions of a governing body of the game and instituted annual national championships, controlled from 1903 by the South African Lawn Tennis Union, formed that year. As a mark of respect to the Port Elizabeth L. T. C. (for its endeavours in advancing the game) its courts were chosen for the first official national championships in 1903.' This year, Mr. L. Giddy retained the Gentlemen's Singles Championship and Mrs. H. Green triumphed in the Ladies' Singles, defeating Miss R. Biddulph (the holder) in the final. Handicap and doubles events were also recorded. £200-300 ($300-450)

Fig. 1.182. **Wimbledon, 1926**
The Jubilee Lawn Tennis Championship Meeting, Wimbledon, 1926, 20pp., 312 x 248mm., single colour throughout. Thursday, June 24th, 1926 (4th Day) with a decorated cover, illustration printed in black showing the meeting of tennis players from the past and the present. The programme includes draw sheets and advertisements from contemporary manufacturers. On this day, Cochet played Lester on the Centre Court in the fourth round of the Gentlemen's singles, while the holder Suzanne Lenglen played Mrs. G. J. Dewhurst in the second round of the Ladies' competition. This turned out to be her last ladies singles match at Wimbledon. Meanwhile the Ladies Doubles saw the proposed match between Misses Ryan and Brown and Mlles. Vlasto and Lenglen on the Centre Court. It was these two matches, scheduled by referee Burrow to be played on the same day, which eventually lead to the withdrawal of Lenglen from the Championships. She never returned. This day also saw H. R. H. Duke of York and his partner, L. Greig, play A. W. Gore and H. Roper Barrett on court two. £150-200 ($225-300)

Fig. 1.183. **Wimbledon, 1929**
The Lawn Tennis Championship Meeting, Wimbledon, 1929, 20pp., 312 x 248mm., single colour covers, black printing throughout. Kelly & Kelly Ltd. E. C. 2. Attractively printed in green ink on green covers this programme features the Ladies Semi-final between Helen Wills (Champion) and Miss E. A. Goldsack and the Men's Doubles Semi-finals. £100-150 ($150-225)

Fig. 1.184. **Wimbledon, 1934**
The Lawn Tennis Championship Meeting, Wimbledon, 1934, 20pp., 313 x 245mm., Ladies Singles Finals Day. Single colour covers, black printing throughout. Kelly & Kelly Ltd. (12th Day) This programme features the Ladies final between Helen Jacobs and Dorothy Round (her first victory). £100-125 ($150-200)

Fig. 1.185. **Wimbledon, 1936**
The Lawn Tennis Championship Meeting, Wimbledon, 1936, 20pp. 309 x 248mm., Ladies Singles Finals Day. Single colour covers, black printing throughout. Kelly & Kelly Ltd. Helen Jacobs played Mrs. S. Sperling on this finals day. £100-125 ($150-200)

Fig. 1.186. **Wimbledon, 1937**
Coronation Year Lawn Tennis Championship Meeting, Wimbledon, 1937, 18pp., 310 x 249mm., two colours front cover, single colour throughout. Kelly & Kelly Ltd. E. C. 2. £125-150 ($200-225)

Fig. 1.187. **Wimbledon, 1938**
The Lawn Tennis Championship Meeting, Wimbledon, 1938, 20pp., 310 x 248mm., single colour, 4pp., cover, black printing throughout. Kelly & Kelly Ltd. E. C. 2. Austin v. Budge in the final. £100-125 ($150-200)

Fig. 1.188. **The New Zealand Open, 1946**
New Zealand Lawn Tennis Championships, Souvenir Programme, Auckland, 1946, 32pp., 214 x 140mm., black printing throughout. Chas. Davy and Sons Ltd., Aukland. £30-50 ($45-75)

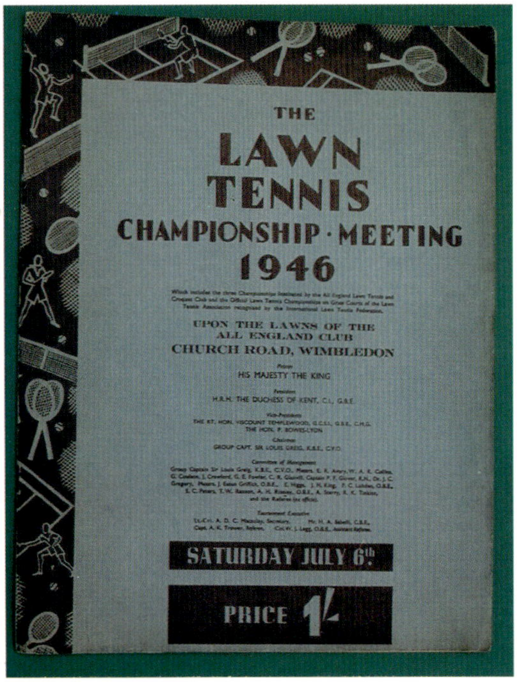

Fig. 1.189. **Wimbledon, 1946**
The Lawn Tennis Championship Meeting, Wimbledon, 1946, 20pp., 308 x 240mm., Gentlemen's Singles Finals Day. Single colour-print. Kelly & Kelly Ltd. London E. C. 2. Ladies Singles Final Day, between P. Betz and L. Brough. £40-60 ($60-90)

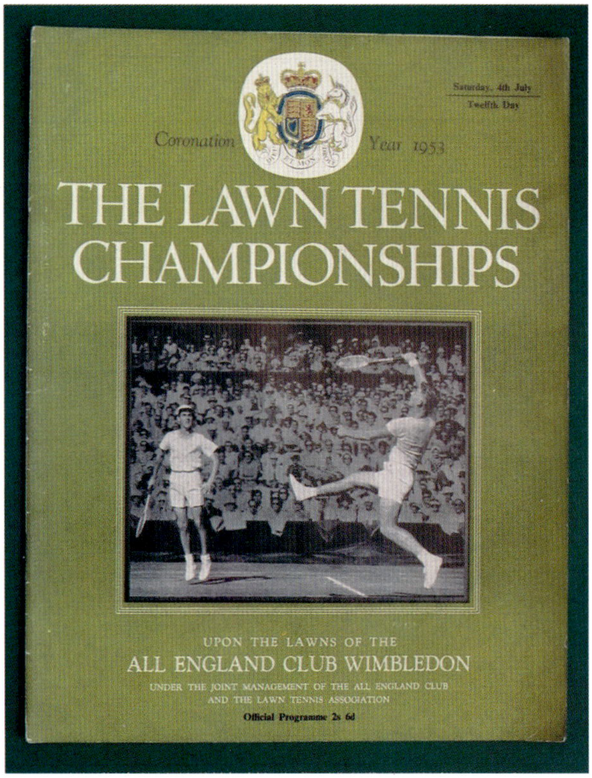

Fig. 1.190. **Wimbledon, 1953**
The Lawn Tennis Championships, Wimbledon, 1953, 36pp., 300 x 235mm., Coronation Year, 12th day. Ladies Singles Finals day. Kelly & Kelly Ltd. London E. C. 2. £20-30 ($30-45)

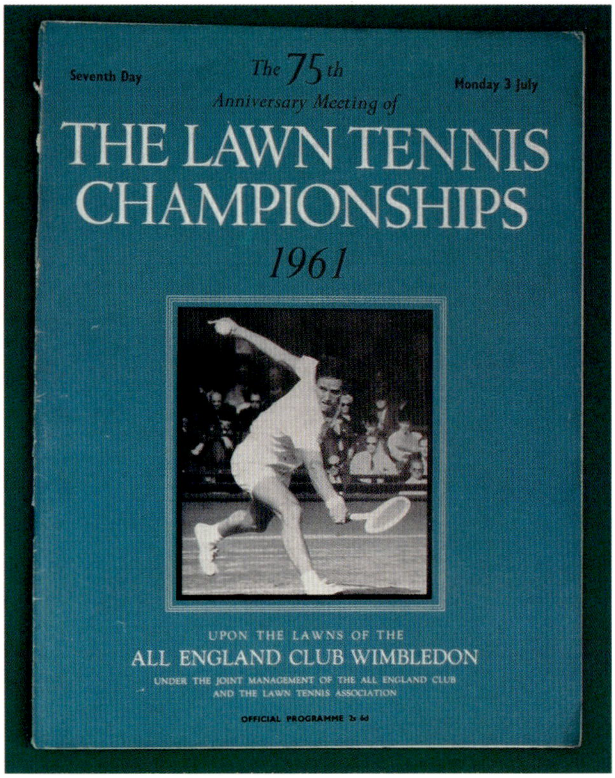

Fig. 1.191. **Wimbledon, 1961**
The Lawn Tennis Championships, Wimbledon, 1961, 36pp. 300 x 235mm., The 75th Anniversary Meeting, 7th day. Kelly & Kelly Ltd. London N.1. £15-20 ($25-30)

Fig. 1.192. **The U. S. Open, 1963**
U S L T A Singles Championships 1963, West Side Tennis Club Forest Hills, New York. The Official Championships Magazine, 32pp., 300 x 226mm., H. O. Zimman Inc., Mass. Complete with large printed draw sheet and a list of competitors. £20-30 ($30-45)

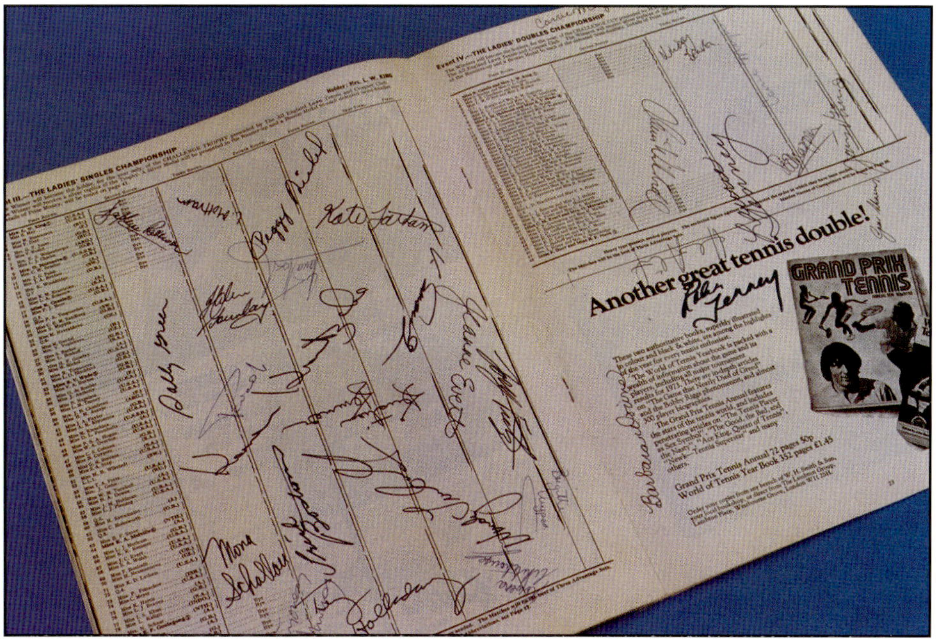

Fig. 1.194. **Wimbledon, 1974**
The Lawn Tennis Championships, Wimbledon, 1974, 48pp. 306 x 233mm.,1st day. Two colour cover, full colour back cover, black printing throughout. Signed by - Mrs. A. J. Pattison, Linda Mottram, Peggy Michel, Kate Latham, Iana Kloss, Helen Gourlay, Sally Greer, Karen Krantzcke, Kristy Kemmer, Jeanne Evert, Miss T. Fretz, Miss P. Bostrom, Mona Schallau, Terry Holliday, Rowena Whitehouse, Wendy Turnbull, Bridgett Cuypers, Barabara Downs, Carrie Meyer, Lindsay Beaven, Greer Stevens, and Sue Mappin. £100-150 ($150-225)

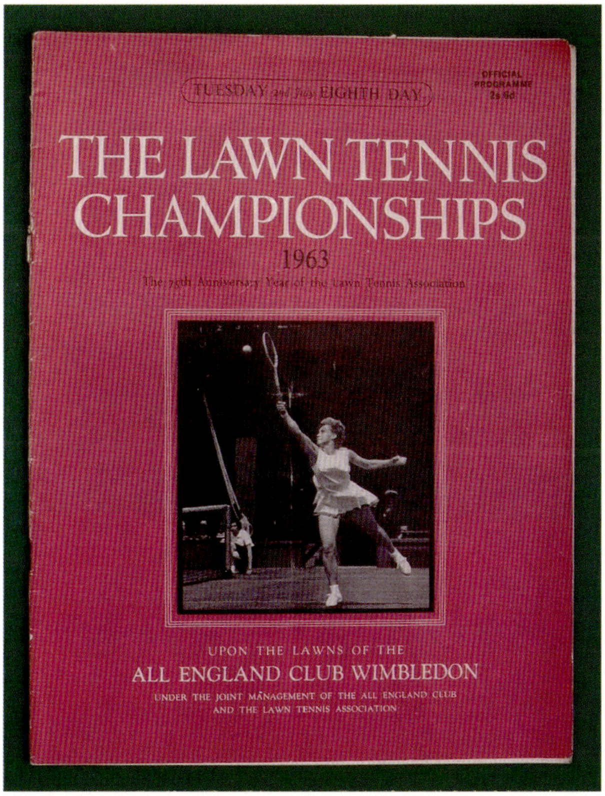

Fig. 1.193. **Wimbledon, 1963**
The Lawn Tennis Championships, Wimbledon, 1963, 36pp., 305 x 234mm., 8th day. 75th Anniversary Year of the Lawn Tennis Association. £10-20 ($15-30)

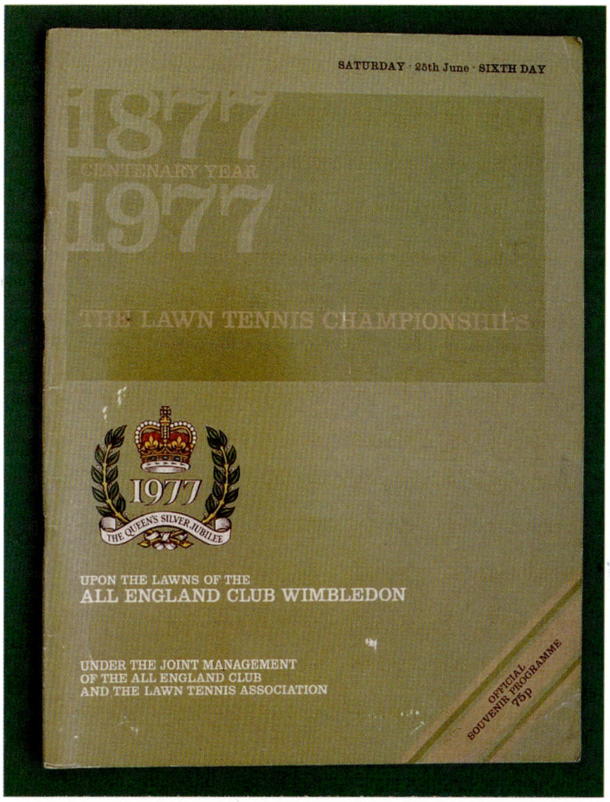

Fig. 1.195. **Wimbledon, 1977**
The Lawn Tennis Championships, Wimbledon, 1977, 80pp., 306 x 234mm., 6th day. Centenary Year. Full colour. £10-15 ($15-25)

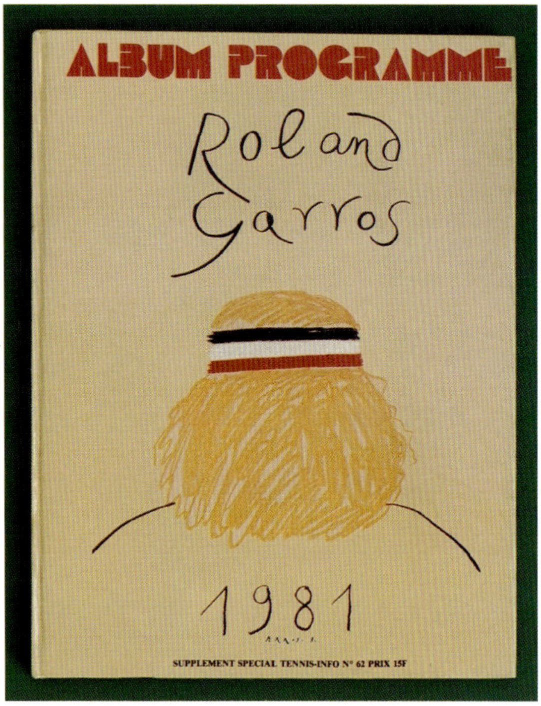

Fig. 1.196. **The French Open, 1981**
Internationaux de France 1981: Album Programme Officiel, Roland Garros, 124pp., 278 x 215mm., hard covers. £20-30 ($30-45)

Fig. 1.197. **The Australian Open, 1984**
Marlborough Australian Open, Kooyong, 1984, 108pp., 273 x 210mm. Full colour throughout. £15-20 ($20-30)

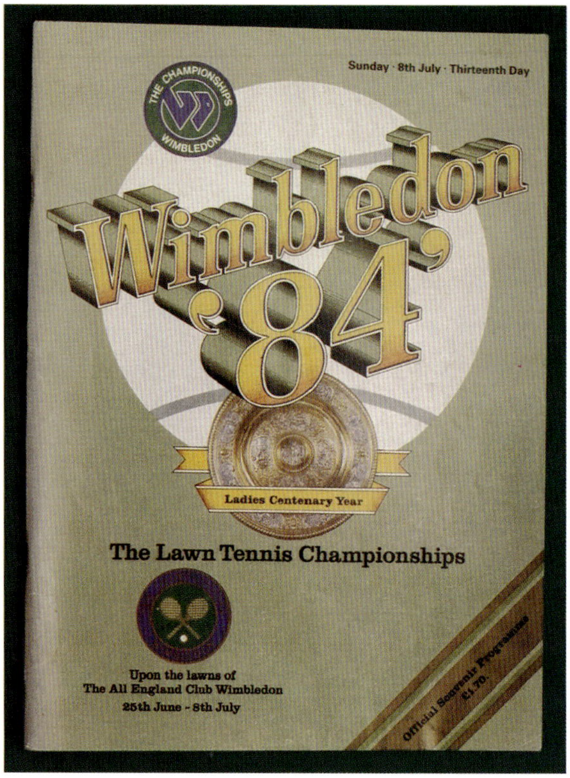

Fig. 1.198. **Wimbledon, 1984**
The Lawn Tennis Championships, Wimbledon, 1984, 104pp., 301 x 220mm., 13th day. Men's Finals Day. Full colour. With separate draw sheet. £10-15 ($15-25)

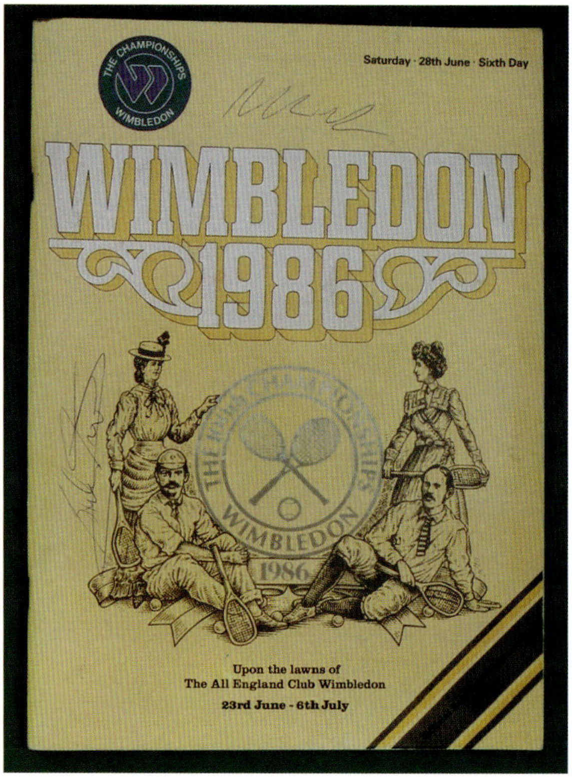

Fig. 1.199. **Wimbledon, 1986**
The Lawn Tennis Championships, Wimbledon, 1986, 124pp., 305 x 220mm., 6th day. The 100th Championships. Full colour. £10-15 ($15-25)

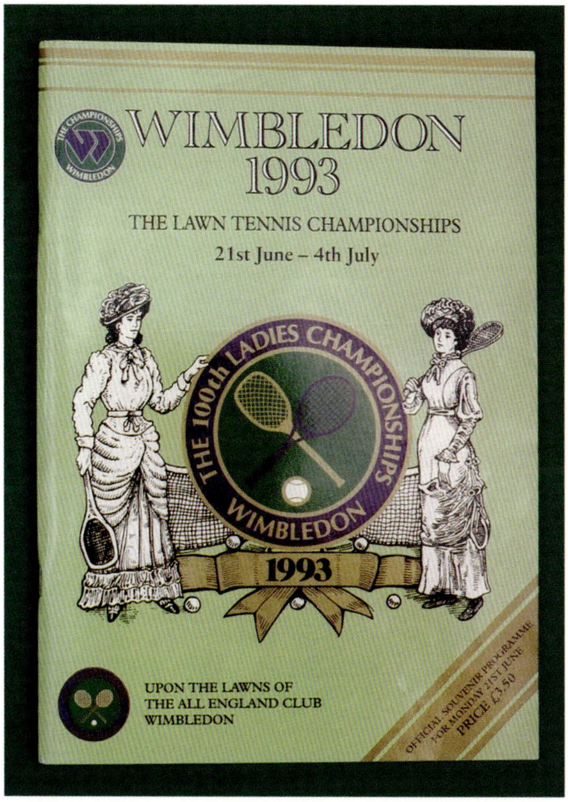

Top left:
Fig. 1.200. **Wimbledon, 1992**
The Lawn Tennis Championships, Wimbledon, 1992, 124pp., 305 x 218mm., 1st day. The 70th Anniversary at the Church Road ground. Full colour. £10-15 ($15-25)

Left:
Fig. 1.201. **Wimbledon, 1993**
The Lawn Tennis Championships, Wimbledon, 1993, 124pp., 305 x 218mm., 1st day. The 100th Ladies Championships. Full colour. £10-15 ($15-25)

Above:
Fig. 1.202. **Wimbledon, 1999**
The Lawn Tennis Championships, Wimbledon, 1999, 124pp., 305 x 218mm., 6th day. Full colour throughout. £10-15 ($15-25)

Newspapers and Magazines

I've always been bewildered by the range of ephemeral items associated with racket sports. At antiques fairs, tickets, passes, clippings, scraps, and a million other items seem to discreetly hide themselves away in cardboard boxes, or scamper away to the very bottom corner the instant that your eye catches a detail of some note.

How many times have I been directed to a distinctly unpromising, battered old box, packed full with all manner of printed paraphernalia? 'Tennis? You might find something in there mate!' Soap powder, corsets, cast iron fencing, and a card of press-studs...yes...lawn tennis, no. Oh well, on to the next. I distinctly remember taking a trip to a small rural town in the English Midlands one spring day. The sun was shining and as a result I was at one with the world, eager to find a new and 'undiscovered' antique or bookshop. 'Where can I find your sports section sir?' (I often resort to asking for 'the sports section' now, because it's more than I can bear, should I ask for lawn tennis, or just 'tennis' to be frowned at and told 'Oh no! we haven't anything like that!') At least if they have a sports section, a lawn tennis book or item might have slipped their notice. It wasn't long before a thoroughly optimistic search turned to doubt and then apathy (the sun had gone in!). I probably dragged my feet a little on the way out (in disgust) wondering where the next emporium of antique treasure was to be found. Before I left, a pile of old newspapers caught my eye in the corner of the room; they were defying the laws of gravity by clinging to the very edge of an old school desk.

The light was poor, so I rescued the whole pile of about thirty copies and carefully placed them on an armchair near to the window. As I worked my way down them I suddenly found an 1868 copy of *Land and Water*, knowing that this was too early for lawn tennis but suitably encouraged I dug deeper, and then...Eureka! It was an issue from May 1874. I was not totally certain when Major Wingfield began to advertise from his French and Company Depot, but I did know that he applied for a patent in February of that year. By now, my heart was beating a little faster, I was searching through the index on page three, hardly able to concentrate, only knowing that should any of the words ...lawn...tennis...or even better...Sphairistike appear before my eyes, I had hit the jackpot. I was lucky enough to find two copies of the newspaper. The first, from 1874, contained one of the earliest advertisements for the game of Sphairistike, the second from 1875 showing how the game had become so popular in just a little over one year.

It just goes to show that there are still many items to be found if you are prepared to search carefully and patiently, and if luck is with you.

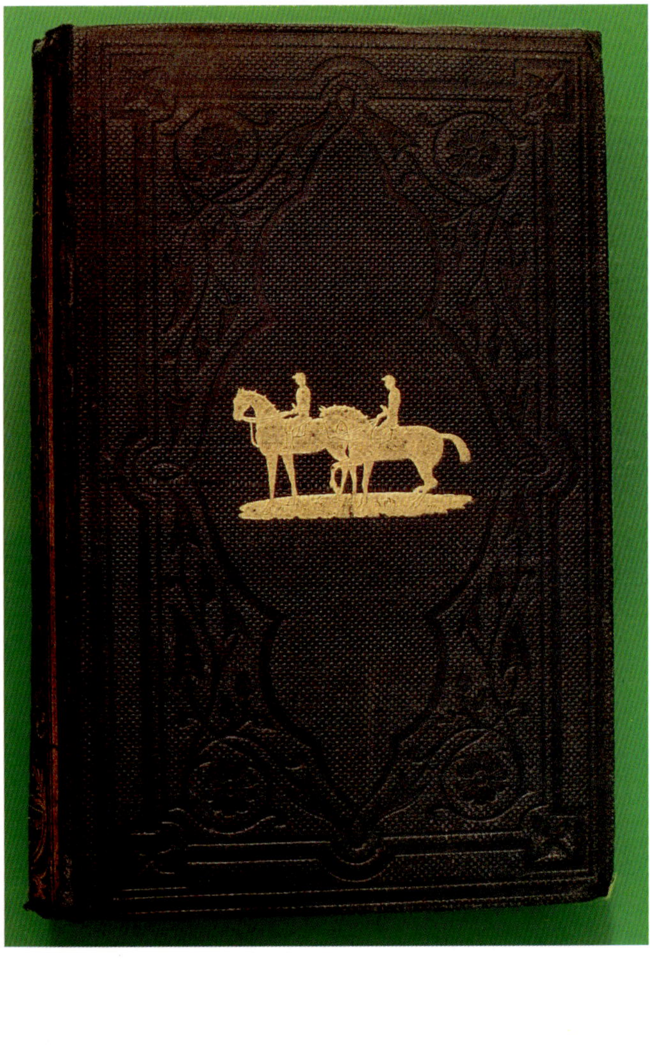

Fig. 1.203. ***Baily's Magazine***
Baily's Magazine of Sports and Pastimes - 1875 Bound Volume XXVII 430pp., 228 x 146mm., hard covers. Bound monthly publications from May until November. The July edition (VOL. XXVII - No. 185 p. 138) contains the: 'Laws of Lawn Tennis - Revised by The M C C.' The single monthly edition can be found individually published in its original soft paper covers. £200-250 ($300-375)

Fig. 1.204. ***Land & Water***

Land & Water, Hunting, Shooting & Practical Natural History, Saturday May 30th. 1874, (Vol. XVII.-No. 436) 28pp., 448 x 292mm. A weekly newspaper which published one of the earliest advertisements for: 'The New Game of Sphairistike or Lawn Tennis' (p. 6). On the same page and column is an advertisement for a new publication by R. D. Norseman: *The Game of Badminton* (I have never heard of or seen a copy of this book!). A review of the new game can be found later in the publication: 'This game is one of the best outdoor games, especially for ladies, that has ever come under our notice.' Under the heading: 'Domestic – The London Season' the paper observes weekly events at one of London's top 'Society' sporting clubs: 'Prince's Club, in Hans-place, is also a wonderful and fascinating place, and certainly bids fair to be the fashion for this season… As you sit under the shade of the row of fine old trees on your right, you might watch marvellous feats of activity in the game of 'Lawn Tennis,' the Indian 'Sphairistike,' which people report to be a good game, and 'Badminton,' which requires some strength and study.' This review and observation of the new game appeared just three months after Major Wingfield had taken out his patent for 'a portable court' Perhaps the reporter was watching the games of Germains Lawn Tennis, Sphairistike, and Badminton? £200-250 ($300-375)

Land & Water, Hunting, Shooting & Practical Natural History, Saturday December 25th. 1875, (Vol. XX.-No.518) 28pp., 448 x 292mm. We are now eighteen months on and lawn tennis is firmly established as a popular pastime. On page six an advertisement for *The New Quarterly Magazine* for January sees an article for: 'Lawn tennis – by John Latouche.' There's also an advertisement for John Wisden and Co., who boast that they are now prepared to supply 'Germain's Lawn Tennis'. Finally there's an advertisement from George Lambert of the Marylebone Cricket club to whom he was the 'tennis player and sole vendor of lawn tennis, rackets and balls' and he was now 'supplying complete sets for lawn tennis, price £5.5s., as used by the club.' £75-100 ($100-150)

LAWN TENNIS CHAMPIONSHIP.

TENNIS AT OXFORD.

CAMBRIDGE.

Fig. 1.205. ***The Field***
The Field, The Farm, The Garden, The Country Gentleman's Newspaper. (Vol.XLIX. – from January 6th to June 30th. 1877, The Field Office, 346, Strand, London. 796pp., 443 x 295mm. A weekly newspaper which was full of information concerning, sports, pastimes, and country pursuits. This volume published (in part) Julian Marshall's Annals of Tennis before it was released as a single volume. It also holds notice of the intention to hold the first Wimbledon lawn tennis championships. These volumes are an amazingly detailed source of information concerning all rackets sports, including tournaments, the development of rules, sports equipment, and the records of players. £300-500 ($450-750)

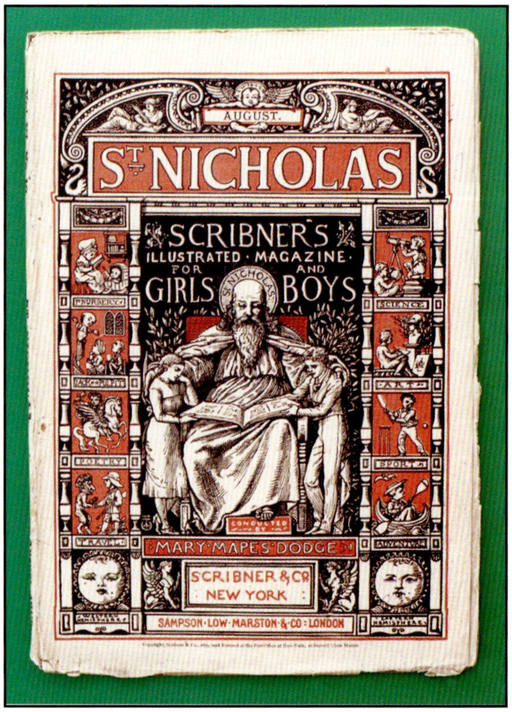

Fig. 1.206. ***St. Nicholas Magazine***
St. Nicholas Magazine, August 1879, Scribner and Co., 743 & 745 Broadway, New York. 254 x 180mm. A four page article (pp. 655-658) by W. H. Boardman, takes a brief look at the history of the game and how it is played just five years after it came to prominence. There's a diagram of an hourglass shaped court and a pleasant engraving by W. Taber looking down onto a similar court while a doubles match is in progress. The article concludes with an engraving of an offset racket and the advice: 'Take your defeats good-naturedly, and wear your honors lightly, but always do your level best.' £75-100 ($100-150)

Fig. 1.207. ***The Queen***[30]
The Queen, The Lady's Newspaper & Court Chronicle, Saturday May 10th. 1884, 64pp., 427 x 287mm. A weekly publication with advertisements, which featured mainly women's costumes, materials, fashions, and other accoutrements. Lawn tennis had become very popular and often there were features or advertisements associated with the game. Notable ones are the: 'Lawn Tennis Blouse from Redfern of Cowes, Isle of Wight; Samuel Winter's Lawn Tennis, boating and Yachting Shoes; and Brown's Patent 'Dermathistic' Corset. Some other fascinating advertisements were those for; 'Melliship and Harris's Lawn Tennis Prizes and Lawn Tennis Requisites; Hamley Brothers; Thomas's Tennis Fencing; Benetfink and Co.'s Lawn Tennis Specialities; F. H. Ayres Lawn Tennis Requisites; and 'Ye Souvenir of ye Season' from D. King & Co. An issue from 1877 published advertisements for; 'George Lambert, Champion Tennis Player; the Lawn Tennis Court Marker; and Hunt's Patent Lawn Tennis Court Marker.' £50-75 ($75-100)

Lawn Tennis and Croquet

PRICE TWOPENCE

THE OFFICIAL ORGAN OF

The Lawn Tennis Association. The Badminton Association.

No. 228.—VOL. IX.] WEDNESDAY, JULY 6, 1904.

THE

"SLAZENGER"

LAWN TENNIS BALL.

The ALL ENGLAND LAWN TENNIS & CROQUET CLUB, WIMBLEDON.

Secretary, ARCHDALE PALMER. 17, Harp Lane, Great Tower Street, London, E.C., 5th July, 1904.

Messrs. Slazenger & Sons, Laurence Pountney Hill, E.C.

Dear Sirs,

Championship Arrangements.

I am directed by the Committee of this Club to express their appreciation of the arrangements you made for the recent Championship Meeting in respect of Nets, Posts, Balls, and the Canvas Belts surrounding the several Courts, which last contributed largely to the improvement of the appearance of the Lawns.

I am also desired to say that the Balls supplied, every one of which was carefully measured and weighed before use in Court by the Referee, gave general satisfaction.

I am, Sirs, yours faithfully,

ARCHDALE PALMER, Secretary.

ILLUSTRATED PRICE LISTS ON APPLICATION.

LAWN-TENNIS AND BADMINTON

THE OFFICIAL ORGAN

2D.

1906. JULY 18. VOL. XI. No. 2

THE CHAMPIONSHIPS,

1906.

THE CHAMPIONSHIP OF THE WORLD, 1906

HAS BEEN WON WITH

The "DOHERTY" Racket.

This is the 11th successive World's Championship won with SLAZENGERS' Rackets.

THE LADIES' SINGLES CHAMPIONSHIP, 1906

HAS ALSO BEEN WON WITH

The "DOHERTY" Racket.

This is the 6th successive Ladies' Championship won with SLAZENGERS' Rackets

THE "SLAZENGER" BALL

WAS USED AT

THE ALL-ENGLAND CHAMPIONSHIP & International Meetings, 1906

Also used for the Championship Meetings in 1902, 1903, 1904 & 1905.

Write for Catalogue to—

SLAZENGER & SONS Laurence Pountney Hill, Cannon St LONDON, E.C.

Top left:
Fig. 1.208. ***Lawn Tennis and Croquet Magazine***
Lawn Tennis and Croquet Magazine, The Official Organ of the Lawn Tennis Association. The Badminton Association. July 6th 1904, 24pp., 304 x 205mm. This magazine started in 1896 and continued to be published weekly until its demise in 1905, when it continued as *Lawn Tennis and Badminton*. Carrying the usual variety of manufacturers advertisements, book reviews, forthcoming tournaments, reports, and commentary. £30-40 ($45-60)

Left:
Fig. 1.209. ***Lawn-Tennis and Badminton***
Lawn-Tennis and Badminton, The Official Organ, July 18th 1906, 28pp., 305 x 205mm. An article entitled 'Ins and Outs' was a regular feature in this magazine, where a correspondent reported on tennis related topics and incidents from the media. In this copy he related that: 'There is an interesting article in *Pearson's Magazine* of the present month on the 'Curse of the Cigarette,' in which it is maintained that cigarette-smoking is undermining the youth of the nation, stunting the growth of boys, blunting their minds, and leading to other vices.' Perhaps he had experienced 'the curse' first hand at his own tennis club? £30-40 ($45-60)

Above:
Fig. 1.210. ***The Illustrated London News***
The Illustrated London News, three issues for July 2nd 1921(40pp.), July 1st 1922 (44pp.) and June 30th 1923,(56pp.) 389 x 274mm. A weekly magazine which, in these cases, carried feature articles on the championships at Wimbledon. The 1921 issue concentrated upon the play at the old Worple Road ground where the championships were taking place for the last time. The other two copies are illustrated with photographs and drawings from the ground at Church Street, where the Centre Court (without the ivy-covered walls) is very prominent. £30-40 ($45-60)

Fig. 1.211. ***Lawn Tennis and Badminton***
Lawn Tennis and Badminton, The Official Organ of the Lawn Tennis Association, issues for August 1922 (24pp., 327 x 203mm), March 1930 (28pp., 320 x 198mm.), August 1957 (32pp., 248 x 184mm.), and August 1967 (48pp., 248 x 186mm.) £20-30 ($30-40)

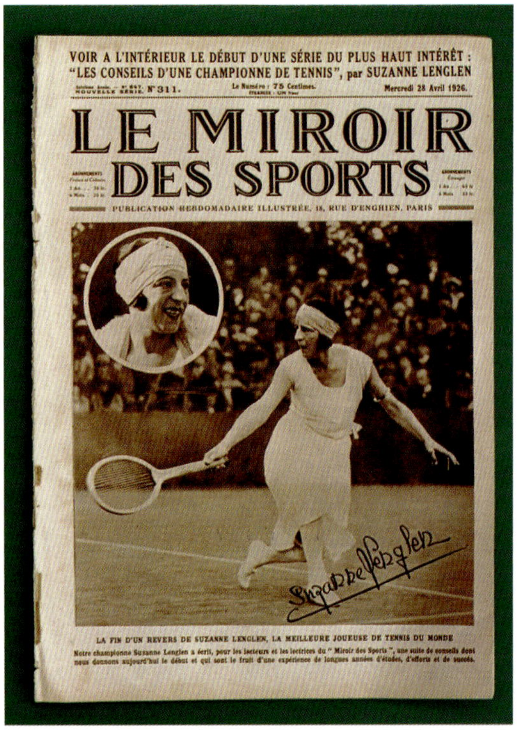

Fig. 1.212. ***Le Miroir des Sports***
Le Miroir des Sports, Avril 1926, 16pp., 327 x 235mm. A French weekly newspaper which covered many sporting events and topics. Printed throughout in brown ink. £20-30 ($30-40)

Fig. 1.213. ***Le Petit Echo de la Mode***
Le Petit Echo de la Mode, Aout 1927, 16pp., 254 x 290mm. A French weekly paper, which often contained a reference to racket sports by the use of a coloured drawing on the cover. £20-30 ($30-40)

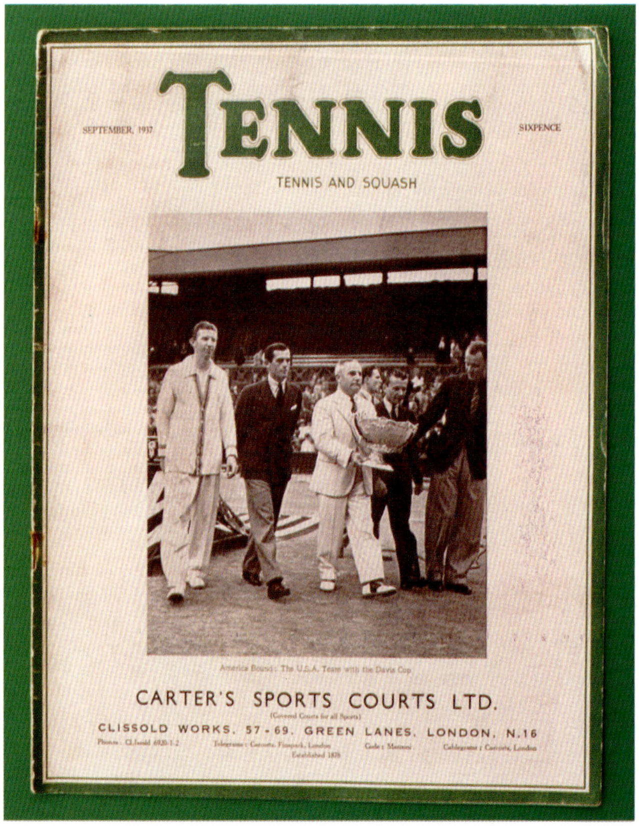

Fig. 1.214. ***Tennis & Squash***
Tennis & Squash, September 1937, 28pp., 309 x 237mm.This title ran from 1933 until 1939. A major review considers the recent loss of the Davis Cup by Great Britain (the holders) to the United States. £15-20 ($20-30)

Fig. 1.215. ***American Lawn Tennis***
American Lawn Tennis, The Illustrated Magazine of the Game, issues for October 1939 and June 1940, 310 x 237mm. Published from 1907 until 1951. £15-20 ($20-30)

Fig. 1.217. ***Illustrated***
Illustrated, Incorporating *The Passing Show* & *Weekly Illustrated*, May 13th 1939, 64pp., 343 x 254mm. A weekly magazine (published during the Second World War), with articles on 'Magic Eye on Jean Nicholl – New tennis star shows how' and 'And This is Real Tennis – as played at Queen's Club'. £10-15 ($15-25)

Fig. 1.216. ***Tennis Illustrated***
Tennis Illustrated, issues for February and November 1937, 28pp., 286 x 223mm. Inside the November issue a cartoon by 'MAC' entitled 'The Winter of our Lawn Tennis' makes an observation on a problem with the British game. The caption reads: 'Far-seeing countries overseas, with a view to fostering their young Davis Cup talent, are going ahead with intensive covered court building. Here in England, with the worst of weather conditions, the lack of covered courts is a serious handicap to any scheme for producing potential Davis Cup players.' Published from 1926 until 1939. £15-20 ($20-30)

Fig. 1.218. ***Picture Post***
Picture Post, issues for July 1939 (76pp.), August 1945 (28pp.), and June 1948 (32pp.), 348 x 258mm. An English 'weekly' which often featured an article associated with tennis during the Wimbledon fortnight. £5-10 ($8-15)

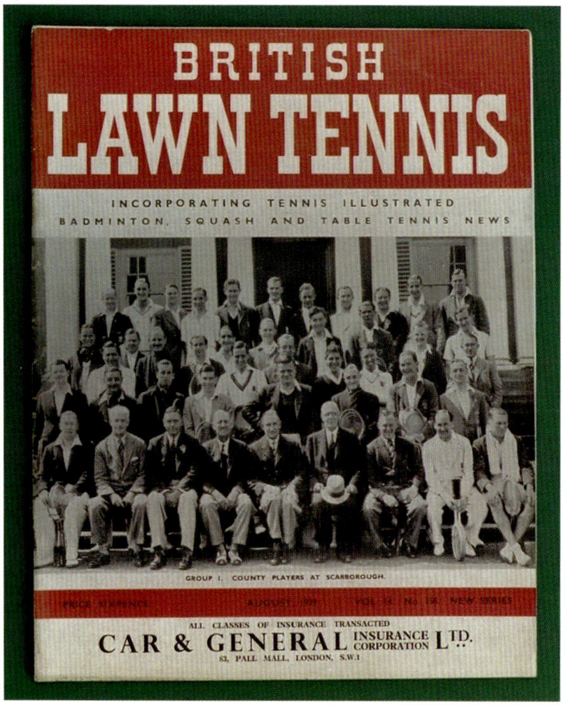

Fig. 1.219. ***British Lawn Tennis***
British Lawn Tennis, Incorporating *Tennis Illustrated, Badminton, Squash and Table Tennis News*, August 1939, 28pp., 285 x 223mm. A time-capsule of European tennis as it stood just before the 'Great Conflict'. The magazine quotes part of a speech made to 13,000 Americans at Madison Square Garden by 'Bunny' Austin. Entitled 'H. W. Austin Speaks to the World' it read: 'Hate, fear and greed are intoxicating the nations of Europe and making the world a madhouse. I learned that the trouble in the world was plain selfishness, not in this individual or that, but in everyone. Moral re-armament is a war on selfishness. There is nothing wrong with the world it is the people in it. To change the world we must change the people in it. I had to begin with myself.' The magazine was published in 1939 and then from 1946 until 1948. £10-15 ($15-20)

Fig. 1.220. ***World Sports Magazine***
World Sports, International Sports Magazine, June 1955, 56pp., 265 x 217mm. A review of the forthcoming Wimbledon Championships: 'Can 'Old Drob' Do it Again' and a major article concerning the question: 'Should Boxing be Banned?' £5-10 ($7-15)

Fig. 1.221. ***British Lawn Tennis & Squash***
British Lawn Tennis & Squash, copies for 1953, 1957, & 1958, 24pp., 278 x 216mm. Published between 1948 and 1967. £5-10 ($8-15)

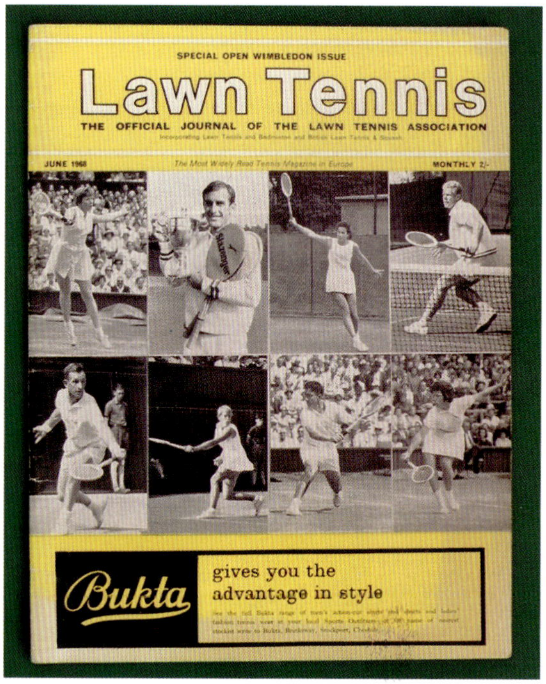

Fig. 1.222. ***Lawn Tennis***
Lawn Tennis, June 1968, 44pp., 275 x 213mm. This title ran from 1968-1976. £5-10 ($8-15)

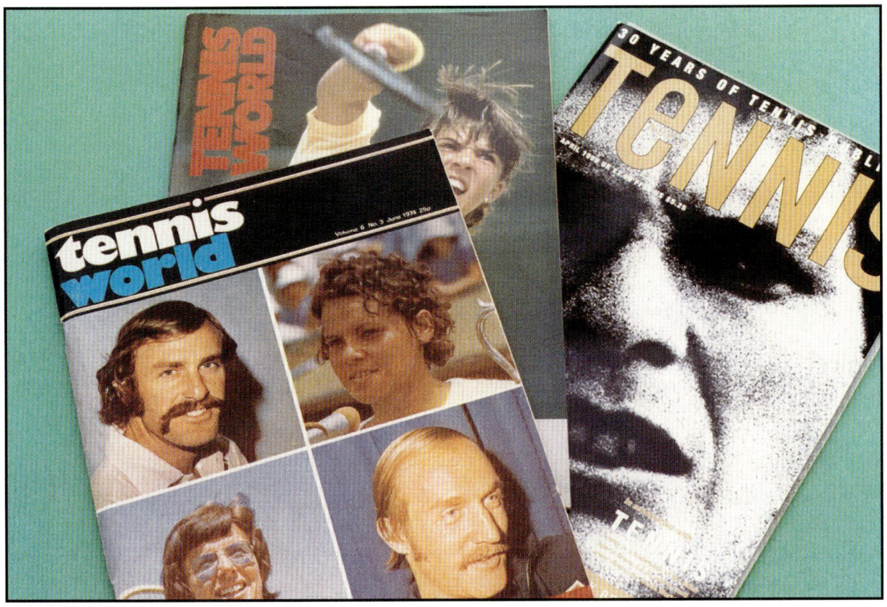

Fig. 1.223. ***Tennis World***
Tennis World, copies for 1974 (278 x 215mm., with supplement) 74pp., 1989 (297 x 210mm., 60pp.) and 1999 (296 x 211mm., 64pp., with 30th birthday supplement). It was first published in 1969 and is still going strong. £5-10 ($8-15)

Fig. 1.225. **The *Radio Times***
Radio Times, June 1977, 68pp., 308 x 250mm. An English monthly guide to television programming which published a special article on the Wimbledon Championships each summer. £3-5 ($5-8)

Fig. 1.224. ***Tennis Today***
Tennis Today, issues for March 1977 (48pp.) and March 1979 (40pp.) 279 x 209mm. The magazine was published between 1976 and 1982. £5-10 ($8-15)

Fig. 1.226. ***'Tennis'* Magazine**
Tennis, Incorporating *Lawn Tennis Magazine*, issues for July 1977 and March 1978, 72pp., 275 x 203mm. A monthly magazine, which was published from 1976 until 1978. £5-10 ($8-15)

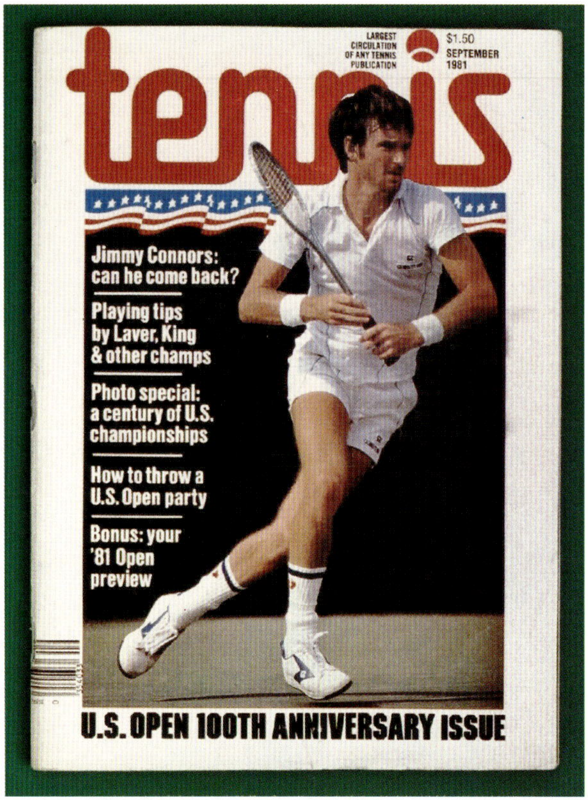

Fig. 1.227. ***'Tennis'* Magazine**
Tennis, September 1981, 160pp., 275 x 201mm. The U.S. Open 100th Anniversary issue, with a seven-page article on the occasion. Published since 1965. £5-10 ($8-15)

Fig. 1.228. ***The World of Junior Tennis***
The World of Junior Tennis, 24pp., 298 x 210mm. Issue no.1 for November 1986 and may have only continued for two years. £5-10 ($8-15)

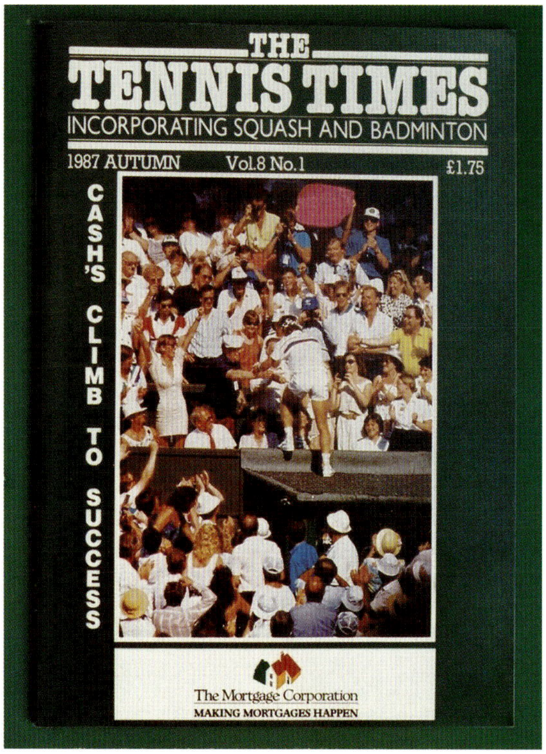

Fig. 1.229. ***The Tennis Times***
The Tennis Times, Autumn 1987, 64pp., 301 x 210mm. Published as four issues a year from 1980. £5-10 ($8-15)

Fig. 1.230. ***Le monde du Tennis***
Le monde du Tennis, August – September 1987, 144pp., 279 x 210mm. Complete with large poster of Gabrielle Sabatini. £5-10 ($8-15)

Fig. 1.231. ***Punch***
Punch, Magazine, June 1988, 60pp., 293 x 212mm. A satirical look at the goings on at Wimbledon: '1900 - The game speeds up beyond recognition as cameras are permitted for the first time – no longer requiring players to pause during tricky shots, to enable portrait artists to sketch notes.' '1927 - Seeding is introduced after all attempts fail to get players to bring their own turf' '1946 - Despite having all the buildings painted camouflage green, foreign tourists still manage to find the club.' £5-10 ($8-15)

Fig. 1.233. ***Serve and Volley***
Serve and Volley, March 1988, 60pp., 297 x 210mm. This edition was dedicated to the Lawn Tennis Association's 100th Anniversary exhibition. The magazine was first published in 1982. £5-10 ($8-15)

Fig. 1.232. ***World Tennis***
World Tennis, issues for July 1987 (82pp.) and July 1989 (100pp.) 266 x 201mm. Issued from 1953-1991. £5-10 ($8-15)

Fig. 1.234. ***Ace Magazine***
Ace Magazine, December 1999, 84pp., 295 x 210mm. £5-10 ($8-15)

Chapter 2.
Printed Ephemera, Games, and Cards

Games and Toys

In a copy of *The Tennis Collector* (January 1995, p.5-7) renowned American collector Chuck Hoey listed over fifty 'indoor racket motif' games, which were manufactured between 1840 and 1950. He astutely described them as: '…a veritable menagerie of thematic imagination, documenting the migration of outdoor racket games to the parlour.' I have included in my list any item which would contain within it an interval of diverting entertainment for young or old. Again, the collector can expect anything and everything to turn up in auctions or at fairs, if you've never seen an example before and you have been making a genuine search for similar items, then it's probably rare. Ultimately you have to decide whether to part with your hard-earned cash. As a general rule, those games which are based upon 'tiddlywinks' type principles are the earliest, and often the most fun to play!

Fig. 2.1. **'Tiddledy-wink' Tennis from Parker Brothers**
A boxed set of the Parker brothers' game, with wooden rackets, plastic counters, and a very thick brown felt court surface. (c. 1895) Box Length 29.3 cms. Depth 20.3 cms. Court Length 53.3 cms. Width 24.3 cms. £100-150 ($150-225)

Fig. 2.2. **A Box of Children's Building Blocks**
A set of pine cubes, each face of which has glued to it a part of a children's coloured picture, or print. Originally, of course, there were six pictures to make up, and each of them had a completed print supplied within the box. The picture on the front of the box is one of children playing lawn tennis; however, there is no court marked on the grass. The box and contents were manufactured in Germany. (c. 1900) Length 25.6 cms. Width 17.8 cms. Depth 5.3 cms. £125-150 ($175-225)

Fig. 2.3. **A Victorian Scrap**
A fine die-cut chromolithograph scrap of a girl holding a tray of four multicoloured lawn tennis balls in one hand and a racket in the other. (c. 1900) Height 24.0 cms. £10-15 ($15-25)

Fig. 2.4. **Old Maid**
A selection of six cards from a complete set of Old Maid playing cards. Each of them shows a member of a Victorian family playing lawn tennis. The remainder of the set shows a number of different sports. (c. 1900) Per set £45-60 ($70-90)

Fig. 2.5. **A Pack of Waddington's Playing Cards**
A full set of boxed gaming cards from Waddington's company, with an image of a 1920s lady player printed on the reverse of each card. Box Length 9.7 cms. Width 6.5 cms. Depth 3.0 cms. (c. 1920) £30-50 ($45-75)

Fig. 2.6. **'Sinnet' from Chad Valley Games**
A board game, which is played by throwing a dice to determine the number of moves around the board. It was manufactured at Chad Valley Works, Harborne, Birmingham, England. The attractive board is chromolithograph printed. (c. 1925) Box Length 30.8 cms. Width 21.8 cms. Court Length 43.2 cms. Width 29.9 cms. £75-100 ($100-150)

Fig. 2.7. **Bridge Tally Cards**
Three American, decorative stand-up bridge tally cards, each with a pencil string attached. They are Art Deco in design. (c. 1930) Length 7.0 cms. £60-80 ($90-120)

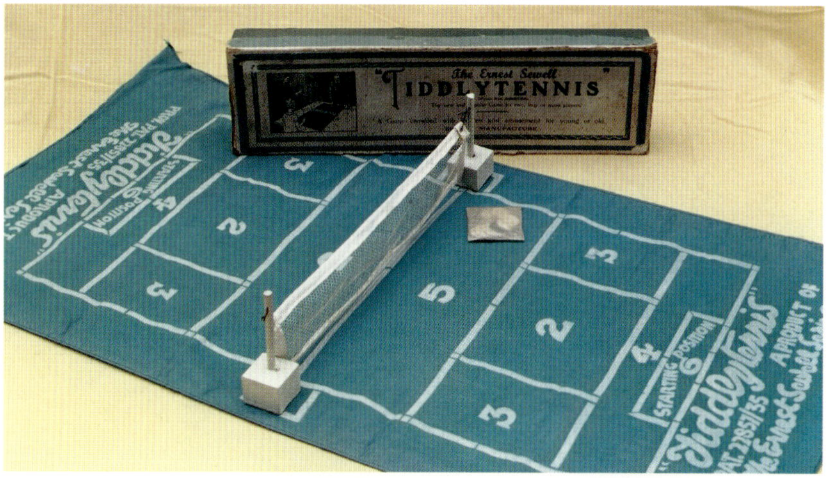

Fig. 2.8. **'Tiddlytennis' from Ernest Sewell**
A complete boxed set with the original cotton court surface, traditional wooden posts, woven net, and play counters. The game is played as one would play tiddlywinks. (c. 1935) Box Length 39.8 cms. Width 10.7 cms. Depth 4.7 cms. Court Length 76.3 cms. Width 40.4 cms. £75-100 ($100-150)

...dition. (c. 1950) Length

Fig. 2.10. **A Children's Doll**
An early children's doll made of felt over a packed straw interior. The racket has a wire frame. (c. 1950) Height 39.5 cms. £50-75 ($75-100)

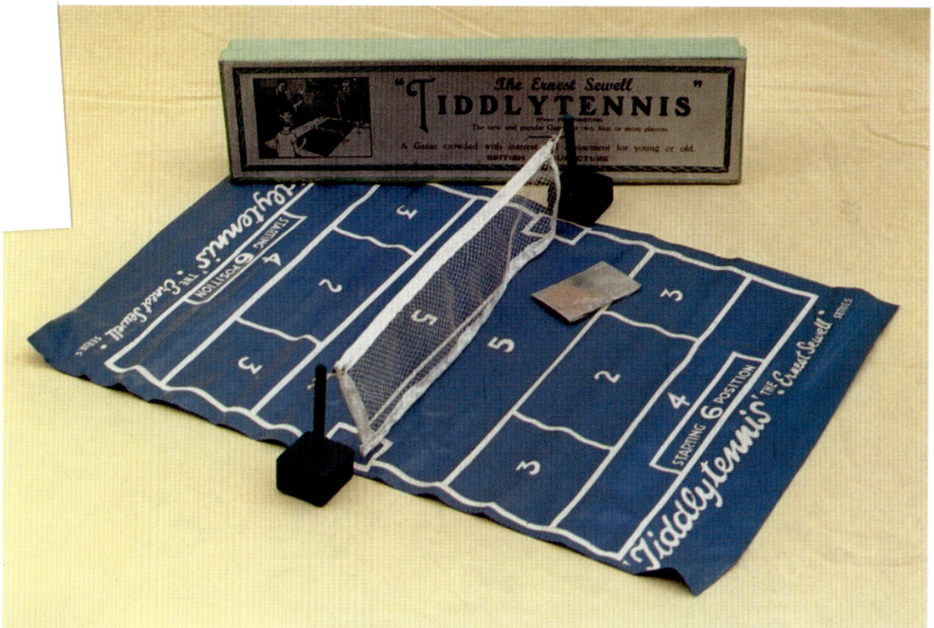

Fig. 2.11. **'Tiddlytennis' from Ernest Sewell**
A complete boxed set with the smaller and later, plastic court surface, traditional wooden posts and woven net, and play counters. (c. 1950) Length 37.3 cms. Width 9.4 cms. Depth 4.0 cms. Court Length 48.8 cms. Width 28.0 cms. £75-100 ($100-150)

Fig. 2.12. **Articulated Tennis Players**
A pair of painted wooden articulated lawn tennis players. Due to their wire sub skeleton, they can be manipulated to show them playing almost any stroke. I have seen similar figures representing other sports. Height approx. 10.0 cms. £35-55 ($50-75)

Fig. 2.14. **A Hand Held Tennis Game**
A game which tests the steadiness of the hands by providing 15 little indentations, into which the player aims to nestle even smaller ball bearings. The whole game is situated upon a printed image of a men's doubles court, and was probably made in the 1970s. It has a patent number of 7670/75. Length 18.5 cms. Depth 11.0 cms. £20-30 ($30-50)

Fig. 2.13. **A Wooden Tennis Player**
A nicely finished souvenir model holding a tennis racket made of wire. Carved into the base are the words: 'Hand made in Italy' Height 31.0 cms. (c. 1975) £20-30 ($30-45)

Fig. 2.15. **World Cup Tennis**
An ingenious table game from the mid-1980s where the players propel a tennis ball into the opponents court while hoping to prevent their return from bouncing twice by catching the ball in a container. Box Length 46.0 cms. Width 28.5 cms. Court Length 85.0 cms. Width 45.0 cms. £25-35 ($40-50)

Tournament and Player Photographic Cards

Fig. 2.16. **Peter Latham from 'The Umpire' Paper**
Although this card is in fairly poor condition, it is quite rare and difficult to find. It features the world tennis champion (real) tennis player, Peter Latham. A short biography extols his virtues as a player: 'the beau ideal of an athlete' and 'it is probable that he will not receive his quietus for a lengthened period.' All the information is reproduced from 'The Umpire' of May 22, 1904. The back of the card is undivided. (c. 1900) £8-15 ($12-25)

Fig. 2.17. **Three Player Cards**
The cards feature Randolf Lycett , Miss Helen Wills, and C. P. Dixon. The Helen Wills card is in fact by Chaplin Jones of Kingston upon Thames; his cards seem to be even rarer than those by Edwin Trim. £12-30 each ($18-45 each)

Fig. 2.18. **Three Edwin Trim Cards**[1]
The cards show Elizabeth Ryan (18), William Tatem Tilden (32), and J. C. Parke. £12-30 each ($18-45 each)

Fig. 2.19. **Three Edwin Trim Cards**
The cards show Mrs. Lambert Chambers (57), Reggie Doherty, and the doubles partnership of Gerald Patterson and A. H. Gobert. £12-30 each ($18-45 each)

Fig. 2.20. **Three Edwin Trim Cards**
The cards show R. B. Powell (O71), Anthony F. Wilding (No.T9), and M. J. G. Ritchie (No.20). £12-30 each ($18-45 each)

Fig. 2.21. **Three Edwin Trim Cards**
Featuring Miss Betty Nuthall (W32), the doubles partnership of Miss Betty Nuthall and Mrs L. A. (Kitty) Godfree, and again Miss Betty Nuthall. £12-30 each ($18-45 each)

Fig. 2.22. **Zenzo Schimidzu of Japan**
An Edwin Trim photograph (115) of one of the finest Japanese players. Also included is a very rare autographed postcard by the same player. (c. 1921) A Davis Cup player, he reached the Wimbledon All-Comers Singles Final in 1920. £12-30 ($18-45)

Fig. 2.23. **Three Edwin Trim Cards**
The cards feature Frank X. Shields (S35), William Tilden, and Elsworth Vines (M29). £12-30 each ($18-45 each)

Fig. 2.24. **Three Edwin Trim Cards**
The cards show Miss Joan Fry (W44), Frauleine Cilly Ausem (A.151), and Miss Kathleen Stammers (R117). £12-30 each ($18-45 each)

Fig. 2.25. **Three Edwin Trim Cards**
The cards feature Miss Bundy (formerly Miss May Sutton) (W146), Miss H. Wills (W138), and Miss D. E. Round (F1). £12-30 each ($18-45 each)

Fig. 2.26. **Three Edwin Trim Cards**
The cards show photographs of H. W. (Bunny) Austin (S47), Fred Perry (wearing his 1930 Davis Cup jacket) (H183), and G. P. Hughes (W55). £12-30 each ($18-45 each)

Fig. 2.27. **Three Player Cards**
The cards show Miss Althea Gibson, Miss Maureen Connolly, and Miss Louise Brough. £8-15 ($12-25) each

Fig. 2.28. **Three Player Cards**
The photographs are of Neil Fraser (with 1963 written on the back), Roy Emerson, and Fred Stolle. £8-15 ($12-25) each

Fig. 2.29. **Three Player Cards**
The cards show Miss M. E. Bueno (dated 1964), Miss B. J. Moffitt and Miss M. Smith (dated 1964). The card showing Miss Moffitt has a hand written message on the reverse: 'Saw this girl beat Margaret Smith on Tuesday. She has only just left school, is really splendid though probably wont win the Champ[ionships] this year.' The year was 1962, and indeed the prophecy was correct as she didn't win that year, losing to Britain's Anne Haydon in the quarterfinals. She did of course make up for this in later years! She was to become Wimbledon Ladies Singles Champion on six occasions. £8-15 ($12-25) each

Fig. 2.30. **Three Player Cards**
Featuring Ile Nastase, Bjorn Borg, and Jimmy Connors (Autographed). £5-15 ($8-25) each

Fig. 2.31. **Three Tennis Cards by Le-Roye Productions**
The players featured are John McEnroe, Chris Evert Lloyd, and Jimmy Connors. They are all under the copyright of Le-Roye Productions Ltd. of Beckenham, Kent, England. The photographer was Michael Cole. (c. 1983) £3-5 ($5-8) each

Fig. 2.32. **Three Topographic Cards**
The humble little monotone card at the top (1918) shows the municipal courts at Teignmouth in Devon, England, and was the first lawn tennis collectible (along with an 'Iris' lawn tennis racket by Surridge) that I ever bought. The price I paid (45p) is still written in pencil on the reverse. The other two show the courts of Crieff Hydropathic Establishment, Tayside, Scotland (c. 1910), and Finsbury Park, London (1925). £2-5 ($3-8) each

Fig. 2.33. **Three Wimbledon View Cards by Edwin Trim**
At the top is a photograph of the Doherty (R. F. and H. L.) brothers playing in: 'THE GENTLEMEN'S DOUBLES II WIMBLEDON No.12'. Straw boaters and huge white hats, festooned with feathers, are in great abundance at the old Wimbledon grounds in Worple Road. Bottom left: (A131. PROMENADE & COURTS) is from a photograph taken in 1928. The 'Order of Play' board can easily be seen in the foreground. Gerald Patterson and Frank Crawford are to play on Centre Court while Hunter, Lycett, Brugnon, and Lee, amongst many others, play on the outside courts. The third (5D O77) clearly demonstrates the popularity of one of the timeless traditions at Wimbledon, 'Tea and Sandwiches'. (c. 1920) £12-30 each ($18-45 each)

Fig. 2.34. **Bad Hamburg 1876**
A rare German slip/card, showing an hour-glass shaped court and competitors at a lawn tennis club in Bad Homburg. For further detailed information on this image, refer to Heiner Gillmeister's *Tennis A Cultural History* (pp. 235-239) 1997 (c. 1925) £15-20 ($22-30)

Fig. 2.35. **Three Wimbledon View Cards**
The card at the top (F104 by Trim) was posted at 5 pm on 30th. June 1938 and shows the main concourse outside the Centre court. The message reads: '…Have been standing for quarter of an hour outside the building watching all the nobility and players arrive. Just 1.30 pm so we shall soon take our seats, crowds here. Don't forget to change the goldfish water…' The card on the left (W122) appears to be from the late 1920s (the Centre Court ivy hasn't grown to its full extent) and shows a mixed doubles match. The third (L153 City Press Photo Agency) takes a view over the outside courts from the Centre Court balcony. On court four, Miss Susan Noel plays a singles match against M. Morphew (South Africa, the victor) in the third round of the 1938 Ladies Singles Championship. £12-30 each ($18-45 each)

Fig. 2.36. **Wimbledon View Cards**
Three photographic studies of Wimbledon, at the height of activity during the 'annual fortnight'. Only the two cards at the bottom can be identified. The card on the left was published by A. V. Fry & Co. Ltd., London. It was posted on 19th October 1959. The card on the right was published by Pamlin Prints of Croydon, England. £8-15 ($12-25) each

Fig. 2.37. **Three Wimbledon View Cards**
At the top a view of the Centre Court shows a mixed doubles match in progress. (c. 1960) Bottom left shows court number one and was posted on June 26th. 1952. It shows a doubles match in progress between P. Abdesselam and his partner P. Remy who are playing Tony Mottram and Geoff Paish of Great Britain. The card on the right is a photograph of the 'CHURCH RD. ENTRANCE' where Fred Perry's Statue now stands. Both of these two cards were issued by the 'PHOTO-STAND SERIES ALL-ENGLAND CLUB WIMBLEDON' and shows a little line drawing of the actual stand which stood inside the club grounds. £8-15 ($12-25) each

Fig. 2.38. **Three Wimbledon View Cards**
At the top, a view of the Wimbledon complex from the air posted in 1963, although the motor cars look as though they're straight from the 1950s. The card at bottom left shows court three, where D. Eklebe (Germany) is about to serve to Owen Davidson, at five minutes past two in the first game of the first set of the first round in 1962! Davidson won the match 6-4 6-2 6-2 before losing in the third round. The third, which shows old court number one, with that huge stand to the right, is from the 1960s. £8-15 ($12-25) each

Fig. 2.39. **Four Views of Wimbledon**
J. Arthur Dixon printed three of the four cards. The other, showing the No1. Court, was printed for the Wimbledon Museum by Clifford Frost Publications. (c. 1985) £8-15 ($12-25) each

Fig. 2.40. **The Devonshire Park Tennis Ground, Eastbourne**
A reproduction of a print, which featured in *The Illustrated London News*, July 23, 1881. Designed and Produced by Adland. (c. 1995) £3-5 ($5-7.50)

Entrance Tickets, Membership Cards, and Related Ephemera

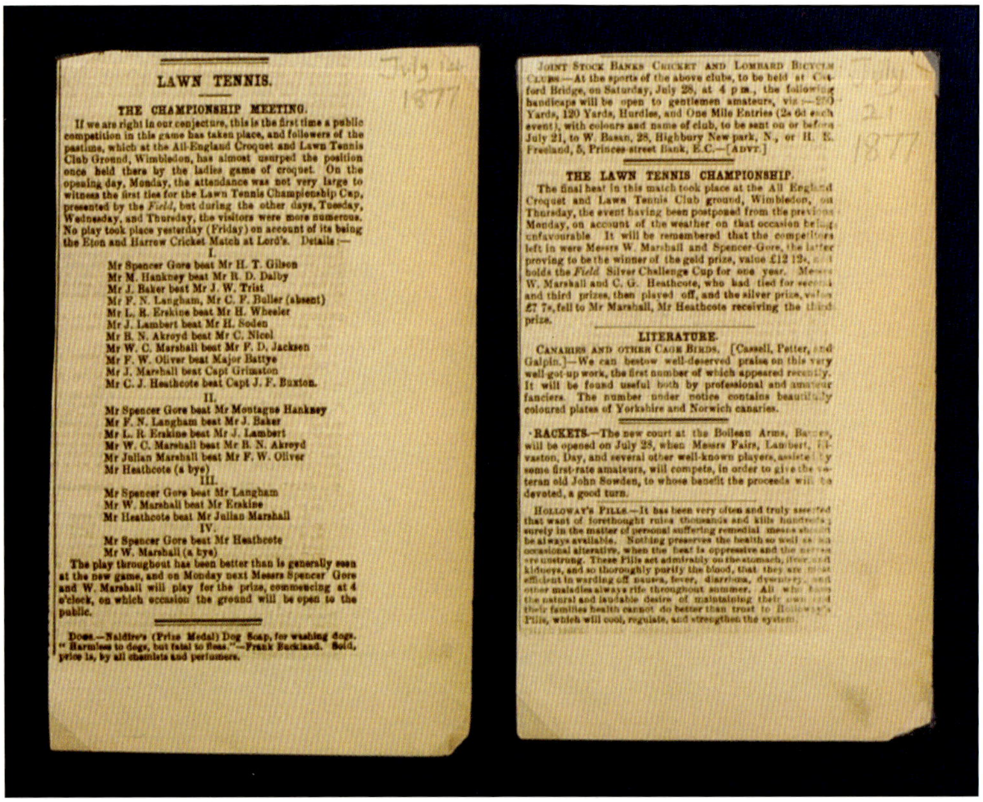

LAWN TENNIS.

THE CHAMPIONSHIP MEETING.

If we are right in our conjecture, this is the first time a public competition in this game has taken place, and followers of the pastime, which at the All-England Croquet and Lawn Tennis Club Ground, Wimbledon, has almost usurped the position once held there by the ladies game of croquet. On the opening day, Monday, the attendance was not very large to witness the first ties for the Lawn Tennis Championship Cup, presented by the *Field*, but during the other days, Tuesday, Wednesday, and Thursday, the visitors were more numerous. No play took place yesterday (Friday) on account of its being the Eton and Harrow Cricket Match at Lord's. Details :—

I.

Mr Spencer Gore beat Mr H. T. Gilson
Mr M. Hankney beat Mr R. D. Dalby
Mr J. Baker beat Mr J. W. Trist
Mr F. N. Langham, Mr C. F. Buller (absent)
Mr L. R. Erskine beat Mr H. Wheeler
Mr J. Lambert beat Mr H. Soden
Mr B. N. Akroyd beat Mr C. Nicol
Mr W. C. Marshall beat Mr F. D. Jackson
Mr F. W. Oliver beat Major Battye
Mr J. Marshall beat Capt Grimston
Mr C. J. Heathcote beat Capt J. F. Buxton.

II.

Mr Spencer Gore beat Mr Montagne Hankney
Mr F. N. Langham beat Mr J. Baker
Mr L. R. Erskine beat Mr J. Lambert
Mr W. C. Marshall beat Mr B. N. Akroyd
Mr Julian Marshall beat Mr F. W. Oliver
Mr Heathcote (a bye)

III.

Mr Spencer Gore beat Mr Langham
Mr W. Marshall beat Mr Erskine
Mr Heathcote beat Mr Julian Marshall

IV.

Mr Spencer Gore beat Mr Heathcote
Mr W. Marshall (a bye)

The play throughout has been better than is generally seen at the new game, and on Monday next Messrs Spencer Gore and W. Marshall will play for the prize, commencing at 4 o'clock, on which occasion the ground will be open to the public.

DOGS.—Naldire's (Prize Medal) Dog Soap, for washing dogs. "Harmless to dogs, but fatal to fleas."—Frank Buckland. Sold, price 1s, by all chemists and perfumers.

JOINT STOCK BANKS CRICKET AND LOMBARD BICYCLE CLUBS.—At the sports of the above clubs, to be held at Catford Bridge, on Saturday, July 28, at 4 p.m., the following handicaps will be open to gentlemen amateurs, viz :—250 Yards, 120 Yards, Hurdles, and One Mile Entries (2s 6d each event), with colours and name of club, to be sent on or before July 21, to W. Basan, 28, Highbury New park, N., or H. E. Freeland, 5, Princes-street Bank, E.C.—[ADVT.]

THE LAWN TENNIS CHAMPIONSHIP.

The final heat in this match took place at the All England Croquet and Lawn Tennis Club ground, Wimbledon, on Thursday, the event having been postponed from the previous Monday, on account of the weather on that occasion being unfavourable. It will be remembered that the competitors left in were Messrs W. Marshall and Spencer-Gore, the latter proving to be the winner of the gold prize, value £12 12s, and holds the *Field* Silver Challenge Cup for one year. Messrs W. Marshall and C. G. Heathcote, who had tied for second and third prizes, then played off, and the silver prize, value £7 7s, fell to Mr Marshall, Mr Heathcote receiving the third prize.

LITERATURE.

CANARIES AND OTHER CAGE BIRDS. [Cassell, Petter, and Galpin.]—We can bestow well-deserved praise on this very well-got-up work, the first number of which appeared recently. It will be found useful both by professional and amateur fanciers. The number under notice contains beautifully coloured plates of Yorkshire and Norwich canaries.

RACKETS.—The new court at the Boileau Arms, Barnes, will be opened on July 23, when Messrs Fairs, Lambert, Gilvaston, Day, and several other well-known players, assisted by some first-rate amateurs, will compete, in order to give the veteran old John Sowden, to whose benefit the proceeds will be devoted, a good turn.

HOLLOWAY'S PILLS.—It has been very often and truly asserted that want of forethought ruins thousands and kills hundreds; surely in the matter of personal suffering remedial means should be always available. Nothing preserves the health so well as an occasional alterative, when the heat is oppressive and the nerves are unstrung. These Pills act admirably on the stomach, liver, and kidneys, and so thoroughly purify the blood, that they are most efficient in warding off nausea, fever, diarrhoea, dysentery, and other maladies always rife throughout summer. All who have the natural and laudable desire of maintaining their own and their families health cannot do better than trust to Holloway's Pills, which will cool, regulate, and strengthen the system.

Fig. 2.41. ***Bell's Life***
One of the earliest 'newspapers' or gentleman's magazines to cover important Victorian sporting events and pastimes was *Bell's Life*. Here we see a cutting, which is a report on the first Wimbledon championships and was printed on July 14th. 1877. £8-15 ($12-25)

Fig. 2.42. **Club Membership Cards**
A range of six booklets from small clubs around England. Generally these booklets contained information about the Officers or Committee of the club, fixtures for the season, and a selection of club rules. (1888-1938) £10-60 ($15-90)

Newton Heath Lawn Tennis Club 1888
This, the oldest of the cards, once belonged to the President of the club, a Dr. B. Steward. I don't know if this club had any association with the present Football Association Club, Manchester United. (The football club began its life as Newton Heath L Y R [Lancashire and Yorkshire Railway Workers] and joined the Football League in 1892.) £50-60 ($75-90)

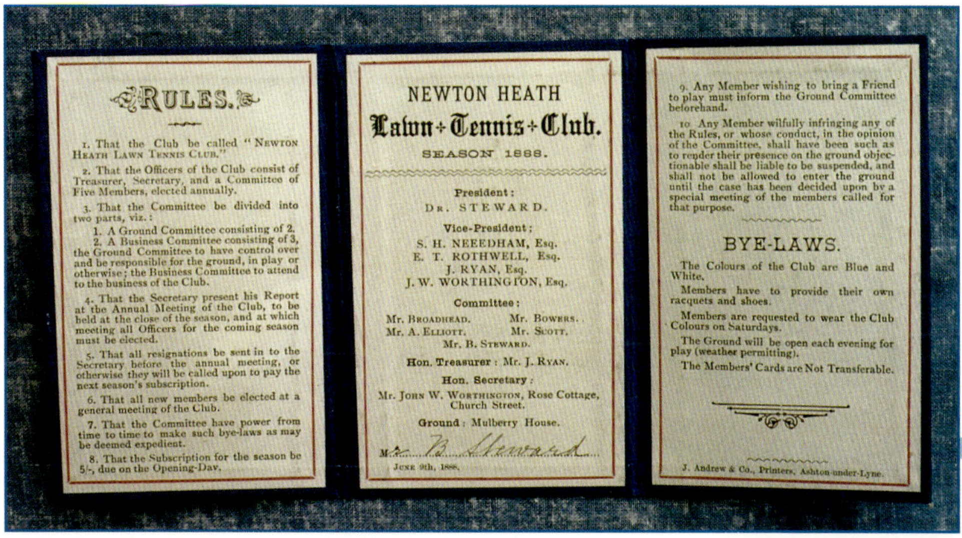
RULES.

1. That the Club be called "NEWTON HEATH LAWN TENNIS CLUB."

2. That the Officers of the Club consist of Treasurer, Secretary, and a Committee of Five Members, elected annually.

3. That the Committee be divided into two parts, viz.:

1. A Ground Committee consisting of 2.
2. A Business Committee consisting of 3, the Ground Committee to have control over and be responsible for the ground, in play or otherwise; the Business Committee to attend to the business of the Club.

4. That the Secretary present his Report at the Annual Meeting of the Club, to be held at the close of the season, and at which meeting all Officers for the coming season must be elected.

5. That all resignations be sent in to the Secretary before the annual meeting, or otherwise they will be called upon to pay the next season's subscription.

6. That all new members be elected at a general meeting of the Club.

7. That the Committee have power from time to time to make such bye-laws as may be deemed expedient.

8. That the Subscription for the season be 5/-, due on the Opening-Day.

NEWTON HEATH
Lawn + Tennis + Club.
SEASON 1888.

President:
DR. STEWARD.

Vice-President;
S. H. NEEEDHAM, Esq.
E. T. ROTHWELL, Esq.
J. RYAN, Esq.
J. W. WORTHINGTON, Esq.

Committee:
Mr. BROADHEAD. Mr. BOWERS.
Mr. A. ELLIOTT. Mr. SCOTT.
Mr. B. STEWARD.

Hon. Treasurer: Mr. J. RYAN.

Hon. Secretary:
Mr. JOHN W. WORTHINGTON, Rose Cottage, Church Street.

Ground: Mulberry House.

Mr. B. Steward
JUNE 9th, 1888.

9. Any Member wishing to bring a Friend to play must inform the Ground Committee beforehand.

10. Any Member wilfully infringing any of the Rules, or whose conduct, in the opinion of the Committee, shall have been such as to render their presence on the ground objectionable shall be liable to be suspended, and shall not be allowed to enter the ground until the case has been decided upon by a special meeting of the members called for that purpose.

BYE-LAWS.

The Colours of the Club are Blue and White.

Members have to provide their own racquets and shoes.

Members are requested to wear the Club Colours on Saturdays.

The Ground will be open each evening for play (weather permitting).

The Members' Cards are Not Transferable.

J. Andrew & Co., Printers, Ashton-under-Lyne.

Fig. 2.43. **Cinderella Dances**
A die-cut card, for the dances to be held at Forest Gate Lawn Tennis Club, Stratford, North London. On the reverse of the card the dances (played by Poole's String Band) are listed and at the side there's a space where one would enter the name or initials of one's partner for that particular dance. The dance dates range from December 1896 to February 1897. This contains the programme for Saturday 9th January 1897. £15-20 ($20-25)

Fig. 2.44. **Exhibition Tennis Tickets**
Two tickets to witness exhibition matches at The Arboretum, Walsall, England, in August 1928. The players were Joan Fry, Dorothy Round, D. Hedges, and H. Lester of Great Britain. £10-15 ($15-25) each

Fig. 2.45. **A Selection of Rules Books**
A selection of five rules books from the 1920s and 1930s. £15-20 ($20-25)

Fig. 2.46. **Three L. T. A. Official Passes**
Three official passes, which would have been given to V. I. P's, enabling them to a seat to watch important tennis events. £15-20 ($20-25) each

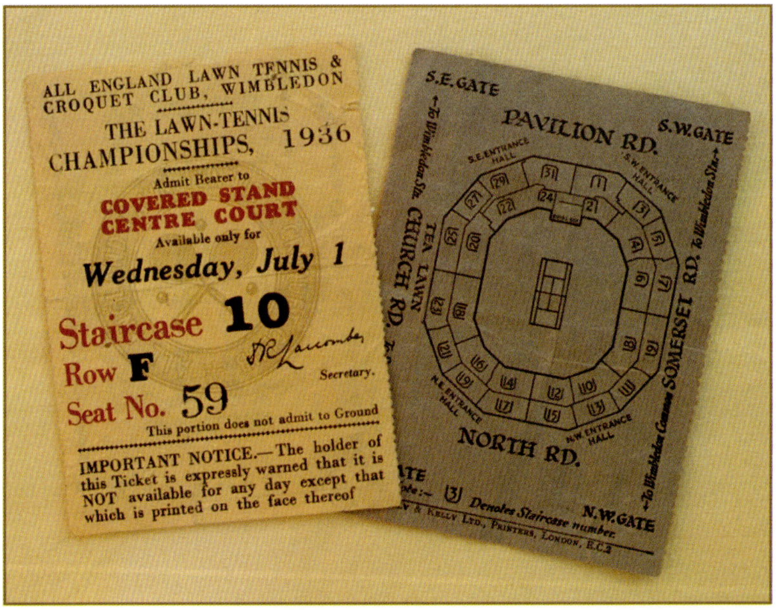

Fig. 2.47. **Centre Court Tickets 1936**
Two tickets for the Championships at the All England Club, Wimbledon. The tickets, although basically the same, were printed on different coloured papers each day. £15-20 ($20-25) each

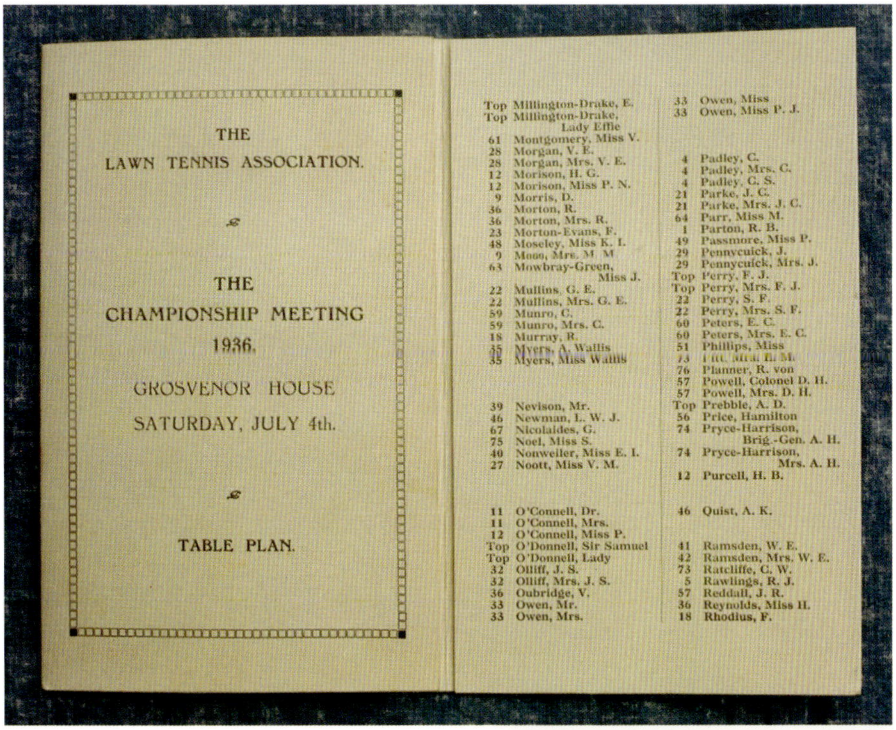

Fig. 2.48. **Grosvenor House, Championship Meeting Table Plan**
An eight page booklet giving a complete list of guests and a guide to which table they were to sit at during the Wimbledon Championship Dinner on Saturday, July 4th. 1936. There was a top table, at which names such as Roper Barrett, Jack Crawford and his wife, and Mr. and Mrs. F. J. Perry were seated. Seventy-five other tables accommodated people such as Viscount Doneraile, Sir Herbert Wilberforce, Sir Samuel and Lady Hoare, and Don Budge. £20-30 ($30-40)

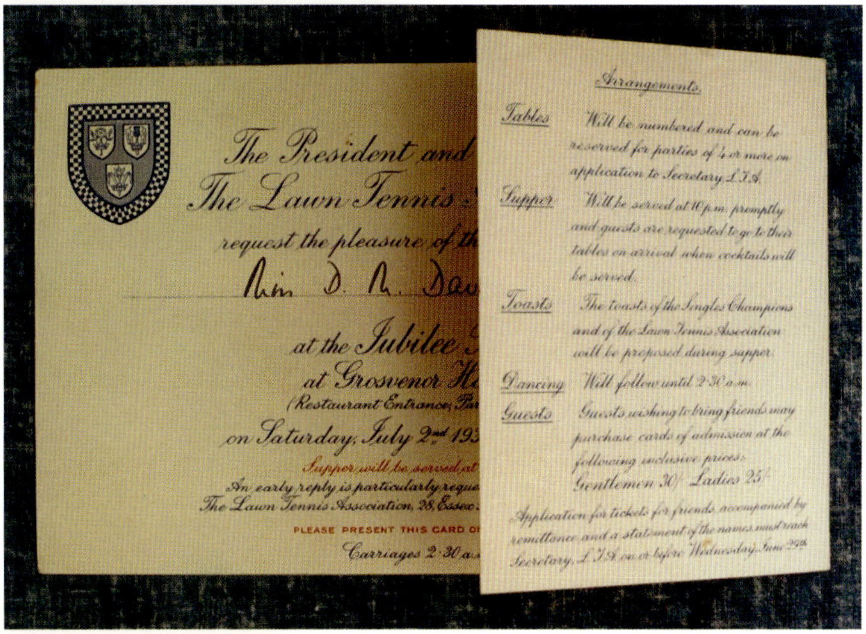

Fig. 2.49. **The Jubilee Ball**
An invitation from 'The President and Council of The Lawn Tennis Association' to attend the Jubilee Ball, at Grosvenor House, London, on Saturday, July 2nd. 1938 at 9.30 pm. 'The toasts of the Singles Champions and of the Lawn Tennis Association will be proposed during supper.' £15-20 ($20-30)

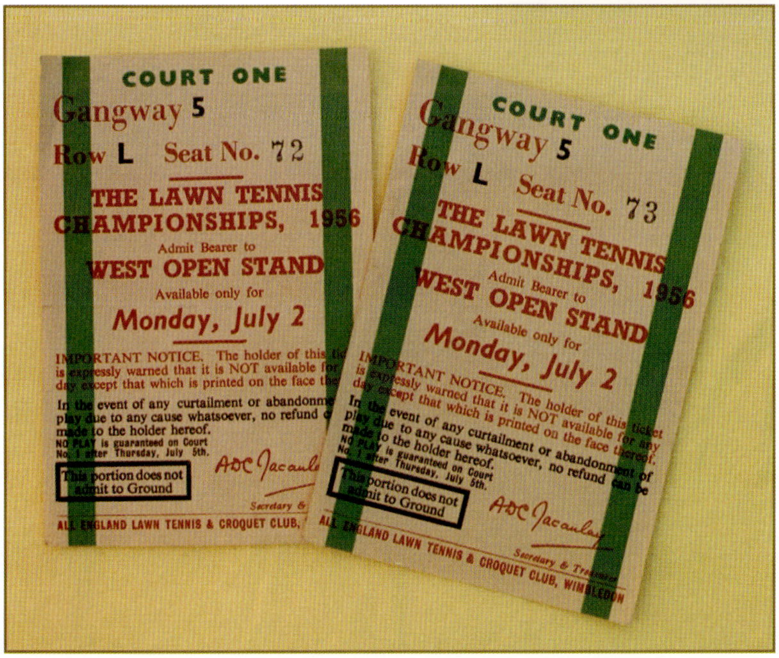

Fig. 2.50. **Court One, Wimbledon 1956**
Two entrance tickets for the West Open Stand on Court One. £15-20 ($20-30) each

Fig. 2.51. **Two Entrance Tickets**
The left-hand ticket is for a reserved seat at the West Hants Lawn Tennis Club in Bournemouth to see the Hard Court Championships of Great Britain in 1958. The second is for the Centre Court at Wimbledon for the same year. £15-20 ($20-30) each

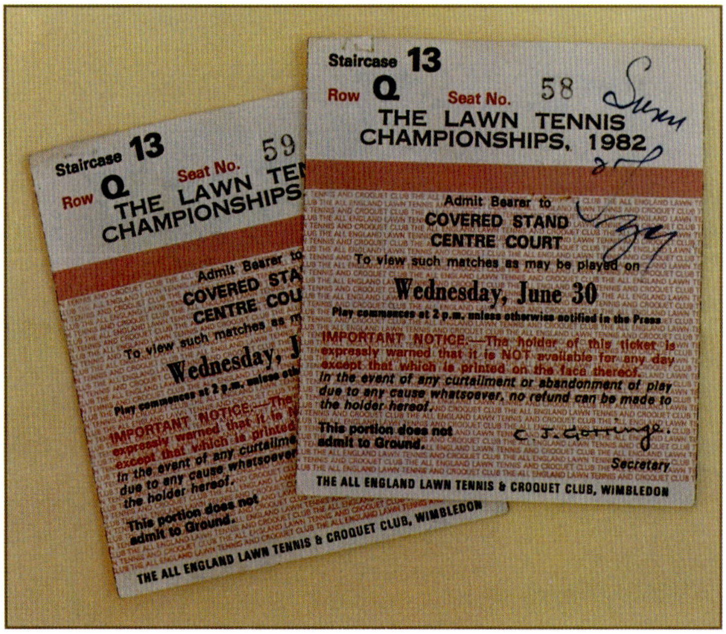

Fig. 2.52. **Centre Court, Wimbledon 1982**
Two tickets for the famous Centre Court Wimbledon, one of which is signed by Susan Fry. £15-20 ($20-30) each

Fig. 2.53. **Wimbledon Tickets**
Tickets for ground admission and a seat on the Centre Court for the year 1986. £10-15 ($15-22) each

Fig. 2.54. **1987 Wimbledon Ephemera**
The selection includes a BBC Staff Pass, a Complimentary Ground Ticket, a Refreshment Enclosure Pass, a Centre Court Ticket, and a Council Members Voucher Booklet. £15-20 ($20-30)

Fig. 2.55. **Three Wimbledon Entrance Tickets**
The Wimbledon authorities have decided to make a special feature of their tickets each year. From left to right these are for the years 1993, 1996, and 1999. £15-20 ($20-30)

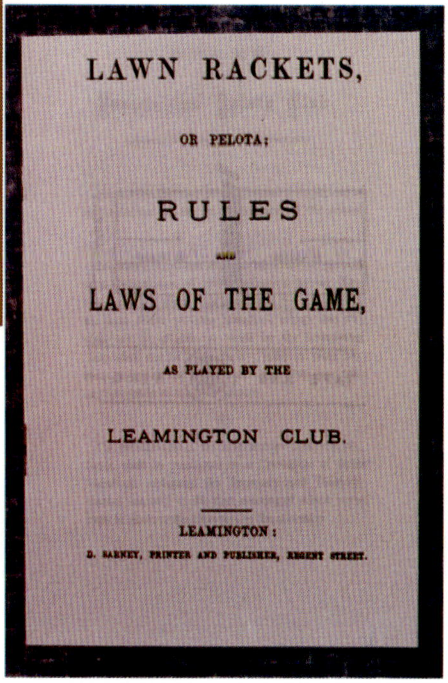
LAWN RACKETS,

OR PELOTA;

RULES

AND

LAWS OF THE GAME,

AS PLAYED BY THE

LEAMINGTON CLUB.

LEAMINGTON:
D. SARNEY, PRINTER AND PUBLISHER, REGENT STREET.

Fig. 2.56. **Lawn Rackets or Pelota (Rules of the Leamington Pelota Club)**
A twelve page photocopy of the rules of the game and laws of the club, as played by Harry Gem, Dr. Haynes, Auguste Periera, and others at the Leamington Club in 1876. The original lies in the archives of Birmingham Public Library, Warwickshire, England. Rule X relates that: 'Every person losing a love game to pay One Shilling to the box.' £15-20 ($20-30)

Photographic Cards

Fig. 2.57. **Three Birthday Cards**
These cards show the variety of effects with which a single photograph, differing frames, and hand painted colour can be achieved. The cards are by The Rotary Photo Company, and on the back of one of them it says: 'This is a HAND PAINTED STUDY from a REAL PHOTOGRAPH of a BRITISH Beauty MISS GLADYS COOPER.' They all show a superb lawn tennis racket with a particularly fine inlaid handle. (c. 1914) £1-3 ($2-5) each

Fig. 2.58. **Two Further Cards from The Rotary Photo Company**
Two glamorous studies of the same model holding an 'Army and Navy-Queen' racket. (c. 1914) £1-3 ($2-5) each

Fig. 2.60. **Two Gladys Cooper Cards**
Two slightly differently posed cards (with printed autographs) by the Rotary Photo Company of London. (c. 1920) £1-3 ($2-5) each

Fig. 2.59. **The Carlton Printing Co.**
Printed in London, these two cards use the same models in different poses. The colour is added by hand. (c. 1914). £1-3 ($2-5) each

Fig. 2.61. **The Girl in a Tam o' Shanter**
Two studio poses (marked 1049a) showing a girl with a racket dressed in a 'sailor-style' blouse. They were printed in France. (c. 1920) £3-5 ($5-8) each

Fig. 2.62. **Three Hand-Tinted Studio Cards**
These three delightful cards show how photographic studios often used studio props to set a scene. In this case the props are a lawn tennis racket and hand sewn lawn tennis balls. The centre card (dated 1943) is by The 'ALPHA' Publishing Co. Ltd., of London. The other two by 'P-C' of Paris (1924) are both numbered '858'. £5-8 ($8-12) each

Fig. 2.63. **Three Hand-Tinted Studio Cards**
Three romantic cards showing a pair of star-crossed lovers who seem determined that a lawn tennis racket should come between them. Published by 'P-C' of Paris they are all numbered '888'. The racket is a 'Championship' model by Williams & Co. of Paris. (c. 1925) £3-5 ($5-8) each.

Fig. 2.64. **Three Hand-Tinted Cards**
The first two cards were printed in Prussia. They used the same model as the third card 'DEUCE', which was published by Jackson & Son of Grimsby. (c. 1930) £3-5 ($5-8) each.

Fig. 2.65. **Three Birthday Cards**
All three use real photographs, have a glossy surface, and have an embossed pattern border. The second is from the W & K Series No.544, and the third is by the Rotary Photo Company of London, with a registered design number of 734734. (c. 1930) £3-5 ($5-8) each.

Fig. 2.66. **Three Birthday Cards**
Sometimes, all a collector needs is the smallest of suggestions that an item should be pursued. Here we have three very similar photocards with embossed floral borders. The only aspect they have in common is a lawn tennis racket. (c. 1930) £3-5 ($5-8) each.

Romantic, Illustrated, and Amusing Postcards

Postcards have been with us for about 130 years. The first appeared when on the 1st October 1870 a plain buff coloured card was already printed with a halfpenny stamp. This was a major departure for the Post Office as at that time letters, at one penny, cost twice as much to post! There was one major disadvantage to the sender and receiver of such cards, and it was that anyone could read the message. The first rules regulated that one side should to be left blank for the stamp and the receiver's address. This meant that any message had to be written upon the illustrated side of the card. This is why quite a few early cards can be found with a blank area below or around the illustration. This procedure ended in 1902, the message was then also written on the back of the card alongside the address, and the front became an area totally devoted to an illustration, or later still, a photograph.

Postcards were an immediate success, and it didn't take long before thematic 'collections' began to form. The subjects were endless, actors and actresses, the Royal Family, seaside towns, and every conceivable topic was available. The age of the postcard had begun and its zenith years were between 1900 and the First World War. As a consequence of the era in which the postcard craze began, the collector can often find wonderfully produced artistic cards with art nouveau designs. These designs weren't restricted to one specific subject, indeed racket sport cards can easily be found.

Although cards can be discovered which are associated with Battledore and Shuttlecock and the game of Racquets, these games probably reached the height of their popularity far too early to be regarded as popular illustrative subjects. You are much more likely to find European or American trade cards which cover these topics. Real Tennis was always regarded as a sport played by the privileged few, and it too was never very popular; but, you may find a topographical card featuring a photograph of Hampton Court or Queen's Club.

By far the most popular subject was Lawn Tennis, and understandably artists seized upon the opportunity to portray images of tennis playing, love struck courting couples, along with a carefully phrased reference to the word 'Love'.

Basically, there are four main collecting themes:

Glamour Cards – often with signed reproductions of artist's drawings, later with photographs of models (male, female, and children) conveniently set in photographic studios with tennis racket, posts, nets, and tennis balls as props.

Humourous Cards – regularly employing cartoon artists (who sometimes became quite famous for their style or sense of humour) or 'staged' scenes taken in studios, with live models.

Topographical – You might find photographic cards of famous clubs, tennis parks and provincial clubs, or seaside resorts.

Photographic Player Cards – These are probably the most sought after, Edwin Trim and Chaplin Jones being the chief exponents from the 1910s until the 1940s.

Fig. 2.67. **A pair of 'Ping Pong' Cards**
This pair of chromolithograph printed table tennis cards from the early 1900s printed by Raphael Tuck and Sons. This new game became very popular extremely quickly, and the company seized the opportunity to produce a whole series of similarly amusing cards on the subject. The cards were part of the company's 'Write Away' series, were designed in England (the artist being L. Thakeray) and printed in Saxony. The backs are undivided. The card, which shows the gentleman in tails, entitled: 'I am sending' has a written entry to an unidentified competition, which was set by Tuck and Sons, of Raphael House, Moorfields, London. It is dated with a company stamp '27th April 1923'. (c. 1900) £8-15 ($12-25) each

Fig. 2.68. **Eight Monochrome Cards illustrated by 'Pirkis'** (?) All eight are based upon a phrase associated with the game. It is uncertain how many cards feature in the series. Divided backs. (c. 1904) £3-5 ($5-8) each

Fig. 2.69. **Three from a Set of Six Comic Postcards**
Three of a set of six comic postcards with a lady taking advantage of her male opponent! Printed in England by Millar and Lang (National Series) (c. 1905). £75-100 ($100-150) per set

Fig. 2.70. **A Montage of Postcards**
A frame containing ten delightful early postcards, many of which are chromolithographs. (c. 1905) £80-100 ($120-150)

Fig. 2.71. **E. P. Kinsella**
A charming series of six postcards illustrated by the artist 'Kinsella'. They are all based upon phrases or words associated with the game of lawn tennis. (c. 1907) They were published by Langsdorff & Co., 19, City Road, London, E. C. £50-75 ($75-100)

Fig. 2.72. **Three Illustrated Glamour Cards**
Three very similar cards as they are all printed copies of hand painted originals. The first, entitled: 'HER GAME' (No.834), was published by Reinthal & Newman of New York, and was printed in America. The second, 'My Chum', was published by A. Vivian Mansell & Co. of London. The third, 'A Love Match', also came from the Mansell Publishing Company. It is also described as: 'The "MAYNARD BROWN" Series. "Sports Girls" Series G2. No. 2613.' by James Henderson & Sons, Ltd., London. (c. 1914) £7-10 ($10-15) each

Fig. 2.74. **A Silhouette**
This card was included because an identical image can be seen hand painted onto a glass vase in another chapter. Entitled 'Tennis', it was produced by A. R. & C. i. B. Nr. 1305/4. (c. 1920) £4-7 ($6-10)

Fig. 2.73. **'Courting Couples'**
The card on the left has an embossed design and is a chromolithograph print (PFB SERIE 6517) (c. 1910). The one in the centre 'THE BEST OF CHUMS' was printed in America by The Knapp Co. Inc. of New York, and was illustrated by T. Earl Christy. (1917) The third is a 'Pocket Novelty Card'. Near the bottom of the card a flap lifts up to reveal a ribbon of twenty or so scenic photographic views of Stratford-On-Avon. (c. 1920) £5-8 ($8-12) each

Fig. 2.75. **A Montage Arrangement**
A modern clip-frame enclosing an attractive arrangement of postcards, cigarette cards, and Victorian scraps. The montage includes postcards of Suzanne Lenglen and Kitty Godfrey by Edwin Trim, as well as two postcards by Wennerberg. £175-200 ($225-300)

Fig. 2.76. **A Modern Clip-Frame**
The frame contains an arrangement of five postcards, one poster, and ten cigarette cards. £75-100 ($100-150)

Fig. 2.77. **A Large Modern Clip-Frame**
It contains nineteen postcards, one advertising card, three Victorian scraps, and a greetings card. £200-250 ($300-375)

Fig. 2.78. **Three Glamour Cards**
The first 'LOVE ALL' was published by Wildt & Kray of London, and has a postmark for 1925. The second and third are chromolithograph prints by the "ALPHASA" Publishing Company of London. The first of which was 'Painted by Alice Luella Fidler' and the second 'Alice Fidler Person'. They were both printed in the U. S. A. and are from a series called 'The American Girl'. (c. 1920) £8-12 ($12-18) each

Fig. 2.79. **Three Tennis Cards**
Three postcards (two embossed and printed in Germany) show the game of lawn tennis. (c. 1920) £20-30 ($30-40)

Fig. 2.80. **Five Amusing Cards from the Regent Publishing Co. Ltd.**
Five from a possible series of six cards which were illustrated by Reg Maurice, who was a very prolific artist for the company. A serial number on the back suggests that one of them may be missing. All have divided backs. (c. 1923) £3-5 ($5-8) each

Fig. 2.81. **G. E. Studdy 'Bonzo'**
Three illustrations showing the activities of 'Bonzo' at the local lawn tennis club. Valentine & Sons Ltd., Dundee and London published the first card. The other two are marked: 'The 'R. P. S.' Series.' (c. 1926) £7-10 ($10-15) each

Fig. 2.82. **Three Comic Postcards**
All three are based upon the aspect of 'Social Tennis' and the circumstances which can arise from it! The first is marked 'P P C', the second was published by The Photochrom Co. Ltd. of London and Tunbridge Wells, and the third was printed in Great Britain. (c. 1927) £7-10 ($10-15) each

Fig. 2.83. **Six Comic 'Bamforth' Cards**
All three cards were published by Bamforth & Co. Ltd. of Holmfirth and New York. From the "COMIC" Series, three of them are signed by the artists Arnold Taylor and David Tempest. (c. 1930) £7-10 ($10-15) each

Fig. 2.84. **Three Modern Re-prints – Pellegrini**
Printed in Switzerland, they are reproductions of illustrations by Carlo Pellegrini. (1866-1937) (c. 1995) £3-5 ($5-8) each

---

Advertising and Decorative Ephemera

A good many early manufacturers seized upon an opportunity to associate with any subject which was particularly interesting to their 'target audience'. Advertising cards, featuring the name of the company and their product, were regularly produced in conjunction with a tennis scene or a tennis player in the background. Greetings card designs were successfully manipulated to meet the celebration of any public holiday or birthday throughout the year. Just occasionally, a spectacular piece will become available, and it's hard to believe that there would be many to rival the figure of 'Wimbledon Winnie' (Fig.2.105).

Far left:
Fig. 2.85. **Kate Greenaway**
A fine chromolithograph printed card illustrated by Kate Greenaway. Note the very small headed offset racket with binding all the way up the racket handle. This style is very similar to those early rackets produced by Jeffries and Malings. (c. 1878) £20-30 ($30-45)

Left:
Fig. 2.86. **Reckitt's Blue**
A large chromolithograph advertisement board for Reckitt's Blue, with ladies in period dress standing and seated in front of a mixed doubles match. The colours are extremely strong. (c. 1880) Height 63.0 cms. Width 44.0 cms. £600-800 ($900-1200)

Fig. 2.87. **Ransomes' Lawn Mowers**
A fine chromolithograph advertisement for 'Ransomes Lawn Mowers The Best in the World'. A tennis party takes place while a young girl trims the grass with a 10 inch Ransomes' Anglo-Paris lawn mower. (c. 1880) Height 36.8 cms. Width 50.0 cms. £600-800 ($900-1200)

Fig. 2.89. **'Served'**
A delightful little chromolithograph printed card entitled 'Served'. The copyright belonged to George M. Hayes in 1881, and the card was printed in 1882. £20-30 ($30-45)

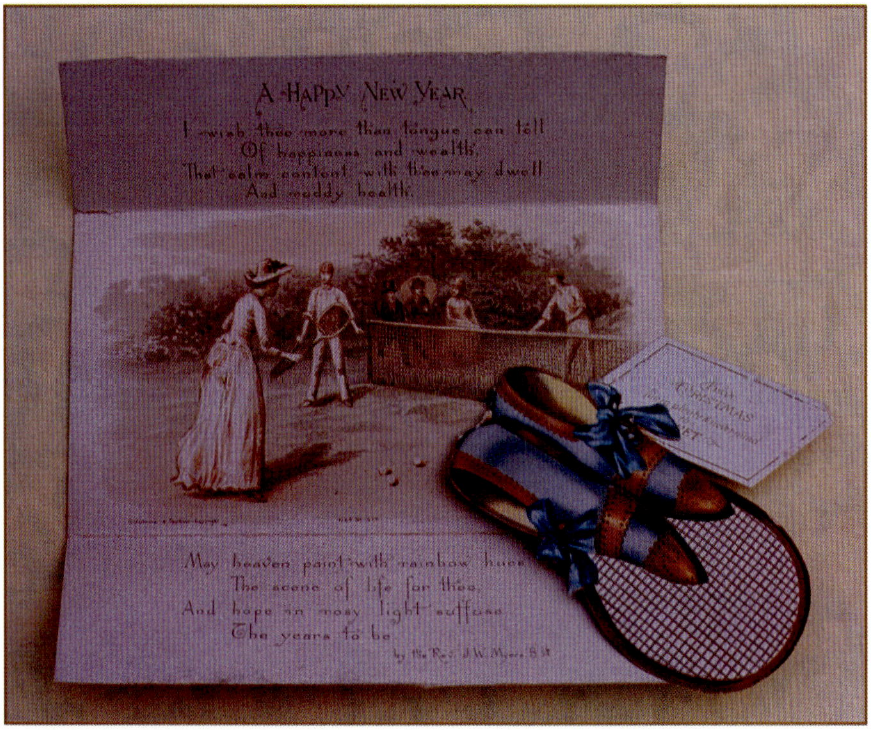

Fig. 2.88. **Folding Greetings Cards**
An early Victorian New-Year folding greeting card with a charming tennis mixed doubles scene with appropriate verse top and bottom. Together with a small Christmas greetings card of a racket and a pair of lawn tennis shoes. (c. 1880) £75-100 ($100-150)

Fig. 2.90. **'The Season's Greetings'**
A chromolithograph printed card by S. Hildesheimer Co. Ltd. The card edged in gold ink. (c. 1885) £20-30 ($30-45)

Fig. 2.91. **A Die-Cut Christmas Card**
A die-cut Christmas card published by Angus Thomas of London. It is interesting in that the racket has been applied to the base card with glue. (c. 1885) £20-30 ($30-45)

Fig. 2.92. **'Lawn Tennis - Humorous'**
A Victorian booklet entitled 'Lawn Tennis – Humorous' by W. J. Hogson, enclosing 4 coloured plates of various tennis scenes. The set is very rare. (c. 1890) £150-175 ($225-250)

'A CHRISTMAS greeting with love'
This single card is typical of the four, it reads: 'When the game may be a trifle slow (to the other side.)' £30-40 ($45-60)

'With every good wish for the NEW YEAR'
The caption reads: 'Who is it? Why that dear curate, the poor man has been overcome by the heat.' £30-40 ($45-60)

Fig. 2.93. **A Christmas Card**
A finely printed chromolithograph card entitled 'A little in the way'. The caption reads: 'At Christmas, if Lawn Tennis you should play, May your score stand at 'one to love all day!' I would have thought it would have been very difficult to find any grass court in England suitable for tennis at Christmas! The card is inscribed on the back 'for Edith from Nellie'. (c. 1895) £20-30 ($30-45)

Fig. 2.94. **A Birthday Card**
A very early chromolithograph printed birthday card with printed gold edges and rounded corners. (c. 1895) £20-30 ($30-45)

Fig. 2.95. **A Christmas Card**
A charming little chromolithograph Christmas card showing a mixed doubles match in progress. The message reads: 'A Happy Xmas – may yours be the winning side' (c. 1895). £20-30 ($30-45)

Fig. 2.96. **Three European Trade Cards**
Three chromolithograph printed cards showing young children playing 'Le Volant'. Only the centre card gives any information as to its origin. It advertises a store in Belgium, 'Grande Maison de Blanc', and on the reverse lists a range of items which were available from the store. (c. 1900) £10-20 ($15-30) each

Fig. 2.97. **Hagoita**
A chromolithograph printed post card from around 1900 showing Japanese children playing a game of the national racket game of Hagoita. £10-12 ($15-18)

Fig. 2.98. **The Eagle Range & Grate Co.**
A twelve page Booklet advertising the range of Eagle lawn tennis court markers. 'For the past 30 years we have supplied many hundreds of Tennis Markers to work with the Endless Rubber Band…' each page shows a different model of marker, along with a description and a list of 'advantages' of that particular model. These lists are quite enlightening as not only do they show advantages but also where problems were to be found with earlier markers. For instance, the 'Eagle Patent Tennis Marker' lists its advantages as: 'No Rubber Band, Marks wide distinct line, Self-cleaning wheel, Stands perfectly firm, Large pan for liquid, Wheels removed for cleaning and replaced in 30 seconds, Indicating pointer to ensure straight line, Cheap, Cannot get out of order, Stove finish in attractive colour.' (c. 1900) £20-30 ($30-45)

Fig. 2.99. **Huntley and Palmers Trade Cards 1900**
Two rare chromolithograph cards from Huntley and Palmers biscuits of Reading and London. £20-30 ($30-45) each

Trade Card
A wonderful card showing spectators (who are being served with Huntley and Palmers 'Pastime' or 'Malta' biscuits) watching a mixed doubles match. £20-30 ($30-45)

Fig. 2.100. **Two Free-Standing Cards**
Two free-standing Victorian cards. The larger item is entitled 'A Love Game' with the players facing each other across a net. 18.0 cms. wide opening to 37.0 cms. £125-150 ($190-225) The little pop-up greetings card has a humorous Christmas romantic verse as well as a stamped envelope which is dated 1906. Width 16.0 cms. Depth 9.0 cms. £75-100 ($100-150)

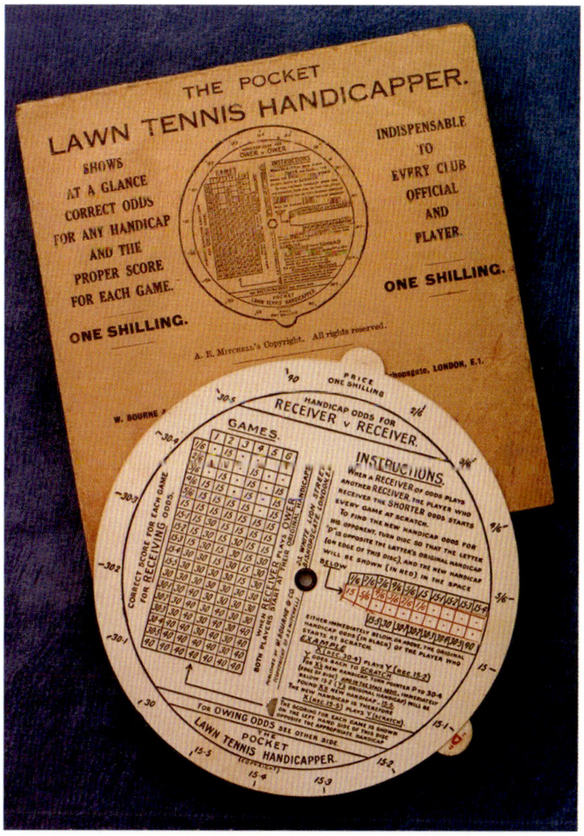

Fig. 2.102. **The Pocket Lawn Tennis Handicapper**
An ingenious gadget for calculating odds for handicap tournaments. Published by W. Bourne & Co. The Score Book People, 23, White Lion Street, Bishopsgate, London, E1. (A. E. Mitchell's Copyright) (c. 1920) £20-30 ($30-45)

Fig. 2.101. **Three Greetings Cards,**
A selection of three Christmas greetings cards, each in the shape of a lawn tennis racket. One of the cards is contained in its own carrying case. These cards are very rare. (c. 1910) Length 18.0 cms., 16.0 cms., 11.0 cms. £50-175 ($225-250)

Fig. 2.103. **A Tea Tray**
A wooden and glass tea tray, advertising the Octagon Tennis Club. As yet there is no clue as to the identity of the club. The image is etched onto the inner surface of the glass and is totally consistent with a design used by the Wilson company in the 1920s. (c. 1925) Width 53.3 cms. Depth 35.9 cms. £125-150 ($185-225)

Fig. 2.104. **Champion Tennis Balls**
A large, heavy, sixteen sided advertising sign for 'Champion Tennis Balls' manufactured from wood and glass. The glass surface area is chamfered at the edge with the text and colours either hand painted or silk screen-printed onto the back. The whole piece is held together with period clips and fittings, and retains the original hanging chain. (c. 1925) Diam. 49.6 cms. £125-150 ($185-225)

Fig. 2.105. **Wimbledon Winnie**[2]
A wonderful, and extremely rare, reinforced plaster of Paris advertising model entitled "Wimbledon Winnie". This model, which would probably have been displayed on a shop counter, features a young tennis girl wearing a 'Liberty Boddice' for Libertyland. The reference to Suzanne Lenglen and Wimbledon suggests a date around 1926, or a little later, when the French star made her last appearance at 'The Championships' and shortly afterwards, turned professional. Base Dimensions 20.2 x 20.2 cms. Height 44.2 cms. £1000-1500 ($1500-2250)

Fig. 2.106. **A Complete Set of Six Advertising Cards** A set of six humorous advertising cards entitled 'Lawn Tennis Balls – Semperit Champion Regulation are the Best'. Shows the 'Soaga' trade mark (European tyre manufacturers) (c. 1930). £120-150 ($180-225) per set

Fig. 2.107. **Dunlop Tennis Rackets** A wonderful six page advertising leaflet from Dunlop, printed in 1934. It is printed in full colour with an additional print in gold ink. All their primary rackets are illustrated, the flagship model being the Maxply Tournament at 72/6 (£3.62). £15-20 ($20-30)

Fig. 2.108. **Dunlop Tennis Equipment**
A full colour, free standing advertising card printed on heavy board, for Dunlop Tennis equipment. (c. 1951) Height 28.3 cms. Width 60.1 cms. £75-125 ($100-185)

Fig. 2.109. **Dunlop Advertising Cards**
The first, printed by Allday Ltd. of Birmingham, shows a list of all rackets, tennis balls, and presses that were available. The most expensive racket was the Dunlop Fort Maxply at 136/6 (£6.83). The Maxply Tournament Model was now 127/6 (£6.38). (c. 1951) Height 38.0 cms. Width 25.4 cms. £40-60 ($60-90)

The large centre card, by J. Howitt and Son Ltd., shows how (in 15 stages) a typical lawn tennis ball is manufactured. (c. 1952) Height 50.7 cms. Width 38.1 cms. £75-100 ($100-150)

The third, by James Cond. Ltd., Birmingham, is die-cut and promotes Dunlop Maxply rackets. (c. 1952) Height 36.3 cms. Width 25.4 cms. £75-100 ($100-150)

Fig. 2.110. **Modern Advertising Cards**
These two cards are reproduced from 19th century originals, which are housed in the Robert Opie Museum of Advertising and Packaging in Gloucester, England. (c. 1995) £1-3 ($2-5) each

Fig. 2.111. **A Pair of Cards with Machine Stitched Details**
These modern cards were made in Spain and their shorts and shirts are sewn with coloured thread. (c. 1995) £1-3 ($2-5) each

Fig. 2.112. **Perrier, Wimbubbledon**
A modern piece of marketing for Perrier Mineral Water. Consisting of a hand held fan and a form to enter a draw. Both of them were given to queuing fans at the Wimbledon Grounds in 1998. £5-10 ($7-15)

English Cigarette Cards

I have included this subsection because, although all those illustrated are English, there are a good many special cards available from other countries, particularly the U.S.A. and Europe.

Fig. 2.113. **Sports of All Nations**
Three chromolithograph cards from a series of 50, issued by W. D. & H. O. Wills Ltd., in 1901. Per set £425-450 ($650-700)

Fig. 2.114. **"Sports" Series**
Three fine, chromolithograph printed cards from the "Sports" Series by Gallaher Ltd., Belfast and London. On the back of each of them are tips on how to play the game. There are ten tennis player cards in the series of 100. (1912) Per set £550-600 ($800-900)

Fig. 2.115. **British Champions of 1923**
Three cards from a series of 75, issued by Gallaher Ltd. in 1923. There are only these three racket sport cards in the set. Per set £110-140 ($165-210)

Fig. 2.116. **Lawn Tennis Strokes**
Three cards from a series of 30, issued by Cope Bros. & Co. Ltd. in 1924/25. (Numbers 26-30 were issued in 1925.) Per set £175-200 ($250-300)

Fig. 2.117. **Lawn Tennis**
Two large cards from a series of 12, issued by W. A. & A. C. Churchman (The Imperial Tobacco Company) in 1928. Per set £100-150 ($150-225)

Fig. 2.118. **Lawn Tennis Celebrities**
Three cards from a fine and much sought after series of 50, issued by Gallaher Ltd. in 1928. Per set £175-200 ($250-300)

Fig. 2.119. **The Game of Sporting Snap**
Three cards from a series of 40, issued by Major Drapkin & Co. Ltd., London, in 1928. There are only four lawn tennis cards in the series. Per set £150-175 ($225-250)

Fig. 2.120. **Men of the Moment in Sport**
Three cards (by 'Mel') from a series of 50, issued by W. A. & A. C. Churchman (The Imperial Tobacco Company) in 1928. There are nine lawn tennis cards in the series. Per set £150-175 ($225-250)

Fig. 2.121. **Lawn Tennis**
Three cards from a series of 50, issued by W. A. & A. C. Churchman (The Imperial Tobacco Company) in 1928. Per set £125-150 ($185-225)

Fig. 2.122. **Lawn Tennis**
Three cards from a series of 25, issued by Godfrey Phillips cigarettes in 1930. Each of the cards illustrates a particular shot both correctly and incorrectly, the merits of both are discussed on the back of each card. Per set £70-80 ($100-120)

Fig. 2.123. **Sporting Celebrities** Three amusing ('Mel') cartoon cards from a series of 50, issued by W. A. & A. C. Churchman (The Imperial Tobacco Company) in 1931. There are eight tennis player cards in the set. Per set £140-160 ($210-240)

Fig. 2.124. **Champions** Three cards from sets of 48 by Park Drive cigarettes, Gallaher Ltd., entitled 'Champions'. The cards of Lee and Hughes are from a second series. (1934 and 1935) There are four cards of tennis players in the first series and six cards in the 1935 series. Per set £20-30 ($30-40)

Fig. 2.125. **In The Public Eye** Three cards from a series of 54, issued by Godfrey Phillips Ltd. in 1935. There are five lawn tennis cards in the set. Per set £25-30 ($38-45)

Fig. 2.126. **Cricket, Tennis, & Golf Celebrities**
Three cards from a series of 50, issued by Ardath Cork cigarettes in 1935. There are twelve lawn tennis cards in the series. Per set £100-125 ($150-185)

Fig. 2.127. **Photographic Cards**
Two photographic cards showing the victorious Great Britain, Davis Cup and Wightman Cup teams of 1936. They are known as the Series 'Z' because they have a small Z printed on the back at the bottom right hand side. The series was numbered from 111-208. The Ardath Tobacco Co. Ltd. issued them in 1936. Per set £50-60 ($75-90)

Fig. 2.128. **Sporting Aces - Tennis**
Two photographic cards from a series of 38, issued by FAX-PAX in 1985. Per set £10-12 ($15-18)

Chapter 3.
Photographs, Prints and Original Artwork

Photographs and Related Items

'The photograph never lies, but sometimes the artist does!' Well, there's certainly some truth in this, but neither method of evidence was particularly reliable in the Victorian era. The main reason that photography was so unpredictable was that the technology was not sufficiently advanced to meet the demands of the photographer; he always had to adapt the scene to meet the limitations of the process. Lighting, exposure, and speed were critical elements as human beings and especially animals were often incapable of holding a pose (to meet the long time exposure required) and the materials with which the photograph were produced were notoriously unreliable. Many people are unaware that originally all the photographs from Victorian times were made up from tones of black and not brown; it was the inability to fix the image that has sent images sepia in colour.

Quite a frustrating fact is that most photographs have never been annotated; one hundred or so years later we haven't the faintest clue of what or who we are looking at, or when, where, how, or why. Nevertheless, from

time to time some very interesting and rare images do surface from the pages of an old family album. The most sought after show images of the earliest players, tournaments, or (the shape of) courts. Crisp and clear images of players holding early rackets, or standing by high nets and tall tottering net poles are fascinating. Any additional information about the subject, which is most often found written on the back, is invaluable.

Before the camera was invented, publications depended upon 'journalistic artists' to reproduce the image of a particular match, tournament, or even the likeness of a famous player. While in many cases the essence of an image has successfully been captured, various details are often not. Rackets without strings (or impossible stringing patterns), courts minus lines, and ludicrous perspective vanishing points are all very common. Nevertheless, as long as the collector keeps this in mind and doesn't regard an illustration as a true rendition, which he claims proves a certain point or other, then everyone is happy.

Fig. 3.1. **Devonshire Park Eastbourne, Summer 1876**
Both the newspaper clipping and the photograph, which are believed to be contemporary, were extracted from the Chappell family album. A Miss Chappell is evident in the newspaper report. This very early photograph shows a ladies singles tournament in progress on two hourglass shaped courts. The rules were those as laid down by the M. C. C. on May 24th. 1875, and this competition was played a year before the first Wimbledon tournament (when a rectangular court was favoured) and eight years prior to Wimbledon's first ladies competition. The game was played over a five foot net, which dropped to four feet in the centre. The service lines were 26 feet from the net (which was altered to 22 feet by 1878) and the court expanded from 24 feet wide at the net, to 30 feet at the baselines. The court was 78 feet long, just as it is today. The newspaper clipping reports that: ' Great interest was manifested in the play and the winners of the various bouts were enthusiastically applauded. There were two events – single ties, for which the prize was a handsome gold brooch, and double ties (handicap), in which the winners each received a tennis bat.' The singles final saw Miss Kent beat Mrs. Famin. (c. 1876) Height 10.8 cms. Width 17.6 cms. £1000-1500 ($1500-2250)

Fig. 3.2. **Merton (Girls) College, Croydon 1881-82**
This amazing photograph shows over 50 attendees and three staff posed in the gardens of the college. They are shown participating in all the 'sporting' activities acceptable to the college authorities. It is very much as if this photograph has been especially arranged for inclusion in publicity material. Dominating the centre of the photograph is a tennis court, and a high net is poorly supported by even higher (6ft.?) poles, which in turn are strengthened by guy ropes. The lines of the court show that the court was rectangular, and to the side you can see a pine lawn tennis equipment box. It appears that the net also has small 'wing-nets' attached to the two ends but they are not extended. (1882) Height 12.4 cms. Width 19.8 cms. £100-150 ($150-225)

Fig. 3.3. **A West Indies Photograph**
A huge party of tennis enthusiasts pose in front of an impressive building in the West Indies. There are 63 people in the group, 24 of whom are holding lawn tennis rackets. What appears to be a postal stamp on the back is very difficult to read. The letters 'S. E. HOUG(?)' are hardly discernible. (c. 1885) Height 17.5 cms. Width 25.2 cms. £30-40 ($45-60)

Fig. 3.4. **The Olympia Photograph Album**[1]
This fine and rare embossed leather album contains ten double-sided pages, which are designed to hold and display between one and four cabinet cards or 'carte de visite'. The cover is blind stamped with a gold border pattern, and shows (in relief) a scene of a lady and gentleman standing to either side of a lawn tennis net situated on the grounds of a large house. The scene is surrounded with a decorative border and has a selection of sporting equipment lying on the grass in the foreground. The album was designed by 'W. H. S. Thompson, H. Bunneft & others.' Each page has at least two chromolithograph illustrations of sporting scenes printed onto it, including a scene which shows two 'tennis' games in progress. A half of the depth of the album (disguised to look like gold edged pages) contains a musical box, with a single brass cylinder. Beside it is stored a key, which winds the mechanism up through a hole in the back of the album. The musical mechanism has a registered number '52196' consistent with the year 1886. Also engraved here are the initials J. G. M. & C. (John G. (Gloag) Murdoch and Company). (c. 1886) Height 29.8 cms. Width 24.5 cms. Width 7.0 cms. £750-1000 ($1250-1500)

Fig. 3.5. **Lawn Tennis – Lewis Volleying**[2]
A positive glass slide (standing on a modern print) showing Ernest Lewis running forward to play a high forehand volley. In the *Graphic* of June 8th. 1889, under the heading: 'Some Instantaneous Photographs' half-tone images of Lewis, Joshua Pim, and Herbert Lawford were reproduced. The 'Lewis' photograph is an identical image to the slide. Mr. L. Meldon, of Dublin, took the photographs at the Fitzwilliam Lawn Tennis Tournament. The article explains how the new high-speed camera is able to capture 'some very curious features…Mr. Lewis is depicted with both feet off the ground evidently hastening to volley the ball.' The writer is quite astonished how in the other photographs both the racket and the ball blurred and distorted. 'These photographs, Mr. Meldon states, were taken by the new Special Paget Plates, and received an exposure of 1-400th of a second, with a Ross Rapid Symmetrical Lens of twelve inch focus.' (c. 1889) Length 8.3 cms. Depth 8.3 cms. £75-100 ($100-150)

Fig. 3.7. **Three Photographs from China**
All three photographs are presented as cabinet cards, and show the same group of tennis players on each card. The card at the top entitled: 'A GREETING FROM CHINA' shows a lawn tennis court, the lines of which have been laid out with tapes and pegs (as a doubles court). The photographic studio's details are printed on the back: 'By appointment to H. H. The Sultan of Linga, H. Salzwedel & Co., Nanking Road, Shanghai.' (c. 1890) Height 10.8 cms. Width 16.6 cms. £25-35 each ($40-60)

Fig. 3.6. **Queen's Club Photograph**
'This is a photograph of the Club's staff assembled just inside the Club's gates. Peter Latham, a Club Real Tennis and Rackets Professional stands on the right; others with lawn tennis rackets are on the left; the gentleman standing in the centre wearing a three piece suit and tall-sided black bowler hat, behind the ball-boys, is the Head Gentlemen's Dressing Room Attendant. The ball boys (who are all wearing Club sweaters – hooped, with the Club's name embroidered in white) were answerable to him as well as the Head of the ground staff. The similarly dressed gentleman on the left is probably the Club's Accountant or Chief Clerk. But what of the mysterious sight of a horse and carriage behind the group and the man clutching a pint of beer? Up until the First World War, a pony and trap would pick up Members from Hyde Park Corner (London) and also Baron's Court Station to transport then to the Club. The chap holding the pint of beer is the Groom, for it was traditional for them to drink beer.' Nice job if you can get it! Contrary to the thoughts of Queen's Club officials, who kindly contributed the information above, (and think that the photograph was taken just before the First World War) I think this photograph is more likely to be from 1890 than 1914. Peter Latham joined the staff in 1888, he was 22 years old. Had this photograph been taken around 1914, Latham would have been 48 years old, which it is obvious he is not. (c. 1890) Height 10.6 cms. Width 14.7 cms. £75-100 ($100-150)

Fig. 3.8. **Three Early Lady Tennis Players**[3]
Miss Dod
A fine photograph of Miss Charlotte Dod, the familiar studio image of her in a white cotton dress and peaked cap, as seen in many lawn tennis books. The photograph has been pasted down onto a presentation board, and was supplied by W. & D. Downey, 57 & 61, Ebury Street, London. (c. 1885) Height 19.6 cms. Width 13.8 cms. £100-150 ($150-225)

A Lady Player
A wonderful image of a young Victorian lady holding a lawn tennis racket manufactured by Thomas Tate. She is dressed in a fine early tennis dress, and has embroidered images of crossed lawn tennis rackets applied to her waistband, and sleeves. It appears very much as though this is more than just a 'studio' photograph but in light of her tennis attire and racket, one of a prominent player of the time. As yet she is unidentified. The photograph was taken by the studio of 'G. West & Son, Artists and Photographers, Palmerston Road, Southsea. And Eagle House, Gosport.' (Neg. No. 53401) (c. 1885) Height 16.6 cms. Width 11.0 cms. £75-100 ($100-150)

All England Tennis 'Miss Garfit'
A photograph of Miss H. M. Garfit (by the London News Agency), who reached the semi-finals of the all comers Ladies Singles Championship in 1909. She lost to Dora Boothby, the eventual winner. (c. 1909) Height 16.5 cms. Width 12.1 cms. £50-75 ($75-100)

Fig. 3.9. **Herbert Chipp's Family Photograph Album**[4]
A photograph album enclosed within padded red leather covers and spine. Complete with a silvered clasp and a patented locking mechanism (Dec. 6. 1881 and Juni. 22. 1875) with seventeen double-sided leaves printed in a simulated walnut pattern and gold line framing. All the leaves have three silvered edges. End papers are printed with a continuous gold and green graphic floral pattern. The album contains thirty-three photographs showing members of the Chipp family, three show Herbert Chipp personally. The first photograph, by Elliot & Fry of 55 Baker Street London, shows him posed holding a racket, and is dated March 19th. 1899. On the facing page an inscription written in ink reads "To Dickie from Herbert". The photographs date from August 1885 until July 18th. 1892 and are by various photographic studios. The album is stamped with the initials 'T. J. S. S. & D.' presumably the manufacturer's monogram. Album Length 22.0 cms. Width 18.3 cms. Depth 6.3 cms. £1000-1500 ($1500-2250)

Fig. 3.10. **Jesus College Cambridge**
A fine university team photograph of Jesus College Cambridge, England, dated May 1893. It shows seven players wearing university blazers. Seated centre picture is the Captain – C. H. W. Johnston. The team's names are written on the mount below, with a hand painted college shield in red, gold, and blue above. The photograph is by Stearn of Cambridge. Height 20.0 cms. Width 25.0 cms. £300-400 ($450-600)

Fig. 3.11. **A Small Leather Photographic Frame**
A Victorian padded leather frame by Walter Jones, 195 & 196, Sloane Street, S. W. London. It contains a 'carte de visite' photograph. (c. 1900) Height 13.2 cms. Width 10.7 cms. £30-50 ($45-75)

Fig. 3.12. **Hebden Bridge Lawn Tennis Club**
A very pleasant image of the club members, posing for the camera outside their wooden clubhouse. There are 35 people in the photograph, and the preponderance of flowered hats, and a little girl dressed in white holding a posy of flowers, suggests that it might have been taken at Easter or some other religious festival. C. Westerman took the photograph. (c. 1900) Height 15.4 cms. Width 20.8 cms. £50-75 ($75-100)

Fig. 3.13. **Cumberland Lawn Tennis Club 1**
A large black and white photograph of the Carlisle (Cumberland, England) lawn tennis tournament of 1905. There are 75 competitors posing in front of the old Victorian pavilion. Height 25.0 cms. Width 36.0 cms. £120-150 ($180-225)

Fig. 3.14. **Cumberland Lawn Tennis Club 2**
A black and white photograph showing the same tournament at Carlisle. Note the layout of the grass courts, with spectators in an informal setting, and the pavilion in the background. Height 25.0 cms. Width 36.0 cms. £85-125 ($125-200)

Fig. 3.15. **The 'World's Tennis Championship for £500 (1907)**[5]
A historic gathering of gentlemen, nearly all of whom had some influence on the development of the game of Real Tennis. The competition was between Peter Latham (Challenger and eventual victor) and Cecil 'Punch' Fairs (Champion), and took place at the Brighton court. The photograph was taken by Hawkins & Company, 62, Preston Street, Brighton. Height 20.6 cms. Width 32.8 cms. £300-400 ($450-600)

Fig. 3.16. **The Alliance Athletic Association 1919**
An extremely crisp and clear photograph of 29 club members posed in a group on the club's grass courts. The image is so clear that you can clearly identify a 'La Belle' and an 'Imperial' racket. Not only that, but also one of the gentleman's watches show that the photograph was taken at five minutes to six in the evening! Wakefields of Ealing, London, took the photograph. Height 15.2 cms. Width 20.4 cms. £75-100 ($100-150)

Fig. 3.17. **Suzanne Rachel Flore Lenglen (1899-1838)**
This must be one of the most elegantly posed images of Suzanne Lenglen that I have seen. She wears her characteristic bandeau, a lucky rabbit foot on her waistband, and manages to hold, very daintily, three lawn tennis balls in her left hand. The image was captured in 1921 and a caption on the back relates that: '...the world's tennis champion will defend her title tomorrow against Miss Ryan.' It was to be her third of six Wimbledon Singles titles. Height 21.5 cms. Width 16.4 cms. £30-40 ($45-60)

Fig. 3.19. **Helen Wills Moody**
A small piece of tissue paper has been glued to the back of the photograph, a press release is typed upon it, it reads: 'Mrs. Helen Wills Moody of 1932: U. S. Tennis Queen coming to Wimbledon. Mrs. Helen Wills Moody, attractive Queen of the U. S. tennis world, has had her hair bobbed. Mrs. Wills Moody has announced her intention of coming to Wimbledon this year. Associated Press photo shows: Portrait of Mrs. Wills Moody after her recent visit to the Barber.' Despite her visit to the "barber" her tennis game remained undiminished! That year she won the Wimbledon Ladies Singles Championship without losing a set. Height 20.8 cms. Width 15.3 cms. £20-30 ($30-40)

Fig. 3.18. **Suzanne Lenglen and Family**
A photograph of Suzanne with 'Papa' (Charles) and 'Mama' (Anais) along with the family pet dog. They await the next round of a tournament, or are they relaxing following yet another Suzanne victory? The photograph is marked '1926' on the reverse. Height 20.2 cms. Width 25.5 cms. £20-30 ($30-45)

Fig. 3.20. **Gussie Moran**
The caption on the reverse reads: 'Gorgeous Gussie Here for Wimbledon June 10th. 1950. Miss Gertrude ('Gorgeous Gussie') Moran arrived at London Airport to day, Saturday, by American Overseas Airways liner from New York. She is here to compete in the Wimbledon tennis championships. Miss Moran, whose lace panties startled Wimbledon last year, has chosen a simple bloomer-girl creation for this year's championships.' I should think so too, whatever next? Height 25.4 cms Width 20.4 cms. £10-20 ($15-30)

Original Artwork, Etchings, Woodcuts, and Others

The expression 'artistic licence' is particularly relevant when it comes to original artwork. I think that what we must keep in mind is that most artists paint or draw because they enjoy producing their own impression of what they can see before them. It is their style, technique, and craftsmanship that are being judged, along with how they have interpreted the subject of the piece. More often than not, only then is the subject a matter of conjecture. Artists have been known to produce many 'sketches' before a work of art is undertaken, and it is quite common to find that buildings, trees, and scenery has been 'moved' in the final rendition to suit the composition of the painting or its aesthetic balance. Beware of forgeries, and always buy from a renowned expert. Be prepared for unwelcome news if you don't. It is a fact that 'artwork' or original paintings enjoy the reputation of commanding the highest figures in the auction world. It could be a total disaster if you part with lots of money without doing your homework first.

Fig. 3.21. **'The First Set'**
A lawn tennis Stevengraph entitled 'The First Set'. A very rare and highly collectable item, woven in pure silk in bright colours. The illustrated scene of a tennis match with spectators is a delight in its intricacy. (c. 1881) Height 5.0 cms. Width 15.0 cms. £700-1000 ($1000-1500)

Fig. 3.22. **'The Tennis Party'**
An original etching by Daniel Mordant after Sir J. Lavery's famous painting, 'The Tennis Party 1888'. The black and white etching has been extremely well executed in every detail, and fully represents the original oil painting. Height 38.0 cms. Width 80.0 cms. £3500-4000 ($4750-6000)

Top left:
Fig. 3.23. **'The Tennis Party' - a Sketch**
An oil on canvas painting (unsigned) of a lady tennis player and spectators. This is a detail from the original Lavery oil painting 'The Tennis Party' and is well executed. Could it be a preliminary sketch for this painting, as the detail is so comparable? Height 54.0 cms. Width 40.0 cms. £1000-1500 ($1500-2250)

Bottom left:
Fig. 3.24. **'The Tennis Girl'**
A watercolour and pastel painting of a girl holding a racket and wearing a tennis-apron. An exceptionally well painted picture in fine detail by J. Bouvier. (c. 1890) Height 29.0 cms. Width 21.0 cms. £2600-3000 ($3900-4500)

Top right:
Fig. 3.25. **Lady and Gentleman in a Garden**
An interesting watercolour by Henry Stephen Ludlow ('Hal') of a lady and a gentleman tennis player in a garden setting, each holding a racket. Besides being a portrait and domestic painter, Ludlow (born 1861) was a very competent all round magazine illustrator, and contributed to *The Sketch* and *The Illustrated London News*. (c. 1890) Height 20.0 cms. Width 16.0 cms. £850-1000 ($1200-1500)

Bottom right:
Fig. 3.26. **Mixed Doubles**
An original finely coloured lithograph of a mixed doubles tennis game in France. A delightful study, with spectators in the foreground and a fountain at the back. The illustration is by Alexandre Lumois. (c. 1895) Length 52.0 cms. Width 40.0 cms. £1100-1300 ($1750-1950)

Fig. 3.27. **'Girl with Her Pets'**[6]
A charming watercolour and gouache painting entitled: 'Girl with her Pets' signed by Arthur Wardle R. I. (1864-1949) The girl is seated with her dog and puppies and her tennis racket lies in the foreground. (c. 1895) Length 22.0 cms. Width 30.0 cms. £4000-4500 ($6000-6750)

Fig. 3.28. **'Une Partie de Lawn Tennis'**[7]
An original coloured French lithograph of a mixed doubles tennis match by George Goursat 'SEM' (1863-1934) The picture is known as 'Une Partie de Lawn Tennis' and was printed in 1897. Height 34.0 cms. Width 48.0 cms. £1250-1500 ($1800-2250)

Fig. 3.29. **'To a Tennis Player'**
An amusing, coloured print of a Victorian lady and gentleman playing a game of lawn tennis. Printed at the base is a humorous verse: 'Lawn Tennis is a jolly game, such lots of fun and flirting. You race about and mash the boys — 'Tis really quite diverting...' (c. 1900) Height 54.0 cms. Width 23.0 cms. £85-100 ($125-150)

Fig. 3.30. **'Une Visite a la Benedictine'** A fine large coloured lithograph, showing a mixed doubles match in France, by M. E. Montaut. It is a view of the Benedictine Monastery with two early aeroplanes in the background. (c. 1910) Height 33.0 cms. Width 73.0 cms. £1000-1200 ($1500-1800)

Fig. 3.31. **A French Chromolithograph** The print features a number of male tennis players in various poses, overlooked by a bearded umpire on a high chair. Each player is named at the base of the print. It was illustrated by Hassan (c. 1910) Height 43.0 cms. Width 63.0 cms. £650-800 ($1000-1200)

Fig. 3.32. **Couple at a Net** A pen and crayon drawing by Carl Toma of a couple standing before a net with spectators taking refreshment in the background. (c. 1910) Height 35.0 cms. Width 24.0 cms. £1600-1800 ($2400-2700)

Fig. 3.33. **A Female Tennis Player**
A woodblock engraving of a female tennis player in action by the Hungarian artist C. Pal Molnar. (c. 1930) Height 20.0 cms. Width 32.0 cms. £650-800 ($1000-1200)

Fig. 3.34. **A Japanese Panel**
A decorative wooden panel, showing (in relief) a game of Hagoita, a very old traditional Japanese game, which appears to be very similar to 'battledore and shuttlecock'. The ladies here are hitting a ball rather than a shuttlecock. (c. 1920) Height 79.1 cms. Width 36.8 cms. £150-175 ($225-250)

Engravings and Prints

Fig. 3.35. **Rackets**
Quite a popular engraving 'Drawn and Etched by Theodore Lane, Eng'd by Geo Hunt.' It shows a scene inside one of the debtors' prisons, where games of (racquets) were often a popular way of making money by placing bets on the outcome. Originally the print was published by Thomas McLean of 26, Haymarket, London in 1827. Height 19.8 cms. Width 29.7 cms. £100-150 ($150-225)

Fig. 3.36. **Prince's Racquet Club Courts**
An engraving showing the interior of Prince's Club in Hans-Place, Belgrave Square, London. It was in these courts that the game of 'Racquets' was played. The engraving appeared in *The Illustrated London News* on August 15th. 1857. Height 14.8 cms. Width 23.5 cms. £15-20 ($25-30)

Fig. 3.37. **The New Game of Badminton in India**
A charming engraving of a mixed doubles game being played on a very small court. The bottom of the narrow net is fringed, and it is supported by a pair of bamboo canes, one of which is placed within the court and the other outside! It was printed in *The Graphic* on April 25th. 1874. Height 22.4 cms. Width 29.8 cms. £30-40 ($45-60)

Fig. 3.38. **Life on Board the Serapis: Lawn Tennis**
A hand coloured engraving, which was originally drawn by an officer of the ship. It was printed in the *The Illustrated London News*, on April 8th. 1876. Height 14.7 cms. Width 21.1 cms. £30-40 ($45-60)

Fig. 3.39. **Sketches at the Championship Lawn Tennis Match – Wimbledon**
A hand tinted engraving, which was printed in the *The Illustrated London News* on July 26th. 1878. The man wearing a helmet, serving tea to the ladies, is believed to be none other than Henry Jones 'Cavendish', the first referee at Wimbledon. The illustration shows the match between Spencer Gore and Frank Hadow. Height 29.8 cms. Width 21.1 cms. £30-50 ($45-75)

Fig. 3.40. **The Champion Lawn Tennis Match**
An original (hand-coloured) engraving, which was printed in the *The Illustrated London News* in 1880. F. H. Ayres supplied the grandstand in the background. The scene shows Mr. Hartley winning the Wimbledon Singles Championship against Mr. Lawford (The scoreboard records his name as Lauford). The umpire is seated on top of a table, as was the norm for early matches. Height 14.5 cms. Width 22.2 cms. £30-50 ($45-75)

Fig. 3.41. **Lawn Tennis**
A black and white engraving of lawn tennis by Shirley Hodson for the *Illustrated Sporting and Dramatic News*, July 23rd. 1881. An excellent early example of a typical game of tennis showing the participants in period costumes. Note the lawn tennis court white line marker, top left. Height 38.0 cms. Width 25.0 cms. £50-75 ($75-100)

Fig. 3.43. **'Battledore and Shuttlecock'**
An engraving from the original painting by Lady Alma Tadema (1852-1909). It shows a young girl concentrating on keeping the shuttlecock up in the air, while counting the hits. Her friend looks on, waiting her turn, while a mother and her young baby are being kept amused. Notice the artist's initials in the floor tiles. (c. 1885) Height 30.4 cms. Width 20.2 cms. £20-30 ($30-45)

Fig. 3.42. **Our Tennis Party**
A wonderful chromolithograph print showing the story of how the ground was cleared to allow for a tennis court: –1. 'Sacrificed to Tennis –2. Victory. –3. The Departure of the Guests.' It was printed in the *Graphic Summer Number* of 1882, and drawn by E. K. Johnson. Height 30.1 cms. Width 19.5 cms. £75-100 ($100-150)

Fig. 3.44. **A Lawn Tennis Tournament**
A very pleasant double-page engraving from the *Harper's Young People*, and printed on July 3rd. 1886. The engraving was by T. de Thulstrup, and shows a ladies doubles tournament in progress. Height 23.2 cms. Width 34.8 cms. £30-50 ($45-75)

Fig. 3.45. **The Lawn Tennis Championship at Wimbledon – 1888**
An illustration by Arthur Hopkins showing Ernest Renshaw's victory over Herbert Lawford. There is the umpire again, seated on top of a table. Height 19.2 cms. Width 25.9 cms. £30-40 ($45-60)

Fig. 3.47. **'Lawn Tennis'**
A pleasant hand coloured engraving of the scene at a lawn tennis garden party. It was printed in France, and has a small 'No.10' printed in the top right hand corner. The artist's name is difficult to read, it might be C. A. Fisch, or it could be Fesch. (c. 1890) Height 15.6 cms. Width 18.3 cms. £30-50 ($45-75)

Fig. 3.46. **The New Prince's Club, Knightsbridge**
A hand coloured engraving entitled: 'Opening of the New Prince's Club, Knightsbridge, by The Prince of Wales.' The opening match was between Mr. A. Lyttleton and Charles Saunders. The engraving is drawn from the hazard end of the court towards the dedans. It was printed in *The Graphic* on May 25th. 1889. Height 16.8 cms. Width 21.8 cms. £30-40 ($45-60)

Fig. 3.48. **Irrepressible Enthusiasts in the Snow**
A fine engraving by Arthur Hopkins RWS, RBA (1848-1930). (c. 1890) Height 19.7 cms. Width 29.1 cms. £30-40 ($45-60)

Fig. 3.49. **Cassiobury Park**
A fine chromolithograph print shows the grand house at Cassiobury Park, near Watford, England. (c. 1890) The postcard shows the park gates and gatehouse in 1910. One of the pine lawn tennis equipment boxes (Fig. 4.16.) relates to this park and a label on the lid shows the house from almost an identical angle. Height 12.8 cms. Width 17.8 cms. £20-30 ($30-45)

Fig. 3.51. **Afternoon Tea at a Lawn Tennis Tournament**
A fine engraving from a superb original watercolour painting by Edward Frederick Brewtnall (1846-1902). It was printed in *The Graphic*, on June 18th. 1892. The original hangs at the Wimbledon Museum. Height 31.5 cms. Width 46.8 cms. £70-100 ($100-150)

Fig. 3.50. **The First Day of the Season**
A hand tinted engraving, which was printed in the *The Illustrated London News* on May 9th. 1891. Height 29.2 cms. Width 23.0 cms. £30-40 ($45-60)

Fig. 3.52. **The Lawn Tennis Championship at Wimbledon**
A small engraving showing Joshua Pim defeating Wilfred Baddeley for the 1894 Singles Championship at Wimbledon. Height 13.7 cms. Width 19.8 cms. £20-30 ($30-45)

Fig. 3.53. **Lawn Tennis – Platz in Homburg**
A wonderful coloured lithograph showing a tournament in progress at Bad Homburg. The ball boys are dressed in the club colours. (1895) Height 21.1 cms. Width 31.5 cms. £75-100 ($100-150)

Fig. 3.54. **'Ping-Pong'**
A delightful engraving illustrated in a Victorian newspaper entitled 'Ping-Pong'. It shows a couple playing a game across a dining room table, while a large audience of ladies and gentlemen look on with great interest. It was illustrated by Lucien Davis R. I. and was supplied in a supplement to *The Illustrated London News* on June 15th. 1901. Someone really should have a quiet word to that lady concerning her backhand! Height 36.0 cms. Width 46.0 cms. £150-175 ($225-250)

Fig. 3.55. **His Majesty at the Lawn Tennis Tournament at Homburg**
An excellent engraving entitled: 'King Edward VII in Germany'. A. Forestier, who was the special artist for the *The Illustrated London News* on September 7th, 1901, was the illustrator. Height 38.0 cms. Width 51.0 cms. £150-175 ($225-250)

Fig. 3.56. **'The Dead Heart'**
An amusing engraving illustrated in the Victorian newspaper *The Sketch* called: 'The Dead Heart'. It shows a couple in tennis attire seated beneath a tree with a caption below: ' The Rejected One: And is this great love of mine to be cast aside? She (wearily): You might have it stuffed!' May 26th 1909, by Frank Reynolds. Height 46.0 cms. Width 30.0 cms. £45-60 ($70-90)

Fig. 3.57. **'Bunny' Austin**
A print from a hand drawn line drawing by the cartoonist 'Mel' in 1932. Height 11.8 cms. Width 12.5 cms. £20-30 ($30-40)

Fig. 3.58. **Slazenger – 75 Years at Wimbledon**
A full colour poster, showing the Doherty brothers at Wimbledon, it was printed as one of a set of three promotional images in 1977. John Beswick was the illustrator. Height 37.0 cms. Width 24.8 cms. £40-60 ($60-80)

Fig. 3.59. **No.5 Court, Wimbledon**
A limited edition print (No. 120 of 950) of a fine watercolour by Kenneth Reed F. R. S. A. (c. 1985) Height 59.0 cms. Width 42.2 cms. £75-100 ($100-150)

Chapter 4.
Racket Sports Equipment

Almost every sport or game requires a player to buy equipment in order to play it. Understandably, manufacturers have been very keen to take advantage of this. A very competitive rivalry has ensured that innovative designs and inventions have continually flooded the marketplace. Unfortunately, varying standards of craftsmanship have been evident too. The speed with which lawn tennis became popular would now be described as an 'overnight sensation'. It literally 'invaded' recreation grounds throughout England, with thousands of wealthy middle class citizens setting up nets and courts wherever there was a suitable plot of land. Within just a few years, there was a summer tournament in every city, town, and village. Lawn tennis clubs were being formed everywhere, and there was much alarm from the 'old stagers' who were taken aback by this 'rude and boisterous' craze. Sports equipment manufacturers probably couldn't have believed their luck! They were in an ideal position to take advantage of this newest game, with a great demand for equipment. In 1876, a correspondent for Bell's Life in London remarked upon its popularity:

> Lawn Tennis is decidedly in the ascendant at the present time, go where we will, amongst the choice assemblages of elegant idlers, or amid the crowds of loungers at sea-side places and agreeable resorts, posts, nets, guy ropes, and courts, demonstrated by white tape or chalk lines, meet the eye in every direction.

In April the following year, a report (on behalf of Bell's Life in London) from the cricket grounds of Oxford University saw lawn tennis as a genuine threat to the English game of cricket:

> We are sorry to observe the increasing prevalence of lawn tennis on this and other cricket grounds, and fear this "ladies game" will interfere with the more manly recreation of cricket.

On 12th July 1879, The Field newspaper reported upon the 'Grand National Tournament' which took place at the Hyde, Hendon.

> Some of the leading makers of bats, nets, balls, &c., used in the game were represented on the ground, making it almost like a small exhibition, and several small tents and marquees were put up just inside the enclosure.

On the very same page, advertisements were taken by companies such as Asser and Sherwin, George Prince, and Parkins and Gotto, all wishing to part with lawn tennis equipment 'at the most competitive prices'.

Quite apart from the 'silverware' on offer to the champion players, tournaments and clubs were already offering other tempting prizes to successful entrants, and sometimes they included equipment too. In a report of a tournament run by the Stour Valley Club at their Kedington Rectory ground, in September 1879, a list of prizes was also included. The tournament was '...witnessed by a large company of the elite of the neighbourhood' and the first prize for gentlemen:

> ...was a handsome inkstand in the shape of a dog's kennel, with two dogs standing outside, quite a novel idea. The first prize for ladies was a hairbrush, with ivory back and a leather waist belt. The second prize in each class was a best racquet bat, with cork handle by Ayres. All the prizes had the club monogram engraved on them.

By 1884 the London Post Office Trades' Directory was listing over forty companies, all of which had some connection with manufacturing lawn tennis equipment. The list included the firm of 'Jefferies and Co.' which until 1880 had been known as 'Jefferies and Malings'. According to the Red Book of Commerce (1923), the firm had been established c.1821 by Jefferies Malings. They had been providing equipment for the game of 'Racquets' many years before lawn tennis became popular and were chosen by Major Walter Clopton Wingfield to provide the rackets in his very first boxed sets of 'Sphairistike'.

George Gibson Bussey & Co.

Another company on that list was George Gibson Bussey and Co. of Peckham, London. George Bussey was born in Ripon, Yorkshire, in 1829. By the time he was twenty-five years old, he was working in Holborn, London, as a 'Saddler'. That year he married Harriet Uphill, and on their daughter's birth certificate he was described as a 'Leather Case Maker' and Master. In 1867 a 'Museum of Fire Arms' had been built by Bussey 'to contain a permanent exhibition of everything connected with gunnery, revolvers, rifles, guns, explosive compounds, projectiles, and cartridges etc.' His company was obviously becoming very successful and trustworthy. (This is why Bussey's business address always included the words 'the Museum Works'.)

The 1871 census returns described Bussey as 'Leather Manufacturer, employing 26 hands.' Well before 1881, Bussey had secured a contract with her Majesty's Army and Navy services to supply 'Accoutrements'. A trade directory of 1876 shows that the building had expanded and now included a skating rink. The following year, he made an application to register a trademark (it was formed from the letters G G B with an arrow passing through them.) This mark was associated with the firm for over fifty years.

Although Bussey had successfully applied for patents related to his leather business in the past, in 1880 we find that he had applied for a patent associated with 'Accessories and Appliances for Lawn Tennis'. He obviously felt that the company was ideally set up to meet the huge demand for lawn tennis and other sporting equipment. His experiences of providing high quality equipment for the British Armed Forces, was redirected into the manufacture of sporting equipment of all kinds. His tennis rackets are now well known for their high degree of finish and detail.

When Bussey died in 1889, he had amassed a considerable fortune. His personal estate was valued at £19,475 10s. 7d. The family home stood as a testament to the fortune he gained through the transactions of his sporting business. The house was called 'Brookfield' and was situated near Ryde Town on the Isle of Wight. Described as a 'Marine Residential Property' with fourteen acres of land, it was comprised of 'The Mansion' (with twelve bedrooms and two 'towers') with a carriage drive, a 'Picturesque Lodge', conservatory, and a 'School Room'. It also had a 'Stabling Department' Coach House, Coachman's Cottage, Small Farmery, Pleasure Grounds and Gardens, Fruit Gardens, Glasshouses, four paddocks, and of course a tennis court.

Manufacturers like Bussey, Wisden, Buchanan, Slazenger, Feltham, and Jefferies (all from England) were there, at or near to the beginning of the game's popularity, supplying pine boxed sets containing everything you would need to play the game.

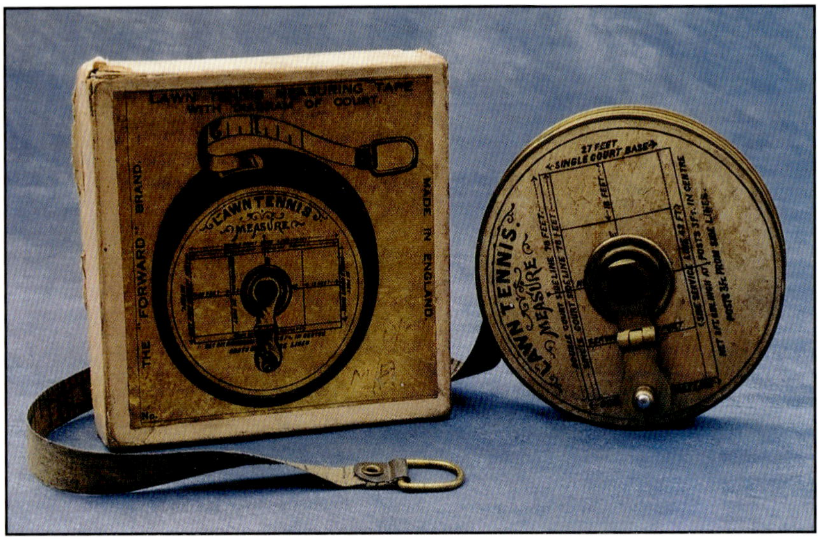

Fig. 4.1. **The 'Forward Brand' Lawn Tennis Measuring Tape**
A neat little tape measure complete in its own original box. The casing of the tape is made of polished brass, and a stiff cardboard label is fitted onto one side. All the dimensions for laying out a lawn tennis court are printed onto it. The tape itself is made of a tough material and is wound back into the casing by turning a handle which will eventually fold away, it is also made of brass. There is no indication of where the tape was made but the box does relate that it was 'MADE IN ENGLAND'. This particular box and lid are covered with a peach coloured paper. I have seen another, this time in a light blue box, but otherwise, it was identical. (c. 1900) Diam. 9.7 cms. £150-200 ($225-300)

Fig. 4.4. **A Brass Cased Lawn Tennis Measuring Tape**
On this example, it appears that the details (or rather the background colour) have been printed onto a brass disc, revealing the dimensional details as a brighter colour. It is not a 'Dean' tape, as the trademark is of two crossed arrows, and at the moment is unknown. What makes this particularly interesting is that the same printing process has been used on the back of the tape to reveal the advertising details of F. H. Ayres. (Frederick Henry Ayres Manufacturing Company). The winder is marked '78 FT.' (c. 1925) Diam. 11.0 cms. £100-150 ($150-225)

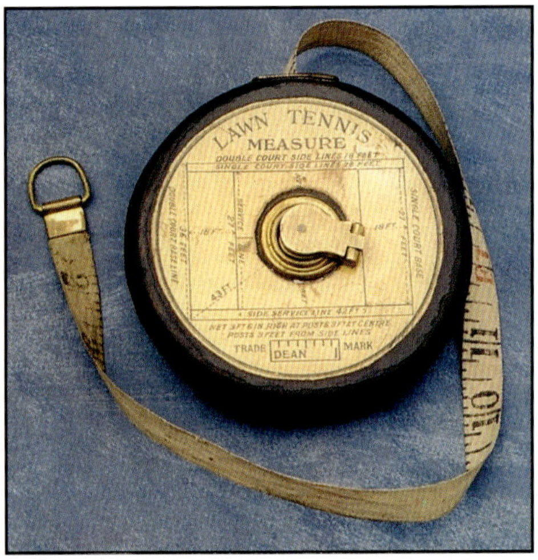

Left:
Fig. 4.2. **A Leather Cased Lawn Tennis Measuring Tape**[1]
A very similar item other than this tape is supplied in a hand sewn leather case. Unlike the previous piece, this label has a trade mark for the company of 'DEAN'. (c. 1910) Diam. 10.7 cms. £125-175 ($185-275)

Bottom left:
Fig. 4.3. **A Brass Cased Lawn Tennis Measuring Tape**
Again manufactured by 'Dean', the surface which formerly displayed a paper disc with the court's dimensions printed on it is now a brass disc, the details are in relief, and the background has been patinated to a darker colour. The winder is marked '78 FT.' (c. 1920) Diam. 10.9 cms. £100-150 ($150-225)

Fig. 4.5. **A Dean-Beddington 'Lawn Tennis Tape and Plan'**
A boxed tape, differing in design from all the others in that it is contained within the centre of two compressed and hardened leather discs, the tape being exposed at the outer edge. The centre of the paper label is identical to that which was used on the leather-cased model. On the inside of the lid a small square paper label reads: 'DEANS SURVEYOR TAPES are made from best woven yarns and then coated with special waterproof paint.' (c. 1925) Diam. 11.0 cms. £100-150 ($150-225)

Top left:
Fig. 4.6. **'The Eclipse Lawn Tennis Marker'**
A very rare Eclipse Lawn Tennis Marker, (Osmond's Patent), manufactured by Jacques and Son, Hatton Garden, London. Markers with a single handle are very difficult to find. The assumption being that very few were made because it was quickly found that they were very difficult to control, the demand for markers with two handles instead of one must have soon prevailed. The box has been replaced and the small transfer wheel has been lost, a common fault with these early machines. The marking wheel at the front is only 3/4" (1.8 cms.) wide. (c. 1880s) Wheel Base 48.0 cms. Height of handle 75.2 cms. £150-200 ($225-300)

Top center:
Fig. 4.7. **An Unnamed Single Handled Line Marker**
A single handled line marker, with two small front wheels, and a system by which a line is marked by the large back wheel. Unfortunately the small transfer wheel which would have sat on top of the wheel, which picks up whiting from the box, is missing. The box itself is sturdy and original and much of the original paint work remains on the surface. (c. 1890s) Wheel Base 52.0 cms. Height of handle 72.0 cms. £150-200 ($225-300)

Top right:
Fig. 4.8. **"The Eureka" Tennis Court Marker**[2]
An ingenious contraption from the U.S.A. It works when the drum is filled with chalk dust or something similar, and the marker is pushed along. There's a small slide mechanism, which allows access to the container. All around the flat circumference of the drum a perforated metal strip allows the material inside to fall through onto the turf. (c. 1890-1920) Diam. 21.5 cms. Width 11.5 cms. (Wheel width 1 1/2" or 4.0 cms.) £125-150 ($200-225)

Fig. 4.9. **The 'Eclipse' Line Marker**
A 'Jacques and Son Ltd. Eclipse Marker, London'. This model has two handles and clever devices for cleaning the wheels. For instance, there is hinged piece of metal at the front of the box, which is directly connected to the front axle. As a consequence, when the marker's pushed along, it acts as a guide pointing outwards along the court, and when the marker is pulled backwards it swings over on top of the box wheel, taking off any excess material. The large marking wheel (wheel width 1 1/4" or 3.3 cms.) has a device for regulating the amount of material transferred to it. (c. 1910) Wheel Base 54.0 cms. Height of handle 71.4 cms. £150-200 ($225-300)

Fig. 4.10. **The "Improved Dale" Line Marker**
A fairly standard construction line marker with a small guide pointer at the front of the container and a cleaning bar to remove excess whiting on the large wheel. The line is achieved by the transfer of whiting onto the large wheel at the back. The marker has been re-painted in the original colours. (c. 1930) (Wheel width 1 1/2 ins. or 4.0 cms.) Wheel Base 47.5 cms. Height of handles 79.2 cms. £100-150 ($150-225)

Fig. 4.11. **Osmond's Patent Eclipse Line Marker**
Manufactured by Jacques and Son, London, it is complete with 2 small wheels at the front, which not only give it stability, but also act as a guide for the user. Again, the line is marked by the large back wheel (wheel width 1 1/4 ins. or 3.3 cms.) and it is also fitted with a wheel cleaner device. (c. 1930) Wheel Base 57.8 cms. Height of handles 74.2 cms. £100-125 ($150-200)

Fig. 4.12. **The S. I. F. 'Comet' Line Marker**
A twin handled marker with a bold construction and a heavy metal container. An extremely robust design, in the original black and green colours. (c. 1950) Wheel Base 48.2 cms. Height of handles 78.8 cms. £100-125 ($150-200)

Fig. 4.13. **The 'B-W' Line Marker**
Another robust twin handled marker with an unusual container lid. Another unusual feature is a small carrying handle, behind which lies a brass manufacturer's plaque. Moulded into the plaque are the words 'Patent applied for' and 'A352/10'. (c. 1950) Wheel Base 43.2 cms. Height of handles 81.3 cms. £100-125 ($150-200)

Fig. 4.14. **A Selection of Ayres Metal Line Corner Markers**
A range of 22 pieces of F. H. Ayres cast iron lawn tennis court line markers. It would be interesting to know what the round head pins are for! (c. 1900) £100-150 ($150-225)

Fig. 4.15. **A Collection of Six Metal Corner Markers**[3]
Back: LAWN TENNIS (no maker); COL. GODFREYS GREENWAY PATENT. Middle: F. H. AYRES LONDON; JAQUES & SON LONDON. Front: JACK SHARP LIVERPOOL; A. G. SPALDING & BROS. (c. 1884-1910) £10-75 each ($15-100)

Fig. 4.16. **The Cassiobury Pine Lawn Tennis Box**[4]
A large green paper label (47.8 cms. wide x 31.0 cms. deep), which has been pasted onto the inside of the lid, reads: 'THE CASSIOBURY GAMES OF BADMINTON AND GARDEN TENNIS' and was printed in black ink by Dean and Son of 160 Fleet Street, London. The illustration is remarkable for several reasons. In the foreground a mixed doubles game is being played on an hourglass shaped court, the net (which is excessively high) is complete with wing nets. In the background, four mixed doubles pairs contest a game of badminton on a rectangular court, and likewise, the net is very high (four shuttlecocks are in mid-flight, so the pairs are certainly not playing competitively!). All the activity takes place within the grounds and immediately in front of Cassiobury House, home of the Duke of Essex. The game was obviously observed as being one which served as a gentle pastime rather than a vigorous, competitive sport. Gentlemen retain their jackets and straw boaters, whereas the ladies wear ground length dresses supported by bustles. Such was the novelty of these new games that the artist obviously thought it was necessary to point out which game was which! Quite apart from items that you would have expected the box to contain, a very small but significant detail appears to show that the lines of the courts were secured at the corners by small pegs. This means that court lines must have been supplied as rolls of tape, and not marked onto the turf with whiting or chalk. The box was fitted with a pair of black enamelled handles and also a lock, but unfortunately the key is missing. (c. 1876) Length 92.3 cms. Depth 18.0 cms. Width 36.4 cms. £700-£800 ($1050-1200)

Fig. 4.17. **An Ayres Army and Navy Pine Equipment Box**
A rare equipment box painted with red, white, and blue stripes on the outside, and a large lithographed paper label pasted onto the inside of the lid. In fact, what appears to be a single label is in fact three. The colourful label in the centre seems to be 'standard' on all the boxes of a similar type manufactured by this company. At the time that these boxes were being produced (c. 1875-1885) the rules of the game were being changed very regularly. In order to keep up with these advances the manufacturers simply printed new labels associated with the dimensions of the latest court and rules, then pasted them on either side of the centre label. This label was printed by W. H. Willcockson, Lithographer and Printer, Cross Steam Works, Baldwins Gardens, London E. C. The label on the left relates to those rules approved by the Marylebone Cricket Club, and The All England Croquet and Lawn Tennis Club in 1878. The right hand label is a very early publication of the rules for 1878, and also gives us a tantalising clue as to the original contents of the box: '6 COVERED AND 12 PLAIN INDIA RUBBER BALLS, POLES JOINTED BRASS FERULED &c. POLISHED OR PAINTED, SUPERIOR TANNED NET, WITH MALLETT DRILL RUNNERS PEGS &c. &c.' There is evidence that there was once a fitted press too. (1878) Length 97.2 cms. Depth 24.0 cms. Width 39.8 cms. £750-£1000 ($1000-1500)

Fig. 4.18. **A Bussey's Lawn Tennis Equipment Box**
A very intriguing box, on the front of which a simple, hand painted two colour border contains the words: 'THE ROYAL LAWN TENNIS SET'. On the inside of the lid, stretching across the whole width and most of the depth (90.8 cms wide x 27.0 cms deep) is a large label with a rather oddly conceived cartoon drawing printed onto it. On the top left and right hand corners, there's the standard Bussey logo of G. G. B. with an arrow passing through the letters from the right to left hand side. In the top centre of the label, it reads: 'BUSSEY'S LAWN TENNIS'. (c. 1880) The style and content of the cartoon is very curious and intriguing; it could easily be that it shows the characters of a theatre group, all dressed in period costume, passing their time playing a game of mixed doubles. Members of the 'cast', look on with interest, others show total apathy. To the left there's a gentleman who appears to be writing the score in a note pad, and nearby a lady is seated in a cane chair and is waiting for the score. Next to her, a man blows a trumpet while his friend has his fingers in his ears to protect them from the noise. At the end of the court a man dressed in black, and wearing an unusual hat, has a conversation with an oriental gentleman. Meanwhile, next to him, a man reclining in a chair is totally oblivious to what is happening only a few feet away, and is content on blowing large soap bubbles from a pipe! Four characters play on a rectangular court while ten other characters are on the right hand side. Here, a man looks on through a pair of binoculars, another is standing on stilts, and a gentleman in a bowler hat walks away while pushing two children in a pushchair. Doublets, hat feathers, and padded trunk hose are worn, but are more in keeping with the dress of the 1540s than the 1880s. The principal line work of the cartoon is printed in black, while green, red, ochre, and blue are printed as solid colours. The label is in two halves (which meet at the centre) and continues off the sheet on each side where a strip of paper is pasted over the top and forms a part of the border. The lid can be supported by a simple two piece locking device, which slots together. Inside the box there's a wooden compartment, which would have held twelve lawn tennis balls, and on each side of the box there's a pair of leather straps which would have secured a set of tennis poles. Tantalisingly, on the bottom of the box there's a ghost impression of the shape of a racket which used to lie there! The box can be locked (but the key's missing) and there are a pair of sliding lever fasteners too. There is a pair of iron handles for carrying the box. (c. 1880) Length 94.0 cms. Depth 16.6 cms. Width 39.7 cms. £600-£700 ($900-1000)

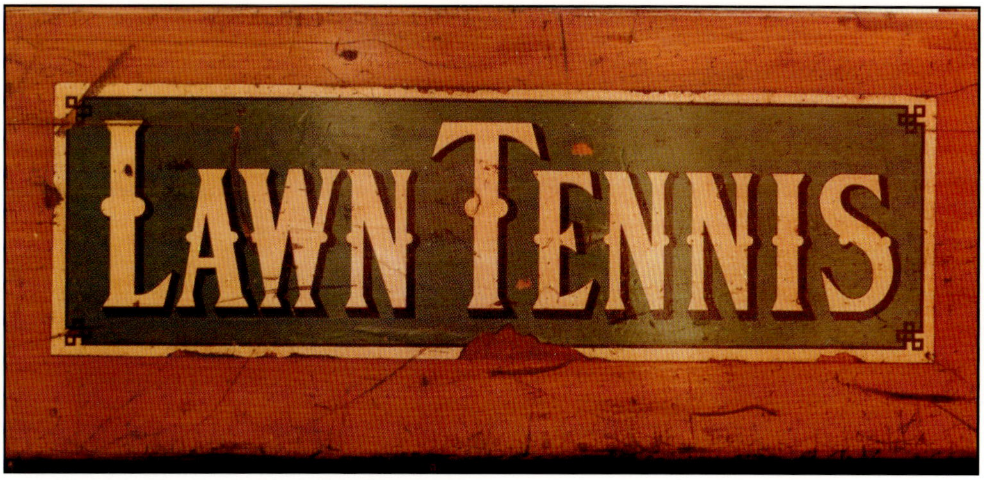

Fig. 4.19. **A Pine Box entitled 'LAWN TENNIS'**
A comparatively small lawn tennis equipment box, which has a vertical wooden divider splitting the inside of the box into two long compartments. I would assume that originally, two or three piece (slot together) lawn tennis poles would have been occupied by one of them, the other by rackets, pegs, mallets, and etc. Above this divider, at either end of the box are two small compartments for lawn tennis balls. I would guess that there would have been room for two balls in each compartment, but it's interesting to note that not a single ball in my collection, from any era, will fit into one of them. A very small green paper label, situated on the centre of the lid inside, is printed in black with the words: 'HARE'S BRUSH, BASKET, AND UMBRELLA WAREHOUSES 32 & 33, WATERWORKS ST. TOY WAREHOUSE 21, SAVILLE ST. HULL'. The box is complete with a pair of enamelled iron handles, one at each end of the box, and a pair of hook and eye fasteners. (c. 1885) Length 95.0 cms. Depth 16.5 cms. Width 26.1 cms. £500-£600 ($750-800)

Fig. 4.20. **A Pine Box for Lawn Tennis Equipment**
On the centre of the inner lid a green paper label (37.9 cms. wide x 25.3 cms. deep) has been pasted. Printed in black it shows an idyllic scene of a Victorian mixed doubles match watched by onlookers, and is taking place on the principal lawns of a typical English country house. The court is not obviously hourglass shaped, in fact there are no lines to be seen, but the net is very high, and there is an absence of wing-nets. In both of the top two corners of the label is the monogram 'E I & S' 'E J & S' or 'E L & S' Drake. (Driver and Leaver of London printed the label.) A retailer's stamp has been printed onto the lid above the label which reads: 'JOHN THOMPSON SOUTH CASTLE ST. KINDERGARTEN DEPOT LIVERPOOL'. There are no fittings in the box at all, but there are the tell-tale signs that the box was once fitted with a lawn tennis racket press. Three perfectly round holes, about 2 cms. in diameter which were originally drilled through the bottom of the box, have been covered (quite early in the life of the box) with small square strips of lead. (It is quite common to find three holes in the bottom of an early equipment box, the press was fixed to the box, and the rackets were fixed into the press simply by removing the top plate of the press.) The box has a pair of black enamelled handles and uses the hook and eye fastening system, although there is a facility for adding a padlock too. (c. 1880) Length 96.0 cms. Depth 22.5 cms. Width 32.8 cms. £500-£600 ($750-800)

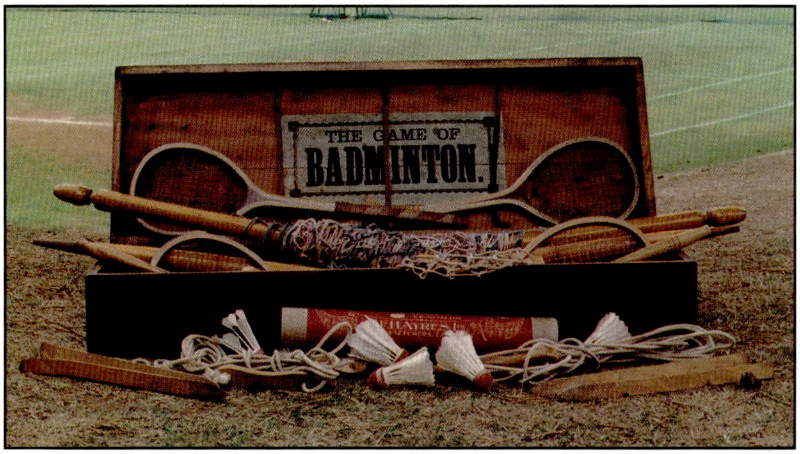

Fig. 4.21. **A Pine Box for Badminton Equipment**
A pine box set of 'THE GAME OF BADMINTON' with a green paper label (38.8 cms. wide x 16.4 cms. deep) printed in black, pasted on the inside of the lid. The set is complete with three original rackets, a set of poles, net, mallets, guy ropes, shuttles, and stakes. When the three-piece poles are slotted together they reach 2.16 m. (7ft. 1 in.) high (not including the 29.0 cms. piece, which is pushed into the ground) and extend to a width of 3.96 m. (13 feet.) The playing height of the net, which itself is only 26.8 cms. deep (10.5 ins.), is 1.85m. (6ft. 1in.) The string net, which has seven tassels hanging down, is coloured red, white, and blue. A pair of metal handles, and hook and eye fasteners, completes the set. (c. 1880) Length 96.0 cms. Depth 22.5 cms. Width 32.8 cms. £500-£600 ($750-800)

Lawn Tennis Net Poles

Fig. 4.22. **A Pair of Early 'Feltham' Lawn Tennis Poles**
These are very rare, and come complete with brass fittings. The brass top piece is nicely decorated with a rope motif. These poles would have been free standing, (with the aid of a spike protruding from the base) and would only have been effective by using guy-ropes which would have been hooked around the brass fittings at the top, and secured into the ground with pegs. A small inlaid ivory rectangle has printed onto it: 'FELTHAM's MAKERS LONDON.' (c. 1890) Length (excluding spike) 42 ins. or 106.6 cms. Diam. 4.3 cms. £400-500 ($600-750)

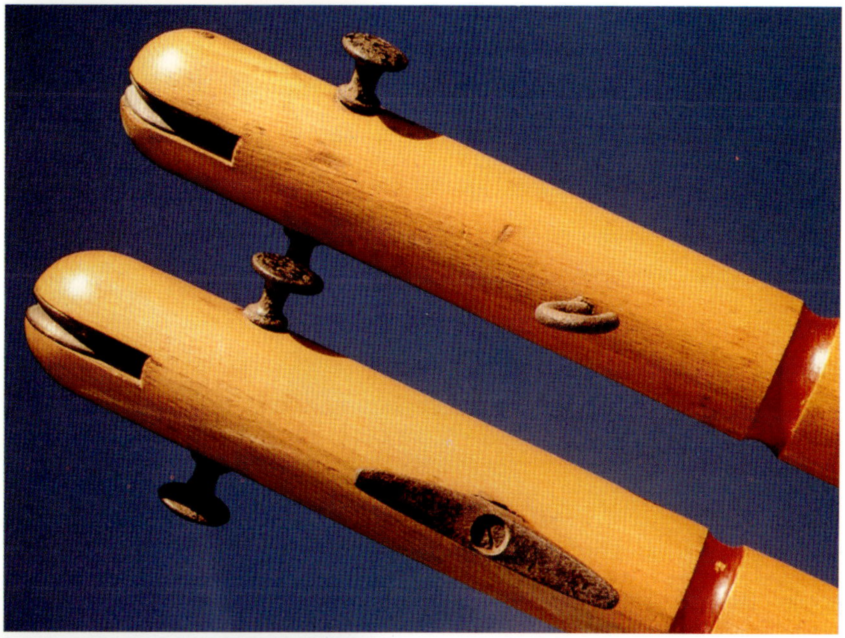

Fig. 4.23. **Decorated Lawn Tennis Poles**
A pair of varnished pine lawn tennis poles with three turned and coloured bands each of which are spaced one foot apart. The poles come complete with black enamelled fittings, a small brass wheel set into the top of the poles, and a brass collar which protects the base of the pole just above the spike. The recessed bands would have supplied convenient anchorage points for tying the net against the poles, and the wheel would have allowed the net to be drawn across the poles more easily. Just like the Feltham's poles these would have been used in conjunction with guy ropes. (c. 1920) Length (excluding spike) 42 ins. or 106.6 cms. Diam. 4.7 cms. £200-300 ($300-450)

Fig. 4.24. **Pair of A. G. Spalding Lawn Tennis Poles**
If we can imagine that these three sets of poles illustrate a logical progression in their design, then this pair incorporate all those improvements which, as a result of past failings, would have made them the most efficient of the three. They slot into a metal fitting, which would have been a permanent court feature, would have alleviated the need for guy ropes and would have stopped the whole net structure from leaning over. The wheel would allow the net to pass easily backwards and forwards for raising and lowering, and the ratchet winder would permit the net to be wound tighter and more accurately, without slipping. A brass metal plaque shows the company details: 'MADE IN GREAT BRITAIN A. G. SPALDING & BROS. ATHLETIC GOODS MANUFACTURERS LONDON & BRANCHES'. (c. 1935) Length (excluding spike) 42 ins. or 106.6 cms. Diam. 6.4 cms. £150-200 ($225-300)

Rackets

It seems that every conceivable size, shape, material, and stringing method has been tried out on rackets, since they were first made. In 1882 The Field featured an article written about steel lawn tennis rackets. Collectible ones are more desirable if they display evidence of any of these experiments, especially if they are from the nineteenth century, or even earlier. It is notoriously difficult to date rackets, but certainly in the English models there are certain details to look for, which can determine the date of origin more closely. For instance, most (but not all) English lawn tennis rackets have no binding around the shoulders until the start of the twentieth century. If you measured the distance between the top of the wedge piece and the very end of the handle, most nineteenth century examples are 40 cms. or more in length, whereas post 1900 models tend to be shorter. This means that earlier manufacturers made rackets where the head size was much smaller in relationship to the overall length of the racket than most twentieth century models. Most of the earlier rackets have smoother handles, which are either round or oval in cross section. Generally, rackets with leather or leatherette handles are from the late 1930s; most of the rackets with plain scored wood handles are previous to this date. The condition of a racket is not everything to a collector, but the appearance of it does help to persuade someone it is worth investing in. Very often, a racket's strings can be in a terrible condition, but the piece has some other rare and desirable detail, which makes their condition of little importance.

Fig. 4.25. **A Henry Malings Lawn Tennis Racket**[5]
A very early offset lawn tennis racket by Henry Malings, Frances St., Woolwich. Probably a mid-1870s racket, with a very small head, original stringing, and a long narrow handle. There are four rows of trebling at both the top and bottom of the head. It has a leather band around the top of the head and a small coat of arms (by royal appointment) is stamped into the convex wedge just above the maker's name. Length 65.8 cms. Width 20.3 cms. Handle 43.0 cms. £2500-£3000 ($3500-4000)

Fig. 4.26. **An Unnamed Early Lawn Tennis Racket**
An unnamed early lawn tennis racket circa 1878, with a decorated leather band around the handle piece where it meets the frame of the racket. The chamfered end to the handle is a very rare feature. Length 70.0 cms. Width 21.6 cms. Handle 42.7 cms. £1500-1750 ($2200-2600)

Fig. 4.27. **An Early Badminton Racket**
An early badminton racket (possibly from the 1870s). Although the racket has an offset head, this is purely because of the tension of the strings pulling more on one side of a weak construction than the other. It is certain that there are no known offset badminton rackets. It is strung in the conventional lawn tennis racket style and even has separate handle pieces. Length 59.8 cms. Width 16.8 cms. £100-£150 ($150-225)

Fig. 4.28. **A Very Early Badminton, or Play Racket**[6]
A very early badminton, or play, racket which may even have been used to hit a tennis ball. The frame is made entirely of cane bamboo, apart from a small concave wedge, which is made of hardwood. The strings are of natural gut with red trebling and they pass through diagonally arranged holes in the head of the racket. The frame comes together to form the handle which is held together with four small pins. Length 65.1 cms. Width 19.6 cms. £100-£150 ($150-225)

Fig. 4.29. **The 'Excelsior' Lawn Tennis Racket**
The 'Excelsior' lawn tennis racket, the retailer or manufacturer is unknown. Possibly a late 1870s frame, it is slightly offset, with original stringing. Five rows of trebling at the top of the head contrast with two at the bottom. Just three strings are broken. It has a long, round, but quite distressed handle. Length 68.3 cms. Width 22.4 cms. Handle 40.3 cms. £1000-1500 ($1500-2000)

Fig. 4.30. **A Feltham Lawn Tennis Racket** An unnamed lawn tennis racket by Feltham of London. A fine 1880s racket with distressed original stringing. A logo impressed on the wedge shows the Prince of Wales feathers a little way below this, a leather band wraps around the handle. Length 65.6 cms. Width 21.0 cms. Wt. 12.5 ozs. Handle 41.2 cms. £1500-1750 ($2250-2625)

Fig. 4.31. **A Richard Whitty Lawn Tennis Racket**
An unnamed lawn tennis racket by Richard Whitty, Tithebarn St., Liverpool. Possibly a late 1880s racket, a flat head, with the original strings, many of which are broken. It has a long handle and a convex wedge with a gold-stamped circular logo on the wedge. Length 67.5 cms. Width 22.8 cms. Handle 40.0 cms. £400-650 ($600-1000)

Fig. 4.32. **A Henry Whitty Lawn Tennis Racket**[7]
An unnamed lawn tennis racket by Henry Whitty, 15, Basnett Street, Liverpool. An 1880s flat-topped racket, probably re-strung in the early 1900s. It has a convex wedge and a very smooth handle. It's constructed from fine dark woods and along one side of the handle an owner has written his name with a fountain pen; it reads: 'M. Richard ? ? Duerry ? or Wiverry ?' Length 67.7 cms. Width 22.9 cms. Wt. 13.5 ozs. Handle 40.2 cms. £700-900 ($1000-1400)

Fig. 4.33. **The 'Old England – Brussels' Lawn Tennis Racket**[8]
The 'Old England - Brussels' lawn tennis racket by an unnamed manufacturer. An 1880s racket with stringing completely replaced. It has a very thick frame around the head and long handle, one side of which has been repaired. The butt end has been replaced. Length 67.5 cms. Width 23.4 cms. Wt. 14.0 ozs. £200-300 ($300-450)

Fig. 4.34. **An Unnamed Offset Lawn Tennis Racket**
An unnamed, slightly offset, concave wedge lawn tennis racket. It is a small racket, and this alone suggests that it may have been one of those which were supplied in a pine boxed set from about the mid-1880s. Length 65.0 cms. Width 20.2 cms. £400-500 ($600-750)

Fig. 4.35. **A Lunn & Co. Lawn Tennis Racket**[9]
An unnamed lawn tennis racket by Lunn & Co., Horncastle. An 1885 racket, with a long handle, original stringing (four broken), three rows of trebling at the top of the head and one row near to the wedge. It has a convex wedge, with the original band of leather around handle. Length 68.5 cms. Width 23.3 cms. Wt. 13.5 ozs. Handle 40.5 cms. £750-1000 ($1000-1500)

Fig. 4.36. **The 'Union' Lawn Tennis Racket**
The 'Union' lawn tennis racket, the retailer or manufacturer is unknown. An extremely rare laminated construction, possibly from the late 1880s. It has the original stringing with three rows of red trebling at the top and bottom of the head. There's a band of leather around the top of the head and it has a long thin handle. The racket is in very good condition. This racket may well be an Ayres model, as when it was found it was secured in one of their "Central" presses. Length 68.7 cms. Width 23.3 cms. Wt. 13.0 ozs. £600-800 ($900-1200)

Fig. 4.37. **A Pair of Rustic Play Rackets**
A pair of very rustic children's 'play rackets' circa 1880, constructed from a single piece of steam bent wood (possibly yew). The stringing is quite standard in design, but the verticals are about twice the gauge of the laterals. The strings feed through a single line of drilled holes in the head of the frame and the whole piece is secured together by the use of half a dozen nailed pins and three bands of material banding. The frame has clearly been stained, possibly with wood dye, as this colour has also been absorbed into the surface of the banding. These rackets could easily be up to 50 years earlier than 1880, as there is so little recorded evidence of the manufacturers. Length 61.4 cms. Width 22.0 cms. £200-300 ($300-450)

Fig. 4.38. **A Matched Pair and a Single Play Racket**
A matched pair and a single 'play racket'. These rackets are all of a similar construction – a single stick of steam bent wood forming a head at one end and a handle at the other. They are most certainly not table tennis bats, as I've seen them described before and could easily have been made prior to the 1860s. The strings, which are of a very coarse flat cross section (fibrous like flax or hemp?) are threaded through a single line of holes, which are evenly spaced around the head. However, the lateral strings are wrapped around the verticals at every junction. According to J. M. Heathcote, this style of stringing ceased (in tennis racket construction) in the early 1850s. One thing is certain, they were never used to hit a tennis ball (of any kind) and it is probable that they did propel a woollen ball or a shuttlecock. The handles are wrapped in an identical 'leatherette' type material, with a small brass stud securing a thin strip of the same material onto a pair of loose wooden pieces, which form the wedge. They do not look English and perhaps the fact that a small piece of early French news text, which has accidentally been glued to the handle of the smaller racket, supports this. Length 52.3 cms. Width 22.3 cms. £200-300 ($300-450); Smaller racket - Length 44.0 cms. Width 17.5 cms. £100-150 ($150-225)

Fig. 4.39. **A Pair of Play Rackets**
An intriguing pair of 'play rackets' constructed from a single piece of steam bent wood. Again, the question of age is a difficult one to answer. Both of them have bands of a red leatherette material, which help to support them, with securing pins through the handle. They also have pairs of holes spaced in a single row around the head. Each of them is strung with thin string. This, however, is where they differ. One of them has the vertical strings wrapped around the laterals every time they meet. The other is knotted at every junction! They are possibly from the first half of the nineteenth century, but someone could have made them the latter part of the century, a person who retained knowledge of and was sympathetic to, earlier stringing methods. Length 48.7 cms. Width 17.2 cms. £200-300 ($300-450)

Fig. 4.40. **An Early Badminton Racket**
An early badminton racket (c. 1880) from a complete set contained in a pine box. The racket is strung, as a lawn tennis racket would be (i.e., gut stringing with diagonal holes around the frame). There are no handle pieces but the leather grip is wound in an unusual manner. Length 57.5 cms. Width 17.0 cms. £150-200 ($225-300)

Fig. 4.41. **A James Lillywhite Lawn Tennis Racket**
An early lawn tennis racket (c. 1880) by Jas. Lillywhite, London, with a concave wedge and retailed by C.A. Moore of Belvedere (London). This is a very good example of a 'flat-top' racket. Although the stringing is in good condition and looks quite old, it may not be the original, as a strip of material (probably leather) has clearly been removed from around the outer edge of the racket head. The frame around the head of the racket has a bevelled edge and the handle is oval shaped in cross section. Length 69.5cms. Width 22.4cms. Handle 40.3 cms. £500-600 ($750-900)

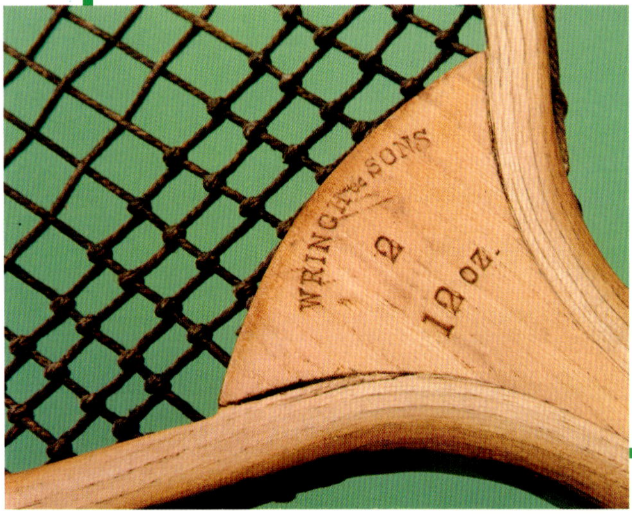

Fig. 4.42. **A Wrinch & Sons Lawn Tennis Racket**[10] The number '2' lawn tennis racket by Wrinch and Sons. An 1885 racket with a square head and constructed of light-toned woods. A rare racket which when purchased had no stringing, collar, band, or butt end. Length 67.1 cms. Width 22.0 cms. Wt. 12 ozs. Handle 41.2 cms. £300-500 ($450-750)

Fig. 4.43. **The 'Champion' Lawn Tennis Racket**
The 'Champion' lawn tennis racket by F. H. Ayres. A fine mid-1880s racket, with the original stringing and a replaced 'collar' piece around the handle. Length 68.8 cms. Width 22.7 cms. Wt. 15 ozs. £300-400 ($450-600)

Fig. 4.44. **A Williams & Co. Junior Lawn Tennis Racket**
Convex wedge lawn tennis racket by Williams & Co. 1, Rue Caumartin, Paris. This racket has the inscription 'J.O. 86' neatly written in ink near to the wedge. It has a smooth, long handle, with a copper collar where the outer handle pieces meet the frame. Length 65.2 cms. Width 19.9 cms. £200-300 ($300-450)

Fig. 4.45. **A Williams & Co. Lawn Tennis Racket**
A French convex wedge racket, with a very smooth oval handle. The original thick, natural stringing has been retained but is in fairly distressed condition. (c. 1885-90) Length 69.8 cms. Width 22.4 cms. Handle 40.3 cms. £150-200 ($225-300)

Fig. 4.46. **The 'All England' Lawn Tennis Racket**[11]
The 'All England' lawn tennis racket by Stanley Morrison & Co. An 1888 racket with a 'square head', a bevelled frame and a smooth long handle. The strings are probably not original, but this is a very rare racket. It has a band of material around the head and there is a little damage to the handle where it meets the frame. Length 67.6 cms. Width 22.2 cms. Wt. 14.5 ozs. £200-300 ($300-450)

Fig. 4.47. **'The Park' Lawn Tennis Racket**
'The Park' lawn tennis racket by Wright and Ditson, Boston. An 1885-90 racket with the original thick stringing and quite a square head. An attractive feature of the racket concerns the handle pieces which are neatly spliced into the surface of the frame where it meets the handle, rather than being glued on to the top surface. Length 68.9 cms. Width 23.2 cms. Wt. 12 ozs. £300-400 ($450-600)

Fig. 4.48. **The 'Triumph' Lawn Tennis Racket**
The 'Triumph' lawn tennis racket by Benetfink & Co., London. An 1890s convex wedge racket. The stringing is complete but of a later date, possibly the early 20th century. A previous owner has coarsely inscribed the letters 'R V' into the frame just above the handle piece. Length 68.8 cms. Width. 22.2 cms. Wt. 12.5 ozs. Handle 40.8 cms. £200-300 ($300-450)

Fig. 4.49. **The 'Prince of Wales' Lawn Tennis Racket**
The 'Prince of Wales' lawn tennis racket by Feltham. An 1890s convex wedge racket, with perfect original stringing. Length 69.4cms. Width 22.4cms. Wt. 13 ozs. Handle 40.9 cms. £400-500 ($600-750)

Fig. 4.50. **The 'Pastime' Lawn Tennis Racket**
The 'Pastime' lawn tennis racket (no information on the maker or retailer). An 1890s racket, probably named after the Victorian gentleman's sporting newspaper of the time, which ceased publication in 1895. Original stringing, but twelve verticals are broken along the top of the frame. There are five rows of red trebling at the top of the frame and near to the wedge. Length 69.0 cms. Width 22.8 cms. Wt. 13.5 ozs. £200-300 ($300-450)

Fig. 4.51. **A Clapshaw and Cleave Lawn Tennis Racket** An unnamed lawn tennis racket by Clapshaw & Cleave (Late Hawcridge). An 1890s flat-topped racket, possibly with the original strings, of which three lateral strings are broken. It has three rows of trebling at the wedge and two rows at the top. Length 68.5 cms. Width 22.3 cms. Wt. 13.5 ozs. £300-400 ($450-600)

Fig. 4.52. **The 'Premier' Lawn Tennis Racket** The 'Premier' lawn tennis racket by Murton of Newcastle. An 1890s racket, which was probably re-strung in the early nineteen hundreds. It has double-centre mains strings, natural verticals and red laterals, two vertical strings are broken. It is complete with a laminated convex wedge construction. Length 68.0 cms. Width 22.0 cms. £250-350 ($375-525)

Fig. 4.53. **A F. J. Bancroft Lawn Tennis Racket** An early Bancroft racket, with an almost perfect transfer situated on the wedge of the racket. The original thick gut stringing is perfect (c. 1895). Length 68.9 cms. Width 23.5 cms. £150-200 ($225-300)

Fig. 4.54. **The 'Handicap' Lawn Tennis Racket**
The 'Handicap' lawn tennis racket. An 1890s convex wedge racket. Although this frame is unnamed, this is almost certainly an 'F. H. Ayres' racket. It looks very much as if this is the original stringing. Length 70.2cms. Width 21.4cms. Wt. 12 ozs. Handle 40.2 cms. £200-300 ($300-450)

An F. H. Ayres Lawn Tennis Racket
An unnamed lawn tennis racket by F. H. Ayres. An 1890s racket with a large head, which has certain features of a square-headed racket as well as a flat-topped one too. The trebling and strings are perfect and a small piece of leather on the very end of the handle shows the Ayres' logo. Length 69.0 cms. Width 23.5 cms. Wt. 14 ozs. Handle 40.2 cms. £200-300 ($300-450)

Fig. 4.55. **An Unnamed Lawn Tennis Racket**
An unnamed 1890s lawn tennis racket, probably French, with the letters 'Jo' inscribed by hand into the wedge. It has a long thin handle with a wax seal on the butt end. The seal shows a knight's helmet situated over a shield, in which the sun's rays pass behind a central band. On the band are the letters T T T. It still has the original thick strings but nine or ten of them are broken near the edge of the frame. Length 69.4 cms. Width 22.8 cms. Wt. 14.5 ozs. Handle 40.2 cms. £200-300 ($300-450)

Fig. 4.56. **The 'Smart' Lawn Tennis Racket**
A late 1890s racket, with a scalloped convex wedge. On the reverse of the wedge there's an attractive silver monogram formed from the letters 'Y' and 'C'. It could be the original stringing but 12 vertical strings are broken where they meet the top of the frame. Below the 'Smart' logo stands a proud cockerel, possibly the company's adopted symbol. Length 69.7 cms. Width 21.9 cms. Wt. 12.5 ozs. £250-350 ($375-525)

Fig. 4.57. **The 'Marvel' Lawn Tennis Racket**
The 'Marvel' lawn tennis racket by Thomas Wallis and Co. Ltd., Holborn Circus, London. An 1890s racket with a long handle and a noticeably round head. It is the original stringing, but all of the verticals are broken next to the convex wedge. There are three rows of trebling at the top of the head and two rows at the base. Length 70.5 cms. Width 22.9 cms. Wt. 13.5 ozs. Handle 42.0 cms. £250-350 ($375-525)

Fig. 4.58. **A Pair of 'Academy' Lawn Tennis Rackets**
A fine pair of 'Academy' lawn tennis rackets by S. H. Co. These fine 1890s rackets are almost certainly American, and retain the original stringing. Length 67.0 cms. Width 21.5 cms. £400-500 ($600-750)

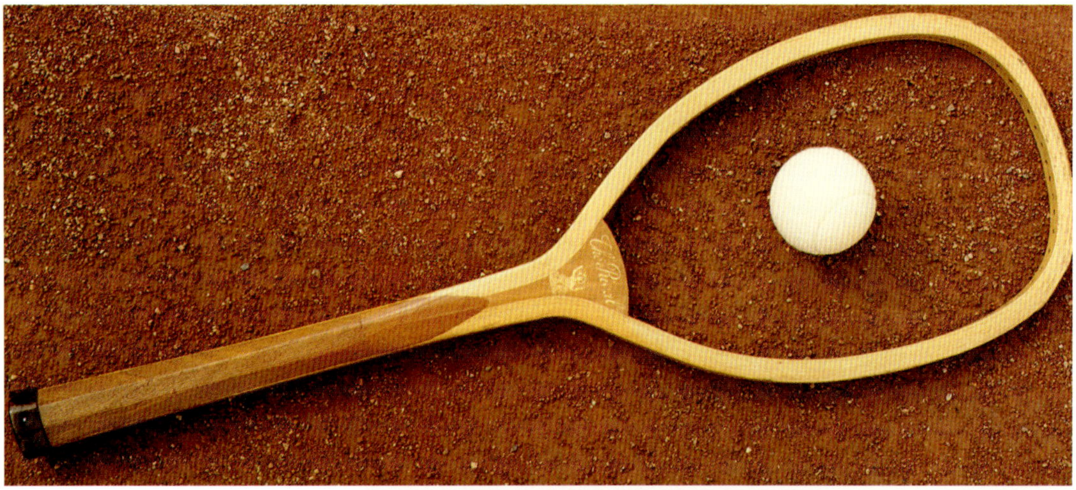

Fig. 4.59. **The 'Rival' Lawn Tennis Racket**
The 'Rival' lawn tennis racket, possibly by Thomas Elvery. From the early 1890s, it once had a band of material, possibly leather, around the top of the head. Length 69.7 cms. Width 21.9 cms. Wt. 12.0 ozs. Handle 40.1 cms. £150-200 ($225-300)

Fig. 4.60. **The 'Eventail' Swallow Tail Lawn Tennis Racket**
The 'Eventail' lawn tennis racket, but the manufacturer is unknown. An 1890s swallow-tailed convex wedge racket, and the racket is slightly offset. With a long handle, twelve original strings are broken. Length 70.5 cms. Width 22.5 cms. Wt. 13.5 ozs. Handle 40.3cms. £175-200 ($275-300)

Fig. 4.61. **The 'All England' Lawn Tennis Racket**[12]
The 'All England' lawn tennis racket by H. Hutton of Durham. An 1890s racket, with a round head and a rare spliced feature in the handle which extends from the butt end right up to the convex wedge. It has the original stringing with three rows of trebling at both the top and bottom of the head. Two vertical strings are broken. Length 68.7 cms. Width 22.8 cms. Wt. 12.5 ozs. £175-200 ($275-300)

Fig. 4.62. **The 'Oxonian' Lawn Tennis Racket**
The 'Oxonian' lawn tennis racket by Geo. G. Bussey & Co. A 1894 racket with original strings, many of which are broken, but this does not defer from the racket's appearance. It has a long handle and the remains of a band around the head of the racket. The letters 'E H' are neatly carved into the centre of the wedge on the reverse side. Length 69.2 cms. Width 22.0 cms. Wt. 12.5 ozs. Handle 40.0 cms. £150-200 ($225-300)

Fig. 4.63. **The 'La Belle' Lawn Tennis Racket**
The 'La Belle' lawn tennis racket, circa 1895, the manufacturer and retailer is unknown. A fine model made from contrasting coloured woods. Length 69.2 cms. Width 22.0 cms. Wt. 12.5 ozs. Handle 40.3 cms. £150-200 ($225-300)

Fig. 4.64. **A Pair of Parkins & Gotto Lawn Tennis Rackets**
A pair of 'Parkins & Gotto' lawn tennis rackets, circa 1895, one flat top, the other more elongated in shape. Length 69.2 cms. Width 22.0 cms. Wt. 12.5 ozs. Handle 40.3 cms. (Length 70.3 cms. Width 21.4 cms. Wt. 13.0 ozs. Handle 39.9 cms.) £300-400 ($450-600)

Fig. 4.65. **'The Club' Lawn Tennis Racket**
'The Club', convex wedge lawn tennis racket by Geo. Halsey, Enfield, North London. Stamped into the wedge, a circular motto proclaims that this company was awarded the 1st Prize Medal and Diploma at the Scarborough exhibition of 1896. Length 67.0 cms. Width 21.7 cms. Wt. 11.0 ozs. £150-200 ($225-300)

Fig. 4.66. **'The Scorer' Fishtail Lawn Tennis Racket**
'The Scorer' lawn tennis racket by Wanless & Co. of South Shields. An early English fishtail racket without any binding around the shoulders, which is a fairly good sign that an English racket may be pre-1900. Length 68 cms. Width 22.0 cms. Wt. 13 ozs. £175-250 ($265-375)

Fig. 4.67. **'The Demon' Fishtail Lawn Tennis Rackets**
'The Demon' fishtail lawn tennis rackets by Slazenger, retailed by R.H. & J. Pearson, Eastbourne Ltd. One racket is probably from the mid-1890s while the other, with the darker wedge piece, is from around 1900. Length 69.0 cms. Width 22.0 cms. Wt. 14 ozs. £200-300 ($300-450)

Fig. 4.68. **An Unnamed Square Fantail Lawn Tennis Racket**
A fine mid-1890s unnamed lawn tennis racket with the image of a 'poised cobra' stamped onto the wedge. This is obviously a 'theme' racket, as the handle is worked so as to produce a coiled grip where one would hold the racket. The handle then extends outwards to form a kind of octagonal 'swallow-tail' effect at the end of the racket. Length 70 cms. Width 21.9 cms. Wt. 13 ozs. £750-1000 ($1000-1500)

Fig. 4.69. **'The Diamond 1' Fishtail Lawn Tennis Racket**
'The Diamond 1' lawn tennis racket, retailed by the L B R Co. (Leyland & Birmingham ? Co. Ltd.). An unusually early 1890s 'fishtail' racket with an equally rare open grooved handle. This racket is absolutely typical of the style and finish provided by Bussey's factory in Peckham, London. Although the stringing is missing, the mesh would have been quite tight, as there are no less than 86 stringing holes around the head of the frame! It has four handle pieces and it is a theory that the racket may well have been strung in a diagonal pattern, hence the name. Length 69.2 cms. Width 22.3 cms. Wt. 14 ozs. £150-200 ($225-300)

Fig. 4.70. **'The Tournament 2' Fishtail Lawn Tennis Racket**
'The Tournament 2' lawn tennis racket by Geo. G. Bussey & Co. A fine 1890s fishtail racket. Length 68.5 cms. Width 23.1 cms. Wt. 13.5 ozs. Handle 40.0 cms. £150-225 ($225-350)

Fig. 4.71. The **'Expert' Lawn Tennis Racket**
The 'Expert' lawn tennis racket by an unnamed manufacturer. This racket, from the late 1890s, has an early laminated frame (the second and inside layer is probably cork) which extends from about four inches above either side of the wedge, down and under each of the handle pieces. The wedge is laminated and the handle is 'waisted' towards the butt end. Length 68.6 cms. Width 23.4 cms. £150-200 ($225-300)

Fig. 4.72. **An Unnamed Fishtail Lawn Tennis Racket**
A fine 1890s fishtail lawn tennis racket with quite a pronounced flat top. The racket has the owner's initials (A I R) inscribed into the wedge. The fishtail effect is very deep and severe. Length 68.0 cms. Width 21.8 cms. Wt. 12 ozs. £150-200 ($225-300)

Fig. 4.73. **The 'E. G. M. Special' Lawn Tennis Racket**
The 'E. G. M. Special' lawn tennis racket from Slazengers, Laurence Pountney Hill, London. A classic racket, circa 1895, which was endorsed by E. G. Meers, a prominent player of the day. Length 70.8 cms. Width 21.0 cms. Wt. 14.5 ozs. £175-250 ($275-375)

Fig. 4.74. **An Unnamed Badminton Racket**
An unnamed badminton racket circa 1900. Length 68.8 cms. Width 20.7 cms. £100-150 ($150-225)

Fig. 4.75. **The 'Paris Special' Fishtail Lawn Tennis Racket**
The 'Paris Special' lawn tennis racket by William Sykes Ltd., Horbury & London. A 1900 fishtail racket with natural verticals and red lateral strings. Two central vertical strings have been replaced while one other remains broken. It has a convex wedge, with two rows of trebling at both the top and base of the frame. Length 69.5 cms. Width 22.0 cms. Wt. 13.5 ozs. £175-250 ($275-375)

Fig. 4.76. **The 'Gold Medal HD Model' Lawn Tennis Racket**
The 'Gold Medal HD Model' lawn tennis racket by A.G. Spalding & Bros., Deodar Road, Putney. A 1905 period racket with a convex wedge. It has the original stringing of white verticals and red laterals. With an attractive transferred logo on the wedge and 'Patent No. 4885 27th Feb. 1904' impressed a little way below it. (This refers to the wedge construction and not the racket design.) It is complete with binding at the shoulders. Length 68.4 cms. Width 22.3 cms. Wt. 14.0 ozs. £200-250 ($300-375)

Fig. 4.77. **The 'Double Main 2' Lawn Tennis Racket**
The 'Double Main 2' lawn tennis racket from G. G. B. (Bussey). A fine racket (c. 1905) which was retailed by Croisdale of Leeds. Do not be misled by the apparent 'flat-top' shape to the head. I believe that these are the original strings, which over time have pulled inwards the top of the racket. On the inside edge of the top of the frame the wood is split a little and the strings have begun to pull through. Length 67.8 cms. Width 21.0 cms. Wt. 14.5 ozs. £175-200 ($225-300)

Fig. 4.78. **'The Fantail 3' Lawn Tennis Racket**
'The Fantail 3' lawn tennis racket circa 1905 by G. G. B. & Co. (Bussey), London. Length 68.3 cms Width 23.5 cms. Wt. 13.0 ozs. £150-200 ($225-300)

Fig. 4.79. **The 'Popular' Lawn Tennis Racket**
The 'Popular' lawn tennis racket, by John Wisden & Co. Ltd., London. An early 20th century convex wedge racket with four sets of double mains strings. Length 67.8 cms. Width 22.2 cms. Wt. 14.0 ozs. £125-150 ($200-225)

Fig. 4.80. **The 'Empire Special' Lawn Tennis Racket**
The 'Empire Special' lawn tennis racket by Sykes Horbury & London. A (c. 1906) racket with bound shoulders and an especially long head. It has the original perfect stringing of natural verticals and red laterals. An attractive logo is impressed in gold on the reverse of the wedge. Length 70.1 cms. Width 21.5 cms. Wt. 14.0 ozs. £200-300 ($300-450)

Fig. 4.81. **The 'Special Club' Lawn Tennis Racket**
The 'Special Club' lawn tennis racket, by Benetfink & Co. Ltd., Cheapside, E. C., London. A fine convex wedge racket, circa 1910, with wonderful feather grained handle pieces. Length 68.5 cms. Width 22.2 cms. Wt. 13 1/2 ozs. £175-250 ($225-375)

Fig. 4.82. **The 'Challenge' Fishtail Lawn Tennis Racket**
'The Challenge' fishtail lawn tennis racket from Slazengers. A good convex wedge racket, circa 1910, which looks as if it was played with once, the strings were broken, and it was never played with again. Length 69.2 cms. Width 22.0 cms. Wt. 14 ozs. Handle 38.8 cms. £175-250 ($225-375)

Fig. 4.83. **The 'Favorite' Junior Lawn Tennis Racket**
The 'Favorite' junior lawn tennis racket, circa 1910. Length 57.5 cms. Width 20.2 cms. £150-200 ($225-300)

The 'Nobby' Junior
The 'Nobby' Junior lawn tennis racket, with double centre mains strings, and made in England by 'APEX'. (c. 1930) Length 57.2 cms. Width 20.5 cms. £100-150 ($150-200)

Fig. 4.84. **The 'College' Junior Lawn Tennis Racket**
The 'College' junior lawn tennis racket, the manufacturer is unknown. From about 1910, the racket head has been completely wrapped in string, presumably to protect it. Length 64.3 cms. Width 20.5 cms. £150-200 ($225-300)

Fig. 4.85. **'The Young' Junior Lawn Tennis Racket**
'The Young' lawn tennis racket, unknown manufacturer (A & B monogram). A junior racket, which may date anywhere between 1890 and 1910. The former owner has inscribed (by burning with a hot implement) his or her name into the handle, it reads: 'L . E. Richault'. Good junior rackets are very difficult to find and this is in fine condition. Length 66.6 cms. Width 21.3 cms. Wt. 11.5 ozs. £200-300 ($300-450)

Fig. 4.86. **The 'Marvel' Fishtail**
The 'Marvel' fishtail lawn tennis racket retailed by Johnson, Burton, and Theobald of Norwich. This is a fine early 20th century racket with the original thick gauge strings. Length 68.2 cms. Width 22.3 cms. Wt. 13.5 ozs. £175-250 ($225-375)

Fig. 4.87. **An Unnamed Racket**
An unnamed convex wedge lawn tennis racket from around 1910. The racket is in superb condition with double centre mains stringing. Length 68.8 cms. Width 21.7 cms. Wt. 13 ozs. £125-150 ($200-250)

Fig. 4.88. **The 'Bedford' Badminton Racket**
The 'Bedford' badminton racket from The M. C. C. Bat Works Ltd., Bedford. A racket from around 1910, with eight pairs of double mains strings. Length 66.4 cms. Width 21.4cms. £75-100 ($100-150)

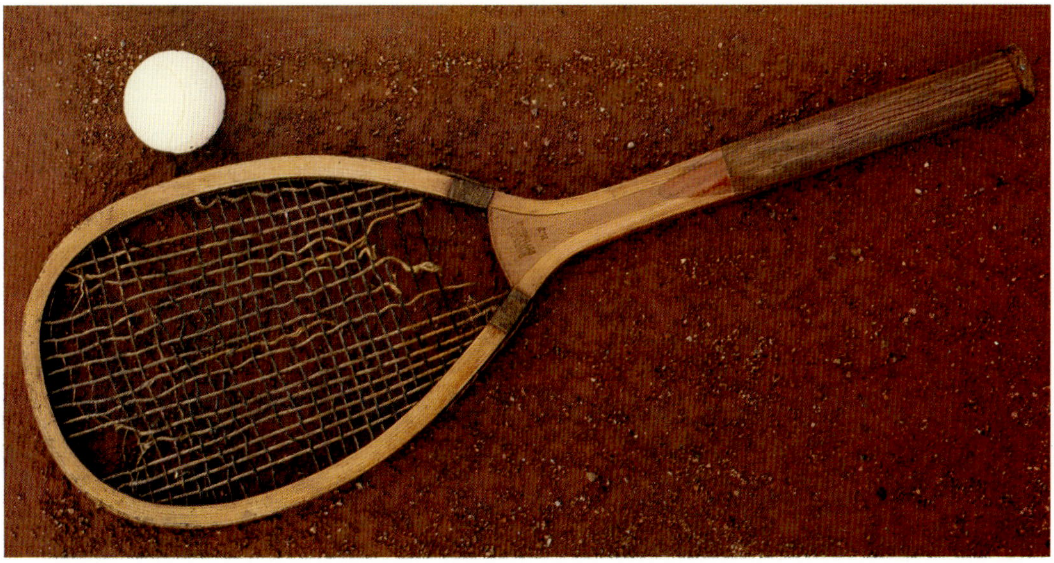

Fig. 4.89. **A Gibbs & Co. Racket**
An unnamed lawn tennis racket retailed by Gibbs & Co., Burton St., Nottingham. A convex wedge racket (c. 1910) with extremely thick, original stringing. The monogram 'E. F.' is stamped into both sides of the wedge. Length 70 cms. Width 22.5 cms. Wt. 12 ozs. £150-200 ($225-300)

Fig. 4.90. **The 'Special Club'**
A 'Special Club' lawn tennis racket retailed by Clouard, Lille. Probably an early 1920s convex wedge racket, but in prime condition and with its original stringing. Length 69.8 cms. Width 22.0 cms. Wt. 14 ozs. £150-200 ($225-300)

Fig. 4.91. **'The Wimbledon'**
'The Wimbledon' lawn tennis racket, the maker is unknown. Original stringing and in fine condition. (c. 1920) Length 68.3 cms. Width 23.7 cms. Wt. 13.5 ozs. £125-175 ($200-250)

Fig. 4.92. **The 'Double Main 5'**
The 'Double Main 5' lawn tennis racket by G. G. Bussey & Co., London. A 1920s racket with the classic Bussey's 'wave' wedge. It has natural verticals, red laterals, two rows of black trebling at the wedge, while there are four rows at the top. An attractive logo is impressed into the wedge. With red cord binding at the shoulders, the manufacturer filled the string-holes around the top of the racket head. A fine racket. Length 68.3 cms. Width 22.9 cms. Wt. 14.0 ozs. £200-300 ($300-450)

Fig. 4.93. **The 'Super Crasmith'**
The 'Super Crasmith' lawn tennis racket by Craske & Smith, The Sports Specialists, Grimsby. A late 1920s racket with double stringing all through the racket head. The frame is laminated and supported by coloured bindings around the shoulders. There is no grip on the handle. Length 68.6 cms. Width 22.8 cms. Wt. 13.0 ozs. £200-300 ($300-450)

Fig. 4.94. **The 'Driva'**
The 'Driva' lawn tennis racket by Williams & Co., 1 Rue Caumartin, Paris. A very clean early 1920s racket bound in white tape at the shoulders. It has natural verticals and red horizontals, many of which are broken. Length 68.3 cms. Width 23.1 cms. Wt. 13.5 ozs. £125-150 ($200-250)

Fig. 4.95. **The 'Excelsior'**
The 'Excelsior' lawn tennis racket, but the retailer or manufacturer is unknown. A 1920s swallow tail convex wedge racket with an unusually long head. It has natural verticals (of which twelve are broken) and green laterals. There is a slight split to the frame along the top edge. Length 70.6 cms. Width 20.5 cms. Wt. 13.5 ozs. £175-250 ($250-375)

Fig. 4.96. **The 'P.B.C. Diadex Special'** The 'P.B.C. Diadex Special' lawn tennis racket, the maker is unknown, but probably this refers to P. B. Cow Ltd. A late 1920s racket with rare diagonal stringing in both black and natural gut. The frame is bound in black cord around the shoulders with 'PP 21162/3' stamped into the top of the frame. Length 67.7 cms. Width 23.5 cms. Wt. 14.0 ozs. £175-250 ($250-375)

Fig. 4.97. **The 'Birmal'** The 'Birmal' all-metal lawn tennis racket by the Birmingham Aluminium Casting (1903) Co. Ltd. A 1923-aluminium racket with wire strings, all of them are intact. In a rare 'Alrak' press. Length 67.8 cms. Width 21.3 cms. Wt. 13.5 ozs. £300-400 ($450-600)

Fig. 4.98. **The 'Argyle'**
The 'Argyle' lawn tennis racket by Stuart Surridge & Co., London. (c. 1925) It has a special feature, which originally depended upon a hoop of steel wire around which the strings on the outside of the frame were threaded. However, this model has a wooden ridge in place of the piece of wire and it could be that this was a further development on the original design concept. Length 68.8 cms. Width 23.0 cms. £100-150 ($150-225)

Fig. 4.99. **An Unnamed Racket**
An unnamed, metal-headed lawn tennis racket from around 1930. The handle is wooden and the racket is strung in thick black gut. Red cord bindings support the frame in various places. Length 68.8 cms. Width 22.9 cms. £200-300 ($300-450)

Fig. 4.100. **The 'National' Fishtail**
The 'National' fishtail lawn tennis racket (c. 1925) by C. J. Withnall and Sons Ltd., Sports Depot. Length 68.1 cms. Width 22.8 cms. Wt. 13.0 ozs. £150-175 ($225-250)

Fig. 4.101. **The 'Rival'**
The 'Rival' Extra Light lawn tennis racket by G. G. B. & Co., London (Bussey). A 1920s racket constructed from light toned woods, which around the wedge piece, neatly contrast with a thin laminate of dark hardwood. The head has a bevelled frame. Length 69.2 cms. Width 23.4 cms. Wt. 13 ozs. £150-200 ($225-275)

Fig. 4.102. **The 'Spalding Metalite'**
A 'Spalding Metalite' lawn tennis racket. This is another fine example from the late 1920s of a fairly successful experiment which combined different materials to form a lawn tennis racket. It has the strength of a metal racket head, with the comfort of a wooden handle. This model has the notification of a patent (probably applied for) on May 4th 1926 and "Patented" February 22nd 1927, stamped onto the handle. Length 68.6cms. Width 22.5cms. £200-300 ($300-450)

Fig. 4.103. **A Miniature Spalding Racket**
A miniature lawn tennis racket by Spalding. A mid-1920s salesman's sample or (more likely) a souvenir gift. This miniature is strung in an identical manner to a full size racket with natural verticals strings, green laterals, and red trebling. The holes through the head of the frame, through which the strings are threaded, are arranged diagonally and the strings are finished off in the traditional way. There are also two handle pieces and a band of leather neatly finishes off the handle. The Spalding logo is found on the very end of the handle. Length 29.0 cms. Width 8.9 cms. £150-200 ($225-300)

Fig. 4.104. **The 'S.N.D.'**
An 'S. N. D.' (named after Stanley Doust) lawn tennis racket from A. W. Gamage Ltd., London. A mid-1920s concave wedge racket. It has an unusual additional piece of wood, which traces the inner curve of the head. (for about 10 cms. either side of the wedge) onto the head of the racket. Length 68.3 cms. Width 22.3 cms. Wt. 13.0 ozs. £125-175 ($200-250)

Fig. 4.105. **The 'Excelsis' Fishtail**
The 'Excelsis' lawn tennis racket by Collard of Grantham. A fine fishtail racket from the early 1920s. Length 67.0 cms. Width 23.0 cms. Wt. 13.0 ozs. £150-200 ($225-300)

Fig. 4.106. **The 'Demon Driver 1'**
The 'Demon Driver 1' (extra light) lawn tennis racket from G. G. Bussey. A mid-1920s racket, which became the firm's premier model. The main features are a bevelled head frame, multiple lines of trebling, the characteristic 'convex wave' shaped wedge, 4 handle pieces, and a handle with cork strips let into the surface. ('Bussey's Tensive Grip') Length 68.4 cms. Width 23.4 cms. Wt. 13.5 ozs. £300-400 ($450-600)

The 'Olympic 1'
The 'Olympic 1' lawn tennis racket from G. G. Bussey. Quite an unusual, slightly flat-topped mid-1920s model, with a large amount of binding around the shoulders and a laminated construction around the wedge which allows for a thin insert of hardwood. This racket also has the 'Tensive Grip' handle. Length 69.3 cms. Width 22.3 cms. Wt. 14.5 ozs. £150-200 ($225-300)

Fig. 4.107. **The 'Wimbledon Hexagon 1'**
The 'Wimbledon Hexagon 1' (light) lawn tennis racket from Bussey. A superbly constructed racket from the mid-1920s, again boasting Bussey's 'Tensive Grip' feature. Length 69.4 cms. Width 22.5 cms. Wt. 14 ozs. £150-200 ($225-300)

Fig. 4.108. **'The Tournament 3' Ball-Tail**
'The Tournament 3' Extra Light lawn tennis racket by G. G. B. & Co. (George Gibson Bussey), Peckham, London. A fine example of a 'ball-tail' racket from the mid-1920s. The racket also has the 'concave wave' wedge design so synonymous with the high-class workmanship of Bussey's employees. As far as I know, other than Bussey, no other manufacturer of lawn tennis rackets has ever produced a model with this ball end feature. Length 68.5 cms. Width 22.7 cms. Wt. 13 ozs. £500-700 ($750-1000)

Fig. 4.109. **A Dayton Racket**
Dayton, Ohio, lawn tennis racket. With a wooden handle, steel head, and strings, circa 1927. Length 67.8 cms. Width 22.2 cms. £100-150 ($150-200)

Fig. 4.110. **The 'Doherty'**
The 'Doherty' lawn tennis racket with 'Slazengers Patent Stringing'. From around 1928, this racket continues the long tradition of using famous player's names to sell products. Even 20 years after their zenith, the legendary brother's name would certainly have not have diminished in its attraction. Length 69.2 cms. Width 22.5 cms. Wt. 14 ozs. £100-150 ($150-225)

Fig. 4.111. **The 'Integral Superflex'**
The 'Integral Superflex' lawn tennis racket by Clement Freres, France. A late 1920s racket with an unusual handle construction which, when the racket is turned sideways, shows that a gap of about one millimetre is retained for about six inches of its length (In all probability, this feature had some connection with its name.) Length 69.0 cms. Width 22.2 cms. Wt. 13 ozs. £100-150 ($150-225)

Fig. 4.112. **The 'Club'**
The 'Club' lawn tennis racket from the late 1920s. The manufacturer is unknown, but this is a very fine example, with original stringing. Length 68.4 cms. Width 23.0 cms. Wt. 12 ozs. £150-175 ($225-250)

Fig. 4.113. **The 'Sport'**
The 'Sport' lawn tennis racket by Sugg of Sheffield, Hull, and Nottingham. A late 1920s racket with a most unusual, multi-layered laminated construction. Fine condition. Length 68.2 cms. Width 23.3 cms. Wt. 12 1/2 ozs. £175-200 ($250-300)

Fig. 4.114. **The 'Match' Fishtail**
The 'Match' fishtail lawn tennis racket, from the late 1920s. A distinctive racket because of the later styled concave wedge and the light coloured woods that were used to construct the whole frame. Length 69.0 cms. Width 23.2 cms. Wt. 13 ozs. £150-200 ($225-300)

Fig. 4.115. **The 'Unique'**
The 'Unique' lawn tennis racket, from the mid-1920s. Retailed by W. H. Johnson, Sports Outfitters of Northampton, this is a superb example of a racket with quite an unusual stringing feature. The strings are perfect and original, with three pairs of vertical main strings, the centre pair actually cross over each other. Length 69.3 cms. Width 22.7 cms. Wt. 13 ozs. £150-200 ($225-300)

Fig. 4.116. **The 'Eland Moth'**
The 'Eland Moth' lawn tennis racket by Lugard & Pulham of Wembley. A racket from the mid-1930s which is in very good condition. Length 68.7 cms. Width 23.1 cms. Wt. 12 ozs. £100-125 ($150-200)

Fig. 4.117. **The 'Gold Medal Ruby'**
'Gold Medal Ruby' Improved (Patent No. 19150), lawn tennis racket by Jefferies and retailed by Stockwin & Co., Birmingham. An unusual early 1930s racket, in that it has two strips of suede material glued on top of the handle pieces. Length 69.0 cms. Width 22.2 cms. Wt. 13.5 ozs. £150-200 ($225-300)

Fig. 4.118. **The 'Wilding'**
The 'Wilding' lawn tennis racket by C. L. Godfrey, Pawtucket, R. I. It has a rare stringing combination of six pairs of vertical strings and five pairs of lateral strings. (c. 1930) Length 68.8 cms. Width 23.1 cms. £200-300 ($300-450)

Fig. 4.119. **'The Stathmore'**
'The Stathmore' lawn tennis racket, manufacturer unknown. A fine example of a circa 1930 racket with two pairs of double mains strings. It has green and natural strings, which are matched with green trebling and bindings. Length 69.0 cms. Width 22.4 cms. Wt. 12.5 ozs. £125-175 ($200-250)

Fig. 4.120. **The 'Streamline Blue Star'**
The 'Streamline Blue Star' lawn tennis racket by Hazell Sports Goods Manufacturers, London. A typical 1930s triple-strut design with eight broken strings. The frame condition is good. Length 68.9 cms. Width 23.3 cms. Wt. 13 ozs. £300-400 ($450-600)

The 'Streamline Red Star'
The 'Streamline Red Star' lawn tennis racket by Hazell Sports Goods Manufacturers, London. A typical 1930s triple-strut design with two broken strings. The frame is in good condition. Length 68.9 cms. Width 23.3 cms. Wt. 13 ozs. £300-400 ($450-600)

Fig. 4.121. **The 'Streamline Blue Star' Badminton Racket**
The 'Streamline Blue Star' Badminton Racket. Based upon the design of its larger tennis cousin, on this model the side struts meet the centre strut nearly half way to the head, instead of next to the handle. It is very difficult to find in good condition, and an even rarer squash racket does exist…somewhere! Length 65.8 cms. Width 20.6 cms. £300-400 ($450-600)

Fig. 4.122. **A Gray's Racquets Racket**
A Gray's Racquets racket from the 1930s. "Strung by R. G. Lay" (or Lang) of Radley College. Length 76.3 cms. Width 19.4 cms. £100-150 ($150-225)

Fig. 4.123. **A Gray's Real Tennis Racket**
A mid-1930s real/royal tennis racket by Gray's of Cambridge. With the distinctive offset design and square section handle. Length 67.8 cms. Width 18.8 cms. £100-150 ($150-225)

Fig. 4.124. **The 'Top-flite'**
The 'Top-flite' (Standard Model) lawn tennis racket by Spalding. A mid-1930s racket, with a characteristic 'open-wedge' design. There is evidence for a lamination technique in the construction of the head of the racket but the stringing is not original. It would have had trebling in a colour which was sympathetic to the ornamental bindings around the frame. Length 68.5 cms. Width 23.0 cms. Wt. 13 ozs. £100-150 ($150-225)

Fig. 4.125. **The 'Dimid' Badminton Racket**
The 'Dimid' badminton racket from Muller, The Strand, London. A racket from the mid-1930s with unusual diagonal stringing which includes 4 double strings too. Length 66.1 cms. Width 19.8 cms. £100-150 ($150-225)

Fig. 4.126. **The'Wisdens Cosmos'**
'Wisdens Cosmos' lawn tennis racket by John Wisden & Co. Ltd., London. A 1930s racket, using a laminated construction method. Length 68.2 cms. Width 22.8 cms. Wt. 13 ozs. £75-100 ($100-150)

Fig. 4.127. **The 'Maxply Dunlop'**
The classic 'Maxply Dunlop' Tournament Model lawn tennis racket retailed by Murton's of Newcastle and Sunderland. A mid-1930s racket which continued to be produced right up until the 1980s. This design set the standard for so many manufacturers to follow. Length 69.1 cms Width 22.4 cms. Wt. 13 ozs. £100-150 ($150-225)

Fig. 4.128. **A Children's Play Racket**
A children's play racket, which by evidence of its laminated construction would probably be from the 1930s. The strings are of gut, but due to their wide spacing and thin gauge, it's very unlikely that it was used to hit a tennis ball. More likely, children played with a shuttlecock, a woollen ball, or most probably a plastic one. The strings are threaded through holes in the head of the frame which are drilled in a single line, not the conventional diagonal arrangement. A specific detail consistent with a 'play racket' is that often there are no handle pieces on either side of the frame. Length 58.0 cms. Width 19.0 cms. £100-150 ($150-225)

Fig. 4.129. **A Pair of 'Victory' Rackets**
A pair of 'Victory' lawn tennis rackets from Slazengers Ltd. (c. 1937) This model, with shoulders bound in white, was retailed by R. G. Pilch Ltd., of Norwich. (This is a descendant of Fuller Pilch, who from the early 1830s was one of England's premier professional cricketers.) The other model was 'Specially selected for Harrods Ltd., London.' Length 68.5 cms. Width 22.4 cms. Wt. 13. ozs. £200-300 ($300-450)

Fig. 4.130. **The 'Victory Sport' Badminton Racket**
The 'Victory' badminton racket from the 1930s. An unnamed manufacturer but with a very typical Art Deco design logo and laminated construction. It is contained in its original press and canvas bag, which has a special pocket in which to place a tube of shuttlecocks. Length 66.7 cms. Width 19.2 cms. £75-100 ($100-150)

Fig. 4.131. **The 'Davis Cup – Model C'**
The 'Davis Cup – Model C' lawn tennis racket by F. H. Ayres. A racket which was probably manufactured during the late 1930s when Great Britain was so successful in the competition. Length 68.7 cms. Width 22.6 cms. £75-100 ($100-150)

Fig. 4.132. **The 'Silver Fox' (Club)**
The 'Silver Fox' (Club) lawn tennis racket by Samuel Fox & Co. Ltd. c. 1950. This racket has a stainless steel head combined with a wooden handle and a patent number 522222. Length 69.0 cms. Width 21.4 cms. £75-150 ($100-225)

Fig. 4.133. **The 'Jet'**
The 'Jet' lawn tennis racket by T. A. Davis. This racket was manufactured between the years 1952 and 1962. Earlier models, such as this one, were strung diagonally. Schreiber and Jones retailed the racket. Length 68.6 cms. Width 23.2 cms. £150-200 ($225-300)

Fig. 4.134. **The 'College Model'**
The 'College Model' lawn tennis racket from Slazengers, retailed by Jackson Young Ltd., Kidderminster. A very clean 1950s racket with a suede grip. Length 68.8 cms. Width 22.2 cms. Wt. 'Light'. £75-100 ($100-150)

Fig. 4.135. **The 'Vanguard'**
The 'Vanguard' lawn tennis racket, manufacturer unknown. From around the mid-1950s, the racket has a distinctive raised centre surface to the shaft which leads to the grip. Transfers proclaim that it has a "laminated frame" and a "handbuilt reinforced shaft". Length 68.8 cms. Width 22.4 cms. £75-100 ($100-150)

The 'Cosmos'
The 'Cosmos' High Velocity Model lawn tennis racket by Wisden. A 1950s racket retailed by Wilkinson's Sports Depot, Penrith. A laminated construction. Length 69.00 cms Width 22.7 cms. Wt. 12.5 ozs. £75-100 ($100-150)

Fig. 4.137. **The 'Pioneer'**
The 'Pioneer' lawn tennis racket from Dunlop. This is a racket from 1954 with a laminated frame. A fine example, with all strings and colour matched trebling intact. Length 68.6 cms. Width 23.3cms. £75-100 ($100-150)

The 'Corinthian'
The 'Corinthian' lawn tennis racket from Robert J. Nash, Racket Maker, Birmingham. Probably a mid-1950s racket with an unusual square cross-section. This probably accounts for three patent numbers, which are applied by transfer to the frame. Length 67.8 cms. Width 22.8 cms. Wt. 13 ozs. £75-100 ($100-150)

Fig. 4.136. **The 'Wimbledon'**
The 'Wimbledon' lawn tennis racket by Slazengers, retailed by Redmayne & Todd Ltd., Nottingham. (c. 1955) Length 68.5 cms. Width 22.8 cms. Wt. 12.5 ozs. £75-100 ($100-150)

Fig. 4.138. **A pair of 'P. M.' Rackets**
A pair of 'P.M.' lawn tennis rackets by Slazengers. This racket from 1960 was preceded by two other versions in 1937 and 1950. It was specially made '…in consultation with World Champion Fred Perry and L.T.A. Training Manager Dan Maskell.' Applied transfers guide the player as to which are the 'FORE-HAND AND SERVICE FACE' and the 'BACKHAND FACE'. You are then advised to be: 'READY! ON YOUR TOES, GET IN POSITION, CONCENTRATE, STROKE FIRMLY, WATCH THE BALL and FOLLOW THROUGH.' By this time the ball has probably passed you! The racket still retains the original owner's name label. The earlier second racket, from 1937, states that Dan Maskell was the 'Coach, All England Club' Length 68.5 cms. Width 22.2 cms. Wt. 'Light'. £100-150 ($150-225)

Fig. 4.139. **The 'Demon'**
The 'Demon' lawn tennis racket by Slazengers, retailed by J. V. S. of Okehampton. A mid-1960s version of a racket, the name of which was used by the firm for very nearly 80 years. It is in wonderful condition. Length 68.7 cms. Width 23.0 cms. £100-125 ($150-200)

Fig. 4.140. **The 'Dunlop Steel'**
The 'Dunlop Steel' lawn tennis racket from the early to mid-1970s. A single shaft, which forms the basis of the handle, and a steel hoop which forms the head, are secured into a 'T'-shaped wedge. Length 69.0 cms. Width 22.6 cms. £100-125 ($150-200)

The 'Steel Master'
The 'Steel Master' lawn tennis racket from Grays of Cambridge. It was retailed in about 1970 by Beales of Bournemouth, and is an interesting experiment combining a steel shaft with a wooden headpiece. Length 68.8 cms. Width 21.5 cms. £75-100 ($125-150)

Fig. 4.141. **The 'T3000'**
The 'T3000' lawn tennis racket from Wilson. Again, these rackets were available between 1973 and 1982. Length 67.8 cms. Width 23.7 cms. £100-125 ($150-200)

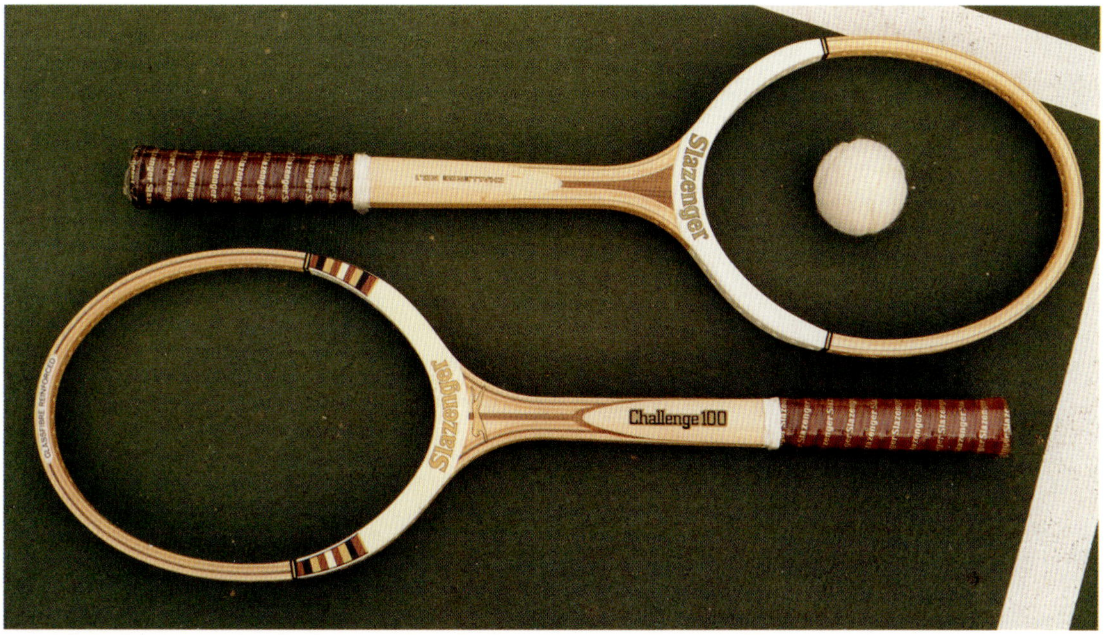

Fig. 4.142. **The 'Challenge No.1'**
The 'Challenge No.1' lawn tennis racket by Slazenger. This is one of the classic wooden rackets, which was manufactured between 1965 and 1975. This is the 'Championship Frame' model and although it is not strung it still retains the original sealed transparent wrapper over the leather handle. Length 68.8 cms. Width 23.2 cms. Wt. 'M6 - Grip 4 3/4.' £150-200 ($225-300)

The 'Challenge 100'
The 'Challenge 100' lawn tennis racket by Slazenger. A further development (from 1975-85) following the success of the 'No.1' racket, which was probably produced during the following ten years. A transfer on the frame boasts a construction of 'Maple, Ash, Leatheroid Fibre, Walnut, Beech, reinforced with Glass Fibre.' Perfect condition. Length 68.8 cms. Width 23.0 cms. 'M4 – Grip 4 1/2.' £75-100 ($100-150)

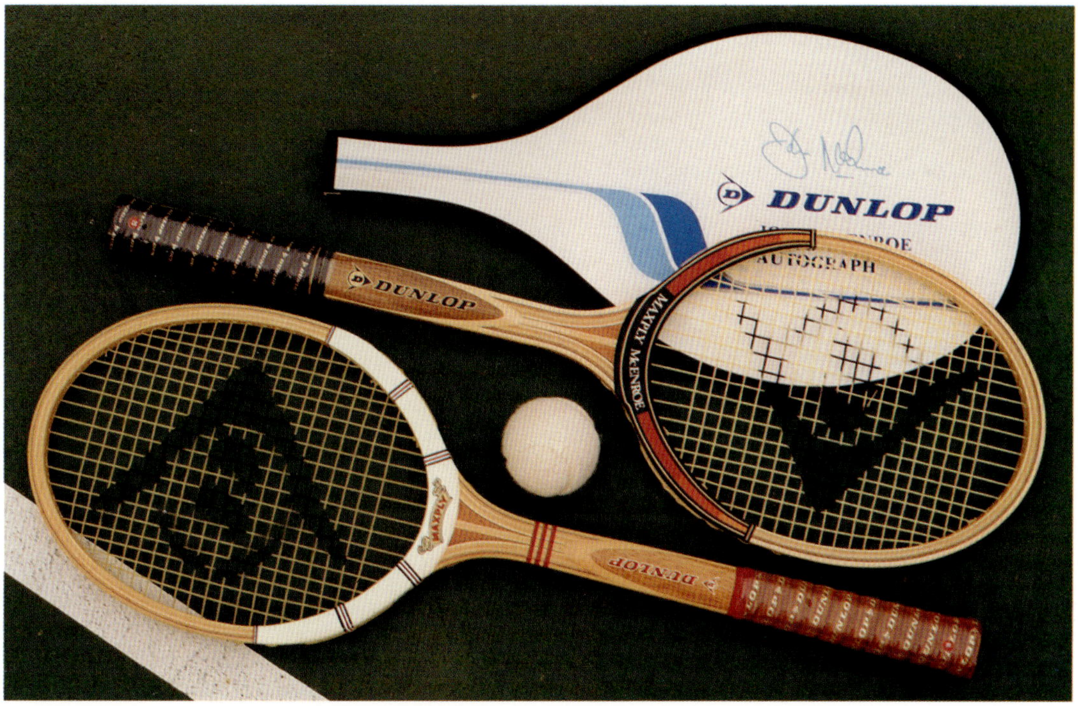

Fig. 4.143. **The 'Maxply McEnroe Autograph'**
The 'Maxply McEnroe Autograph' lawn tennis racket by Dunlop. This racket was made between 1985-87, with a laminated construction of five different materials. They are: glass fibre; maple; hickory; vulcanised fibre; beech; and ash. Complete with its original three-quarter length cover and factory fitted, shrink-wrapped leather handle. The racket is in mint condition. Length 68.8 cms. Width 22.8 cms. 'M6 - 4 3/4'. £75-100 ($100-150)

The 'Maxply Fort'
The 'Maxply Fort' lawn tennis racket by Dunlop. This is surely one of the 'flagship' wooden rackets, which was produced in massive numbers between 1954-80. Length 68.0 cms. Width 22.9 cms. 'M6 – 4 3/4'. £75-100 ($100-150)

Fig. 4.144. **The 'Arthur Ashe Competition'**
The 'Arthur Ashe Competition' lawn tennis racket by Head. Produced in 1979, it has a fibreglass core with brushed aluminium veneers on each side. Length 68.7 cms. Width 22.8 cms. £75-100 ($100-150)

Fig. 4.145. **The 'Edge'**
The 'Edge' lawn tennis racket by Head. Produced between 1981 and 1985, the wedge is made from nylon. Length 68.0 cms. Width 23.8 cms. £50-75 ($75-100)

The 'World Class'
The 'World Class' lawn tennis racket by Wilson, c. 1982. Apparently there was a '110' model with a large hitting area and a '27' model, of which I think this is an example. Length 68.3 cms. Width 22.4 cms. '4 3/4 M'. £50-75 ($75-100)

The 'Classic 110'
The 'Classic 110' lawn tennis racket by Prince, from 1982 but first produced in 1976. The original 'oversize' racket (110 sq.ins.), with an extruded aluminium body and a nylon wedge. Length 68.4 cms. Width 27.7 cms. '4 5/8'. £50-75 ($75-100)

Fig. 4.146. **The 'Graphite Challenge'**
The 'Graphite Challenge' lawn tennis racket by Slazenger. Probably manufactured during the early 1980s, in its original cover. Length 68.8 cms. Width 23.0 cms. 'M4 – Grip 4 1/2'. £50-75 ($75-100)

Fig. 4.147. **The 'Vite Professional'**
The 'Vite Professional' lawn tennis racket from Jaguar. The racket was made in Taiwan in the 1980s. It appears to be a wooden racket with veneered surfaces, but apart from that there is little I can find out about it. It is unused and retains the original transparent plastic cover on the grip. Length 68.7 cms. Width 23.2 cms. 4 5/8 ins. Top. £75-100 ($75-100)

The 'Glaflex'
The 'Glaflex' lawn tennis racket by Yonex. Possibly produced in the 1980s. Length 67.7 cms. Width 23.8 cms. 'MEDIUM 4 5/8'. £75-100 ($100-150)

Fig. 4.148. **The 'Ergonom'**
The 'Ergonom' lawn tennis racket from Snauwaert. A revolutionary new design for a tennis racket, which was made between 1983 and 1985. The head is turn by an angle of about 30 degrees from the vertical. Length 67.8 cms. Width 28.5 cms. Wt. 'L-3'. £100-150 ($150-225)

Fig. 4.149. **A Set of Three Miniature Rackets**
A set of three miniature lawn tennis (Length 22.9 cms. Width 7.9 cms.), Real tennis (Length 22.9 cms. Width 6.9 cms.), and racquets rackets (Length 25.4 cms. Width 6.8 cms.) by the late Mr. Maurice Smith of Norfolk. Three wonderfully manufactured rackets in the style of the 1930s models supplied by Grays of Cambridge. The rackets are photographed with a full size lawn tennis ball. £250-300 ($375-450)

Fig. 4.150. **A Yonex Miniature Racket**
The 'PRO RD70 LONG' miniature racket by Yonex, and comes complete with a carrying bag. The racket is photographed with a tennis ball alongside. Length 23.5 cms. Width 9.2 cms. £75-100 ($100-150)

Fig. 4.151. **The 'Big Bubba Titanium XL'**
A modern racket complete with 'in your face' advertising and promotion. An all action, all shouting item accompanied by 'Film Star Status' propaganda! 'GAMMA BIG BUBBA Titanium XL SUPER OVERSIZE! 25% larger hitting area for more winning shots. MASSIVE POWER! Hit the ball harder and faster with less effort and shock. EXTRA LONG 29"! Reach more balls and improve your serve. NEW TITANIUM! Alloyed with Titanium for lightness and strength', and on, and on it goes! I'm now convinced that all I have to do is stand on the court with it and all adversaries will fall to their knees in submission! But seriously, the moment it arrived here, it appeared so large compared to the standard racket, that I started laughing. It's two inches longer than standard, and the head seems enormous. (c. 1995) Length 73.8 cms. Width 31.0 cms. £100-150 ($150-225)

Racket String Restorers

Fig. 4.152. **Racket Gut Reviver**
A small collection of bottles showing various firms' attempts at producing 'reviver', 'restorer', or 'preservative' whatever that is! From left to right: A bottle of 'No.1 Gut Reviver – to be applied when the racket is in use'. The price of 71/2d is hand written on the label in ink; A box of Slazengers 'Lawn Tennis Racket Gut Reviver' containing two bottles and two small hard bristled application brushes. The bottle with a green label 'No.1' contains a preparation which should be applied before the racket is used, the second bottle 'No.2' when the racket has been 'laid aside'. A bottle of 'The Ace' Dual Purpose Gut Preservative – Contents sufficient to cover at least 3 rackets. The final bottle from the Atlas Manufacturing Company, Woodford, London, is: 'Lawn tennis Racket Gut Reviver for Rackets OUT OF USE.' A pleasant detail concerns the company's name and address, which is moulded into the surface of the bottle at the back of the label. (c. 1920-50) Bottles range in size from 7.0 cms. to 9.5 cms. £20-50 each ($30-75)

Racket Presses

Until recently, one of the most underrated pieces of racket equipment was the press. If there's one item that has challenged inventors to the limit of their ingenuity, then the press takes first prize. Some years after I started collecting, I was aware that collectors were beginning to buy rackets at antique fairs, only to discard the racket and keep the press in which it was kept. Keep an eye open for absolutely anything that is a little different from the normal, and collect them from every era; your investment will not go unrewarded.

It appears that the earlier presses, consisting of two flat pieces of hardwood with similar shaped spacers in between them, were often made much earlier than at first thought. For instance, the 'Cape Town' press (Fig.4.153.) will only accommodate two of the earliest lawn tennis rackets in my collection. It is dated 1880, and the width between the pegs of presses may well have some correlation with their age. Isn't it reasonable to assume that as racket heads increased in size the presses did also? With the invention of metal rackets the press finally became an irrelevance and obsolete; it is probable that there will never be another made.

Fig. 4.153. **A 'Cape Town' Lawn Tennis Press**
A heavy oak lawn tennis press with three metal screw pegs and a single dividing plate. A small 'silver' shield has been fitted to the centre, and has the following information engraved onto it: 'WON BY MISS E. M. HASSARD at the LADIES LAWN TENNIS CHAMPION TOURNAMENT CAPE TOWN 1880.' (Very little is known concerning South African tennis prior to 1881.) Length 37.4 cms. Width 26.0 cms. Max. Racket Width 21.0 cms. £250-300 ($375-450)

Fig. 4.154. **A Brass-Handled Lawn Tennis Press by Henry Malings**
Impressed into the surface of the wood, just above the handle plate, there's a coat of arms and the words: 'HENRY MALINGS FRANCES ST. WOOLWICH'. All the fittings are of brass, apart from the threads of the pegs, which are of iron. It has three dividing plates, and would have held four rackets. (c. 1880) (See Fig. 4.25.) Length 34.5 cms. Width 26.8 cms. Max. Width of Racket 22.0 cms. £200-250 ($300-375)

Fig. 4.155. **The Murton 'Star' Lawn Tennis Press**
A very rare lawn tennis press with clever corner fasteners which depend upon a lever and pivot mechanism. The screw is tightened, and because it is anchored to the arm by another screw (the 'pivot'), the small 'foot' tightens against the racket, pushing it up against the arm of the press. Cast into the surface of the press are the words: 'STAR RACKET PRESS PATENTED MURTON MAKER NEWCASTLE ON TYNE' A particularly attractive detail concerns the four locking mechanisms, where a small racket and ball is cast into the surface. (c. 1885) Length 20.9 Width 24.9 cms. £150-200 ($225-300)

Fig. 4.156. **A Feltham 'Handicap' Lawn Tennis Press**
A triangular shaped press, fastened with three screw-threaded iron pegs. Impressed into the surface are the words: 'Feltham London Handicap Regd. No.57245' (c. 1886). Length 24.8 cms. Width 28.0 cms. £50-75 ($75-100)

Fig. 4.157. **A Pair of Ayres 'Central' Lawn Tennis Presses**
These presses were available in ash, walnut, or mahogany and work on the principle of a single screw, which tightens the two cross pieces together on either side of the racket. A disadvantage was that, in order to use the racket, the press had to be completely taken apart. The arms are impressed with the words: 'F. H. AYRES PATENT CENTRAL RACKET PRESS'. (c. 1890) Width 30.1 cms. £100-150 ($150-225) each

Fig. 4.158. **A 'Pear' Shaped Lawn Tennis Press**
An unusual 'pear' shaped lawn tennis press for a single racket, with three hand-turned softwood screw-in pegs. There are no identifying marks on the piece. (c. 1890) Length 35.0 cms. Width 26.8 cms. Max. Width of Racket 23.0 cms. £200-300 ($300-450)

Fig. 4.159. **An Unusual Triangular Lawn Tennis Press**
A sturdy racket press, with the additional feature that it was deliberately designed to enable it to be hung from a hook or nail. A registered number '249135' (1895) has been stamped onto the bottom arm of the press. Length 32.3 cms. Width 28.8 cms. £75-100 ($100-150)

Fig. 4.160. **An Ayres 'Grip' Lawn Tennis Press**
A typical 'triangular' highly polished wooden press with the name: 'The Grip'. Length 26.9 cms. Width 28.7cms. (c. 1900) £75-100 ($100-150)

Fig. 4.161. **A 'Conventional' Shaped Lawn Tennis Press**
A bold and hefty lawn tennis racket press complete with brass fittings, a leather carrying handle and three wooden spacers enabling it to hold four rackets. The three iron, screw-thread pegs are 18.0 cms. long and are tightened with large brass wing nuts. (c. 1900) Length 35.0 cms. Width 26.8 cms. Max. Width of Racket 24.0 cms. £150-175 ($225-250)

Fig. 4.162. **A Brass-Handled Lawn Tennis Press**
An aesthetically pleasing 'tear-drop' shaped lawn tennis racket press, with brass fittings. The brass carrying handle is hinged, and forms part of a neat recessed centre plate, which is screwed in at all four corners. The threads of the pegs are of iron but the turning heads are of brass. There is one dividing plate and the whole piece is polished to a high finish. (c. 1900) Length 37.6 cms. Width 27.8 cms. Max. Width of Racket 24.1 cms. £175-200 ($250-300)

Fig. 4.163. **A Pair of Free Standing Lawn Tennis Presses**
A pair of oak multiple presses, one for three rackets the other for five. Despite the fact that they are different in shape, they are based upon identical design principles, and are complete with three screw-thread pegs, dividing plates and leather carrying handles. Neither of them have any identifying marks. (c. 1900) Three Racket Press Length 39.8 cms. Width 29.0 cms. Five Racket Press Length 35.6 cms. Width 29.2 cms. £150-200 ($225-300) each

Fig. 4.164. **The 'Tenax' Lawn Tennis Press**
A uniquely designed press by John Wisden and Company of London. The mechanism depends upon the tightening of a central screw, which pulls two parallel pieces of the wooden frame tightly around the racket. A patent number of 255730 is stamped into the surface of the wood along with a reminder that the company is endorsed by Royal appointment. (c. 1910) Length 24.4 cms. Width 27.0 cms. £30-50 ($45-75)

Fig. 4.165. **The 'Gigans D. R. G. M. S.' Lawn Tennis Press**
A 'triangular' wooden press made for the 'Gigans' racket, fastened by four butterfly wing nuts. (c. 1920) Length 27.7 cms. Width 31.0 cms. £30-50 ($45-75)

The 'Gigans 1'
The 'Gigans 1' lawn tennis racket from D. R. G. M. S. of Germany. A difficult racket to date, due to its unusual strengthened wedge design, but probably from the early 1920s. Length 70.0 cms. Width 21.8 cms. Wt. 12 ozs. £125-175 ($200-250)

Fig. 4.166. **An Unusual Sliding Mechanism Lawn Tennis Press**
A square wooden press, which allows a racket to be placed inside by the use of a sliding mechanism in one corner. Each wing nut is permanently fastened to the thread below and has a patent number cast into it. (No. 18566) Although there are two 'stamps' on the surface neither of them are readable. (c. 1920) Length 28.4 cms. Width 21.6 cms. £50-75 ($75-100)

Fig. 4.167. **The 'Perfect' Lawn Tennis Press**
A wooden press by F. H. Prosser and Sons of London. On one side of the press the pegs are at the two ends of a single metal bar which is bent into a 'U' shape. (c. 1920) Length 25.2 cms. Width 20.7 cms. £30-50 ($45-75)

Fig. 4.168. **The Bussey Lawn Tennis Press**
A fairly standard 'triangular' wooden press stamped: 'GEO. G. BUSSEY & CO. LTD.' (c. 1920) Length 28.0 cms. Width 28.4 cms. £30-60 ($45-90)

Fig. 4.169. **A Wooden Bussey Lawn Tennis Press**
A wonderfully constructed wooden press by G. G. Bussey and Co. Ltd. (c. 1925) Length 28.2 cms. Width 20.2 cms. £50-75 ($75-100)

Fig. 4.170. **The 'Maltese' Lawn Tennis Press**
A wooden two piece press in the shape of a rectangle, with tightening screws in each corner. One of the screws is fastened (by means of a metal plate) to a hinge. This allows the racket to slide out of the press more easily. The press was made by F. H. Ayres, and has a patented number '6281' stamped into the surface. (c. 1930) Length 28.9 cms. Width 21.5 cms. £30-60 ($45-90)

Fig. 4.171. **A Two Racket Plywood Lawn Tennis Press**
A fairly standard triangular wooden press with an unusual plywood divider in the centre, enabling it to hold two rackets. (c. 1930) Length 27.1 cms. Width 28.4 cms. £40-80 ($60-120)

Fig. 4.172. **A 'Racquets' Press**
A traditionally designed square wooden press. Each half of the press is 21 mm thick and one of the corner screws works on a hinged pivot principle. (c. 1930) Length 21.7 cms. Width 20.0 cms. £30-50 ($45-75)

Fig. 4.173. **The 'Alrak' Lawn Tennis Press**
An unusual press, the shape of which was loosely based upon a figure eight. It was made from aluminium, and can be found finished in either blue or red and gold paint. The Sports Utilities Co. of Oldham, England, made them. A registered number of 768128 suggests the year 1931 or 1932. These presses are often associated with 'The Birmal' lawn tennis racket, but literature from that company always maintains that their racket never needed a press. Therefore, we can assume that it was strictly intended for use with the wooden rackets of the era. Length 24.6 cms. Width 21.0 cms. £50-75 ($75-100)

Fig. 4.174. **A Folding Metal Press**
An aluminium press marked 'T. S.' by D. R. G. M. S. A neatly conceived press which folds around a central pivot. In 1931, an application for a patent on the design was filed, the inventor was Theodor Stoik of Berlin. Length when folded 31.0 cms. £50-75 ($75-100)

Fig. 4.175. **A Slazenger Metal Lawn Tennis Press**
An aluminium press from Slazengers: 'PATENTS AND REGISTERED DESIGNS GRANTED AND PENDING IN GREAT BRITAIN AND OTHER COUNTRIES'
When activated, a lever in each corner of the press compresses a small spring situated inside the two halves. (c. 1947) Length 24.2 cms. Width 26.8 cms. £30-50 ($45-75)

Fig. 4.176. **The 'Zephyr' Lawn Tennis Press**
An aluminium press in the shape of a cross. It works upon the principle of tightening a single screw in the centre onto a threaded tube, which is situated on the other half. Consequently you have to completely open the press into its two halves before it can be used. There's a small oval pad of felt on the end each 'arm' to protect wooden rackets from damage. Inside the 'arms' of the press, moulded into the surface are the words: '65 MADE IN FRANCE MODEL DEPOSE BREVETE S.G.D.G.' (c. 1950) Length 26.4 cms. Width 26.4 cms. £30-50 ($45-75)

Fig. 4.177. **The 'B. A. G.' Lawn Tennis Press**
A press, which is made from two pieces of aluminium, in the form of a figure '8'. It is effective by the use of a screw at each side of the press, and has no need to be taken apart before use. Moulded into the surface of the inner face are the words: 'MADE IN ENGLAND PAT. NO. 598525' (c. 1950) Length 27.8 cms. Width 19.2 cms. £40-60 ($60-90)

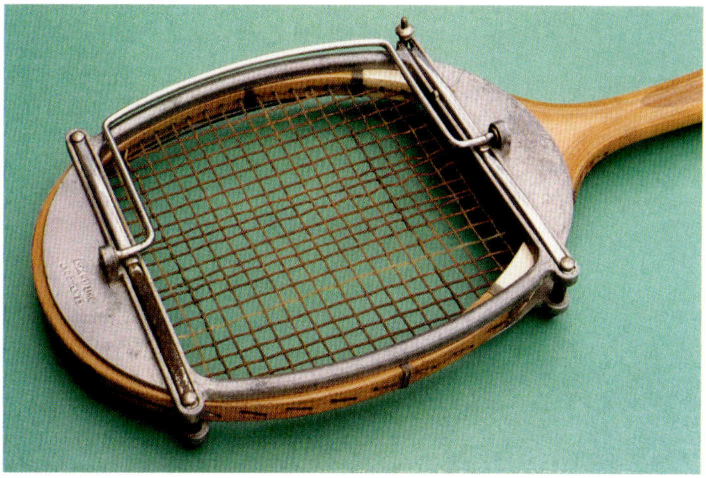

Fig. 4.178. **The 'Centa Cort' Lawn Tennis Press**
An intriguing aluminium press which will maintain contact (by means of its shape) with the entire perimeter of the head of a racket. There are four tightening pins, one of which is arranged on a pivot allowing the racket to slide out of the press. When these pins are secure, a lever arm is pivoted across the press tightening down on a series of levers. It is marked: 'CENTA CORT BRITISH MADE PAT. NO. 361023' (c. 1950) Length 30.6 cms. Width 22.4 cms. £30-60 ($45-90)

Fig. 4.179. **The 'Dyna Imperdable' Lawn Tennis Press**
A very similar press to the 'Zephyr' model but this time marked: 'VIS ACIER IMPERDABLE' (c. 1950) Length 26.4 cms. Width 26.4 cms. £30-60 ($45-90)

Fig. 4.180. **A Plywood Press Marked SBK**
An unusual press, possibly from the mid-1950s with a three colour transfer showing a pair of British Union flags. The surface of the wood has also been stamped with the initials 'AGP' Length 31.2cms. Width 23.2 cms. £50-75 ($75-100)

Lawn Tennis Balls, Boxes, and Tins

Fig. 4.181. **A Slazengers 12 Ball Box**
A very rare lawn tennis 12 ball box by Slazengers Ltd. Although the box has printed paper labels pasted onto all four sides, which date the box to 1913, they are intended to cover silk screen information originally printed upon a vellum surface, which dates from a year earlier. The two sides of the box which can't be seen from the photographs, proclaim that this make had been "Used at The Championships for the last Eleven Years" and was "Used at The Olympic Games 1904, 1908 AND 1912" The balls that it contained would have had hand-sewn seams and been supplied in individual tissue paper wrappers. Length 26.8 cms. Width 20.3 cms. Depth 7.1 cms. £150-200 ($225-300)

Fig. 4.182. **A Slazenger Box of Tennis Balls with 'Hand Sewn Seams'**
An extremely rare box of six unused Slazenger lawn tennis balls, with hand-stitched seams. (c. 1927)
Length 20.4 cms. Width 14.2 cms. Depth 7.2 cms.
£350-450 ($500-675)

Fig. 4.183. **The Jacques 'LTA Official'**
A rare box of Jacques 'LTA Official' lawn tennis balls from 1929, containing four original balls, three of which are in their original greaseproof wrappers. The two-colour label, which is on the inside of the lid, is exactly the same as the one on the top of the box. If we consider that two of the balls are certainly unused after 72 years of life, the depth of the 'nap' or covering on the ball is almost non-existent. (This would have made the ball very difficult to control). The seams are very narrow and dark in colour too. Length 20.4 cms. Width 13.8 cms. £150-200 ($225-300)

Fig. 4.184. **The Bussey (No.1) LTF**
An extremely rare box of six unused, Bussey (No.1) LTF International lawn tennis balls. A leaflet contained inside advises: "Do not throw these Balls away after the season for they can be re-inflated and their resiliency restored to play as new balls… If direct return is desired please enclose 1/6." (A remarkable claim – I wonder if they were cleaned too?). The other side contains a declaration that the company will only produce balls which conform to the strictest rules of Lawn Tennis Association. "MERIT AND VALUE Is the slogan of Geo. G. Bussey & Co. Ltd." It appears that the balls would have been stamped separately and individually under the LTF logo with the year of manufacture, which in this case is 1930. Each box is numbered and the other box in the photograph remains unopened. Length 20.9 cms. Width 14.1 cms. Depth 6.9 cms. £350-450 ($500-675) each. Depth 7.1 cms. £300-500 each ($450-750)

Fig. 4.185. **Slazenger Lawn Tennis Balls (1931)**
A box of Slazenger lawn tennis balls. The box contains two unused balls marked for the year 1931, one of which retains its original tissue paper wrapper. (The four other balls are not original.) Length 20.4 cms. Width 13.9 cms. Depth 7.2 cms. £100-150 ($150-225)

Slazenger Lawn Tennis Balls (1936)
A box of six unused Slazenger lawn tennis balls from 1936. The box contains six original balls.(13/6 per dozen) Length 20.3 cms. Width 13.6 cms. Depth 6.8 cms. £150-200 ($225-300)

The Slazenger 'Stitchless' Box
A rare, but distressed box for six Slazengers' 'Stitchless' lawn tennis balls. The very fact that the firm advertises the fact that they are stitchless, informs us that this is from the mid-transition period before the onset of the permanent seam ball. (c. 1925) Length 20.4 cms. Width 14.0 cms. Depth 7.1 cms. £50-75 ($75-100)

Fig. 4.186. **Pope & Smith "Tournament" Lawn Tennis Balls**
A cardboard tube (without the lid) for three white Pope & Smith "Tournament" balls, with a 'Reinforced Wool-Nylon Cover'. A clue to the age of the box is given in a copy line which says 'Pope and Smith Ltd. Essex County Cricket XI'. Dudley Fairbridge Pope was born in 1906 and was killed in a road accident in 1934. He played first class cricket for Essex between 1928 and 1934. The text also suggests that they had retail premises in Chelmsford and Colchester. The price of 8/3d is written on the box. (c. 1930s.) Height 20.3 cms. £30-50 ($45-75)

Fig. 4.187. **Slazenger Lawn Tennis Balls (1938)**
A box for six Slazenger lawn tennis balls from 1938. (14/6 per dozen) Length 20.3 cms. Width 13.6 cms. Depth 6.8 cms. £ 30-40 ($45-60)

Fig. 4.188. **'Peradin Vanessa' Lawn Tennis Balls**
A very scarce box of six 'Peradin Vanessa' lawn tennis balls. This box was: "Manufactured and Guaranteed by:- VANESSA BALL COMPANY, Ltd. PERADIN MILLS. BATH. SOMERSET. ENGLAND". The lid shows a superb Art Deco design in three colours and the inside lid gives advice on how to mark out a court. It contains six balls (dated 1938), five of which are in their original greaseproof paper wrappers. Length 20.6 cms. Width 14.1 cms. Depth 7.0 cms. £200-250 ($300-375)

Fig. 4.189. **Slazenger Lawn Tennis Balls (1939)**
A scarce cardboard tube with rounded sides from 1939, to hold six Slazenger lawn tennis balls. (14/6 per doz.) This was a revolutionary new design for a tennis ball container which, prior to the Second World War, was also adopted by Dunlop. Notice of the application for a provisional patent in 1938 is printed on one of the curved sides. Length 20.5 cms. Width 14.2 cms. Depth 7.3 cms. £100-150 (£150-225)

Dunlop Lawn Tennis Balls (1940)
A cardboard, Dunlop 'Fort' lawn tennis ball box, for six balls from 1940. It was almost identical to the Slazenger box, which also has a metal lid. I've only seen this particular design of container for the years 1939 and 1940. Length 21.2 cms. Width 14.2 cms. Depth 7.3 cms. £100-150 (£150-225)

Right:
Fig. 4.191. **A Box of Dunlop 'Fort' Lawn Tennis Balls (1950)**
A box for six Dunlop 'Fort' lawn tennis balls, made in 1950. The box contains 2 original unused balls. Especially made 'with the new long lasting deep-nap cover' they retailed at 29/- per dozen. Length 20.5 cms. Width 13.9 cms. Depth 7.0 cms. £40-60 ($60-90)

A Box of Dunlop Lawn Tennis Balls (c. 1950)
A box for six Dunlop lawn tennis balls. (c. 1950) Length 20.4 cms. Width 14.0 cms. Depth 7.1 cms. £30-50 ($45-75)

Center right:
Fig. 4.192. **A Box of Slazenger Lawn Tennis Balls (1952)**
A box of six Slazenger lawn tennis balls, manufactured in 1952. Curiously, all of the unused balls inside are marked for the previous year. Length 20.4 cms. Width 13.9 cms. Depth 7.0 cms. £150-200 ($225-300)

Bottom right:
Fig. 4.193. **A Tin of Slazenger Lawn Tennis Balls for 'Tropical Play' (c. 1959)**
A tin of early 1950s Slazenger lawn tennis balls, "EXPRESSLY MADE FOR TROPICAL PLAY". The balls are unused and individually wrapped in tissue paper. An unusual feature is that it does not appear to be a key-opened can. Underneath a metal end cap there's a separate inner disc of metal which one is asked to press firmly to release. This must have formed the original inner seal and this tin must have been one of the earliest to be produced without a key. Length 27.1 cms. Diam. 7.9 cms. £175-225 ($250- 350)

Fig. 4.190. **A Tin of Slazenger Lawn Tennis Balls (c. 1940s)**
An attractive, much sought after, unopened tin of Slazenger lawn tennis balls, c. 1940s. This tin is very difficult to date but due to the evidence of a logo entitled 'SERVICE' which features on the side of the tin, it is my guess that it was made in the early 1940s. This logo or device was used by Slazengers on advertising booklets prior to, and just after, the Second World War. Length 27.7 cms. Width 7.3 cms. £150-250 ($225-375)

A Tin of Dunlop "The Service" Lawn Tennis Balls
An unopened tin of four Dunlop "The Service" tennis balls circa 1939-45, containing 4 original unused balls. The fragile remains of a printed label, with the heading 'IMPORTANT', glued to the side of the tin informs us that: "This tin was packed under pressure for an Export ... market. Owing to the Rubber Restrictions Order prohibiting exports, it has been possible to divert stocks to home supplies. If the tin is not opened, the balls will retain their playing qualities for an indefinite period. (I wonder if this applies after 60 years?)...Users are requested to hand discarded tins to their LOCAL SALVAGE ASSOCIATIONS. Price 20/- per doz. balls." The tin would have been opened with a key, which was affixed to the tin. Height 27.8 cms. Diam. 7.3 cms. £150-250 ($225-375)

Fig. 4.194. **Slazenger Demon Lawn Tennis Ball (c. 1957)**
A box of six Slazenger Demon lawn tennis balls, circa 1957. The box contains six unused and unwrapped balls. Length 20.5 cms. Width 14.0 cms. Depth 7.0 cms. The other box of four balls is in fairly distressed condition. Length 27.2 cms. Width 7.1 cms. Depth 7.0 cms. An accompanying Slazenger booklet (1957) states that boxes of six were 18/6d or the box of four 12/4d. £125-175 ($200-250)

Fig. 4.195. **Gamages Lawn Tennis Balls**
A superb box of six unused Gamages "SPECIAL" lawn tennis balls, circa 1955. Quite probably sold directly from the A. W. Gamage Ltd. sports department, of Holborn, London E. C. Length 20.4 cms. Width 14.0 cms. Depth 7.2 cms. £125-175 ($200-250)

Right:
Fig. 4.196. **Slazenger 'Nylon-armoured' (c. 1960)**
A box of four white Slazenger 'Nylon-armoured' lawn tennis balls as 'Selected for THE CHAMPIONSHIPS WIMBLEDON 1960'. Length 27.0 cms. Width 7.2 cms. Depth 6.8 cms. £100-150 ($150-225)

Slazenger 'Nylon-armoured' Open Ended Box (1960)
A box of four white Slazenger 'Nylon-armoured' lawn tennis balls as 'Selected for THE CHAMPIONSHIPS WIMBLEDON' (c. 1960) This box opens at each end, rather than the usual method of a single lid. Length 27.0 cms. Width 7.2 cms. Depth 6.8 cms. £75-100 ($100-150)

Bottom right:
Fig. 4.197. **A Box of 'Nylon and Terylene' Lawn Tennis Balls**
A box of four Dunlop Fort 'nylon & terylene reinforced cover' lawn tennis balls from 1961. It appears that these balls were originally individually wrapped in a transparent cellophane cover. 'Price 14/- for 4 balls, inclusive of purchase tax.' There's an advertisement for Maxply Fort tennis rackets on the inside of the lid. Length 27.0 cms. Width 7.2 cms. Depth 7.1 cms. £75-100 ($100-150)

'The Dunlop' Lawn Tennis Ball Box 1961
A box of four white 'The Dunlop' (Reinforced with Nylon) lawn tennis balls from 1961. 'Price 12/- for 4 Balls, inclusive of purchase tax.' Length 27.1 cms. Width 7.5 cms. Depth 7.1 cms. £50-75 ($75-100)

Fig. 4.198. **A Tin of Three 'Aeroplane' Lawn Tennis Balls**
A sealed tin of three white1960s Chinese 'Aeroplane' tennis balls, with a key for opening the tin. They were made in Shanghai for hard or grass courts. Height 21 cms. £75-100 ($100-150)

Fig. 4.199. **Four Boxes of Slazenger 'Nylon-armoured' Lawn Tennis Balls**
A box for four white Slazenger 'Nylon-armoured' lawn tennis balls for (1967-1976). Length 27.0 cms. Width 13.8 cms. Depth 6.6 cms. £50-75 ($75-100)

Fig. 4.200. **A Box of Three Dunlop Fort Lawn Tennis Balls (c. 1970)**
A box of three white Dunlop Fort lawn tennis balls. (c. 1970) Length 20.3 cms. Width 7.0 cms. Depth 6.9 cms. £75-100 ($100-150)

A French Box of Dunlop Fort Lawn Tennis Balls (c. 1970)
A French box of four white Dunlop Fort lawn tennis balls. (c. 1970) Length 27.1 cms. Width 7.1 cms. Depth 6.8 cms. £30-50 ($45-75)

Fig. 4.201. **A Tin of White Slazenger 'Nylon-armoured' Lawn Tennis Balls (c. 1970)**
A tin of three white Slazenger 'Nylon-armoured' lawn tennis balls (c. 1970). Complete with a key for opening the tin. Height 21.1 cms. £75-100 ($100-150)

Fig. 4.202. **A Tin of Three Spalding 'Davis Cup' Lawn Tennis Balls (c. 1970)**
A sealed tin of three yellow Spalding 'Davis Cup' lawn tennis balls, with a key for opening them. Both the tin and the contents were manufactured in Australia (c. 1970). Height 20.5 cms. £75-100 ($100-150)

Fig. 4.203. **Phillips 'Official' and Slazenger 'Victory' Lawn Tennis Ball Boxes**
The Phillips box was manufactured at 'A. W. Phillips Ltd., Albion Works, Nuneaton, England'. (c. 1974) (Length 20.6 cms. Width 14.0 cms. Depth 6.5 cms.) £10-20 ($15-30)
The Slazenger 'Victory' box, containing six original balls, was the kind which were supplied for use by lawn tennis coaches. (c. 1974) (Length 20.2 cms. Width 13.7 cms. Depth 6.5 cms.) £10-20 ($15-30)

Fig. 4.205. **Slazenger 'Panther' Lawn Tennis Balls (c. 1980)**
A tin for three yellow Slazenger 'Panther' lawn tennis balls (c. 1980). Height 20.5 cms. £30-50 ($45-75)

Wilson 'Optic Yellow' 1984
A tin of three 'Optic Yellow' Wilson Championship lawn tennis balls (c. 1980s). 'Heavy duty felt for hard courts'. Height 20.5 cms. £15-20 ($20-30)

Fig. 4.204. **Dunlop Warwick Lawn Tennis Balls (c. 1983)**
A tin of three white Dunlop Warwick lawn tennis balls. (c. 1983) Height 20.6 cms. £50-75 (75-100)

A Tin of Dunlop Fort Lawn Tennis Balls (c. 1975)
A tin of four yellow Dunlop Fort lawn tennis balls. (c. 1975) Height 27.2 cms. £50-75 ($75-100)

Dunlop Fort Lawn Tennis Balls (c. 1983)
A tin of three yellow Dunlop Fort lawn tennis balls. (c. 1983) Height 20.4 cms. £30-50 ($45-75)

Fig. 4.206. **3 Boxes of Dunlop Lawn Tennis Balls**
On the left we have a four ball box containing 4 mint lawn tennis balls. (1979) (Length 14.0 cms. Width 13.8 cms. Depth 6.5 cms.) £30-50 ($45-75)
The box in the centre is a six ball box from 1972 containing 6 lightly used balls. (Length 20.3 cms. Width 14.0 cms. Depth 6.8 cms.) £30-50 ($45-75)
The other box, from 1982, contains four yellow unused balls. (Length 13.7 cms. Width 14.0 cms. Depth 6.6 cms.) £20-40 ($30-60)

Fig. 4.207. **Slazenger White L. T. A. Official Lawn Tennis Balls (c. 1985)**
A sealed tin of three white Slazenger L. T. A. Official lawn tennis balls (c. 1985). Height 20.5 cms. £30-50 ($45-75)

A Tin of White Slazenger Balls
A sealed tin of three white Slazenger 'Nylon-armoured' lawn tennis balls (c. 1985). Height 20.5 cms. £30-50 ($45-75)

Fig. 4.208. **Slazenger L. T. A. Official 1984**
A tin of four yellow Slazenger L. T. A. Official 1984 lawn tennis balls, a small orange sticker proclaims that they were the 'Official Ball' at Wimbledon, Roland Garros, Monte Carlo, and the Volvo Masters. Height 27.2 cms. £30-50 ($45-75)

Slazenger Yellow L. T. A. Official Lawn Tennis Balls (c. 1985)
A tin for three yellow Slazenger L. T. A. Official lawn tennis balls (c. 1985). Height 20.5 cms. £10-20 ($15-30)

Fig. 4.209. **Penn Championship 1984**
A tin of four yellow Penn Championship lawn tennis balls from 1984. Significantly, part of the graphic displays that this is the year of Penn's '10th. Anniversary in Europe – 1974-1984', and it's probably in recognition of this that the company were giving away one ball 'Free' with each tin. Height 27.2 cms. £10-20 ($15-30)

Penn 1
A tin of four yellow Penn 1 pressurized lawn tennis balls c. 1990. Distributed by Donnay U.K. Ltd. Height 27.1 cms. £10-20 ($15-30)

Fig. 4.210. **Dunlop Fort 'Premium Quality'**
A tin for three yellow Dunlop Fort 'Premium Quality' lawn tennis balls (c. 1998). Height 20.5 cms. £10-20 ($15-30)

Dunlop Fort 1986
A tin of four yellow Dunlop Fort L. T. A. Official lawn tennis balls from 1986. This tin featured a special offer: 'Serve an Ace and win a Dunlop holdall worth £15 R. S. P.' Inside the tin there was a small circular four page leaflet, with a photograph of a player serving into a tennis court. If you could guess correctly what the apparent result of the service was, you could send off for your free holdall. Having full recall of this tantalising offer, I can remember that almost everyone I knew who opened a tin of these balls eventually sent for a holdall! It would be interesting to know if Dunlop thought that the offer was a success or not, but there must have been thousands of bags travelling through the post. Height 27.2 cms. £10-20 ($15-30)

Fig. 4.211. **Slazenger Wimbledon Lawn Tennis Balls 1985**
A tin of 3 white unused and sealed tennis balls from Slazenger, 1985. Height 20.5 cms. £10-20 ($15-30)

Slazenger 'Wimbledon' Lawn Tennis Balls 1987
A tin for three yellow Slazenger 'The Wimbledon' lawn tennis balls from 1987. The advertising on the tin offers an opportunity to win a British 2.8 litre Panther Kallista (in keeping with the panther symbol). Height 20.5 cms. £10-20 ($15-30)

The NEW Slazenger 'High Visibility' Lawn Tennis Ball
A sealed tin of four yellow Slazenger Wimbledon 'High Visibility' lawn tennis balls, c. 1999. Height 27.2 cms. £10-20 ($15-30)

Fig. 4.212. **Dunlop 'Volley'**
A tin of three yellow Dunlop 'Volley' lawn tennis balls (c. 1990). Height 20.5 cms. £10-20 ($15-30)

KLM Promotional (c. 1985)
A tin of three KLM Airline promotional tennis balls (c. 1985). A paper label is quite simply pasted around a standard tin of Dunlop Fort lawn tennis balls. Height 20.5 cms. £20-30 ($30-45)

Fig. 4.213. **Tretorn 'Championship'**
An attractive commemorative tin for six unused Tretorn 'Championship' lawn tennis balls, circa 1995. Although this was advertised as a 'limited edition' there is nothing to state how many the edition is limited to! Nevertheless, it's a very presentable item with miniature versions of period tennis art posters on the exterior and a short introduction to the history of the company on the hinged inner lid. Length 20.7 cms. Width 16.0 cms. Depth 7.9 cms. £30-50 ($45-75)

Lawn Tennis Ball Cleaners

Fig. 4.214. **A 'Patent' Cast Iron Lawn Tennis Ball Cleaner**
A very rare, large cast iron lawn tennis ball cleaner, which is designed to be free standing or attached to a bench or flat surface via bolt holes through each of its four legs. Cast into the flat surface of the drum are the words: 'PATENT J. OSMOND THORNHILL WORKS LEE LONDON'. A lawn tennis ball is placed onto the surface of a revolving brush, which is situated around the central axis. As the handle is turned, the ball is guided into the drum by a series of clever cast iron guide arms, and the friction against the brushes cleans the ball. At the base of the device, under the drum, a small sliding trap door keeps the ball rotating inside or it can be left open, allowing the clean ball to drop through. (c. 1895) Height 34.0 cms. Width 34.8 cms. Depth (of drum) 16.4 cms. £350-400 ($475-600)

Fig. 4.215. **The 'Rotor Tennis Ball Cleaner'**
This amazing cast-iron hand activated machine would originally have been wall mounted. A pivoted trap door on the top of the 'drum' allows a tennis ball to be positioned between a series of four rotating metal arms. The trap door is closed and as the handle is turned the ball is forced between two walls of stiff bristle matting which line the flat surfaces of the drum, so cleaning the tennis ball. The device has a patent number 203108. (c. 1925) Diam. 20.0 cms. Depth 17.8 cms. £200-300 ($300-450)

Fig. 4.216. **The 'Kleenball' Tennis Ball Cleaner**
A wooden, machine-turned two piece tennis balls cleaner, with a series of short (1 cm.) concentrically arranged bristles mounted into each half. The tennis ball was placed inside one half of the cleaner and the other half was rotated against it by hand, effectively removing debris and restoring some of the original colour. A neat little ivory disc with the name of the cleaner is set into the surface of one of the halves. (c. 1905) Diam. 10.5 cms. £150-200 ($225-300)

Lawn Tennis Clothing and Equipment

Fig. 4.217. **A Lawn Tennis Bag**
A very special leather-carrying bag supplied by W. W. Bridge of London. A small red leather label inside gives details of the company: 'W. W. BRIDGE, PORTMANTEAU, BAG, Saddle and Harness Manufacturer, 22 & 24 Wormwood Street, OLD BROAD STREET, LONDON E. C.' The inside of the bag is lined with beige cotton, and a small pocket is provided (possibly for personal items) on the inside of the lid. The bag has a metal sub frame and a lockable spring catch. (Sadly the key is missing) Additionally a pair of straps and buckles provides more security. The bag was once provided as a lawn tennis prize, as a brass plaque (11 cms. by 4.5 cms.) has been securely fastened to the front of the bag. It reads: 'RACING CLUB DE FRANCE CHAMPIONNAT DOUBLE DE TENNIS 1893'. Just below it, the initials M. C. C. have been stamped into the surface of the bag. This famous French club was founded in 1882. (1893) Length 71.6 cms. Width 11.0 cms max. Depth 25.0 cms. £150-200 ($225-300)

Above:
Fig. 4.218. **Gentleman's Lawn Tennis Clothing**
The photograph features a range of items including a modern jacket by 'DAKS', a Bilston Lawn Tennis Club Tie (c. 1970), a pair of heavy duty cotton trousers (with the utility mark c. 1945), a gentleman's belt, and a pair of white lawn tennis shoes. The last two items warrant further examination.

A Gentleman's Lawn Tennis Belt
The belt, which is 82.6 cms. in length, incorporates an ingenious 'stretch' mechanism. All the metal links are interconnected by means of a thin cotton twine, which weaves in and out of them. This enables the belt to be extended (to match all sizes!) to more than 20.0 cms. beyond its original size. The centrepiece of the buckle features a pair of 'open-throat' lawn tennis rackets and two lawn tennis balls. On the other side, stamped into the coupling are the words: "Martin" Pat. No. 660336 Made in England. (c. 1920) Length 82.6 cms. Width 3.8 cms. £150-200 ($225-300)

Lawn Tennis Shoes
The handsome pair of leather shoes were supplied by Bartley and Sons, 493, Oxford Street, London. They have crepe soles, and are thought to have once belonged to the Fleming family of Sarsden Hall in Oxfordshire. (c. 1920) £75-125 ($100-175)

Right:
Fig. 4.219. **A Lawn Tennis Dress**
A hand-made, short sleeved lawn tennis dress, made in the 1920s or 1930s for a special tennis party, event, or tournament. It features all the elements that make up a tennis court. The tennis balls are made of felt, the rackets are of silk, with fine strings, the net tape, posts and netting are of cotton, all on a grass green base. (c. 1925) £150-200 ($225-300)

Fig. 4.220. **Ladies Lawn Tennis Clothing**
The photograph shows two cotton dresses from the 1960s and 1970s, a pair of ladies shoes, and a silk lawn tennis dress.

Lawn Tennis Shoes
The lawn tennis shoes have a high loop button fastening and 3.0 cms. high heels. Moulded into the sole are the words: 'NORTH BRITISH MADE IN BRITAIN' along with the image of a thistle. (c. 1920) £75-100 ($100-175)

A Silk Lawn Tennis Dress
A finely made lawn tennis dress, with mother of pearl buttons and a club badge (MLTC) upon which is embroidered the image of a prancing dragon. The dress also features a pair of culottes. (c. 1930) £150-200 ($225-300)

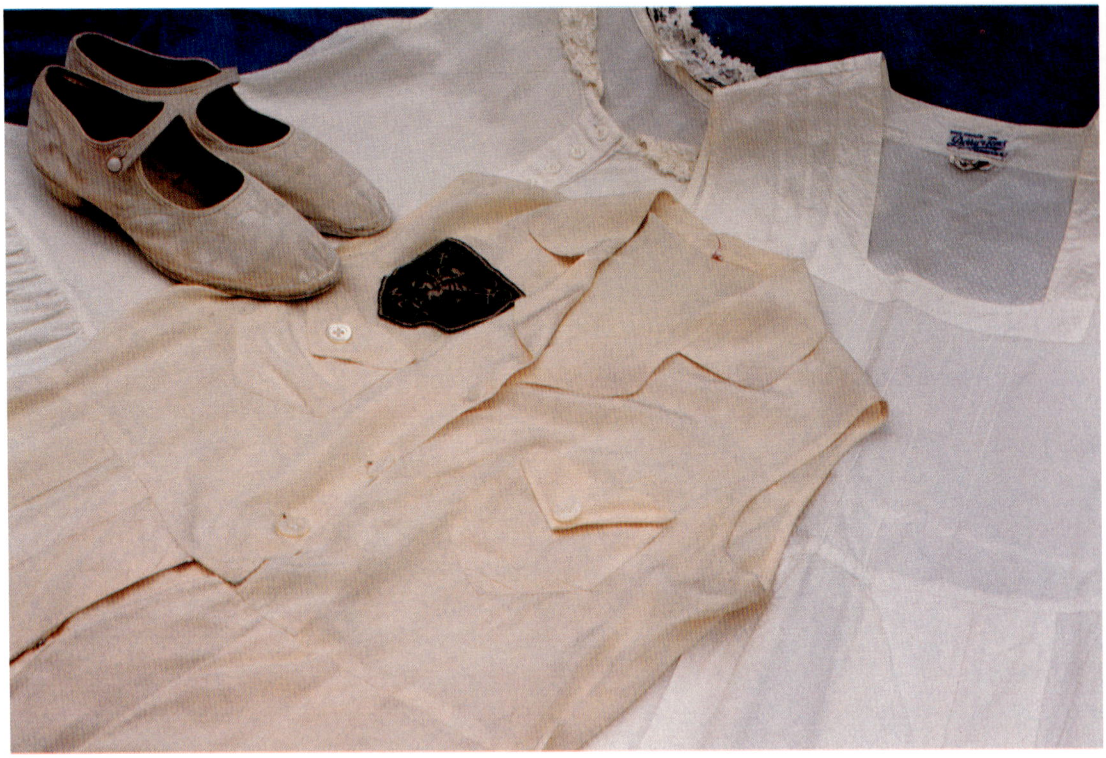

Badminton Equipment, Table Tennis Boxes, and Equipment

Fig. 4.221. **A Battledore (c. 1875)**
A very rare battledore with one side of the head strung with gut, and the other stretched with vellum. The handle is laminated. (c. 1875) Length 48.2 cms. Width 15.2 cms. £100-125 ($150-200)

Fig. 4.222. **A Free Standing Net**
The net is stretched over the two wooden poles, which in turn screw into a hard wooden base. The base is in two equally sized halves, which neatly push together in the centre via two wooden pegs. In his booklet, *Table Tennis The Early Years*, (p.27) Gerald Gurney attributes their manufacture to Grays of Cambridge. (c. 1890) Length 98.2 cms. Width 6.5 cms. £100-125 ($150-200)

Fig. 4.223. **Two Long Battledores**
The model at the top of the photograph could possibly have been used to play Ping-Pong; it has a number 4 printed onto the wedge piece. It has a leather loop attached to the end of the handle. (c. 1900) Length 49.5 cms. Width 16.6 cms. £30-50 ($45-75)

The 'Spratt'
The second model appears to be much older, and was probably used to play Battledore and Shuttlecock. It has a long tapering handle and 'SPRATT' and '3' printed onto either side of the wedge piece. (c. 1880) Length 49.6 cms. Width 16.1 cms. £50-75 ($75-100)

Fig. 4.224. **Two Pairs of Battledores**
Two pairs of identical vellum covered battledores (other than that one pair is 43.6 cms. long, the other 35.4 cms.). They were almost certainly made for the game of Ping Pong. (c. 1900) £50-75 ($75-100) each pair

Fig. 4.225. **A Table Tennis Battledore**
A fine old vellum faced battledore with an unusual, calf hide covered handle, which is finished with a narrow band of leather. (c. 1900) £50-75 ($75-100)

Top:
Fig. 4.226. **Two Battledores**
Both of these would have been used to play table tennis or Ping-Pong. The larger model is 44.3 cms. long and just 12.8 cms. wide. (c. 1900) £50-75 ($75-100)

The smaller model was made by George Bussey's Company in Peckham, London. Length 29.6 cms. Width 14.2 cms. (c. 1900) £20-40 ($30-50)

Middle:
Fig. 4.227. **A Pair of 'Ping-Pong' Bats or Rackets**
A pair of 'Ping-Pong' bats or rackets, the maker of which is unknown. Some early table-tennis bats were strung like lawn tennis rackets until protagonists realised that it was very difficult to control a celluloid ball off a strung surface. With very fine 'natural' verticals and red laterals and trebling, the rackets are very nicely made. Apart from the stringing pattern, which depends upon the strings being threaded through holes which are in a straight line around the head rather than on the diagonal, they are almost identical to their larger lawn tennis cousins. They also have small hardwood wedge pieces with a single screw through each of them, two handle pieces, and a thin leather butt-cap. (c. 1900) Length 38.2 cms. Width 13.8 cms. £200-300 ($300-450)

Cavendish Table Tennis Posts
A pair of identical table tennis posts manufactured by F. H. Ayres. They are modelled upon their lawn tennis counterparts, except that there is no provision for the cord of the net to be wound tight. The bases are of cast-iron and the posts are of turned and varnished pine. (c. 1900) Height 19.8 cms. £75-125 ($100-200)

Bottom:
Fig. 4.228. **'The New Table Game of Ping Pong or Gossima**
A material covered box, containing a set with 'Sole Publishers & Manufacturers, J. Jaques & Son. Ltd. & Hamley Bros. (Jointly Concerned)'. The interior of the box is covered entirely in an attractive glossy pink paper, and the inside of the lid has a label printed as a caution to the public: 'The only genuine PING-PONG Games are those which bear the Registered Trade Marks..."PING-PONG" AND "GOSSIMA"...' Inside the box is a pair of adjustable wooden posts with brass bases, a fine green string net, and a pair of 'Best Vellum' covered 'No.3' battledores. A 12 page 'Standard Edition' booklet of 'Rules and Directions' is also included in the box. (c. 1900) Box Length 46.8 cms. Width 17.8 cms. Depth 8.1 cms. £100-150 ($150-225)

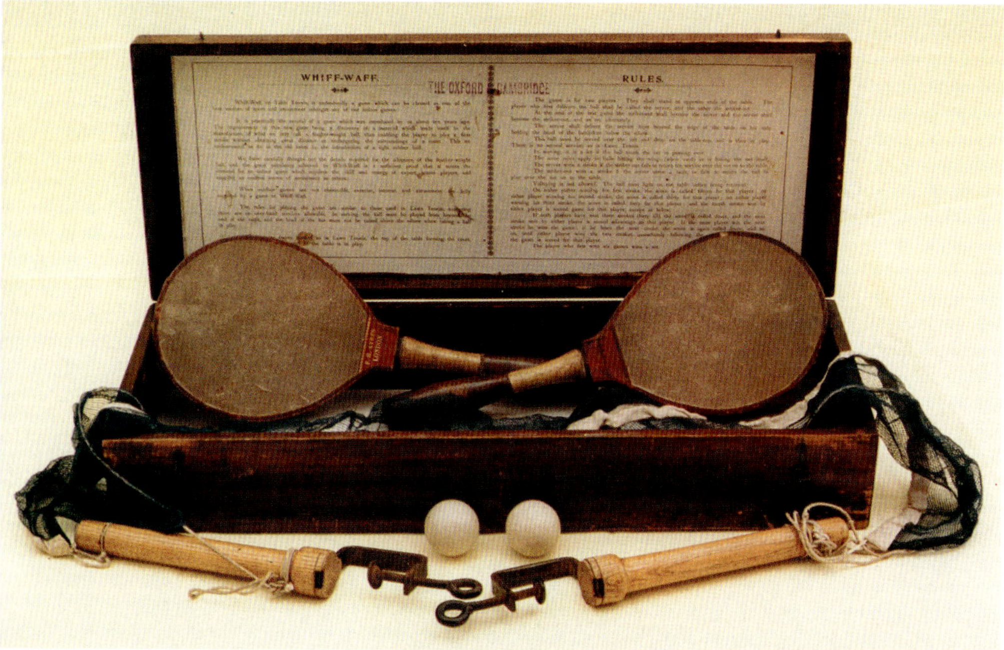

Top:
Fig. 4.229. **Whiff-Waff**
A wooden box set of Whiff-Waff. This is the 'OXFORD & CAMBRIDGE' set, which has the rules of the game printed on a label glued onto the inside of the lid. The two vellum-covered battledores have the manufacturers F. H. Ayres name printed on them, but this doesn't mean that Ayres made the set. Battledores often get swapped around if they're broken or missing. The exterior of the box has very little decoration other than a small diamond shape in the centre of the lid, which is meant to simulate a veneer. (c. 1900) Box Length 54.0 cms. Width 20.5 cms. Depth 10.0 cms. £100-125 ($150-200)

Middle:
Fig. 4.230. **The New Game of Whiff-Waff or Table Tennis**
A vellum covered cardboard box, containing a set of Whiff-Waff. A label has been pasted onto the inside of the box lid. On the right hand side of the label the rules (of the game) are printed. The rules mention the presence of 'wings (when used)'. This refers to an addition to the standard net, which is positioned in the middle of the table. They were small nets, which extend from the posts a little way along the edge of the table. The scoring system was as in lawn tennis, but without a second service. On the left hand side of the label there are a few enlightening sentences concerning the development of the game: 'It (Whiff-Waff) is practically the revival of a game which was introduced by us about ten years ago. The improvement in this new game being a discovery of a material which lends itself to the manufacture of what we may call a feather-weight ball (celluloid), thus enabling the player to play a firm stroke without obtaining great distance or endangering the surroundings of a room. This we endeavoured to do in the old times by the introduction of a light rubber ball.' The battledores are very recognisable with their 'square copper banded' collars. On one side of the vellum is printed: 'VELLUM WHIFF-WAFF' and on the other: 'THE CHISWICK S & S LONDON' (Slazenger and Sons) The cloth rim of the net is also printed: 'WHIFF-WAFF REGD.'(c. 1900) Box Length 48.9 cms. Width 18.6 cms. Depth 6.8 cms. £100-125 ($150-200)

Bottom:
Fig. 4.231. **Table Tennis Bats, Posts, and Net**
A pair of unusual bats with plain wooden blades and flat hardwood handles. The posts are of turned hardwood with metal fittings. (c. 1900) Bat Length 27.9 cms. Width 16.9 cms. £60-80 ($90-120) Posts Length 25.0 cms £30-50 ($45-75)

Fig. 4.232. **A Pair of Fretwork Bats**
A very rare and fine pair of bats, each cut as a symmetrical pattern. The round bat has hardwood handle pieces. (c. 1900) Length 32.4 cms. Width 15.5 cms. £50-75 each ($75-100)

Fig. 4.233. **Three Table Tennis Bats**
The bat on the left is formed from a single piece of hardwood, the blade being scored on one side and plain on the other. The handle is formed by the addition of two thin pieces of additional wood on either side of the blade piece. (c. 1900) Length 29.5 cms. Width 15.2 cms. £10-20 ($15-30)

The bat in the centre is made by the addition of two semi-circular hardwood handle pieces to either side of the laminated blade piece. The end of the handle is finished off with a band of leather. (c. 1900) Length 28.0 cms. Width 13.8 cms. £50-75 ($75-100)

The bat on the right is formed in a similar way but this time the handle pieces are of stained cork, finished with a band of tooled leather. (c. 1900) Length 29.4 cms. Width 15.2 cms. £20-30 ($30-45)

Fig. 4.234. **'The Amersham Table Tennis' Set**
A British made table tennis set, supplied in a varnished pine box. The lid shows a coloured label with a man and lady from the late 1920s playing table tennis. On the inside of the lid a small label is printed with the rules of the game. The inside of the box is divided into five compartments, two small ones reserved for holding table tennis balls. There are two tubular adjustable posts, a diagonally-strung green string net, four standard bats and an unusual 'practice bat'. Two of the standard bats have pimpled and sandpaper covered blades, where the other pair are pimpled and cork. All the standard bats have cork covered handles. The 'practice' bat is very intriguing. It measures 28.8 cms. long, but the blade (which is diagonally scored on one side and plain on the other) is only 5.7 cms. wide. Even the original tissue paper is at the bottom of the box. (c. 1920s) Box Length 48.5 cms. Width 31.8 cms. Depth 8.0 cms. £100-150 ($150-225)

Fig. 4.235. **'Stag' Table Tennis**
A pine box, which contains a 'Stag' table tennis set. A wooden divider provides an area for table tennis balls, a net, metal posts, and two bats lie on the other side. The bats have nicely turned, varnished handles, and the plywood blades are faced with cork on one side, but are plain on the other. A leaflet describing the table tennis laws is included. The registered number '325094', which suggests a year of 1898, refers to the registration of the stag symbol rather than the age of the box. (c. 1930) Box Length 37.0 cms. Width 16.6 cms. Depth 7.6 cms. £75-100 ($100-150)

Fig. 4.236. **'Table Tennis'**
A boxed set of table tennis equipment, which includes wooden nets posts with metal bases, a finely strung green net, and a pair of bats, the blades of which are covered with sandpaper on both sides. The original tissue paper remains in the bottom of the box. The lid has a very attractive Art Deco design printed onto it in black and gold. There is no clue to the identity of the manufacturers. A label is printed with the rules of the game, and is pasted to the inside of the lid. (c. 1930) Box Length 41.0 cms. Width 20.1 cms. Depth 5.2 cms. £75-100 ($100-150)

Fig. 4.237. **'The Cleashaw Bros. Ltd., Regulation Table Tennis'**
A stained and varnished pine box containing a table tennis set, which was quite possibly made by the firm of Clapshaw and Cleave. It contains a pair of turned wooden posts with metal bases, a widely strung green net, four bats, and a four-page rules booklet. There are two pairs of bats, one pair has blades covered with very fine sandpaper, the other pair with cork. All four cork-handled bats have one side of the blade which is plain wood, but it is highly varnished. An attractive label is pasted to the inner lid. (c. 1930) Box Length 37.7 cms. Width 17.2 cms. Depth 10.4 cms. £75-100 ($100-150)

Fig. 4.238. **A Pair of Table Tennis Bats**
A pair of square pimple covered bats with attractive ornate copper handle collars. The handles are made of cork. (c. 1930) Length 29.2 cms. Width 14.8 cms. £60-80 ($90-120)

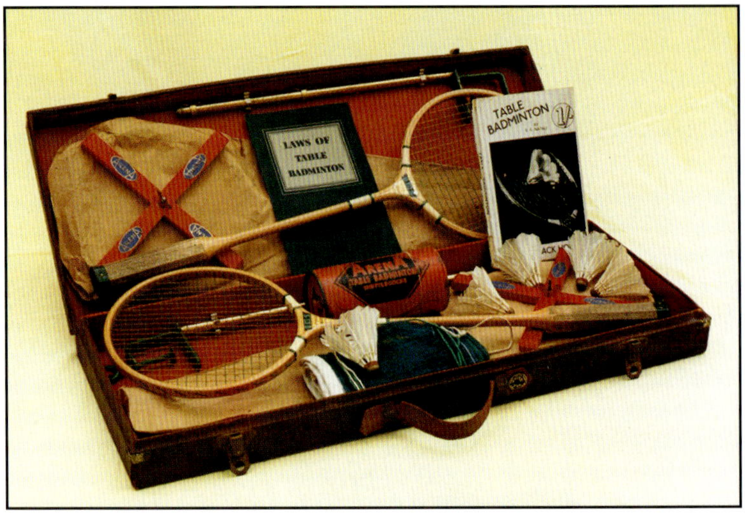

Fig. 4.240. **'Arena' Table Badminton**
A hard brown Rexene-covered case containing a set of 'table badminton' by the Table Badminton (Patent Rights) Ltd., 46 Basinghall Street, London. It contains two 22 inch rackets with circular heads, 7 ins. in diameter (with original paper container sleeves), two 13 1/2 inch metal posts, a net, a round carton of 6 small shuttlecocks, The 'Laws of Badminton' 12pp. Booklet, and a 'Table Badminton' book (48pp.) written by E. E. Natali. Scoring is the same as table tennis. (c. 1934/35) Box Length 59.9 cms. Width 23.2 cms. Depth 8.2 cms. £100-125 ($150-200)

Fig. 4.239. **Krazy Table Tennis**
A wooden box containing a set of 'Krazy Table Tennis' by B. G. L. of London, England. An interesting set containing four plywood bladed bats designed in very unusual shapes. The net too, can be hung from the metal posts as a standard net with a top rim parallel to the table, or it can be turned upside down whereby the centre of the net is higher than the sides. The original price of 3/6d. is written on the inside of the lid. (c. 1940) Box Length 34.8 cms. Width 24.5 cms. Depth 4.5 cms. £75-100 ($100-150)

Fig. 4.241. **A Table Tennis Ball Box**
A small box entitled 'Dunlop BARNA Table Tennis Balls' manufactured by the Dunlop Sports Co. Ltd., St. James's House, St. James's Street, London S. W. 1. It contains twelve table tennis balls. (c. 1950) Box Length 16.0 cms. Width 12.0 cms. Depth 4.3 cms. £10-20 ($15-30)

Fig. 4.242. **Three Modern Table Tennis Bats**
The bat on the left is a 'Victor Barna' model, with pimpled rubber on both sides and a suede-covered handle. (c. 1970) Length 26.6 cms. Width 16.1 cms. £10-12 ($15-18)

The Klemmer Souvenir Bat
The tiny bat in the centre is a 'KLEMMER Tischtennis CONNY' souvenir model. (c. 1950) Length 16.4 cms. Width 8.8 cms. £20-30 ($30-45)

The Wakaba S88
On the right is a 'Wakaba S88' (c. 1980) Length 25.8 cms. Width 15.4 cms. £10-20 ($15-30)

Badminton Shuttlecocks

Fig. 4.243. **F. H. Ayres 'Association' Shuttlecocks**
The tube in the background 'Association Badminton Shuttlecocks' is quite fragile and was manufactured in about 1914. Tube Length 40.5 cms. £20-30 ($30-40)

The tube in the foreground is a more up to date version from around 1931. Tube Length 39.2 cms. £25-45 ($40-70)

Fig. 4.244. **F. H. Ayres Velvet Bottom Shuttlecocks**
The shuttles have 16 feathers but no cotton binding. They are also very narrow, and you would imagine that they would 'fly' quite quickly. (c. 1900) Tube Length 40.5 cms. £25-45 ($40-70)

Fig. 4.245. **Slazengers No.1 'Precision' Shuttlecocks**
A cardboard tube containing Slazengers No.1 'Precision' Shuttlecocks, described as 'Tournament Tested, Medium Pace.' The shuttles have 16 feathers and are decorated with a band of green ribbon. (c. 1935) Tube Length 40.0 cms. £25-45 ($40-70)

Fig. 4.246. **The Windsor Badminton Shuttlecocks**
The shuttles have 16 feathers, two bands of supportive cotton binding, and a decorative band of green plastic. (c. 1935) Tube Length 40.0 cms. £25-45 ($40-70)

Fig. 4.247. **R. S. L. Shuttlecocks**
Tubes of 'Gold Seal' and 'Silver Feather' Shuttles. (c. 1990) Tube Length 40.0 cms. £12-15 ($18-20)

A Range of Battledore Associated Items

Fig. 4.249. **A Ladies' Glove Box**
Being very stiff cardboard in form, the lid of the box is covered in a brittle white 'celluloid' type of material which shows (in relief) a 'Kate Greenaway' style illustration of children playing in a large field, situated next to country cottages. One of the children has a strung racket in her hand, while three others appear to be waiting to catch a small ball. The whole scene is very detailed, even down to the 12 tiny buttons on the boy's shirt. Originally, the box was decorated in gold all around the edge of the scene. (c. 1900) Length 32.4 cms. Width 11.0 cms. Depth 5.8 cms. £30-40 ($45-60)

Fig. 4.248. **A range of Battledore Associated Items**

A Wooden Tray
At the back of the photograph is a beautiful little hardwood tray, with two bands of brass stringing. Under the glass surface a decorative scene has been hand-sewn from hundreds of various sized sequins on a plain silk ground. In the centre of the tray a paper print has been applied and framed in the smallest sequins. It shows a hand tinted steel engraving of two gentlemen hitting a large feathered shuttlecock up into the air, with hand strung rackets. (c. 1840) Length 27.8 cms. Width 9.2 cms. £150-200 ($225-300)

A Large Shuttlecock
The large shuttlecock, which sits at the front of the tray, is very similar to the one illustrated in the engraving. It is believed that the body of the shuttle was probably made from a champagne cork, covered with felt and calf skin, and then pierced with goose feathers, in this case, 34 of them! (c. 1840) Length 12.0 cms. £75-100 ($100-150)

A Square Headed Play Racket
The square headed racket to the left is very difficult to date. Its frame is made from a single piece of plywood, formed to give the racket a very square head. It has a convex wedge and two handle pieces at the end to make this area thicker. It is finished with a small decorative band of material fastened around the frame where the handle pieces end. As you can see, the stringing passes through the frame at regular intervals, but the holes are arranged in a straight line, not in diagonal pairs as a lawn tennis racket would be. (c. 1900) Length 50.3 cms. Width 17.9 cms. £75-100 ($100-150)

A Shuttlecock
The large feathery shuttlecock which lies on the above play racket's strings, is a total mystery. I have no idea what game it was designed and made for, other than to say that it has many feathers (unidentified) and a turned wooden body. (c. 1900) Length 10.5 cms. £50-75 ($75-100)

A Play Racket
The play racket to the right is made from a single piece of wood, which has been bent into a hoop and fastened together to form a handle. The handle has then been bound with green and red material. The stringing is fairly conventional in design, and is very widely spaced. There is no possibility that this racket was ever used to hit a heavy ball. (c. 1900) Length 47.5 cms. Width 16,2 cms. £75-100 ($100-150)

A Small Victorian Tin
A pretty little hinged Victorian tin, which has the name 'TUDNO' printed on the bottom edge. It is Art Nouveau in design. On one side it shows an illustration of two children playing with a rocking horse, on the other, a girl with her sister or friend, playing battledore and shuttlecock. Originally, there would have been some kind of carrying mechanism fastened through the holes on the top, or it might have had a ribbon attached to form a simple carrying handle. (c. 1900) Length 14.5 cms. Width 10.8 cms. Depth 4.2 cms. £20-40 ($30-60)

Postcard
The card is a very modern reproduction of a page from a book (*Book of Games*, 1899), which was illustrated by Kate Greenaway. It shows two children playing battledore and shuttlecock. (c. 1990) £2-3 ($3-5)

Chapter 5.
Porcelain, Ceramics, and Glass

I have chosen this title because there are so many specific terms and types of 'pottery' (to name another!) that the terminology can become bewildering. Porcelain is described as a fine white ware with a translucent body, and 'Ceramic' is a general term describing anything that is made from clay. The word 'bisque' (from the Old French word bescoit, [to bake twice] referring to unglazed but fired porcelain) is used to describe a large number of racket sports related items in this chapter. It was first produced in England in the mid-eighteenth century, and huge quantities of cheap bisque figures, which were produced in Germany and France in the late nineteenth century were imported into Britain. Pieces from the 'great' factories of Europe can be found (some of which are illustrated here) but the vast majority of figurative porcelain associated with racket sports appears to be bisque.

Bisque

A problem for the collector is the preponderance of pieces do not even look like tennis or badminton players! The great majority that were produced are attired in nineteenth or even eighteenth century costumes, holding totally impractical rackets, and are usually decorated in very light pastel colours. When they were produced, they were inexpensive; but, there has been much more interest in them lately, and higher prices bear out this fact. Many collectors find them engaging and they are undeniably decorative. Large figurines can be quite fine and detailed and are similar to their smaller cousins in that often they are not decorated on the back of the piece. The smaller items are sometimes regarded as coarse and garish with little apparent thought as to their appearance. Nevertheless, many pieces from both ends of the spectrum are illustrated here and, at the very least, serve to demonstrate the vast differences in craftsmanship and quality.

Restoration

Collectors should be very aware that these and other ceramic figures can be easily broken. There are many experts who are capable of doing a fine job at putting them back together again too! It is difficult to know whether or not some pieces will turn up for purchase again, so if you are going to buy a repaired piece, remember that the asking price should reflect this fact. Small cracks can often appear at the firing stage and they will regularly show at the base of the piece. Do not be discouraged, but concentrate more on trying to discover major imperfections that have been painted over or cosmetically disguised. I have bought more than one figure, only to find at home that a body had been decapitated sometime during its past!

You can often detect fine repairs by lightly running the back of your fingernail over the surface of a suspect piece. You will easily feel the line of a consistent crack which has been quite successfully disguised. Occasionally, adhesive has been squeezed from the repair or even the filler and cosmetic paintwork has left a residue nearby via the repairers fingertips. It is extremely difficult to match existing colours too. Take the piece out into natural daylight to discover differences in colour more easily.

Always look for factory marks, which indicate that these pieces are often from the better factories; those marked '(E B S) Ernst Bohne', 'Amphora', and 'Keramos' were fine quality pieces.

Of course, not all ceramic pieces are figurative in design, but almost all of them are decorative. Flower vases, spill vases, jugs, tiles, cups and saucers, and even cruet sets can be found, but the same rules apply when it comes to condition.

Glass

Among the most collected tennis items made of glass are the so called 'Mary Gregory' pieces. Often found in the shape of glasses or vases, varying in colour from cranberry to deep blue or green, they always depict small children holding rackets and hitting a ball. Sometimes, usually on the larger pieces, there's an illustration of a diagonally strung lawn tennis net and posts too. Beware of forgeries, copies, or imitations … or whatever you wish to call them. Enterprising 'artists' are taking undecorated coloured glass items and are simply painting them with a white image of a child. For the finest genuine examples, look for crisp and confident image making with fine details such as buttons, curls in the hair, and even evidence of eyebrows and clearly defined folds in the children's clothing. Other items, such as vases, plaques, and remarkable stained glass windows have made an appearance at auctions in the past.

Fig. 5.1. **A Delft Tile**
A Delft tile believed to be 18th century in origin. It shows a hand painted scene of two men playing battledore wielding hand-strung rackets and a large long feathered shuttlecock. Dimensions 12.9 x 12.8 cms. £100-125 ($150-200)

Fig. 5.2. **A Pair of Wax Figurines**
An intriguing pair of wax figurines contained in their original glass domes and wooden bases. The girl holds a bat and ball while the boy's favourite is a whip and top. The style of their clothing and the fact that they are made of wax suggests a date of manufacture around the 1840s. Height 24.5 cms. £200-£300 ($300-450)

Fig. 5.3. **A Delft Tile**
A Delft tile (c. 1900) showing a hand painted figure running while hitting a shuttlecock up into the air. Dimensions 12.7 x 12.6 cms. £50-75 ($75-125)

Fig. 5.5. **A 'New Hall' Vase**
A 'New Hall' pottery vase with a 'Buck' pattern transfer showing a lady and a young girl holding rackets and a single shuttlecock. Designed in brown on a cream coloured ground, an ornamental frieze showing a grapevine is painted around the widest circumference of the vase. A further transfer on the reverse shows a lady and a little girl reclining on a chaise longue while playing with a tambourine. (c. 1840) Height 16.0 cms. Rim Diam. 12.3 cms. £150-200 ($225-300)

A 'New Hall' Cup
A 'New Hall' pottery cup and saucer with an identical transfer to that shown in Fig. 5.5. applied to both items. (c. 1840) Cup Height 5.8 cms. Saucer Diam. 13.9 cms. £60-80 ($90-120)

Fig. 5.4. **A Printed Tile**
A transfer-printed tile showing a couple playing battledores, this time with vellum covered bats. The corners of the tile show a pair of crossed (strung) rackets and a shuttlecock. (Date unknown) Dimensions 15.3 x 15.3 cms. £75-100 ($100-150)

Fig. 5.6. **A Children's Plate**
A children's soft paste porcelain plate with a hand coloured transfer scene of four boys playing 'Shuttlecock' c. 1880. Diam. 13.6 cms. £60-80 ($90-120)

Fig. 5.7. **An Early Children's Mug**
A very rare pottery children's mug decorated with a hand-coloured transfer of two young girls playing lawn tennis (c. 1880). Height 7.6 cms. £300-400 ($450-600)

Fig. 5.9. **A Parian Ware Figurine of Ernest Renshaw**
A rare Parian ware figure of a Victorian tennis player, sculptured in 1884 by R. J. Morris (signed and dated on the base). At his feet lies a lawn tennis ball and his racket is held across his body. The figure bears a strong resemblance to James Ernest Renshaw and a similar coloured painted figure is displayed in the Wimbledon Museum. Height 45.0 cms. £1650-1800 ($2475-2700)

Fig. 5.8. **An Early Children's Mug 'Lawn Tennis'**
A very rare pottery children's mug decorated with a transfer of two young girls playing lawn tennis (c. 1880). Height 9.0 cms. Diam. 9.0 cms. £300-400 ($450-600)

Fig. 5.10. **A Hand Painted Cup and Saucer**
A cup and saucer hand painted with a honeysuckle and exotic birds on a pink ground. The cup has an asymmetrical tennis racket handle, which could be representative of either 'Real Tennis' or a very early 'Lawn Tennis' racket. The saucer has the number '6976' hand painted on to the base. (c. 1890) Cup Height 6.5 cms. Saucer Diam. 13.6 cms. £150-200 (225-300)

A Hand Painted Cup
A similar cup to the above without a saucer, this time with a white ground and strawberry pattern illustration. To date I have discovered only one other example of this pattern, this with a light green ground. (c. 1890) Height 6.5 cms. £40-60 ($60-90)

A Children's Cup and Saucer
An attractive cup and saucer, both with a hand painted transfer of a child's lawn tennis game in action. An applied transfer relates that this was: 'A present from Newport' (c. 1885) Cup Height 7.1 cms. Saucer Diam. 14.1 cms. £150-200 ($225-300)

Fig. 5.11. **A Victorian Tennis Figurine**
A very rare glazed lady tennis figurine in Victorian costume, with a diagonally strung racket. Ochre glazes. A number '15' is pressed into the solid base. (c. 1890) Height 31.5 cms. £150-200 ($225-300)

Fig. 5.12. **A Large Pair of Matching Bisque Figurines**
A rare matching pair of bisque lawn tennis players decorated in peach, light purple, and light green tones. The modelling on these pieces is extremely fine and there are several subtle differences between them and their slightly smaller counterparts. The boy's hair has a wider parting beneath the cap and his eyes are looking towards his left-hand side. His vest beneath the collar is of a button-up design. The design of his collar is far more elaborate and his left-hand actually grips the lawn tennis ball. The racket which he holds, also has a concave wedge rather than a convex one, as on the smaller models. The most notable difference concerning the girl figure is that the bow extending down from her waist-band is a completely different design; the criss-cross lacing on her shoes is very pronounced and she too looks slightly to one side. (c. 1890) Height 36.5 cms. £500-750 ($750-1000) the pair

Fig. 5.13. **A Pair of Large Bisque Figurines**
A fine pair of early bisque figures in pastel colours, wearing small caps and decorated with racket and ball symbols. The boy figure has a small number '27' pressed into the interior surface of the base while the girl figure has a number'3' hand painted. (c. 1890) Height 32.0 cms. £200-300 ($300-450) each

Fig. 5.15. **A Pair of Figures Decorated in Gold**
A very striking but fine pair of matching boy and girl lawn tennis figurines, both wearing straw hats, their gold painted shirts being the principle decoration. Both of them hold diagonally strung lawn tennis rackets. They both have the number '9' (or '6'!) painted inside their bases. (c. 1890) Height 23.8 cms. £150-200 ($225-300) the pair

Fig. 5.14. **A Matched Pair of Figurines**
A fine matched pair of large bisque figurines of a boy and girl holding tennis rackets and balls, predominantly decorated in ochre colours, which are heightened with gold. Both figures are wearing close fitting caps (much like one of those often worn by Lottie Dod). As with all similar versions of this model, the rackets are quite small for lawn tennis; this could quite probably have been a concession to firing problems. A particularly attractive detail is the 'racket' pattern, which is repeated in the surface of their clothing. They have the numbers '26' and '30' impressed into their bases. (c. 1890) Height 31.9 cms. £200-300 ($300-450) each

Fig. 5.16. **Two Victorian Candlesticks**
A matched pair of small candlesticks decorated pink and light blue, showing a young girl and boy holding very small rackets and tennis balls in their hands. They both stand in front of (and are integral with) a tree stump. Into each is moulded a small loop handle but both sconces are missing. There are no identifying marks, other than a hand painted number '3' inside the base. (c. 1890) Height 14.4 cms. £60-80 ($90-120) the pair

Fig. 5.17. **A Pair of Blue and White Candlesticks**
A similar pair of small blue and white tennis candlesticks (complete), showing a girl and boy both standing at a tree stump, colours are heightened in gold. One of them is hand marked on the base with the number '33'. (c. 1890) Height 18.2 cms. £100-150 ($150-225) the pair

Fig. 5.18. **A Large Bisque Tennis Figurine**
A fine and very rare bisque figure of a man dressed in shirt and tie, trousers and cummerbund, complete with a jauntily angled Tam o' Shanta. He stands against a lawn tennis post and the diagonally strung net drapes between his feet. The base is decorated with a Shamrock. (c. 1890) Height 35.2 cms. £150-250 ($225-375)

Fig. 5.19. **A Boy in a Feathered Hat**
A bisque tennis figurine of a boy wearing a large hat with a feather, a light blue shirt, orange breeches, and blue shoes. The racket is strung diagonally. Height 25.0 cms. £40-60 ($60-90)

Fig. 5.20. **A Pair of Glazed Porcelain Figurines**
A very rare pair of 'E. B. S.' (Ernst Bohne [and] Sons) glazed porcelain tennis players in Victorian clothing. They are very finely modelled, are hand painted, and have the number '350' impressed into the base. (c. 1890) Height 11.5 cms. £150-250 ($225-375) the pair

Fig. 5.21. **A Larger Pair of Glazed Porcelain Figurines**
A very rare and fine pair of 'E. B. S.' tennis figures dressed in bold black and white chequered clothing. Highlights are in pink and other pastel colours. The stringing in the long handled rackets is diagonal in manner. The bases are impressed with the number '659' and '22' (c. 1890) Height 16.3 cms. £150-250 ($225-375) the pair

Fig. 5.23. **A Bisque Posy Vase**
A bisque posy vase designed as a boy holding a tennis racket and ball, dressed in breeches and other period clothing. (c. 1900) Height 15.0 cms. £30-50 ($45-75)

A Bisque Tennis Figure
A bisque figure of a boy holding a lawn tennis racket, wearing a straw hat and a blue coat draped over his left shoulder. The number '3586' is impressed into the reverse of the figure and a number '141' is painted onto the base. (c. 1900) Height 22.6 cms. £40-60 ($60-90)

A Girl with a Racket and Ball
A bisque figure of a girl holding a racket and ball, the figure is painted in pastel tones. (c. 1895) Height 20.0 cms. £50-75 ($75-125)

Fig. 5.22. **A Pair of Small Spill Vases**
A pair of small spill vases of a boy and girl wearing white hats, each of them stand beside a small tree. Colour is applied to the front surface only. They are both marked '542' on the reverse. (c. 1900) Height 11.7 cms. £60-80 ($90-120)

A Children's Plate
A small children's soft paste porcelain plate with an applied brown transfer showing a game of trap ball. (c. 1890) Diam. 9.9 cms. £30-50 ($45-75)

Fig. 5.24. **A Girl with a Flat Top Racket**
A glazed porcelain lady tennis player, predominantly white in colour, holding an ochre coloured racket and a golden lawn tennis ball. The racket is quite unusual in that it has a very flat top to the head and is strung diagonally. Number '40' is hand painted inside the base. (c. 1895) Height 17.5 cms. £75-100 ($100-150)

Fig. 5.27. **A Toast Rack**
A rare glazed soft paste porcelain toast rack with five pairs of crossed lawn tennis rackets forming four divisions. Each pair of rackets is surmounted with a tennis ball, and there's a tennis ball at the base of each of them too. There are traces of gold heightening around the piece and the two ends of the piece are conveniently turned slightly upwards to form carrying handles. (c. 1890) Height 9.0 cms. Length 21.5 cms. Width 8.5 cms. £75-125 ($100-185)

Fig. 5.25. **A Pair of French Figurines**
A decorative pair of French glazed porcelain tennis players with jeu de paume and longue paume rackets, both with diagonal stringing patterns. The decoration is predominantly blue and white and heightened with gold. Both of them are supported by (leaning against) a small dilapidated brick wall. They are both hand-numbered '38' inside the base, but neither of them has any hand colouring on the reverse. (c. 1895) Height 23.5 cms. £100-150 ($150-225) the pair

Fig. 5.26. **A 'Mary Gregory' Glass**
A 'Mary Gregory' Drinking Glass, 'Cranberry' in colour: the glass is hand painted in white enamel and the initials ' E A H' are engraved onto the reverse. These pieces are often called 'Mary Gregory' and although she was well known for painting scenes with children in them, she didn't necessarily paint any of these models. Similar glass pieces can be found with two children playing over a net, or as a single child hitting a ball into the air. Very poor attempts at copies can be found at fairs and boot sales but I can suggest that they would probably omit the 'cross seams' on the ball. (A feature which is often found on early play balls) (c. 1895) Height 11.3 cms. £100-150 ($150-225)

Fig. 5.28. **A Matching Pair of Bisque Figurines**
A pair of bisque tennis figures, hand painted in light greens, lemon, and peach, both wearing straw boaters and carrying diagonally strung rackets. Neither figure is decorated at the back. He has a hand painted number '14' on the base and she records a number '8'. (c. 1895) Height 30.0 cms. £200-250 ($300-375) the pair

Fig. 5.29. **A Small Bisque Figurine**
A smaller, but almost identical model of the girl figure in Fig. 5.28, this time decorated in yellow and green. Her pose and garments are almost indistinguishable, but the gap between her right leg and a wooden post next to it is not apparent on the smaller model. (c. 1895) Height 24.8 cms. £75-125 ($100-185)

A Large Single Girl Figurine
Identical to that in Fig. 5.28. but decorated in a range of pastel colours. (c. 1895) Height 30.0 cms. £100-125 ($150-185)

A Single Girl Figurine
A single girl figurine predominantly decorated in pink. She is stamped '29' and hand painted '22' and stands at 27.8 cms. (c. 1900) £75-125 ($100-185)

Fig. 5.30. **A Fine Cut Glass Trophy**[1]
A two handled trophy with a 'Bucket' shaped bowl which is engraved with a pair of crossed rackets and three tennis balls. Above this there is believed to be the 'Rose' family emblem or badge, showing the profile of the head of a racehorse and the motto: 'I PUSH?' Engraved on the reverse is the monogram: 'CDR', believed to be that of Sir Charles Day Rose. (c. 1900) Height 21.0 cms. £350-500 ($525-750)

Fig. 5.31. **A Pair of Austrian (Turn) Figurines**
A fine pair of Victorian Austrian china figures in high blue glaze. Each lady is holding a metal racket, one is about to serve, the other receiving. They were made in Vienna. (c. 1900) Height 26.0 cms. £850-1000 ($1300-1500)

Fig. 5.32. **A Pair of Amphora Spill Vases**
A very rare fine pair of "Turn" Amphora Austrian tennis figures/spill vases decorated with pastel tone colours. The designs are very consistent with Art Nouveau designs using flowing organic forms. Each piece is stamped with 'Imperial Amphora Turn – Austria 4293 43 G' along with the coat of arms and a crown. (c. 1900) Height 21.6 cms. £200-300 ($300-450)

Fig. 5.34. **A Girl Tennis Player**
A coarse glazed tennis figure of a girl dressed in a yellow dress with blue collar and trimmings. She has a blue base with '4773' moulded into the surface at the back. (c. 1900) Height 18.1 cms. £30-50 ($45-75)

Fig. 5.33. **A Jelly Mold**
A china ironstone jelly mold in white glaze made by the English Copeland china factory. (c. 1900) Length 15.5 cms. Width 13.0 cms. £500-700 ($750-1000)

Fig. 5.35. **A Pair of White Bisque Vases**
A pair of white bisque posy vases (one damaged) showing a boy and girl holding a lawn tennis racket and ball whilst leaning against small trees and rustic fencing. Each of them is impressed with 'GERMANY 4275' on the base. (c. 1900) Height 15.1 cms. £50-75 ($75-100)

Fig. 5.36. **A Girl with a Racket and Ball**
A bisque tennis player in floral patterned dress decorated with pink bows. The size of the racket suggests that this might be representative of a 'racket and ball' game rather than lawn tennis. (c. 1900) Height 20.4 cms. £30-50 ($45-75)

Fig. 5.39. **A Small Pair of Seated Players**
A pair of small white bisque, seated tennis players marked 'GERMANY 13354' (c. 1900). Height 8.5 cms. £60-80 ($90-120)

Fig. 5.37. **A Small Posy Vase**
A small bisque spill/posy vase of a young girl with a tennis racket, the whole piece is decorated in blue and pink. (c. 1900) Height 14.0 cms. £30-50 ($45-75)

Fig. 5.38. **Two Seated Players**
A pair of quite early glazed white porcelain tennis players sitting on stools. For some strange reason her racket is extremely elongated with a conventional stringing pattern. His racket is traditional in shape but the strings are diagonal. These figurines are extremely difficult to find in perfect condition, and were also manufactured in at least one other size. They both display the number '11988' moulded into the surface near the base at the back of the stool. (c. 1900) Height 12.6 cms. £70-100 ($100-150)

Fig. 5.40. **A Lady Lawn Tennis Player**
A glazed porcelain lady tennis player figure, hand painted in brown, pink, and lemon, wearing a brown hat. The figure has no colour on the reverse but does show a small imprint number of '4479'. (c. 1900) Height 22.6 cms. £40-60 ($60-90)

Fig. 5.41. **A Match Container**
A heavy 'match strike' complete with a hand coloured transfer of crossed rackets and lawn tennis balls. Marked S & G Ltd. MCINTYRE B1812 (c. 1900) Height 6.0 cms. Diam. 7.0 cms. £200-250 ($300-375)

Fig. 5.42. **A Little Girl with a Racket**
A small white bisque figure of girl with racket seated on a potty, formed as a spill vase. Traces of the original colour remain. Impressed into the reverse of the figure is a number 13422 and the word 'GERMANY'. (c. 1900) Height 8.4 cms. £20-40 ($30-60)

Below:
Fig. 5.43. **A Pair of Small Tennis Figurines**
A pair of blue and white tennis figures in glazed porcelain with colour applied to the front surface only. (c. 1900) Height 12.7 cms. £40-80 ($60-120)

A Seated Boy
A small glazed white porcelain model of a seated boy holding a tennis racket. This would have been one of a matching pair and an identical pair of figures can be found in a larger size. He has the number '11989' impressed into the surface at the back of the figure. (c. 1900) Height 9.9 cms. £30-50 ($45-75)

Fig. 5.44. **A 'Demitasse' Cup and Saucer**
A 'demitasse' cup and saucer designed as a tennis ball cup, with hand-sewn seams and an early lawn tennis racket handle. The cup sits upon a saucer made up from eight identical lawn tennis rackets arranged together forming a circle. Both of the items are stamped with a registration mark '352978' giving an approximate date of 1900. Cup Height (to rim) 4.6 cms. Saucer Diam. 10.3 cms. £100-150 ($150-225)

Fig. 5.45. **A Large Porcelain Table Centrepiece**
A large porcelain table centrepiece, with two children (one of whom holds a racket and ball) climbing a tree which acts as a posy vase. The base is marked with a windmill placed within a shield emblem. Blue and white heightened in gold. I have seen two similar pieces both with different colour schemes. (c. 1900) Height 18.8 cms. Width 20.5 cms. £120-175 ($180-250)

Fig. 5.46. **'Antediluvian' Tennis Players**
A very unusual, and even grotesque, matching pair of 'Antediluvian' (after the flood) tennis player spill vases, the figures using hand made clubs to engage battle (presumably) with each other. There are no identifying marks other than hand written pattern numbers (4153 & 4152) which are also impressed into the surface of each base. Very reminiscent of those characters illustrated in Albert Guillaume's *Le tennis a travers les ages* (*Tennis throughout the ages*) 1890. (c. 1900) Height 11.1 cms. £100-120 ($150-180)

Fig. 5.47. **A Lemonade Jug**
A very rare 'Denby' pottery lemonade jug in a light brown ground with a dark brown glaze. Decorated in relief with two crossed convex wedge lawn rackets and three lawn tennis balls. The base of the handle has a vine leaf and grapes applied in relief. (c. 1900) Height 16.3 cms. £150-250 ($225-375)

A Lemonade Beaker
A lemonade beaker applied with a relief panel showing two crossed lawn tennis rackets, 3 lawn tennis balls along with a lawn tennis net, posts, and guy ropes. (c. 1900) Height 11.3 cms. Rim Diam. 8.2 cms. £100-150 ($150-225)

A Lemonade Jug
A 'Denby' pottery lemonade jug (as above) but applied with the identical pattern as the beaker and heightened in gold. Height 16.6 cms. £150-250 ($225-375)

Fig. 5.48. **A Pair of German Bisque Figurines**
A pair of German bisque figures (c. 1900) showing a boy and girl holding tennis rackets and a ball. They are both decorated with traces of red, brown, and grey glaze. On the back of their heels is impressed the number '10986'. Height 19.6 cms. £70-120 ($100-180) the pair

Fig. 5.51. **An 'Elizabethan' Tennis Player**
A bisque male lawn tennis player, wearing a tri-corn hat, and Elizabethan costume. He holds a diagonally strung racket. (c. 1900) Height 33.2 cms. £75-120 ($100-180)

Fig. 5.49. **A Bisque Tennis Figurine Wearing a Tam o'Shanta**
A small bisque tennis figure wearing pink breeches and a Tam o'Shanta. The number '361' is impressed into the surface at the rear. (c. 1900) Height 11.8 cms. £30-40 ($45-60)

A Young Girl Tennis Player
A bisque figure of young girl with a lawn tennis racket wearing a blue dress and a jacket. The piece is hand painted number '30' inside the base. (c. 1900) Height 11.9 cms. £30-40 ($45-60)

A Small Lawn Tennis Figurine
A very small bisque lawn tennis figure impressed with the number '82' at the reverse. (c. 1900) Height 9.6 cms. £30-40 ($45-60)

A Small Boy with a Racket
A glazed figure of a boy holding a racket up to his waist in one hand and a lawn tennis ball in the other. (c. 1900) Height 12.4 cms. £30-40 ($45-60)

Fig. 5.50. **A Small Figurine with a Badminton Racket**
A small bisque figure of a seated little girl who holds a badminton racket in her right hand. (c. 1900) Height 10.6 cms. £30-40 ($45-60)

Fig. 5.52. **A Warwick Plate**
A 1903 Warwick Ware plate entitled 'Tennis Deuce' with an illustrated cartoon by Victor Venner. The reverse is stamped with the company crest and a registered number: 'Rd. No. 516465' Diam. 26.6 cms. £80-150 ($120-225)

Fig. 5.53. **A Present From...**
A small porcelain figure of a girl with a tennis racket, decorated in browns, ochres, and flesh tones. The reverse of the figure is left unpainted and the small white panel at the front is often transferred in gold as 'A present from...'; which more often than not is the first detail to wear away. Moulded into the surface at the back of the figure are the words: 'Made in Germany 2672'. (c. 1910) Height 15.7 cms. £40-60 ($60-90)

Fig. 5.55. **A Glazed Spill Vase**
A highly decorated tennis girl spill vase holding a blue tennis ball and lawn tennis racket. The vase is formed to represent a lawn tennis net. There is a matching boy figure in this size. (c. 1910) Height 20.0 cms. £50-80 ($75-90)

A Smaller Glazed Spill Vase
A smaller spill vase similar to that above, this time a boy player but smaller in size. There is a matching girl player in this size. (c. 1910) Height 17.7 cms. £40-60 ($60-90)

Fig. 5.54. **A Glazed Porcelain Posy Vase**
A glazed porcelain posy vase, showing (in relief) the figure of an elegant young lady, who is about to hit a high forehand drive. It is decorated in pastel colours heightened with gold, and a matching vase with a boy tennis player can be found. (c. 1910) Height 14.7 cms. £80-120 ($120-180)

Fig. 5.56. **A Small Bisque Spill Vase**
A small bisque figurine/spill vase modelled as a girl with a tennis racket and ball. She is quite well detailed and the many tresses of her long blonde hair reach her waist just above a large blue bow of ribbon, which is tied around her hips. (c. 1910) Height 16.9 cms. £40-60 ($60-90)

Fig. 5.57. **A Pair of Wall Plaques**[2]
A pair of small cold-decorated tennis wall plaques moulded in relief, one showing an Edwardian man in a curious pose (this is how to balance a lawn tennis racket on one finger!) and lady about to play a backhand over a tennis net. They are respectively impressed into the reverse with model number and code – 'G538' and '539', and are each provided with a pair of small holes and a string loop with which they can be hung. (c. 1910) Diam. 15.2 cms. Depth 2.5 cms. £120-150 ($180-225)

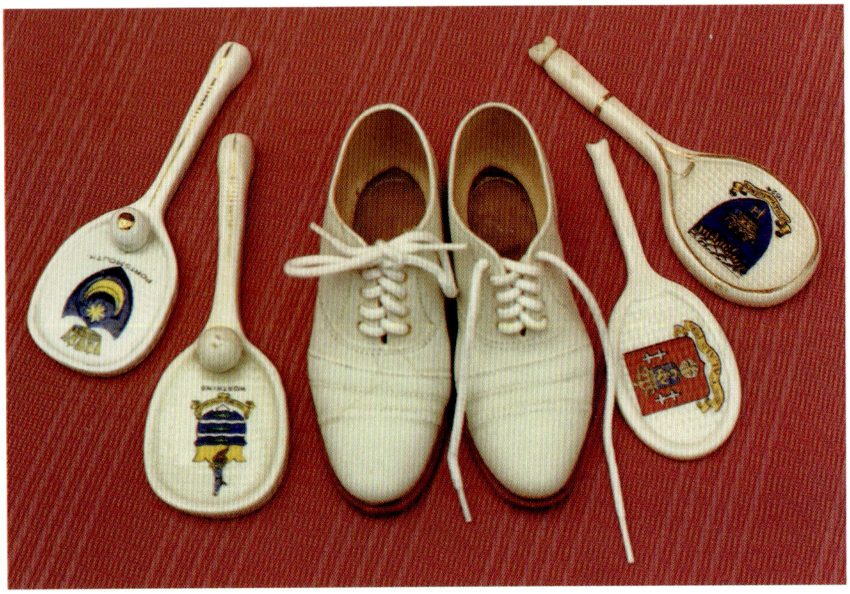

Fig. 5.58. **A Grouping of Five China items**
A crested china lawn tennis racket complete with a tennis ball positioned on the strings. A transfer of the coat of arms of Portsmouth is shown on the head of the racket. (c. 1910) Length 13.2 cms. £25-40 ($35-60)

An identical piece, except that the transfer features the town of Worthing. (c. 1910) Length 13.2 cms. £25-40 ($35-60)

Pair of fine white china tennis shoes with brown soles and real laces (not original). They are very susceptible to hair-line cracks. On the sole of each is painted the number '35'. This was possibly a pattern number, as it is known that other types and colours of shoe can be found, some of them with a patent number too. (c. 1905) Length 12.5 cms. £120-150 ($180-225)

A small crested china lawn tennis racket representing Calais. The piece is interesting in that it shows a 'fishtail' style handle and a convex wedge. (c. 1920) Length 10.9 cms. £25-40 ($35-60)

A crested china lawn tennis racket with a 'fishtail' handle. It has the coat of arms for Henley on Thames with the number '1624' beneath it. On the reverse there's a circular transfer for 'GROSVENOR-WARE ENGLAND'.(c. 1910) Length 13.2 cms. £25-40 ($35-60)

Fig. 5.59. **A Souvenir of Llandudno**
A glazed porcelain fairing in the form of a horseshoe surmounted by a dove, crossed rackets, flowers, and lawn tennis balls. An applied transfer declares that the piece is a 'Souvenir of Llandudno'. Many other similar pieces have been found, all souvenirs of towns and popular resorts. Inside the base is stamped the word 'FOREIGN'. (c. 1910) Height 6.4 cms. £30-60 ($45-90)

Girl in an Orange Dress
A tennis girl dressed in an orange dress and carrying a racket and ball. The based is marked 'FAIRYLITE FOREIGN'. (c. 1925) Height 11.9 cms. £70-100 ($100-150)

A Pair of Cake Decorations
A pair of small bisque cake decorations styled as lawn tennis players. These are very difficult to find in perfect condition. (c. 1920) Height 7.2 cms. £80-120 ($120-180)

A Small Spill Vase
A small spill vase of a young girl with a racket and ball dressed in yellow, with green and brown trimmings. Height 8.0 cms. The back of the figure is marked 'GERMANY 5829'. (c. 1910) £30-50 ($45-75)

Fig. 5.60. **A Breakfast Set**
A breakfast set of a plate, cup and saucer, each decorated with a green transfer showing a pair of convex wedge rackets below a shield which encloses the image of a captured mythical bird. The letters 'F' and 'P' flank the shield. The plate is unmarked but the cup has a transfer on the base which says 'J. ABRAHAMS CANTERBURY'. The saucer is impressed 'COLLINGWOODS ENGLAND'. (c. 1920) Plate Diam. 15.2 cms. Cup Height 6.4 cms. Saucer Diam. 13.5 cms. £120-150 ($180-225)

Fig. 5.62. **A French Tennis Girl**
A petite glazed porcelain tennis girl figure standing alongside three containers, the purpose for which has been quite strongly debated. Are they for spills, matches, buttons or quite simply for small items of virtue or of no value at all? I'll let you decide. For some reason the piece looks French, but is unmarked. (c. 1920) Height 10.8 cms. £40-60 ($60-90)

Fig. 5.63. **A Pair of 1920s Lawn Tennis Players**
A fine matching pair of 1920s lawn tennis players, both of which are marked 'Foreign' along with the impressed numbers '8770' and '8771' on their bases. Height 14.0 cms. £150-250 ($225-375) the pair

Fig. 5.61. **'Lobster Jnr.'**
A small cartoon-like bisque figure/spill vase of a player modelled as 'lobster jnr.' (c. 1920s). His wooden racket is strung diagonally, and he wears a black cummerbund around his waist. I wonder if there is a 'Lobster senior' anywhere out there, to accompany this piece. (c. 1920) Height 13.8 cms. £30-50 ($45-75)

Fig. 5.64. **'Love all'**
A small and amusing glazed porcelain spill vase in the 'Mabel Lucie Attwell' style, showing a bemused young boy figure holding a flat top racket. The piece is entitled "Love all". I have seen a similar football-playing figure, which may well make up a matching pair. (c. 1925) Height 15.3 cms. £75-100 ($100-150)

Top left:
Fig. 5.65. **A Yellow Glass Vase**
A bold yellow glass vase (c. 1930) showing a red and black, hand painted silhouette of an elegant young girl holding a lawn tennis racket over her shoulder. Several black vertical lines divide the remainder of the surface. The vase is painted yellow upon the inner surface. Height 27.2 cms. £150-200 ($225-300)

Top right:
Fig. 5.66. **A Glazed Porcelain Bookend**
A glazed porcelain bookend, showing a boy with a lawn tennis racket, seated upon two library books. The base is marked: 'HAND PAINTED ITALY'. (c. 1930) Height 15.5 cms. £40-60 ($60-90)

Bottom left:
Fig. 5.67. **A Goldscheider Figurine**
A pretty highly glazed porcelain figure of a girl holding a tennis racket at her back. Made by the famous Austrian porcelain factory Goldscheider, modelled by Dakon in the Art Deco style. (c. 1930) Height 23.0 cms. £1350-1500 ($2025-2750)

Bottom center:
Fig. 5.68. **A 'Keramos' Lawn Tennis Figure**
A very rare and fine figure of a 1930s tennis girl in a yellow shirt, grey pullover, green scarf, and cheque skirt. She supports a racket at her waist and stands on a black rounded base. On the bottom of the base a transfer reads 'Wiener Kustheramia "Keramos" made in Austria L58'. (c. 1925) Height 29.3 cms. £300-500 ($450-750)

Bottom right:
Fig. 5.69. **A Pair of 'Keramos Knight' Ceramics**
A pair of glazed porcelain figures of a young girl and boy wearing casual clothing while holding lawn tennis rackets. Information on the bottom of the base reads 'DAKON 2083 98 Modell Dakon MADE IN AUSTRIA WIEN KERAMOS KNIGHT CERAMICS' (c. 1930) Height 23.6 cms. £80-120 each ($120-180) the pair

Fig. 5.70. **A Pair of Bookends**
A pair of white plaster(?) bookends showing two ladies crouching near to a lawn tennis net, about to play a shot. The bookends themselves are formed by solidly moulded tennis nets and posts. The back of each piece is impressed 'MADE IN LONDON RD. 771848' (1932). These pieces could well represent Helen Wills Moody and Helen Jacobs who played each other in the Wimbledon final of that year. Height 13.1 cms. £100-150 ($150-225) the pair

Fig. 5.71. **Arthur Wood Tankards**
An 'Arthur Wood Royal Bradwell Sports Series' tankard, with a cream ground showing hand coloured transfers of what it is believed to be Jack Kramer and Margaret Osborne from the 1947 Wimbledon Championships. The handle is modelled as a lawn tennis racket with a lawn tennis ball mounted on top. Height 11.6 cms. £30-50 ($45-75)

A Wood's tankard which is similar to the above but predominantly with a brown ground and heightened in silver. Height 13.3 cms. £20-40 ($30-60)

A Wood's tankard, which is very similar to the first, but this is a larger model. Models of this tankard can be found in various sizes, but less desirable pieces have a standard loop handle. Height 13.5cms. £30-50 ($45-75)

Fig. 5.72. **A 1950s Tennis Girl**
A 1950s china tennis girl holding a racket. She's dressed in a white top, blue shorts, and orange shoes. She has a typical 'bobbed' hair cut. The piece is stamped on the base 'FOREIGN'. Height 15.3 cms. £30-60 ($45-90)

Fig. 5.73. **A Children's Pottery Tea Set**
An English mid-1950s 'Teddy Bear Pottery Tea Set' featuring twelve pieces, each moulded in relief with a teddy bear and several toys placed around them, including a tennis racket and ball. Max. Height 9.2 cms. £50-75 ($75-100)

Fig. 5.74. **A Deauville Figurine**
A fine limited edition bone china figurine of a 1920s 'Flapper' girl by Royal Doulton, England. The base shows a typical factory mark and the following information: 'SWEET & TWENTIES COLLECTION, DEAUVILLE. Designed by Peggy Davies and produced in a world-wide limited edition of one thousand five hundred.' This piece is hand numbered at no. '885' and is dated 1981. Height 20.8 cms. £80-120 ($120-180)

A 1930s Tennis Girl from Royal Worcester
An equally detailed bone china figurine of an elegant 1930s tennis girl, wearing a bandeau and holding two wooden lawn tennis rackets under her left arm; in her right hand she holds a white lawn tennis ball. The Royal Worcester factory in England manufactured the piece. (c. 1990) Height 21.2 cms. £50-75 ($75-100)

A Coalport Tennis Figure
An Edwardian tennis girl, modelled in bone china, holding a metal racket in her right hand. A transfer on the base reads: 'EARLY DAYS Tennis Lady Circa 1914 From a MARY ROBERTS Design. Modelled and decorated by hand. A Limited Edition of 500.' The piece is hand numbered as '161' and was manufactured by the Coalport factory in England in the late twentieth century. Height 20.2 cms. £70-100 ($100-150)

Fig. 5.75. **A Goebel Cruet Set**
A cruet set, consisting of small boy salt and tennis ball pepper pot sitting on a crossed racket stand. The base of the stand is marked 'M 70A c. by W.Goebel 1957' Height 8.0 cms. Length 11.4 cms. £70-100 ($100-150)

Fig. 5.76. **A Centenary Tankard**
A Lawn Tennis Association Centenary tankard (1988). A very fine, decorative transfer showing Victorian Tennis Matches. Height 12.5 cms. £30-40 ($45-60)

A Sylvac Tennis Mug
A lawn tennis mug (c. 1977) by Sylvac in the shape of a white tennis ball on a grass base with lawn tennis racket as a handle. The number '4723' is impressed into the base. Height 9.0 cms. £20-40 ($30-60)

Fig. 5.77. **Bone China Wimbledon Souvenirs**
A souvenir bone china plate, especially made to celebrate the centenary of the Wimbledon Championships. (1977) The plate is decorated with a black hand coloured transfer showing a scene of the entrance to the Centre Court, Wimbledon, from across court number 5 (without the large green screens at the back of the court). On the reverse of the plate is a short paragraph of text outlining the history of the Championships, the club, and the opening of the new lawn tennis museum. Reli Washbourne of England manufactured it. Diam. 21.0 cms. £20-40 ($30-60)

A small bone china coaster with an almost identical black hand coloured transfer of Centre Court, Wimbledon, and (a longer!) history of the club and game on the reverse. The item is marked 'RWL' (Reli Washbourne Limited) London. Diam. 10.6 cms. £10-20 ($15-30)

Fig. 5.78. **Seven Modern China Souvenirs**
A grouping of seven modern 'souvenir' glazed china lawn tennis toys, along with one articulated plastic figure. The only pieces with any identification are 'The Pink Panther', which was distributed in the United Kingdom by James Winchester of London (c. 1981), and 'Garfield' manufactured in Korea by Downpace Ltd (c. 1981). Heights vary between 5.5 cms and 13.0 cms. £20-50 ($30-75) each

Fig. 5.79. **"Centre Court 1903"**
A modern china figure of tennis girl entitled "Centre Court 1903" by Goebel of West Germany. Dressed entirely in white except for a salmon pink tie and orange boater. The piece is impressed with the number '16 293 22' on the base. (c. 1985) Height 21.7 cms. £50-75 ($75-100)

A Lady Tennis Player
An attractive lady tennis figure marked "S" surmounted with a crown on the base. Height 20.1 cms. £30-50 ($45-75)

Fig. 5.80. **A 'Georgian' Tennis Player**
A Georgian tennis player wearing a tri-corn hat and a pink over-jacket. Marked "S" (c. 1950). Height 18.6 cms. £40-60 ($60-90)

Fig. 5.82. **Sport Goofy**
Sport Goofy Figurine standing over a vanquished Donald Duck. (c. 1985) Height 23.2 cms. £20-40 ($30-60)

Fig. 5.81. **'Alexandra' by Spode**
A very pleasant white bone china figurine of an Edwardian tennis girl wearing a full-length dress and straw boater. The piece is entitled 'Alexandra', a model by Pauline Shone of the Spode factory in England. There is another version of this piece available, this time decorated with gold highlights. (c. 1985) Height 24.4 cms. £70-100 ($100-150)

Fig. 5.83. **A Wedgwood Trinket Box**
A Wedgwood trinket box, showing a detailed white figure (in relief) of a Victorian lady tennis player wielding a square-headed lawn tennis racket on a plain green 'Jasper' ground. The original box shows a label with the title: 'WIMBLEDON THE CHAMPIONSHIP 1986 FLUTED BOX.' Height 4.4 cms. Diam. 9.0 cms. £30-40 ($45-60)

A Trinket Box by Minton
A small trinket box by the Minton factory of England. The lid shows a coloured transfer of 'THE TENNIS PARTY'. The base explains that the design is 'From the Original by E. F. Brewtnall, displayed in The Wimbledon Lawn Tennis Museum.' The design has a copyright for Royal Doulton in 1988 by appointment to The All England Club, Wimbledon, and also shows the (by then) newly adopted 'W' Wimbledon logo. Height 3.1 cms. Diam. 9.8 cms. £20-40 ($30-60)

Fig. 5.84. **A Bone China Sandwich Plate and Cup**
A modern bone china sandwich plate by the Royal Doulton, Minton factories, with a matching cup. The set is complete with a full coloured transfer of a Victorian tennis scene and is entitled 'ON THE LAWN'. (1988) Cup Height 5.7 cms. Plate Width 25.0 cms. £40-60 ($60-90)

Fig. 5.85. **'Between Sets'**
A modern pottery (c. 1990) model of a young girl in bed with her coach, entitled 'Between Sets – an undercover story by Margaret Howard'; the bed cover is removable. Height 7.3 cms. Length 10.5 cms. £30-40 ($45-60)

Fig. 5.86. **'Centre Court' by Emilio James**
A limited edition round vase, by Emilio James of England in the manner of the Clarice Cliff 'Tennis' patterns of the Art Deco period. This pattern is named as 'CENTRE COURT' and as a limited number 10 of 50 pieces. (c. 1995) Height 18.0 cms. Rim Diam. 7.0 cms. £40-60 ($60-90)

Fig. 5.87. **A Souvenir Plate by Wedgwood**
A bone china souvenir Wimbledon plate by Wedgwood. The transfer details on the reverse that it forms part of the 'WIMBLEDON COLLECTION – IN A LIMITED EDITION OF 2000' The front surface features a hand painted transfer of an Edwardian scene outside Centre Court with the words 'The Championships Wimbledon 20th June - 3rd July 1994.' Diam. 20.5 cms. £30-50 ($45-75)

'An Edwardian Summer'
A souvenir bone china Wimbledon plate entitled 'An Edwardian Summer' by the Royal Worcester factory. It was designed by Edward Mortelmans, Dip.F.A.(Lond) and supplied in a limited edition of 4000. The front surface shows a decorative Edwardian tennis scene of people sitting taking tea on the Wimbledon lawns. (c. 1995) Diam. 20.7 cms. £30-50 ($45-75)

Fig. 5.88. **A Hand Painted Vase**
A hand painted glazed vase, made to commemorate the recipient's attendance of the 1996 Wimbledon Championships. This piece is number 19 of 33 'limited edition' pieces given by 'Girobank' to the company's most valued VIP's. The piece is predominantly decorated in blues and ochres, with small amounts of accent colour. Height 24.0 cms. £70-100 ($100-150)

Fig. 5.89. **A Derby Dwarf**[3]
A hand painted glazed figure, originally manufactured by the 'Royal Crown Derby' factory. On his hat a message reads: 'Grand Treat for the Fancy at the Tennis Court'. A hand drawn illustration on his back shows two men hitting a ball back and forth. Unfortunately, the piece is damaged and has been extensively repaired. Otherwise the figurine would be quite a valuable one. Height 24.1 cms. £50-75 ($75-100) repaired value; £300-500 ($450-750) mint value

Chapter 6.
Silver and Metalware

Trophies

There are hundreds if not thousands of racket sports items fashioned in metal, and the reason for this is more than just a practical one. Silver is a favourite metal; it exudes confidence, permanence, and precision. In Victorian households silver was regarded as a statement of wealth. It was used to make trophies of all shapes and sizes, but most of all it represented strength, superiority, and victory. An engraved trophy is unique too; if it shows the name of a tournament, the victor(s), and sometimes—very rarely—the score, it is truly a 'time capsule' without equal. As you will see, a trophy can often be researched to the extent that the item itself represents the result of a whole series of events in a tournament. If you can research deeply enough, its immediate provenance is there waiting to be discovered. Tournament organisers would have simply visited their local silversmith or shop and ordered the prizes 'off the shelf', the engraving being added following the tournament. It is believed that often players were presented with a voucher, and they chose the prize for themselves.

I would advise collectors to find out as much as they can about the early tournaments, who ran them, where they were played, and the people who played in them. Look for trophies associated with important clubs and players. Should the item also include an engraved tennis scene or be embellished with a racket, then all the better. During the Victorian era, lawn tennis tournaments were played everywhere; a cursory glance through the pages of a Victorian 'sporting weekly' in the height of June will reveal tens, if not hundreds, of tournaments being played in the coming weeks. Each tournament was comprised of several events: singles, doubles, mixed, handicap, and more often than not, both winners and runners-up were awarded a prize, often in the form of a silver trophy.

Fig. 6.1. **An Irish Silver Belt Buckle**[1]
A unique Irish silver belt buckle with the front inscribed with the letters: 'F. W. T. C.' surmounted by two crossed lawn tennis rackets. Arranged around this are the words: 'DUBLIN CHAMPION DOUBLES DUBLIN 1880'. The obverse is inscribed to the winners: 'H. F. Lawford & A. J. Mulholland Dublin 29 May 1880.' Width 8.0 cms. Depth 6.0 cms. £1500-2000 ($2250-3000)

Fig. 6.2. **A Silver Plated, Oak-Lined Tankard Trophy**
A very rare, silver-plated, straight-sided tankard, lined with strips of oak, which are strengthened with four concentric bands, fixed with small silver screws. The top band is engraved: 'Uva Autumn Meet', the second: 'H. H. Capper', the third: 'Lawn Tennis Singles'. A small silver shield, situated between the third and fourth bands records that this was the 'First Prize 1882'. Frustratingly, neither the engravings nor the maker's initials on the base (JB & S), give any clues as to where this tournament took place. It has been suggested that the inscription might refer to Auriel College at the University of Virginia, but as yet there is no specific evidence. Height 10.5 cms. Diam. 7.3 cms. £400-500 ($600-750)

Fig. 6.3. **An American Hammered Silver Trophy Bowl**[2]
Stamped: '900 STERLING' this hammered silver bowl by Whiting is engraved: 'ALL PHILADELPHIA Lawn Tennis Tournament, 1st PRIZE SINGLE WON BY Clarence M. Clark JUNE 1883.' Height 8.0 cms. Diam. 17.4 cms. £1000-1500 ($1500-2000)

Fig. 6.4. **A Small Electroplated Silver Goblet Trophy**
The body is engraved with a pair of symmetrical sprays of ferns and reeds, at the centre of this the words: 'NEWMARKET (Suffolk, England) LAWN TENNIS CLUB TOURNAMENT SEPT. 10th. 1884 GENTLEMENS DOUBLE FIRST PRIZE WON BY W. I. L. SHEPPARD & A. S. MANNING.' are engraved. The maker is R P & Co. It has a knopped stem and the foot of the goblet is decorated with rings of beads and a lightly engraved irregular band. Height 14.6 cms. Diam. 6.3 cms. £250-300 ($375-450)

Fig. 6.5. **An Early Victorian Silver Trophy from Cheltenham**[3]
A beautiful sterling silver bowl supported by three interlocking offset rackets, which in turn are surrounded by a victory wreath. The rackets stand upon a plain circular base with a raised centre piece, in the middle of which is a single silver (tennis) ball, which is fastened to the stand by a silver wing-nut from below. The rackets are in the style of typical early 'quality' rackets, complete with long handles and leather butt pieces, leather bands around the middle of the handles, and, surprisingly, double lateral stringing. The detail is so fine that you can see where the strings pass through the side of the frame and are tied off. The pins, which secure the leather band just below the throat of the rackets, can clearly be seen. Each racket is marked with a registration diamond for the date 23rd. July 1883. The bowl is engraved: 'CHELTENHAM L. T. T. (Tournament) 1884 OPEN GENTLEMANS DOUBLES 1st Prize Won by: - Capt. C. K. Wood R. E. AND C. L. Sweet' Height 21.5 cms. Diam. 9.8 cms. £750-1000 ($1000-1500)

Fig. 6.6. **A Victorian Silver Trophy Cup**[4]
A goblet shaped half-fluted trophy with a simple flared foot and engraved: 'WEYBRIDGE LAWN TENNIS CLUB Challenge Cup.' (Weybridge, Surrey) Made in London 1886 by 'E H', all the victor's names from 1888 until 1897 are engraved on the reverse. This would have been the club trophy presented by Weybridge Lawn Tennis Club for its annual club tournament. Remarkably, during all these years, there were only two different winners, Wilfred Milne in 1889 and E. J. Avory on eight occasions. Inexplicably the winner in 1896 is not recorded. Weight. 14ozs. Height 24.7 cms. Diam. 12.1 cms. £400-500 ($600-750)

Fig. 6.7. **A Selection of Items formerly in the ownership of Harold Segerson Mahony (1867-1905)**

A Photograph of Harold Segerson Mahony
A large black and white monochrome framed photograph taken at his home in Dromore Castle, County Kerry, Ireland. This photograph has been used in many books featuring his achievements in the tennis world (i.e., *Lawn Tennis at Home and Abroad* by Wallis Myers, p. 145). Image Size Height 28.0 cms. Width 23.0 cms. £250-350 ($375-525)

A Silver Mounted Glass Jug and Beakers[5]
A textured glass jug and a pair of glass beakers, each with silver mounts. The claret jug has a flat hinged cover and boar tusk handle. Inscribed: 'All Comers Doubles 1st Prize G. W. Hillyard and H. S. Mahony.' Heath and Middleton made it in Birmingham. Jug Height 24.0 cms. Beaker Height 11.5 cms. £3000-3500 ($4500-4750)

A Fine, Round Silver Rose Bowl Trophy[6]
This bowl was awarded to Harold Mahony on his victory in the 1890 Cheltenham gentlemen's singles championship. It is engraved: 'CHELTENHAM LAWN TENNIS TOURNAMENT 1890. RESIDENTS CHALLENGE CUP 1st PRIZE. H. S. MAHONY', and suggests that a trophy, possibly owned by the club, was also presented. It has a shaped border, bands of embossed leaves and scrolls, and vertical shell topped flutes. The prize was made by F. Sibray and J. F. Hall in London (1889) and has a registered number (144476) clearly stamped on the base, which is consistent with this date. Wt. 36 ozs. Height 17.1 cms. Diam. 26.0 cms. £1000-1500 ($1500-2250)

'The All England Mixed Doubles' Ebonised Plinth[7]
The plinth (along with the cup which originally stood on top!) was awarded to Harold Mahony in 1896 when he and his partner, Miss Charlotte Cooper, won the 'All England Mixed Doubles Championship' for the third time. This particular plinth is engraved 'Gentleman's Cup' implying that there was also a 'Ladies Cup' which we can assume was also presented 'for keeps' to Miss Cooper. Evenly spaced around the plinth are seven oval and a further three rectangular silver 'shields', each of which has been engraved with the winners names since the inauguration tournament in 1888. Many of the names featured are 'legendary' in lawn tennis history and include: Ernest Renshaw, Mrs. Hillyard, Lottie Dod, and Wilfred Baddeley, as well as Mahony and Cooper. Height 8.0 cms. Diam. 22.6 cms. £3000-4000 ($4500-6000)

Fig. 6.8. **An Octagonal Electroplated Trophy Tray**
The tray is mounted on four 'shell' feet, and has an engraved wildlife scene, the rim decorated with a band of flowers. In the centre of a decorative panel the tray is engraved: 'Burton on Trent Lawn Tennis Tournament 1888 LADIES & GENTLEMEN'S DOUBLES 1st PRIZE WON BY MISS L. JOHNSTONE & E. EVERSHED.' Height 2.6 cms. Width 29.8 cms. Depth 20.2 cms. £150-200 ($225-300)

Fig. 6.9. **A Two Handled Silver Plated Trophy**[8]
Manufactured by W B [&] B Co. for 'CHELTENHAM L. T. T. 1890 GENTLEMENS SINGLES HANDICAP WON BY R. Grist.' It has two scroll and mask handles and part reversed fluting on a knopped stem and round foot, which is decorated with a beaded border. Height 23.5 cms. Diam. 9.5 cms. £100-150 ($150-225)

Fig. 6.10. **Five German Silver Trophies**

Three Silver Trophies from the Uhlenhorst Club, Hamburg[9]
All three trophies were awarded to Mr. F. K. Horley at the Hamburg Championships of September 1893.

The trophy on the left, made by 'B & C', was awarded as a first prize (presumably one of two identical prizes) 'Doppelspiel für Herren' in the open doubles championship. Horley's partner was a Dr. A. H. Williams. The trophy stands upon three round (tennis ball) feet, and gently tapers outwards toward the rim from an oval cylinder base. Two very simple engraved patterned lines, parallel to each other, circumvent the body of the trophy. Height 17.7 cms. Diam. 10.4 cms. £500-700 ($750-1000)

The trophy second from the left is a small silver tankard awarded for a second prize in the singles competition to Horley, following his defeat by W. Bonne who was the defending champion from the previous year. The engraving reads: 'Lawn Tennis Turnier, Septbr.1893, II Preis, EINZELSPIEL FUR HERREN, UM DIE MEISTERSCHAFT VON HAMBURG, - Hamburg' Height 10.7 cms. Diam. 6.7 cms. £500-700 ($750-1000)

The rather unusual but beautiful trophy on the far right, also made by 'B & C', was a prize for the victors of the handicap doubles 'mit Vorgabe' tournament, which was also secured by Horley and Williams. Height 21.2 cms. £500-700 ($750-1000)

A Silver Mounted Glass Vase Trophy 1903[10]
An extremely fine, beautiful, and very rare trophy awarded to Curt von Wessely for his defeat of R. Schindler in the final of the Championship of Prussia Tournament in Berlin. The silver rim is inscribed: 'Dem Gewinner der Meisterschaft von Preufsen Internationales Tennis Tournier zu Berlin, Pfingsten 1903'. The base is also engraved. It reads: 'Gestiftet von Eugen Lifsner Berlin' (Donated by Eugen Lifsner of Berlin). The vase is cut glass and neatly fits into the mounts at the base and the top rim. The base is also stamped: 'J. H. WERNER BERLIN 800' Height 29.4 cms. Diam. 16.9 cms. £1000-1500 ($1500-2000)

A Small Silver Trophy from Berlin[11]
A very distinctly designed little trophy based upon a simple round bowl, raised upon a straight sided, 'studded' stand. The trophy is engraved: 'Hamburg Lawn Tennis Tournament, August 1897. Gentlemen's Singles (Handicap) Class B. First Prize. Henry W. Brooke. Owes 15 5/6. Beat Budelmann receives 5/6 6-1 9-7. Beat C. M. Winter owes 15 7-5 6-3. Beat R. Schutt receives 15 2/6 6-4 4-6 6-4. Beat Col. Lane owes 2/6 6-3 6-4. Beat Westergaard owes 4/6 6-4 6-3.' It is the only time I have ever seen the actual tournament scores engraved upon a trophy. Height 15.2 cms. Diam. 11.5 cms. £300-400 ($450-600)

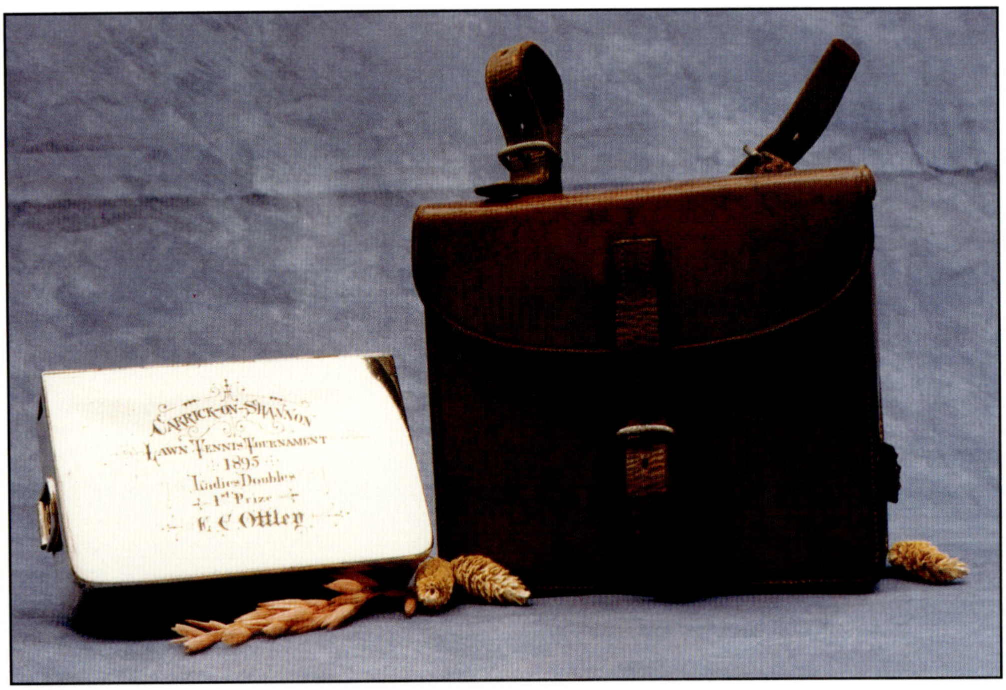

Fig. 6.11. **A Silver Plated Brittania Metal Sandwich Box Trophy**[12]
A small expanding sandwich box by James Dixon and Sons, in its original leather case. The lid of the box is engraved: 'CARRICK-ON-SHANNON LAWN TENNIS TOURNAMENT 1895 Ladies Doubles 1st. Prize E. C. Ottley.' The box has a hinged lid as well as a hinged back edge which allows easy access to the contents (the sandwiches must have been mighty small!). The leather case, with straps for securing it to a belt or even a saddle, has a compartment for the box and, presumably, a bottle for liquids (sadly missing). The monogram E. C. O. is stamped into the front of the case. Box Length 12.0 cms. Width 7.4 cms. Depth 3.6 cms. £125-175 ($200-250)

Fig. 6.12. **A Silver Plated Tankard Trophy**[13]
A silver-plated 'pint' tankard of a shallow concave form, with a skirt support. The makers are unknown. The engraving reads: 'EDGBASTON ARCHERY & LAWN TENNIS SOCIETY CHALLENGE CUP, HOLDERS - S. C. WATSON 1896, A. D. WATSON 1897, A. D. WATSON 1898.' This very important piece was presented at one of the oldest lawn tennis clubs in the world. Height 15.5 cms. Diam. 10.7 cms. £750-1000 ($1000-1500)

Fig. 6.13. **A Decorative Plated Wine Coaster**
Sitting on four little 'claw' feet, a decorative band of flowers and leaves surrounds the body of the coaster. These are matched in style by a raised relief cartouche situated in the centre of the bowl. A pair of 'hook' handles are balanced by the addition of two early flat-topped lawn tennis rackets both of which are decorated by a bow of ribbon. The rim is styled in a flowing regular ribbon pattern. It was made by the Pairpoint Manufacturing Company in the mid-1890s, and it is also stamped 'quadruple plate'. Height 5.1 cms. Diam. 13.3 cms. £150-200 ($225-300)

Right:
Fig. 6.14. **A Silver Plated Goblet**
A highly decorated goblet, with a knopped step and round foot, which has a beaded and floral decoration. The bowl is engraved with a shield surrounded by an ornate symmetrical pattern of flowers and leaves, in the centre of which is engraved the words: 'S. C. C. LAWN TENNIS TOURNAMENT SPRING 1903 2nd PRIZE "C" SINGLES 'HANDICAP' WON BY' Height 11.7 cms. Diam. 7.6 cms. £100-150 ($150-225)

Far right:
Fig. 6.15. **A Large Silver Goblet Trophy**
A large silver trophy cup inscribed: 'Bexley Lawn Tennis Club Presidents Cup won by Maurice E. Ford, July 1904'. It was made in London in 1897. Height 30.0 cms. £130-175 ($200-250)

Fig. 6.16. **A Silver Wimbledon Umpiring Notebook**
An unusual and very rare item being A Wimbledon Umpire's notebook inscribed 'Lawn Tennis Championships 1905 – Umpiring'. The notebook has several pages with ink hand written results of matches from June 1906 to June 1909 including Davis Cup, Wimbledon, and Olympics 1908. The front and back are silver with fine hinging. Made by Elkington & Co. Ltd, Birmingham, in 1904. Length 8.5 cms. Width 6.0 cms. £850-900 ($1275-1350)

Fig. 6.17. **A Pair of Silver Plate Tankard Trophies**
Both are of very similar design — concave in shape, on a raised base with plain loop handles. The first is engraved: 'INTER STATION TENNIS CLUB XMAS 1909' on one side and: 'WON BY BANGKOK W. W. WOOD & H. PRICE' on the other. Between these two inscriptions there is a detailed engraving of a three-headed elephant with an eastern style temple in the background. The second tankard has the words: 'INTER-STATION TENNIS CUP XMAS 1913' with: 'WON BY BANGKOK E. J. WALTON. HAMILTON PRICE.' The tankard is engraved with the image of a mythological creature complete with a horse's head, dragon's wings, and fish's tail. Both of them are made by The Alexander Clark Manufacturing Company, London, and are marked - WELBECK PLATE. Height 13.9 cms. Diam. 9.5 cms. £150-200 ($225-300 each)

Fig. 6.18. **A Silver Presentation Inkwell**
This inkwell was 'presented to Mr. W. T. Davies Esq. ON THE OCCASION OF HIS OPENING THE GLAN ABER TENNIS CLUB MAY 30th. 1908'. It was made by W & H and has Mr. Davies initials, worked as a monogram, engraved into the lid. It is lacking an ink container. Height 5.1 cms. Diam. 10.7 cms. £100-150 ($150-225)

Fig. 6.19. **A Silver Two Handled Trophy**
A large trophy bowl engraved: 'MIXED DOUBLES TOURNAMENT CAIRO JANUARY 1911' by Levi & Salaman, Birmingham. Height 15.2 cms. Diam. 17.7 cms. £100-125 ($150-200)

Fig. 6.20. **A Silver Preserve Dish with Original Glass Liner**
A neat little dish mounted upon three simple claw feet and inscribed: 'WINDSOR LAWN TENNIS CLUB LADIES SINGLES WON BY KATHLEEN F. PERCY 1918'. Made by Huskin and Heath of Birmingham in 1917. Height 3.6cms. Diam. 8.4 cms. £150-200 ($225-300)

Fig. 6.21. **South Shore Lawn Tennis & Croquet Club** A fine, large silver challenge cup, with a pair of attractive swan shaped handles. It is inscribed: 'Presented to the South Shore Lawn Tennis and Croquet Club by J. Nuttal, President 1919. (The club was situated in Squires Gate Lane, Blackpool, England.) This mixed doubles trophy is inscribed with all the winners from 1919 until 1971. Height 17.0 cms. Diam. 21.0 cms. Made in Sheffield, 1918. £200-250 ($300-375)

Fig. 6.22. **A Small Electroplated Trophy** A neat little egg cup style trophy supported by three 1920s style interwoven lawn tennis rackets. The rackets are 'held' together with a hoop of woven 'rope' and a solitary tennis ball sits upon the resulting inverted tripod. The trophy is unmarked and stands upon a contemporary ebonized wooden base. Height 17.2 cms. Diam. 5.7 cms. £75-100 ($100-150)

Fig. 6.23. **A Silver Plated Sweet Dish** An elegant shallow dished table-ornament supported by three interlocking 1920s style lawn tennis rackets standing on a round base. The dish is scalloped and has a decorative perforated edge. The makers are J C & Co. Ltd. Height 11.4 cms. Diam. 12.6 cms. £175-200 ($250-300)

Fig. 6.24. **A Badminton Trophy** An attractive silver-plated trophy, complete with 16 'feathers' 'stitched' with a thread of copper wire. There is no indication of the date that this item was manufactured but the style suggests mid-1920s. There is no evidence of engraving. Height 15.0 cms. Base Diam. 7.7cms. £75-100 ($100-150)

Fig. 6.25. **A Racquets Trophy**
A very unusual silver-plated trophy formed as a trio of 'rope' bound racquets rackets standing upon on a scalloped, square cornered triangular base. The rackets have bound handles and support a simple bowl, which is gilded on the inner surface. A racquets ball sits neatly in the centre of the base. The piece is unmarked but probably dates from the mid-1920s. Height 21.4cms. Base Diam. 11.7cms. £125-175 ($200-250)

Fig. 6.28. **A Collection of Small Silver Trophies**
A personal collection of trophies, which originally belonged to R. W. Hazel of Stone Lawn Tennis Club, Staffordshire, England. They represent a cross section of prizes as a result of her participation in small provincial tournaments and league competitions. The trophies range in date from 1931 to 1935 and are all hallmarked silver. Heights range from 4.9 cms. to 13.0 cms., including the plinth. £100-125 ($150-200)

Fig. 6.26. **A Small Silver Trophy**
A small silver bowl supported by three fine concave wedge rackets which stand on a circular base. The racket strings are formed by the use of a fine silver mesh and the trophy is mounted upon a turned wooden base. The bowl is engraved: 'THORNDALE LAWN TENNIS CLUB Gentlemens Singles Handicap'and at the foot of the rackets, on the circular base: 'Winner 1923. T. G. Davies.' The maker's were Adie Brothers Ltd. of Birmingham. Thorndale Lawn Tennis Club is in Wallasey, Cheshire. Height 14.0 cms. Diam. 5.7 cms. £150-200 ($225-300)

Fig. 6.29. **Cup with Lady Tennis Player**
An attractive silver rose bowl with finely scalloped rim and a pair of swan shaped handles. On the front a small shield is embossed with a lady playing tennis. Made in Birmingham in 1938. Height 12.0 cms. Diam. 18.0 cms. £75-100 ($100-150)

Fig. 6.27. **A Fives Trophy**
An unusual silver-plated trophy presented to: 'G. W. NORRIS, HOUSE FIVES, ETON 1924'. Fives was the hand ball game popularised by the boys at private schools like Eton, Harrow, and Winchester, where 'House' matches frequently took place. The piece is indistinctly marked on the base. Height 18.6 cms. Diam. 8.7 cms. £75-100 ($100-150)

Fig. 6.30. **A Lawn Tennis Trophy**
A small silver trophy which was possibly made in the Far East. The base is stamped: 'TUCK CHAN[G]?' accompanied by a small monogram. The inscription reads: 'SWIRE TENNIS CLUB Won by A. V. T. DEAN 1933'. It is mounted upon a square hardwood base. Height 14.7 cms. Width 12.8 cms. £75-100 ($100-150)

Fig. 6.31. **A Small Silver Dish**
A fine, round silver dish incorporating a two sided reversible medal in the centre. The piece was manufactured by Garrards & Co. of London, to commemorate Wimbledon's Centenary year in 1977. Both pieces are hallmarked. Height 1.8 cms. Diam. 9.2 cms. £50-75 ($75-100)

Fig. 6.32. **A Silver Mounted Glass Claret Jug**
A beautiful modern claret jug (c. 1995) engraved with a scene portraying a mixed doubles match. The piece is marked: 'S. P. & Co.' and the spout is decorated with a grapevine design. Height 30.8 cms. Base Diam. 9.4 cms. £150-175 ($225-250)

Figurative Metalwork

In the case of a trophy, it's the engraving that makes it unique. Figurative pieces were probably originally manufactured in their hundreds, but in most cases cannot be related to any particular event. They have their own special potency. Often they are decorative pieces; sometimes they are functional too. Silver, bronze, or spelter figurines are very popular and collectors are quick to determine the most successful or rare manufacturers, as well as the more aesthetic question of figuratively correct poses! Now and again, the figure will be based upon a particular player, but as you can imagine only the finest players have ever received this honour. I have seen figures representing Anthony Wilding, Suzanne Lenglen, and Arthur Gore, but not many more. France is the country most associated with the production of bronze figurines, and a trip to Paris could well be very worthwhile.

Fig. 6.33. **A Spelter Victorian Gentleman Tennis Player**[14]
A marvellous little figurine, showing a Victorian gentleman posing with his tennis racket. He wears a cap, a long sleeved sweater, and long socks over the top of his trousers. (c. 1880) Height 12.0 cms. £150-250 ($225-375)

Fig. 6.34. **A French 'Figurative' Mantle Clock**
A rare French Victorian marble mantle clock surmounted by a gold coloured spelter lady tennis player. She holds a tennis racket and has a tennis case at her feet. The chiming clock has an attractive floral porcelain face with enamelled numerals by A. Dupuy, and a gold metal surround. Scrolled metal feet support the black and green marble base. The tennis figure is modelled and signed by the French sculptor G. Demange and entitled 'Jeu de Tennis'. (c. 1895) Height of Figure 40.0 cms. Total Height 60.0 cms. £2000-2500 ($3000-3700)

Fig. 6.35. **A Spelter Bust**
An Art Nouveau patinated spelter bust of an allegorical young lady entitled "L'ete" (The Summer). She is complete with a diagonally strung lawn tennis racket, which is tied around the handle with a bow of ribbon, and is indistinctly signed on the base. (c. 1900) Height 30.4 cms. £150-200 ($225-300)

Fig. 6.37. **A Spill Vase**
A spelter match or spill vase, complete with its original lining. The piece features a young girl posed holding an early racket while standing upon a decorative tray. The spill container has a hinged lid and a metal liner sits inside. (c. 1900) Height 15.5 cms. Width 15.8 cms. £100-150 ($150-225)

Fig. 6.36. **A Silver Plated Condiment Set**
An attractive large Electro-plated table condiment set with two inverted long handled rackets with open mesh stringing, on an oval base. Behind the nets are six cut glass bottles, three with plated covers and the others with cut glass stoppers. (c. 1900) Height 27.0 cms. Width 22.0 cms. £800-1000 ($1200-1500)

Fig. 6.38. **An Art Nouveau Figurine**[15]
An Art Nouveau, pewter tennis girl figure, in a serving position, mounted upon a square marble base. The racket is original and the piece is signed "Fraisse" in the surface of the pewter. Although the base appears slightly incongruous or awkward, I have seen an identical figure at a recent antique fair which was mounted in exactly the same way. (c. 1910) Height 18.8 cms. £100-150 ($150-225)

Fig. 6.39. **A Kayzerzinn Figurine**
A Kayzerzinn silvered metal figure of a male tennis player, cast from a model by W. Zwick, the figure being in mid-service. The stringing to the racket, which is original, is extremely fine. Height 33.0 cms. £850-1000 ($1300-1500)

Fig. 6.41. **A Small Silver Gentleman Tennis Player**
A small silver figure, in the shape of a gentleman playing a forehand stroke. A hallmark dates this item as 1922. Height 5.8 cms. £75-100 ($100-150)

Fig. 6.42. **A Brass Tennis Figure**
A male tennis figure moulded in brass, playing a running forehand. The figure is mounted upon an attractive marble base. The racket has been replaced. (c. 1925) Height 21.0 cms. £75-100 ($100-150)

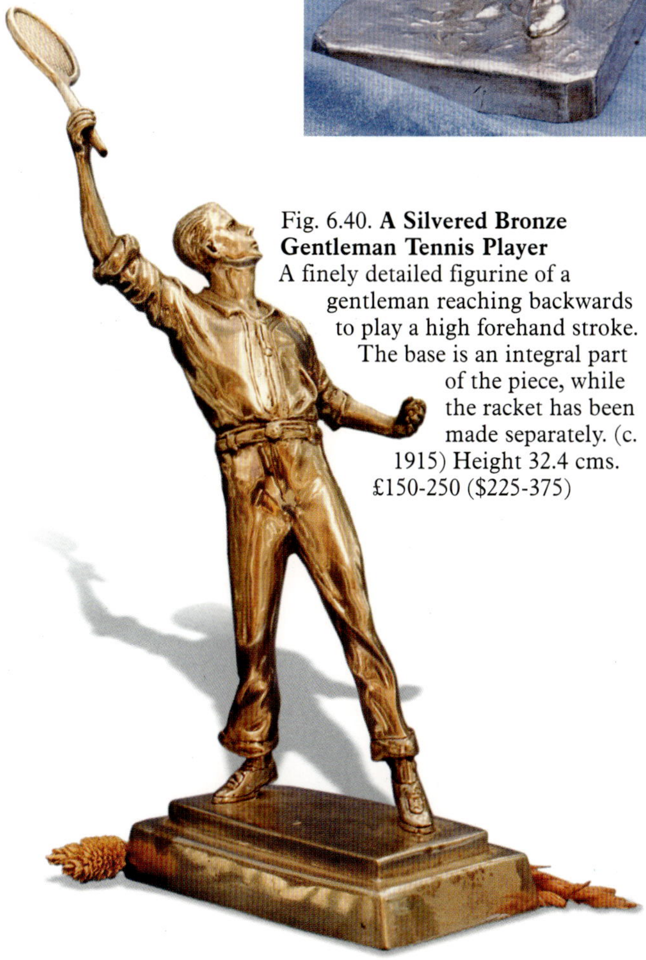

Fig. 6.40. **A Silvered Bronze Gentleman Tennis Player**
A finely detailed figurine of a gentleman reaching backwards to play a high forehand stroke. The base is an integral part of the piece, while the racket has been made separately. (c. 1915) Height 32.4 cms. £150-250 ($225-375)

Fig. 6.43. **A Small Bronze 1920s Lady Lawn Tennis Player**
A finely modelled figurine of a lady, playing a high backhand volley. The whole piece fits onto a piece of soapstone. The figurine might well have been modelled upon Kitty Godfree, the former British Wightman Cup player and Wimbledon Champion. The racket is not original. (c. 1925) Height 13.0 cms. £200-250 ($300-375)

Fig. 6.44. **A Silver Plated Photo Frame**
A small photo frame (or a calendar holder) in the form of a symmetrical rectangular stand, surmounted by two 1920s lawn tennis rackets. (c. 1925) Height 6.5 cms. £100-150 ($150-225)

Fig. 6.45. **A Bronze Lady Tennis Player**
An attractive Lady lawn tennis player reaching forward to play a forehand drive. The racket is moulded as a separate piece, but the figure is very detailed. It is often paired with a gentleman player, very much in the pose of the brass figurine already mentioned. The piece sits upon a rectangular marble stand. (c. 1925) Height 24.7 cms. £150-250 ($225-375)

Fig. 6.46. **'A Girl Tennis Player' by Ferdinand Preiss**[16]
A cold painted bronze and ivory figure, which is cast and carved from a model by Ferdinand Preiss. It is in the form of a young woman, wearing a pale green dress, playing a backhand shot. She stands on a rectangular green and black banded onyx base. Height 29.0 cms. (c. 1930) £8500-10000 ($12750-15000)

Fig. 6.47. **A Small Chrome Figurine of a Lady Tennis Player**
An Art Deco style figure styled as flat silhouette positioned on a round base. (c. 1930) Height 7.0 cms. £30-40 ($45-60)

Far left:
Fig. 6.48. **A Chrome Candlestick**
Consisting of a figure of a 1930s lady about to hit a forehand smash. The figure is cut from a flat sheet of chromed metal, which has been fixed onto a tubular central supporting rod. The base is stamped with the registered number 760405 in two places, and the piece is often seen with another, the figure of which is in a similar, but not identical pose. (c. 1931) Height 23.5 cms. £75-100 ($100-150)

Bottom:
Fig. 6.49. **A 'Pompeian Bronze' Lady Tennis Player**
A wonderful figurine of a 1930s lady lawn tennis player made by The Pompeian Bronze Company. The company is much better known for their production of bookends and lamps. The base is covered with felt upon which a small round company label has been fixed. (c. 1930) Height 40.4 cms. £450-550 ($675-800)

Left:
Fig. 6.50. **A Small Figurative Tennis Trophy**
A small trophy showing a 1920s lady holding a lawn tennis racket behind her back. The piece is quite finely detailed. The figure stands on the top of a Bakelite base. (c. 1925) Height 11.0 cms. £40-60 ($60-90)

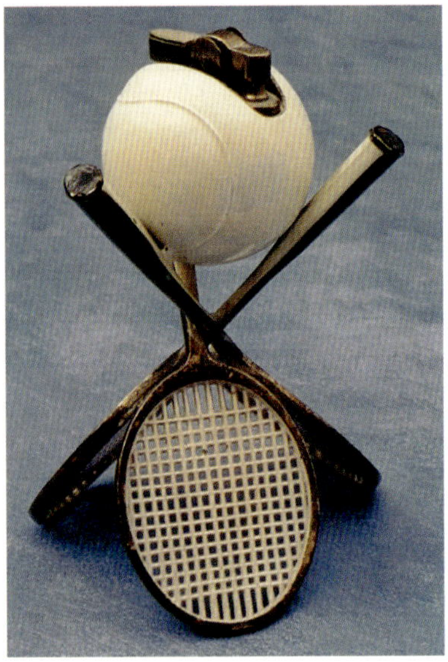

Fig. 6.51. **A Cigarette Lighter**
A base metal cigarette lighter in the form of three 1950s interlocking lawn tennis rackets, which support a lawn tennis ball. A small cigarette lighter neatly fits into a slot at the top of the ball. The whole piece is enamelled in white and gold. (c. 1950) Height 12.6 cms. £100-150 ($150-225)

Fig. 6.52. **A Bronze Frog Tennis Player**
A decorative, bronze frog figurine, holding a racket up in the air. He stands upon a leaf on which a tennis ball sits near to the edge. (c. 1950) Height 21.1 cms. £75-100 ($100-150)

Coins and Medals

Although its obvious that medals are not comparable to trophies in size and intricacy (many of which are supposed to be permanent possessions of the clubs that present them), they are often the prize that a player will take home for 'keeps'. And so, in many ways they are just as important and significant. Larger and more expensive coins and medals were produced in gold and silver, while less expensive and smaller examples tend to be bronze and copper. Specific details of a club or tournament are often included too, because they can be designed as 'bespoke' quantity commissions.

Fig. 6.53. **Oxford Trade Tokens**[17]
An extremely rare Oxford trade token made for Thomas Wood vintner, in 1652. The obverse shows a short handled racket, with Wood's initials on the reverse. Diam 1.5 cms. £400-500 ($600-750)

A similar extremely rare Oxford trade token for Thomas Burnham "Tennis Court," 1650s, showing a tennis racket on the obverse and Burnham's initials on the reverse. Diam. 1.6 cms. £400-500 ($600-750)

Fig. 6.54. **Argosy Braces Token**[18]
A brass trade token for 'ARGOSY BRACES' (c. 1885). The design shows a very detailed image of a bearded gentleman holding a lawn tennis racket; his trousers are obviously supported by the aforementioned braces and the title is repeated in extremely small type. The reverse shows a detailed image of the braces themselves and again the legend is repeated. The token has a milled edge. Diam. 2.1 cms. £75-100 ($100-150)

Fig. 6.55. **Hendon Lawn Tennis Club Medal**[19]
A fine and rare silver medal by 'J.A.R.' The medal is engraved on the reverse: '1886 Hendon L. T. C., Lady and Gentleman Doubles, Miss Last & R.H. Langton' There's a detailed image of a man playing a forehand volley on front. Diam. 3.8 cms. £150-200 ($225-300)

Fig. 6.56. **Princes Club Medals**[20]
A pair of silver commemorative medals, made for the Princes Club Racquet Challenge Cup. The front of each medal is deeply moulded with the Prince of Wales feathers and the Doubled Handicap event. The obverse describes the winners as: 'Louis Mieville & Nigel Holmes in 1891 and L. Mieville & P. Grenfell in 1893. The medals are set in the original presentation box with 'Princes 1891-1893' printed on the lid. Diam. 4.0 cms. £550-650 ($800-1000)

Fig. 6.57. **A Gold Lawn Tennis Club Medal**[21]
An extremely rare gold medal presented by the Dean Lawn Tennis Club of Edinburgh. H. S. O'Connor won the medal for his victory in the club's Championship Cup in 1893, the fifth year it was held. The Dean Club was one of the first eight Clubs to join the Scottish L. T. A. The medal was found with a small booklet, published by the club to celebrate their centenary year. Diam. 2.1 cms. £300-400 ($450-600)

Fig. 6.58. **Cambridge University Medals**[22]
A very rare pair of cased silver Cambridge University medals. The first is inscribed: 'SINGLES P. W. COBBOLD TRIN COLL 1896'. I would assume that he was presented the medal for winning his University's singles championship. The second medal is not engraved but was manufactured with the words: 'CHAMPION RACQUET MEDAL' which he was awarded for his victory in the racquets singles championship of the same year. They are both encased in glass with a silver rim and are contained in their original silk-lined cases. Each item is marked: 'D.Munsey, Goldsmith & WatchMaker Cambridge. (By appointment to his R. H. The Prince of Wales.) Medal Diam. 5.0 cms. Case Dimensions 8.0 x 8.0 cms. £200-250 ($250-375) each

Fig. 6.59. **A Gold Glamorgan Championships Medal**
A fine gold (15 ct.) and enamelled medal for the Glamorgan Championship of Wales. It is marked: 'Gentlemen's Doubles – B. W. Freeman 1912'. The obverse shows the county coat of arms. Height 3.5 cms. Width 2.5 cms. £150-200 ($225-250)

Fig. 6.60. **Le Touquet Lawn Tennis Club Medal**
A French bronze medal prize from Le Touquet Lawn Tennis Club, in 1921. It features a figure of Gallia, below which are the words; 'LE TOUQUET LAWN TENNIS CLUB 17 e me TOURNOI INTERNATIONAL SEPTEMBER 1921.' It is contained in its original case of issue. Extremely fine condition. Medal Width 3.5 cms. Depth 5.0 cms. £125-150 ($190-225)

Fig. 6.62. **Warwickshire L. T. A. Medal**
A small round silver medal with an enamel shield applied to the centre. The hand painted enamel shows an illustration of Warwick County's emblem (a brown bear). On the obverse are the words: 'WARWICKSHIRE COUNTY L.T.A.' The reverse has been engraved: 'JUNIOR DOUBLES CHAMPIONSHIP – 1920 – PRIORY L. T. C. I. B. JENKINS AND D. G. BIRCH.' A hallmark shows the manufacturer as V & S of Birmingham in 1921! The medal is contained in a box made by 'VAUGHTONS LTD., Goldsmith & Silversmith BIRMINGHAM'. On the lid of the box are stamped the words: 'WARWICKSHIRE COUNTY LAWN TENNIS ASSO'N. 1914'. Diam. 2.6 cms. Box length 6.1 cms. Width 5.5 cms. Depth 1.7 cms. £100-125 ($150-200)

Fig. 6.61. **B. C. Eveleigh Medal**[23]
A large bronze medal minted to celebrate the life and works of Wimbledon Umpire B. C. Eveleigh. The obverse is inscribed: 'B. C. Eveleigh Lawn Tennis Referee 1882-1910' complete with bust of Eveleigh. The reverse: 'Eveleigh Memorial Medal for level Mixed Doubles won by' with a laurel wreath. Diam. 5.0 cms. £100-125 ($150-200)

Fig. 6.63. **A Dutch Medal**
A finely detailed medal showing an Edwardian lady playing a low forehand. Engraved on the reverse: "NAT. Tenniswedstrjden T.I.O.D. Gouda Wisselbeker Dames Single 1921" Diam. 3.0 cms. £50-75 ($75-100)

Fig. 6.65. **A Dutch 1923 Medal**
A large finely detailed medal showing a gentleman playing a smash, in mid-court. The reverse is engraved with the words: "KKAMPIOENSCHAP OVERDEKTE BANEN1923" which is enclosed with a border of decorative leaves. Diam. 4.1 cms. £50-75 ($75-100)

Fig. 6.66. **A Fernlea Tennis Club Medal**
An attractive silver medal in the shape of a shield. The reverse is engraved: 'FERNLEA TENNIS CLUB HANDICAP 1931'. The medal is hallmarked William Adams of Birmingham, 1925. A small 'D A' monogram is engraved onto a raised shield on the front. £15-20 ($20-30)

Fig. 6.64. **A Gouda 1921 Medal**
A small medal, showing a gentleman playing a low backhand drive whilst taking part in a mixed doubles match. On the reverse are engraved the words: "KAMPIOENSCHAP GOUDA 1921 DAMES DOUBLE". Diam. 2.8 cms. £50-75 ($75-100)

Fig. 6.67. **An Enamelled Lawn Tennis Medal**
A finely detailed silver medal with a blue enamelled panel. The obverse is engraved: 'W. Y. M. C. A. B.' while the words: 'LAWN TENNIS CLUB' are also engraved on the medal. The design also incorporates a pair of crossed lawn tennis rackets and a ball superimposed over a lawn tennis net. T & Co. of London manufactured the medal in 1926. Length 3.7 cms. Width 2.6 cms. £40-60 ($60-80)

Fig. 6.68. **A Wimbledon Jubilee Championships Medal**[24]
An extremely rare brass medal, which is believed to have been presented to Cyril Eames in 1926 (but is not engraved). These medals were presented (on the Centre Court) to all the competitors who took part in the Jubilee Championships at Wimbledon. The reverse shows the inscription "Wimbledon 1877-1926". Diam. 5.1 cms. £200-250 ($300-375)

Fig. 6.69. **A Birmingham Evening Despatch Lawn Tennis Medal**
A silver tennis medal with a laurel wreath surrounding a medallion with crossed rackets, the whole surmounted by a crown. The reverse is engraved: 'EVENING DESPATCH TENNIS TOURNAMENT SEMI-FINALIST 1928 F. E. BATES'. The Evening Despatch was the name of an English newspaper, which sponsored the tournament. The medal is hallmarked for V & S Birmingham 1925. Length 3.5 cms. Width 2.8 cms. £30-50 ($45-75)

Fig. 6.70. **A Streatham Lawn Tennis Cup Medal**
A small round silver medal issued as a prize for 'STEATHAM LAWN TENNIS CUP COMPETITION'. The medal is engraved: '1929 JUNIOR MISS E. PRATT'. A hallmark reads: F. Fattorini and Son Ltd., Birmingham 1928'. Diam. 3.3 cms. £20-30 ($30-45)

Fig. 6.71. **A Cambridge University Medal**
A large bronze university lawn tennis medal. The obverse reads: 'UNIVERSITAS CANTABRIGIENSIS' which encloses a representation of the Cambridge University coat of arms. Within a symmetrical enclosure of laurel leaves the reverse has been engraved: 'CAMBRIDGE UNIVERSITY LAWN TENNIS CLUB FRESHMENS HARD COURT TOURNAMENT DOUBLES RUNNER UP R. N. A. LEYTON CAIUS [COLLEGE] J. R. ATTREE CORPUS [COLLEGE] 1929'. Diam. 5.0 cms. £75-100 ($100-150)

Fig. 6.72. **A Silver Mixed Doubles Medal**
A fine ornate silver lawn tennis medal with its original ribbon and pin. It dates from 1935 and is engraved on the reverse: 'C. A. T. C. – E. BIRD MIXED DOUBLES'. A hallmark reads: 'William Adams Ltd., Birmingham 1933'. Length of medal 3.3 cms. Width 2.2 cms. £30-40 ($45-60)

Fig. 6.73. **A Pinches of London Medal**
A finely detailed 1930s tennis medal (gold colour) by Pinches of London, showing ladies playing a game of doubles. The reverse shows a blank area surrounded by a sprig of leaves. Diam. 3.3 cms. £30-50 ($45-75)

Fig. 6.75. **A Gentleman's Enamelled Silver Medal**
A decorative silver medal with a finely detailed enamel of a gentleman playing a high volley on the obverse. A hallmark on the reverse shows that it was made by William Adams of Birmingham in 1947. Length 5.0 cms. Width 3.0 cms. £20-30 ($30-45)

Fig. 6.74. **A Wimbledon Umpire's Medal**
A bronze Wimbledon umpire's medal from 1938. 'Fattorini & Sons Ltd., Bradford Works, Barr St. Birmingham' manufactured the medal. On the obverse side the design reads: 'ALL ENGLAND L. T. C.' which is superimposed over the image of a pair of crossed lawn tennis rackets. The reverse reads: 'THE LAWN TENNIS CHAMPIONSHIP UMPIRE'S SOUVENIR H. R. S. DUNCAN 1938'. This was the year that Don Budge and Helen Wills Moody won their respective singles championships. The medal is contained in its original box. A few of these medals have been seen in various auction houses and sales, but I've never seen one dated after the Second World War. £75-100 ($100-150)

Fig. 6.76. **A Gentleman's Lawn Tennis Medal**
A 1950s copper and silver plate tennis medal showing a gentleman tennis player wearing shorts. Length 4.3 cms. Width 3.0 cms. £10-15 ($15-20)

Fig. 6.77. **Three Brass Lawn Tennis Medals**
Three similarly designed, brass lawn tennis medals from the 1950s. Ave. Diam. 3.3 cms. £10-15 ($15-20) each

Fig. 6.78. **A Circular White Metal Medal**
A circular white metal lawn tennis medal showing a pair of gentlemen playing a singles rally over a net. The engraving on the reverse reads: 'N. L. A. C. Ladies' Singles CHAMPION 1952 MRS. A. LAKIN'. Diam. 2.9 cms. £10-15 ($15-20)

Fig. 6.79. **A 1950s Gentleman's Medal**
A large brass medal with a gentleman playing a running backhand on the obverse. Engraved on the reverse is: 'W. L. V. '57' Diam. 4.0 cms. £10-15 ($15-20)

Fig. 6.81. **The Junior Championships of Great Britain**
A silver medal engraved: 'Mixed Doubles 1965 Winners'. The championships would probably have been played at Wimbledon. It is contained in its original box and was made by Fattorini and Sons of Birmingham. Diam. 3.2 cms. £30-50 ($45-75)

Brooches and Pins

In the main, brooches and pins have always been produced for ladies to wear, but there have been a few exceptions. The most popular design features a racket or a pair of crossed rackets, and is quite interesting because they are often styled as miniature replicas of the rackets of the day, in every detail. They will often feature flat top rackets, diagonal or double mains stringing, leather collars, head bands, and sometimes even the screws which helped hold the wedge and head of the racket together.

Fig. 6.82. **An Early Silver Racket Brooch**
An early silver racket brooch with diagonal mesh stringing and a ball in the centre of the head. This design, with a long handle and straight tear-drop shape head, may well represent the game of 'Racquets' rather than 'Lawn tennis'. As a result, its date of manufacture could be anywhere between 1840 and 1890. Length 6.1 cms. Width 1.4 cms. £75-100 ($100-150)

Fig. 6.83. **Crossed Rackets, Tennis Ball, Posts, and Net**
A very rare Victorian silver brooch with fine crossed rackets and ball superimposed above an early pair of posts and net with a very detailed grass base. The piece is hallmarked with a registration diamond – 11th. January 1880 J : T STD Length 4.3 cms. Width 3.0 cms. £300-350 ($450-475)

Fig. 6.84. **Racket and Ball**
A large continental silver offset racket brooch with solid string surface and ball. (c. 1880) Length 7.0 cms. Width 2.1 cms. £100-150 ($150-225)

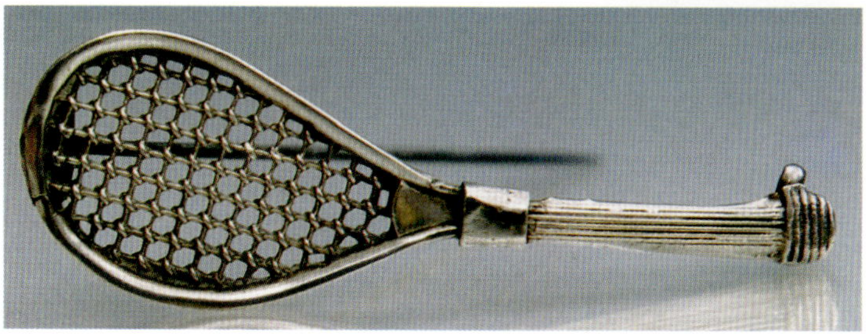

Fig. 6.85. **An Offset Lawn Tennis Racket**
A rare silver offset-racket brooch with a collar and a grooved handle. Quite apart from its unusual shape, a specific detail is that each of the strings in the head of the racket are wound around each other at each junction. The design suggests a date of from the late 1870s to perhaps 1883, although it's too difficult to be more precise than that. Length 5.9 cms. Width 1.9 cms. £100-150 ($150-225)

Fig. 6.86. **Hearts and Flowers**
A Victorian silver-plated racket brooch with a symbol of two entwined hearts and flowers. (c. 1885) Length 4.4 cms. Width 1.2 cms. £100-150 ($150-225)

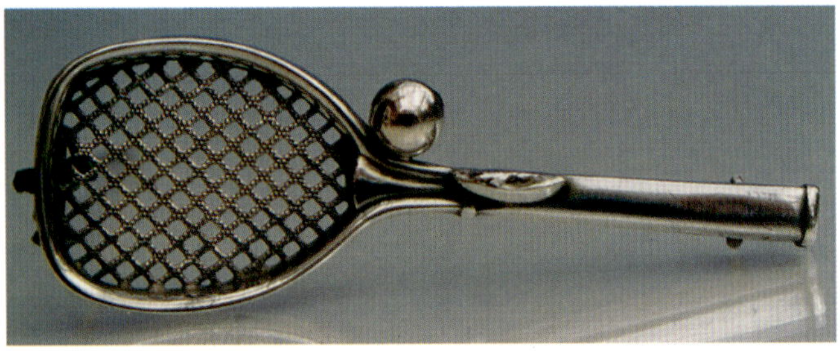

Fig. 6.87. **A Flat Top Racket**
A fine unmarked Victorian silver flat top racket brooch with a diagonal stringing pattern and a lawn tennis ball (manufactured from a hollow sphere) fixed to the side. (c. 1885) Length 5.4 cms. Width 1.9 cms. £100-150 ($150-225)

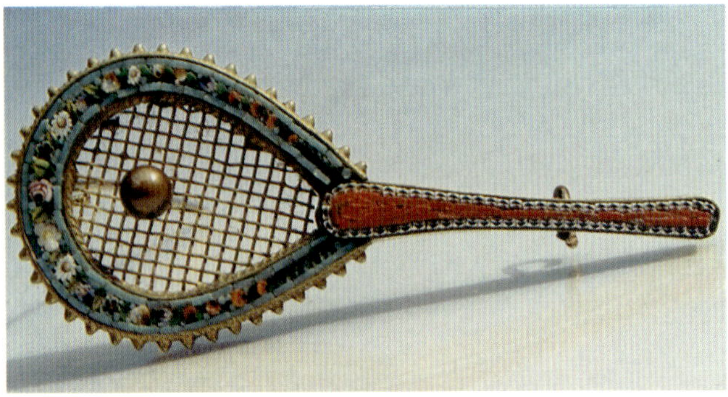

Fig. 6.88. **A Gold Metal Racket**
A very pretty gold metal brooch with painted floral decoration around the head of the racket, and a red handle. It has fine gold stringing with a lawn tennis ball in the centre. (c. 1885) Length 3.0 cms. Width 2.5 cms. £60-80 ($90-120)

Fig. 6.89. **Crossed Lawn Tennis Rackets**
A silver Victorian brooch designed as crossed lawn tennis rackets. Each has a lawn tennis ball in the centre of a diagonal stringing pattern. Although the method of dating is notoriously unreliable, evidence from the design of the rackets suggests a date in the early 1880s. Length 4.8 cms. Width 2.1 cms. £70-100 ($100-150)

Fig. 6.90. **A Brooch from Chester**
A silver hallmarked Victorian brooch with a racket set across a floral decoration in a crescent shape. Hallmarked for Chester 1887. Length 4.0 cms. Width 2.5 cms. £65-85 ($100-125)

Fig. 6.91. **Rackets on a Horseshoe**
A Victorian silver brooch with two crossed rackets positioned in the middle of a horseshoe with a marquisette stone representing a lawn tennis ball. Hallmarked – Murdoch and Jones of Birmingham, 1888. Diam. 3.0 cms. £75-100 ($100-150)

Fig. 6.92. **A Scarf Brooch**
A silver Victorian scarf brooch, decorated with a racket, (love) birds, flowers, and ball, all in relief on an oval base. The item is hallmarked Thomas Walker of Birmingham, 1888. Length 4.2 cms. Width 2.6 cms. £100-150 ($150-225)

Fig. 6.93. **A Racket and Tennis Shoes**
A Victorian solid silver brooch showing a strung racket surface with two lawn tennis shoes and a ball set onto the surface. A hallmark on the rear indicates that Plante & Co. made the brooch at Birmingham in 1889. Length 5.0 cms. Width 1.75 cms. £120-150 ($180-225)

Fig. 6.97. **A Flat Top Racket with Shamrock**
A silver Victorian flat top racket brooch with shamrock and imitation diamond lawn tennis ball. (c. 1890) Length 3.4 cms. Width 1.2 cms. £50-75 ($75-100)

Fig. 6.94. **A Brass Dress Brooch**
A brass dress brooch in the form of a very detailed lawn tennis racket and a pair of tennis shoes. An imitation diamond is mounted on the head of the racket forming a lawn tennis ball. (1889) Length 4.1 cms. Width 2.4 cms. £75-100 ($100-150)

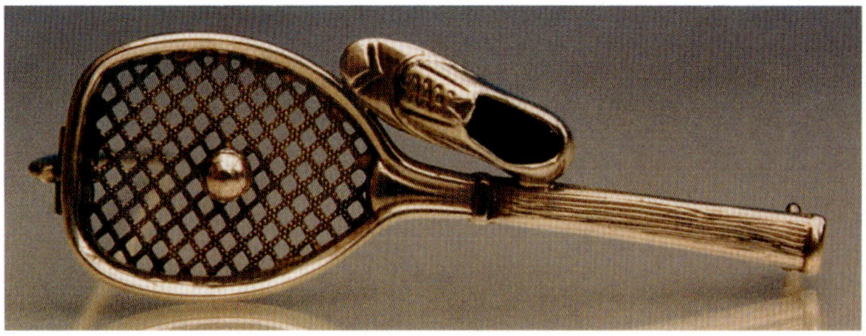

Fig. 6.98. **A Flat Top Racket with a Single Shoe**
A fine rare silver brooch in the style of a flat top racket with tennis shoe attached to one side. The piece is very detailed (c. 1890). Length 5.3 cms. Width 2.0 cms. £100-125 ($150-185)

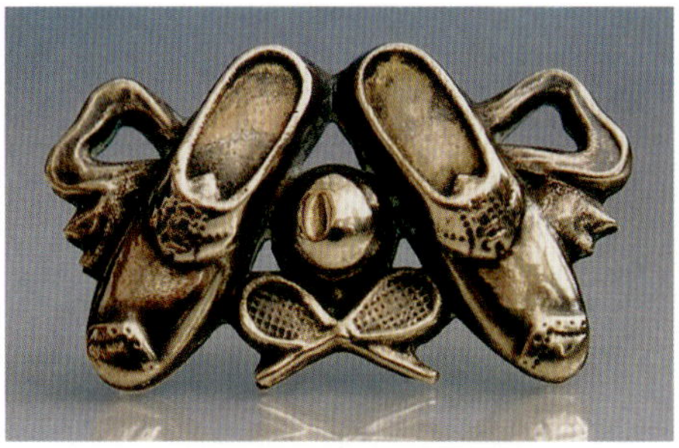

Fig. 6.95. **Tennis Shoes and a Racket**
A symmetrical hollow-ware brass or copper tennis brooch, the design of which is based upon a pair of early lawn tennis shoes, behind which is a pierced bow of ribbon, and in the foreground a lawn tennis ball and two crossed tennis rackets. The item is quite detailed. (c. 1890) Length 3.5 cms. Width 2.0 cms. £50-75 ($75-100)

Fig. 6.99. **A Silver Racket and Ball**
A finely decorated silver Victorian racket brooch with a tennis ball on the strings. The piece has a silver hallmark and is very difficult to decipher, but was probably made in Birmingham in 1892. Length 5.4 cms. Width 1.6 cms. £100-125 ($150-185)

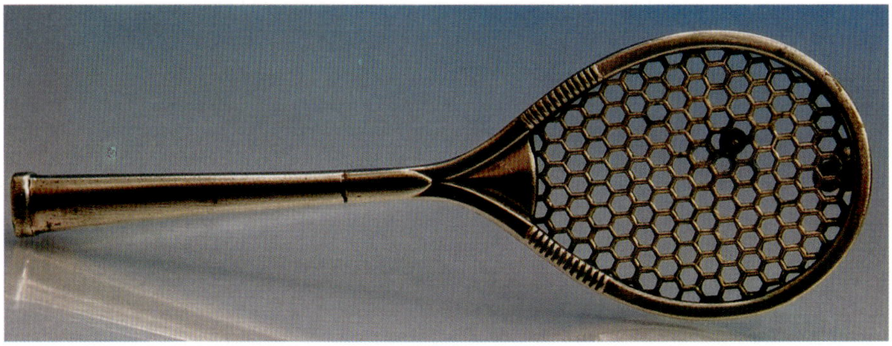

Fig. 6.96. **A Hexagonal Strung Racket**
A large but elegant brass Victorian tennis racket brooch with a mesh of hexagonal shaped stringing which is sandwiched between two identical halves of the racket. A simulated pearl 'tennis ball' was once positioned slightly to the left centre of the strings. (c. 1890) Length 7.5 cms. Width 2.4 cms. £100-125 ($150-185)

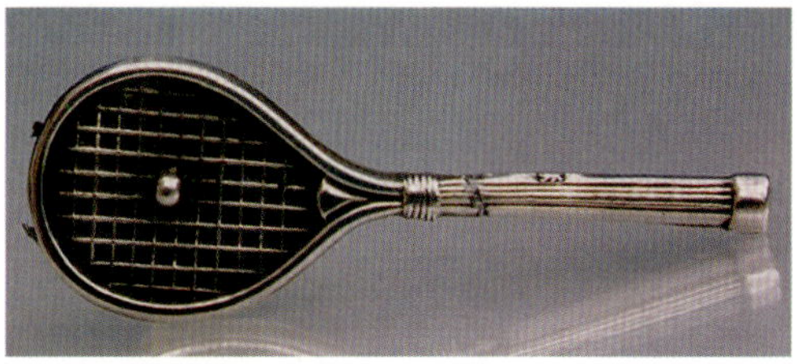

Fig. 6.100. **A Racket showing a Leather Collar**
A fine Victorian sterling silver racket brooch showing a collar around a grooved handle and a small ball in the centre of the strings. Hallmarked – H : H Birmingham 1895. £100-125 ($150-185)

Fig. 6.101. **A Horseshoe Brooch**
A silver horseshoe shaped Victorian brooch with racket and ball, decorated with flowers. Hallmarked – Birmingham 1896 S. Brothers. Length 3.3 cms. Width 2.9 cms. £75-100 ($100-150)

Fig. 6.105. **A Jet Brooch**
A rare black jet Victorian brooch with a dainty ladies hand holding the racket which has diagonal stringing and a lawn tennis ball in the centre of the strings. (c. 1900) Length 5.4 cms. Width 2.0 cms. £75-100 ($100-150)

Fig. 6.102. **A Tournament Brooch**
A rare German (?) silver, brass, and enamel prize brooch. The text reads – V. OEST L. T. TURNIER JUNI 1898. The colours (red and yellow) quite probably relate to the club at which the brooch was awarded. Length 4.8 cms. Width 4.2 cms. £150-200 ($225-250)

Fig. 6.106. **A Silver Table Tennis Brooch**
A rare silver table tennis brooch showing a string net and posts with a table tennis ball perched at the top of the net band, behind which are a pair of vellum battledores with what appears to be a representation of wound calf-skin handles. The brooch is hall-marked P & T Birmingham 1900, a prime era for the development and popularity of the table-top game. Length 4.0 cms. Width 1.1 cms. £100-150 ($150-225)

Fig. 6.103. **An Enamelled Copper Brooch**
A very unusual small enamelled copper brooch in blue and orange. (c. 1900) Length 3.4 cms. Width 1.3 cms. £40-60 ($50-90)

Fig. 6.107. **A Brass Table Tennis Brooch**
A small brass or gilt brooch with two ornately decorated table tennis bats and a silver metal table tennis ball. Marked – T+H and G.F (c. 1900) Length 3.2 cms. Width 1.2 cms. £100-150 ($150-225)

Fig. 6.104. **A Gold Metal Brooch with a Leather Handle**
A very pretty gold metal brooch with painted floral decoration around the head of the racket, and a red handle. It has fine gold stringing with an imitation pearl lawn tennis ball slightly off centre on the strings. (c. 1900) Length 7.5 cms. Width 3.5 cms. £120-150 ($180-225)

Fig. 6.108. **A Gold Table Tennis Brooch**
An extremely rare Victorian gold table tennis brooch, with two crossed rackets set below an ornate gold net with mesh stringing. A gold ball surmounts the net. The rackets have mother of pearl faces and the handles have gold stringing. (c. 1900) Length 5.0 cms. Width 1.75 cms. £250-300 ($375-450)

Fig. 6.109. **A Silver Table Tennis Brooch (Two Table Tennis Balls)**
A small but elegant brooch with a pair of small battledores behind a table tennis net. It was made in Birmingham in 1906 by 'P & T'. Length 4.0 cms. Width 1.3 cms. £100-150 ($150-225)

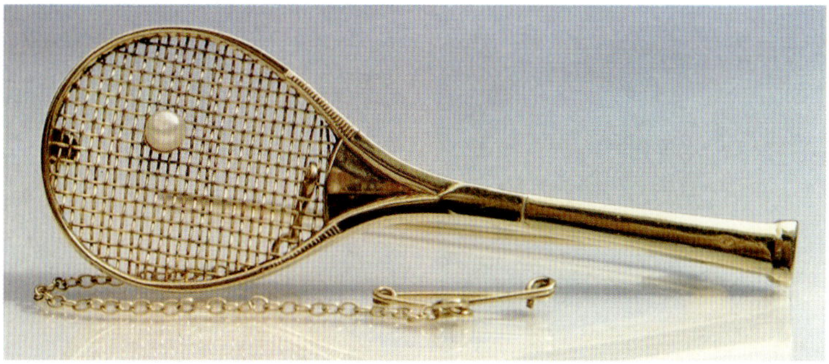

Fig. 6.110. **A Gold Tennis Brooch**
A beautiful gold brooch with gold mesh stringing and fine filigree to the racket head. There is a full-length gold pin on the back with a safety chain attached. (c. 1900) Length 7.0 cms. Width 2.25 cms. £800-1000 ($1200-1500)

Fig. 6.111. **An Offset Racket with a Shamrock**
An Edwardian silver offset racket brooch with a green agate shamrock decoration, and a tennis ball on the strings. Hallmarked S & C Birmingham 1909. Here is a prime example of how misleading the design of a racket can be. Without a hallmark one would assume this was certainly a Victorian piece, possibly from the late 1870s! Length 3.5 cms. Width 1.3 cms. £50-75 ($75-100)

Fig. 6.112. **A Flat Top Racket Decorated with Flowers**
This unusual piece has separate decorative pieces added to a flat top racket. It was made in Birmingham and has a hallmark for 1917. Length 5.4 cms. Width 1.6 cms. £50-75 ($75-100)

Fig. 6.113. **Two 1930s Brooches**
The first is stamped from a flat piece of brass and shows a lady playing a low forehand. The piece is simply decorated with a small piece of red 'plastic' at the base. Height 5.4 cms. £30-40 ($45-60)

The second is an enamelled copper figure of a girl holding a tennis ball in her left hand, about to hit a backhand. Height 3.4 cms. £40-50 ($60-75)

Fig. 6.114. **A Red 'Plastic' Racket**
An attractive 1930s racket, which consists of a red plastic racket mounted onto a copper base by means of copper wire decoration around the handle and the head. A simulated pearl represents a lawn tennis ball. Length 6.6 cms. Width 2.1 cms. £20-30 ($30-45)

Fig. 6.115. **Three 'Art Deco' Brooches**
Three attractive 'Art Deco' style sterling silver brooches, the first having a red enamelled shirt and green grass base. The centre figure has a marcasite setting. (c. 1930) Height 4.0 cms. £120-150 ($180-225) each

Fig. 6.116. **A Scarf Brooch**
A white metal Victorian scarf brooch (circular) showing two crossed rackets and three lawn tennis balls. (c. 1910) Diam. 3.3 cms. £50-75 ($75-100)

Fig. 6.117. **A Flat Topped Racket**
A white metal tennis brooch (possibly silver) in the form of an early flat-topped racket with diagonal stringing and a shamrock decoration. The back is stamped 'MADE IN ENGLAND'. (c. 1910) Length 4.5 cms. Width 1.8 cms. £50-75 ($75-100)

Fig. 6.118. **A Crossed Racket Brooch**
A small metal gilt crossed racket brooch with mesh strings, each racket surmounted by a pearl ball. (c. 1910) Length 4.0 cms. Width 2.0 cms. £50-75 ($75-100)

Fig. 6.119. **A Decorative 'Art Deco' Brooch**
An 'Art Deco' style metal racket brooch with a black decorative front and cross stringing, surmounted by a metal ball. (c. 1925) Length 5.0 cms. Width 1.5 cms. £55-75 ($80-120)

Fig. 6.120. **A Silver Crossed Racket Brooch**
A pretty silver metal crossed racket brooch with solid stringing and an attractive decorative relief to the front surface. (c. 1925) Length 4.0 cms. Width 2.5 cms. £30-50 ($45-75)

Fig. 6.121. **Crossed Rackets and Ball**
A pair of two crossed rackets with a ball, with minimum surface detail, marked – silver. (c. 1925) Length 3.6 cms. Width 2.0 cms. £50-75 ($75-100)

Fig. 6.122. **A Round Silver Brooch**
A small round silver badge or brooch showing crossed rackets and the letters – T R C. Hallmarked – C. Usher of Birmingham 1926. Diam. 2.3 cms. £50-75 ($75-100)

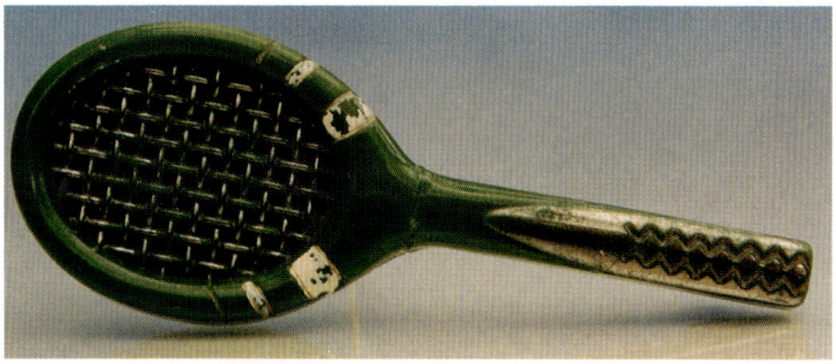

Fig. 6.123. **A Lead Based Metal Brooch**
An 'Art Deco' lead based metal brooch with green and silver decorative banding. (c. 1930) Length 7.1 cms. Width 2.5 cms. £40-60 ($60-90)

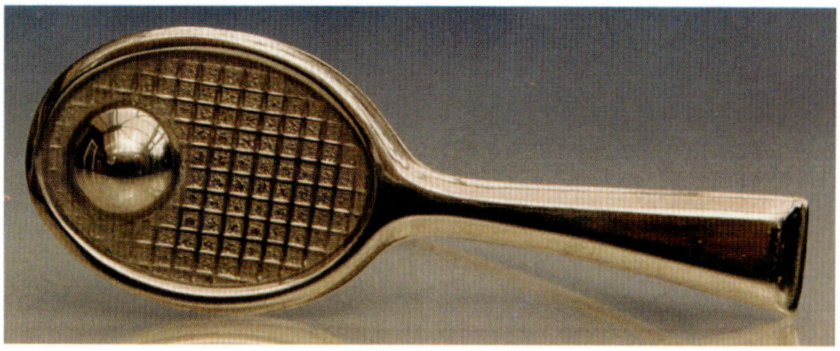

Fig. 6.127. **A White Metal Racket Brooch**
An artistic white metal brooch in the shape of a lawn tennis racket, with a tennis ball sitting on the strings. The whole piece is stamped out of a single piece of metal. The back of the head of the racket is formed from an additional oval piece. (c. 1935) Length 6.4 cms. Width 2.2 cms. £40-60 ($60-90)

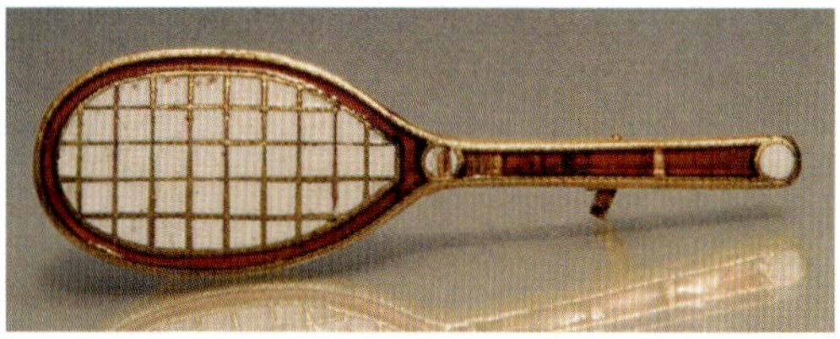

Fig. 6.124. **A Red and White Enamelled Brooch**
A neat little red and white enamelled brooch with white string area. (c. 1930) Length 3.8 cms. Width 1.1 cms. £40-60 ($60-90)

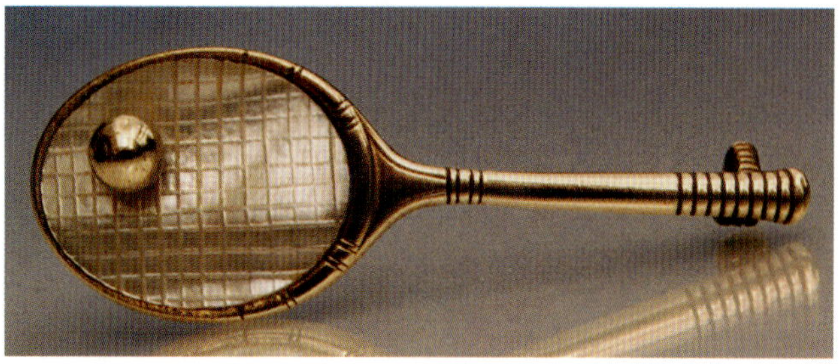

Fig. 6.128. **A Brass Racket Brooch with Mother of Pearl**
An attractive brass racket brooch with mother of pearl inlay strings and brass tennis ball. (c. 1940) Length 5.2 cms. Width 1.7 cms. £40-60 ($60-90)

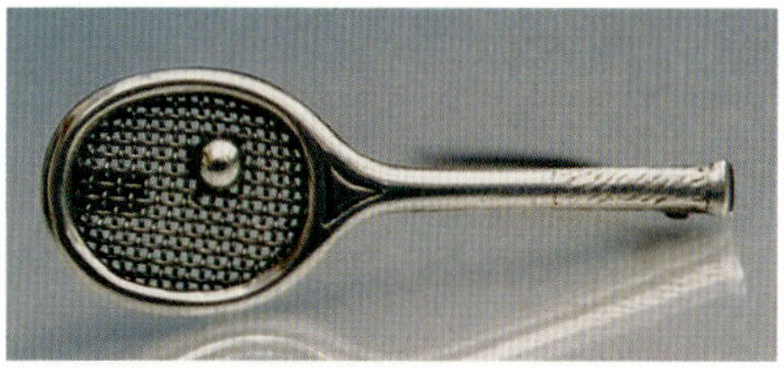

Fig. 6.125. **A Silver Racket Brooch**
A small, fine silver racket brooch, with a tennis ball fixed into the centre of mesh strings. (c. 1930s) Marked STERLING SILVER. Length 3.2 cms. Width 1.1 cms. £60-80 ($90-120)

Fig. 6.129. **A Large Silver Gilt Racket**
A large silver gilt racket brooch, with a rather large head in comparison with the size of the racket. This item was most certainly made before the trend for oversize rackets! (c. 1950) Length 7.0 cms. Width 2.5 cms. £30-50 ($45-75)

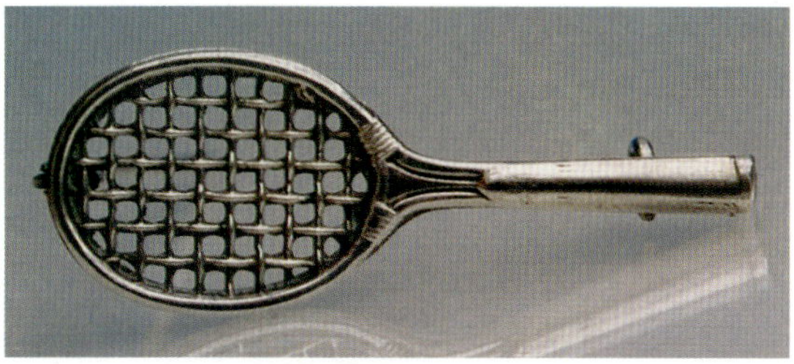

Fig. 6.126. **A Sterling Silver Brooch**
A silver tennis racket brooch from the 1930s. The item is marked STERLING SILVER and is particularly fine as the strings are represented in an 'open' manner. Length 4.4 cms. Width 1.6 cms. £40-60 ($60-90)

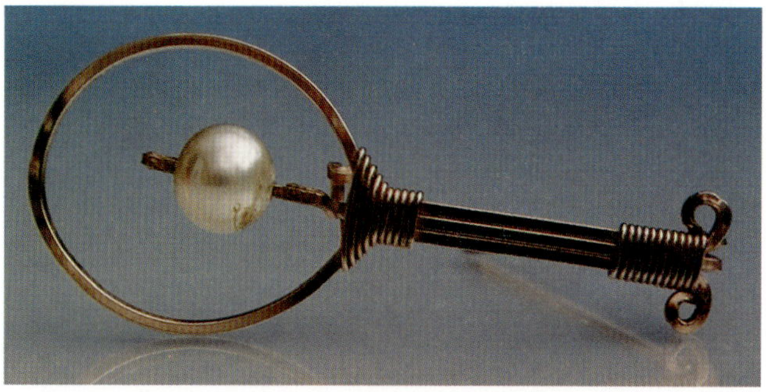

Fig. 6.130. **A Gilt Metal Single-Piece Brooch**
A modern gilt metal gold brooch in the shape of a lawn tennis racket, with simulated pearl tennis ball. It has a curious and yet ingenious construction, in that the whole of the main body of the 'racket' (including the catch mechanism) appears to be constructed from a single length of metal. (c. 1950) Length 5.0 cms. Width 2.1 cms. £20-40 ($30-60)

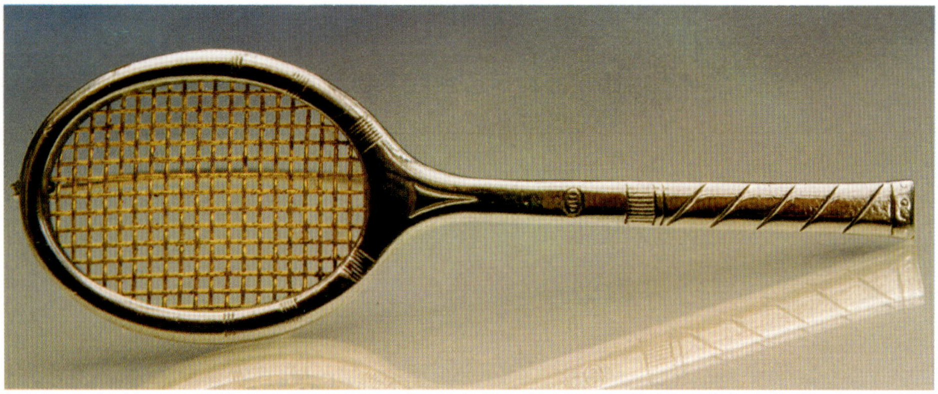

Fig. 6.131. **A White Metal Brooch with Copper Wire Strings**
A large white metal tennis racket brooch with fine copper wire strings and accurate detailing. Marked W. B. S. PAT. APP. FOR (c. 1950) Length 7.6 cms. Width 2.4 cms. £30-50 ($45-75)

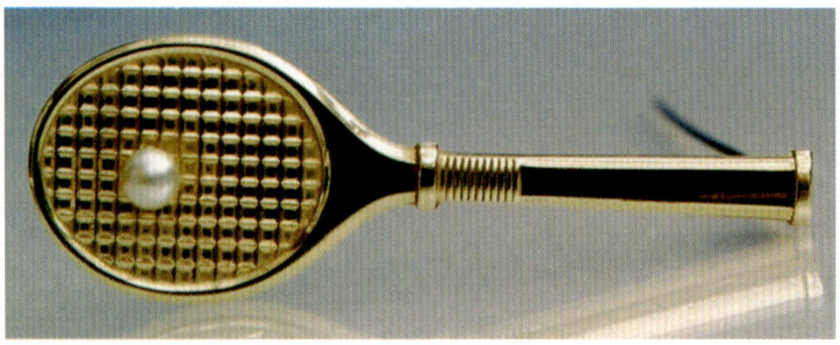

Fig. 6.132. **A Gold-Plated Racket Brooch**
A neat little gold-plated racket brooch with a simulated pearl tennis ball. Marked on the pin - ROLLED GOLD (RW?)(c. 1960) Length 4.9 cms. Width 1.6 cms. £40-60 ($60-90)

Fig. 6.133. **Three Robinson's Golliwog Brooches**
Quite a modern brooch, with the words: '©JAMES ROBERTSON & SONS P. M.' impressed into the surface at the back. (c. 1985) Height 3.0 cms. Width 2.1 cms. £20-30 ($30-45)

A Robinson's brass 'golliwog' tennis badge advertising 'GOLDEN SHREAD' marmalade. Made for James Robertson & Sons, Paisley, England, by Fattorini and Sons, 36, Barr Street, Birmingham, England. This particular model was made anywhere between 1946 and 1969. Height 3.4 cms. Width 1.7 cms. £50-75 ($75-100)

A Robinsons golliwog badge marked 'R.E.V.COMM FREDERICK ST. B'HAM 1985' on the reverse. Buyers should be aware that fakes are in the market place; the maker's name should be stamped on the rear of a genuine piece. Height 3.4 cms. Width 1.7 cms. £30-50 ($45-75)

Fig. 6.134. **A Silver Brooch with Fine Stringing**
A fine modern silver brooch with a pair of crossed rackets and a simulated pearl ball. The strings are actually interweaving and the piece is marked MG SILVER. (c. 1970) Length 3.6 cms. Width 2.2 cms. £40-60 ($60-90)

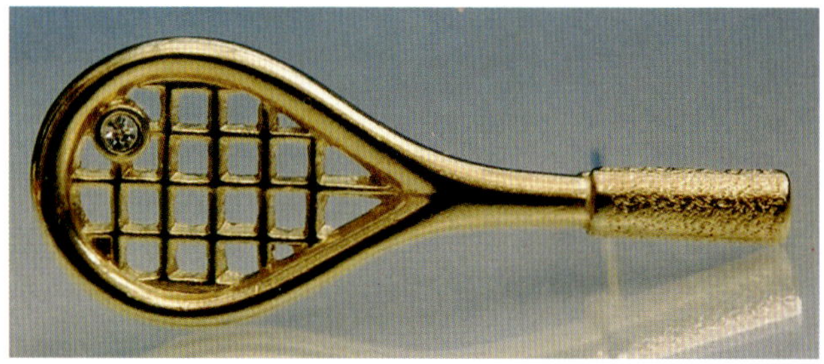

Fig. 6.135. **A Modern Gilt Metal Racket**
A modern gilt metal lawn tennis racket brooch, with a glass 'diamond' tennis ball and a safety catch. (c. 1995) Length 4.9 cms. £40-60 ($60-90)

Fig. 6.136. **A Gilt Metal Racket with Faux Diamonds**
A modern gilt metal crossed racket brooch with imitation diamonds. (c. 1995) Length 4.1 cms. Width 3.5 cms. £30-60 ($45-90)

Fig. 6.137. **A Marcasite Brooch**
A very decorative silver and marquisette brooch formed as a lawn tennis racket. Ornamented with reproduction diamonds on the handle and frame with a pair of coloured stones simulating tennis balls. (c. 1995) £40-60 ($60-90)

Utilitarian Items

Manufacturers have always grasped the opportunity to produce any kind of item that can be an aid in the home or for personal use. It could be that the item is merely 'decorated' or printed to suggest association, or they may have ventured a little further and produced something that looks like a racket, a tennis post or a ball, but is fact used to contain, clip, hold, fasten, or even draw. The type of things that turn up are sometimes very surprising, and the collector should be prepared for absolutely anything to relate to racket sports in some way. If you have previously thought that you would never see cocktail sticks, cigar cutters, a long case clock, a letter rack, or a propelling pencil, then you have a surprise in store! Some delightful, very good quality, but very unusual items can be found, so take a look at everything just in case.

Fig. 6.138. **A Longcase Clock by Thomas Pyke, Bridgwater**[25]
A magnificent eight-day longcase clock, showing an extremely rare automaton scene of two people hitting a ball backwards and forwards to each other. The unusual square brass dial has illustrations of the four seasons engraved into the corners. Engraved within a ribbon motif in the centre are the words: 'Thomas Pyke, Bridgwater'. Pyke was from a family of bellfounders in Somerset. The twelve inch brass breakarch dial has Roman hour and Arabic minute numerals, a seconds ring below twelve o'clock, a half-moon date aperture, and contemporary blue steel hands. Within the arch is a wonderfully painted scene showing a gentleman and lady hitting a ball to each other. (The ball passes to and fro, as if they are counting the seconds as they pass.) The mahogany case has a swan neck pediment, supported by fluted columns which are in turn surmounted with brass Corinthian capitals. It is believed by Wimbledon Museum that the scene might possibly show a game of 'Field Tennis' in progress. (c.1790-1830) Height 217.0 cms. Width 52.0 cms. Depth 28.0 cms. £10000-12000 ($15000-18000)

Fig. 6.139. **A Silver Napkin Clip**
A very rare and fine silver napkin clip, with a moveable collar. Based upon the style of a square-headed flat top racket with a banding around the base of the 'head'. The clip has a registration diamond stamped onto the back of the collar. Apparently, the 'hook' was placed inside the buttonhole of a shirt or blouse and the napkin eased between the two rackets, then the collar was pushed towards the racket head tightening the grip on the napkin. Frustratingly, the registration numbers are difficult to read because it is stamped across a joint in the collar. It suggests that the design was registered on 3rd July 1876, but the specific year is in doubt. The presence of a registration diamond, however, does prove that the design is pre-1883. Length 4.9 cms. Width 1.2 cms. £250-300 ($365-450)

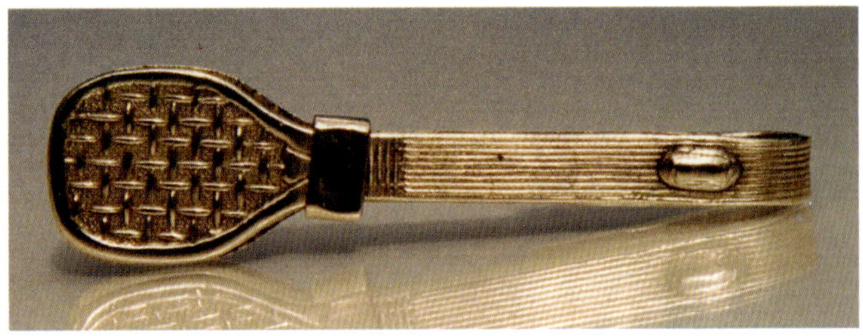

Fig. 6.140. **A Lop-Sided Silver Racket Pencil**
A fine and early pencil designed as a lawn tennis racket. Even the screws in the wedge, the stringing pattern around the frame, and the leather band at the end of the handle are represented. It has a silver registration mark for 1879 and is also marked: '& Co. N. Y.' The pencil is fitted with a pin and a safety catch too. Retracted Length 6.6 cms. Width 1.8 cms. £500-700 ($750-1000)

Fig. 6.141. **A Silver Tennis Stick Pin**
A Victorian gold and silver 'Tennis' stick pin by Edwin Umfreville of Birmingham in 1879. Length 4.0 cms. Width 1.5 cms. £260-300 ($390-450)

Fig. 6.142. **A Silver Racket Pencil**
An exceptionally fine rose gold (9ct.) racket pencil by S. Mordan and Co. with a lop-sided head and gold stringing. (c. 1880) Length 7.0 cms. Width 2.0 cms. £950-1100 ($1400-1650)

Fig. 6.143. **An Early Set of Six Brass Buttons**
A finely manufactured set of buttons, showing a symmetrical arrangement of two pairs of lop-sided (diagonally strung) rackets, and four balls on a tennis net background. On the back is a very large diamond registration mark, which covers the entire surface of the button. It shows that this design was registered on the 15th. November 1881. Diam. 1.7 cms. £150-200 ($225-300)

Fig. 6.144. **A Silver 'Choker'**
An exceptional Victorian silver 'choker', with a pendant locket, the locket having an embossed lady tennis player (set in gold) playing a game across a net, with trees and a house in the background. The choker chain is light metal with individual links in typical Victorian style. Made in Birmingham by Hardman, Powell & Co. 1882. £350-400 ($475-600)

Fig. 6.146. **A Leather and Brass Book Cover**
A wonderful book cover with an unusual moulded brass panel fixed to the front cover. It shows a mixed doubles match in progress. Notice the tripod-supported ball carrier and the diagonally strung net, which is supported by at least five vertical posts. The inside is lined with grey silk and there's provision for a small pencil. It comes complete with a carrying handle. (c. 1885) £150-200 ($225-300)

Fig. 6.145. **A Silver Bangle**
An early Victorian silver bangle inscribed with a tennis racket amidst floral decorations. It is hall-marked 'Chester 1885.' Diam. 7.0 cms. £250-300 ($375-450)

Fig. 6.147. **A Pair of Glass 'Pendants'**
The pendant is secured within a narrow copper rim. The crossed rackets and balls are moulded into the surface of the glass and are then hand painted. (c. 1885) Diam. 2.1 cms. £30-50 each ($45-75)

Fig. 6.148. **Victorian Bookmarks**
Two rare Victorian bookmarks. The top figure is a large brass item of excellent quality with extremely fine stringing and handle. The blade is thin and delicate. Length 12.0 cms. Width 2.5 cms. £180-250 ($270-375)

The lower marker is silver and again has fine stringing with a flat top racket head. Length 8.0 cms. Width 2.0 cms. Made in Birmingham by L. Spiers in 1886. £300-350 ($450-525)

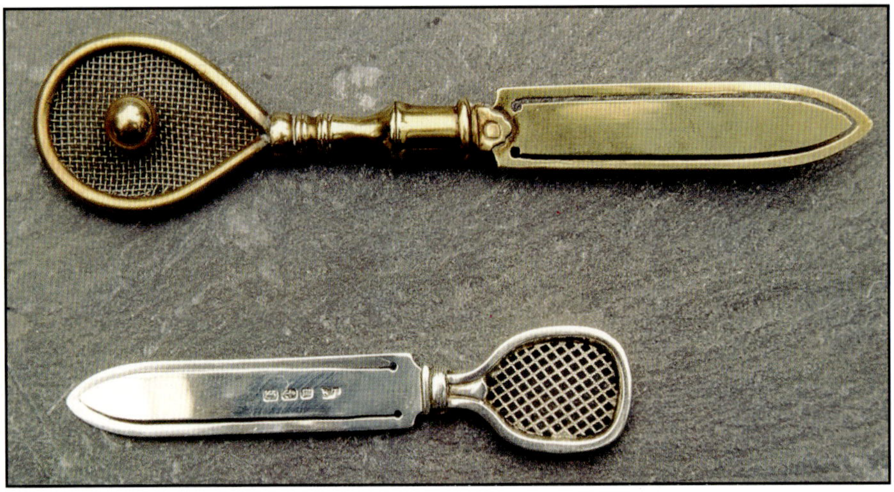

Fig. 6.149. **A Victorian Paper Clip**
A large Victorian bronze metal heart shaped paper clip with a detailed crossed racket and floral design. A very strong spring is attached to the rear plate with the registered mark 74173. (1887) (A similar example is displayed at the Wimbledon Museum shown as a belt clip on a ladies dress!) Height 8.0 cms. Width 7.0 cms. £250-300 ($375-450)

Fig. 6.151. **Victorian Cigar Cutters**
Three Victorian cigar cutters. The one on the left is an ivory-faced racket with a silver blade, which is released by the two tennis balls at the top. It is marked 'Gesetzlich Geschutzt' and is probably German in origin. (c. 1890) Length 5.0 cms. Width 1.5 cms. £250-300 ($375-450)

The cutter in the centre is in the form of a silver flat top racket, with the handle releasing the cutter. The hallmark is for Birmingham in 1888. Length 5.0 cms. Width 2.0 cms. £140-175 ($210- 250)

The third and final cutter is made of brass, and has a pivoted sliding cutting action. There is a registration mark for 1889. Height 5.0 cms. Width 2.0 cms. £95-125 ($135-190)

Fig. 6.150. **A Brass Napkin Clip**
A very rare Victorian brass napkin clip with a moveable collar. The clip is formed as a pair of crossed rackets and ball tied around the handles with a symmetrical bow of ribbon. On the inner surface of the hook there's a registration number which reads 139053, consistent for late 1889. Length 5.2 cms. Width 2.1 cms. £150-200 ($225-300)

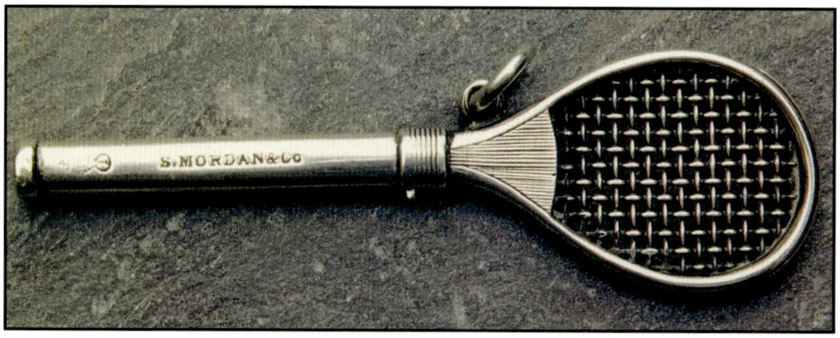

Fig. 6.152. **A Silver Tennis Racket Pencil**[26]
A silver tennis racket pencil by S. Mordan and Co., with fine silver mesh stringing and chased throat decoration. (c. 1890) Length 7.5 cms. Width 2.0 cms. £700-800 ($1000-1200)

Fig. 6.155. **A Belt Attachment**
A brass 'S' shaped attachment for an elasticised tennis belt, showing a snake superimposed with an early lawn tennis racket. The reverse is stamped with a registered number (185042) for the year 1891. Length 5.0 cms. Width 3.2 cms. £50-75 ($75-100)

Fig. 6.153. **A Set of Six Brass Buttons**
Nicely cast buttons showing a scene of two ladies playing tennis over a low net, with a small pet dog in the foreground. (c. 1890) Diam. 1.8 cms. £80-100 ($120-150)

Fig. 6.156. **A Belt Buckle**
An excellent example of a Victorian man's belt buckle. An embossed brass with copper centre boss, showing crossed rackets and balls with a floral surround. They are often marked on the back: 'Martin's Patent'. (c. 1895) Height 4.0 cms. Width 6.0 cms. £80-100 ($120-150)

Fig. 6.154. **'Austrian Tiny' Buttons**
Seven buttons, probably from a set of eight, finely manufactured from brass and base metal, complete with a hoop at the back with which to attach it to a garment. The detail is amazing, with both the frames of the rackets and the shamrocks around the edge being hand coloured. (c. 1890) Diam. 0.9cms. £100-150 ($150-225)

Fig. 6.157. **A Gold Pendant**
An exceptional rose gold racket inscribed presentation pendant, with a fine decorative front having three pearls on the throat and a gold ball with solid string surface. On the rear with the registration and hallmark is the following inscription: 'Presented to Miss A. Butler by members of Morancell Tennis Club and Friends.' The location of this tennis club has not been identified but could possibly be in Ireland. (c. 1900) Length 2.0 cms. Width 1.75 cms. £275-350 ($400-525)

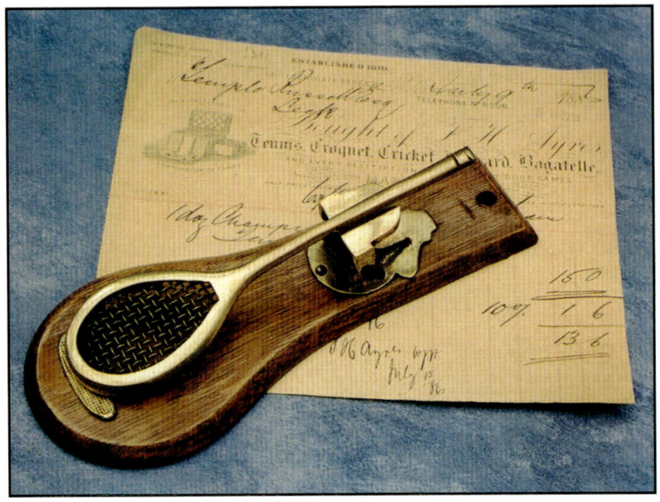

Fig. 6.159. **A Wooden and Brass Paper Clip**
A boldly designed paper clip fixed onto a hardwood base, which can be hung on a wall. (c. 1900) Length 20.9 cms. Width 8.2 cms. £100-150 ($150-225) It is shown sitting on top of an 1886 receipt for one dozen 'Championship' lawn tennis balls from the F. H. Ayres establishment in London (13s.6d.) Frederick Henry Ayres signed the receipt.

Fig. 6.158. **A Gentleman's Pocket Watch**
A wonderful watch with a fine embossed image showing a gentlemans doubles match on the reverse of the case. The image is marked: 'HOLY f r s DEP'. (c. 1900) Diam. 4.6 cms. £150-200 ($225-300)

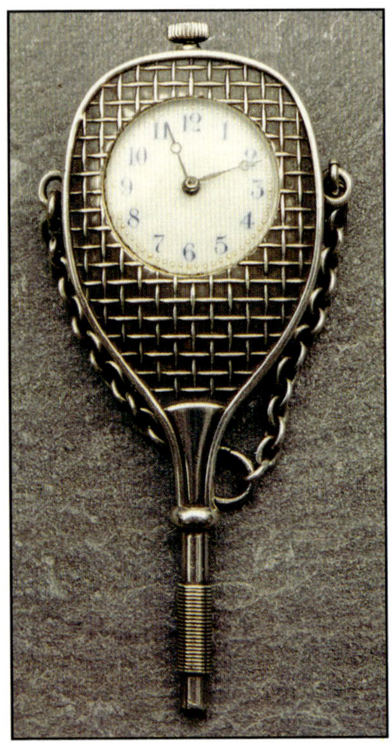

Fig. 6.160. **A Victorian Ladies Dress Watch**
An unusual Victorian sterling silver ladies dress watch with solid stringing and decorative handle and throat, the watch dial having blue numerals and black fingers. The reverse has sterling silver marks and the initials 'N. E.' (c. 1900) Length 8.0 cms. Width 3.0 cms. £275-325 ($400-450)

Fig. 6.161. **A Ladies Coin Case**
A fine, early, ladies sovereign and half-sovereign case. (c. 1900). The fastening device is released by pressing a small lever on the top of the case. The top of the case is stamped in relief with a very detailed scene of a Victorian mixed doubles match. Length 6.6 cms. Width 3.1 cms. £150-200 ($225-300)

Fig. 6.164. **Cuff-Links**
An unusual pair of oval enamelled copper cuff-links (c. 1910) One of them shows a pair of square head lawn tennis rackets with three tennis balls on a white ground, the other an image of a lady player holding her racket, while standing next to the net. Each of them is predominantly green, white, red, and pink in colour. Length (of enamel) 1.6 cms. Width 1.3 cms. £75-100 ($100-150)

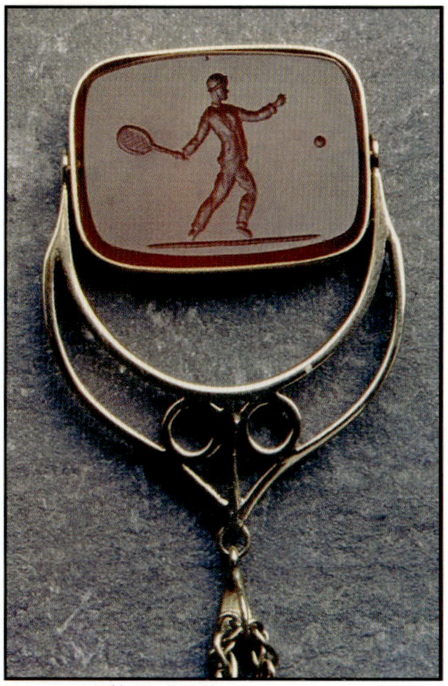

Fig. 6.162. **A Tennis Pendant**
A rare and unusual tennis pendant with a deep amber Cornelian stone setting. Delicately carved into the stone, the design shows a player making a forehand shot. The pendant has a gold chain swivel setting (c. 1910) Height 2.0 cms. Width 3.0 cms. £225-250 ($335-375)

Fig. 6.165. **A Cachous Tin**
A small French Edwardian cachous tin showing a scene (cleverly printed in combinations of only the three colours of red, yellow, and blue) of a lady playing a high forehand stroke. Printed upon the bottom edge of the lid are the words: 'Marque Deposee "FEMINA SPORTS".' Length 4.4 cms. Width 3.8 cms. Depth 1.3 cms. £50-75 ($75-100)

Fig. 6.163. **A Cuff-Link Box**
A round copper cuff-link box with a felt lining and Victorian style crossed brass rackets mounted upon the lid. (c. 1910) Diam. 6.5 cms. Depth 3.4 cms. £100-125 ($150-200)

Top left:
Fig. 6.166. **Decorative Tennis Spoons**
A very fine and detailed silver teaspoon with applied crossed lawn tennis rackets and lawn tennis balls. The base design features a royal crown and engraving on the bowl, which reads: 'C. T. C.' suggests a 'Royal' town, such as Cheltenham. On the reverse, the hallmark reads: 'W. J. D. Birmingham 1924'. Length 12.4 cms. £100-150 ($150-225)

A very similar sugar spoon, the engraving reads: 'L. T. C.' possibly from Leamington. The hallmark shows that 'W. J. D.' made it in Birmingham in 1909. Length 11.3 cms. £100-150 ($150-225)

Bottom left:
Fig. 6.167. **Three Tennis Racket Spoons**
An E. P. N. S. teaspoon with a typical 1920s design lawn tennis racket at the end of the handle. Length 11.7 cms. £30-40 ($45-60)

A very detailed Edwardian silver spoon with a seamed tennis ball placed in the middle of the head and coloured enamel wedge. The detail is very fine, and includes double centre-mains strings as well as binding around the shoulders of the racket. A registered number of 586782 dates the item to 1911, and the hallmark is for Birmingham 1913 by Jones and Stephenson. Length 11.4 cms. £75-100 ($100-150)

An E. P. N. S. teaspoon with crossed rackets and tennis balls as part of an 'Art Deco' design. (c. 1930) The back of the item is engraved 'B. G. S. C.' Length 11.6 cms. £30-40 ($45-60)

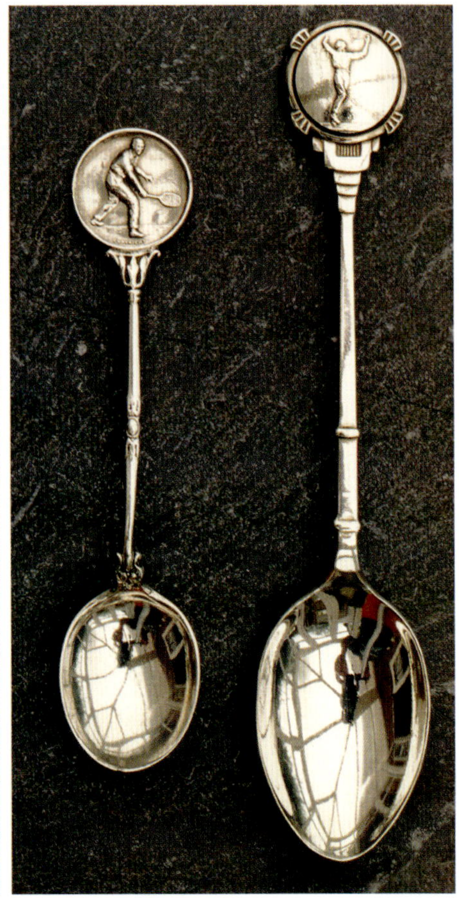

Top right:
Fig. 6.168. **Two Spoons Showing a Gentleman Tennis Player**
A small silver teaspoon, showing a gentleman in long trousers playing a backhand stroke. A hallmark shows that it was made by J.F. of Birmingham in 1927. Length 9.4 cms. £30-40 ($45-60)

An E. P. N. S. tea spoon showing a man playing a service or smash. The spoon has a very strong Art Deco design. (c. 1930) Length 12.5 cms. £20-30 (30-45)

Bottom right:
Fig. 6.169. **Three Tennis Spoons**
A pair of silver spoons engraved "Penns Hall Lawn Tennis Club A.V. Jerome". The hallmark shows the manufacturers were C.B.& S. of Sheffield in 1924. Length 13.9 cms. £30-50 ($45-75)

A silver tennis spoon, showing a scene of a gentleman's singles match. A hallmark indicates that 'RB' of Birmingham made it in 1922. Length 11.2 cms. £20-30 ($30-45)

Top left:
Fig. 6.170. **Three Tennis Spoons**
An electroplated tennis spoon with enamelled scene of lady tennis player. The reverse shows an identification mark of: 'PITCHER E. P. N. S. A1 MELB.', c. 1950. Length 11.7 cms. £10-20 ($15-30)

A silver spoon with a tennis racket engraved into the handle, and 'W. T. C.' on the bowl. C. B. & S. of Sheffield manufactured the spoon in 1937. Length 11.7 cms. £20-30 ($30-45)

An enamelled silver lawn tennis presentation tea spoon. It was presented in 1961 to Mrs. N. S. Wagstaff for her part in achieving the runners-up spot for the county of Surrey in the inter-county hard court championships. Length 11.8 cms. £40-60 ($60-90)

Bottom left:
Fig. 6.171. **Three Decorative Spoons**
A very unusual spoon with the handle design based upon a rectangle, within which a gentleman appears to be hitting a smash. It is marked: 'MADE IN ENGLAND ANCORA EPNS'. (c. 1930) Length 12.4 cms. £30-50 ($45-75)

A finely detailed silver spoon by D. G. C. of Birmingham in 1933. An engraving on the back reads: 'HARRINGAY MIXED DOUBLES CUP RUNNER UP 1933 S. J. B. LOUDEN ESQ.' Length 11.8 cms. £40-60 ($60-90)

Small silver tennis spoon showing two men on a badminton court playing a rally over a high net. The hallmark shows that the spoon was made by R B of Birmingham in 1936. Length 11.8 cms. £20-40 ($30-60)

Top right:
Fig. 6.172. **Two Lady Player Spoons**
A silver spoon by J F of Birmingham in 1921 which shows a lady playing a backhand. On the reverse are engraved the initials B. H. L. T. A. Length 11.5 cms. £30-50 ($45-75)

An E.P.N.S. tea spoon with a 1950s lady (in shorts) playing a backhand. Length 11.5 cms. £20-30 ($30-45)

Bottom right:
Fig. 6.173. **Three 'Racket' Spoons**
A silver spoon with the symbol of a lawn tennis racket moulded into the handle. The reverse shows a shell-like design and the letters J D & S and was made in Sheffield (1935). Length 11.4 cms. £30-50 ($45-75)

A silver lawn tennis spoon with quite an intricate detailed handle design. The bowl is engraved: 'M. S. C. 1937' and a hallmark on the reverse shows that it was made by W. A. of Birmingham in 1937. Length 11.7 cms. £30-50 ($45-75)

An E. P. N. S. teaspoon with a 1950s crossed tennis rackets emblem. Length 11.5 cms. £20-40 ($30-60)

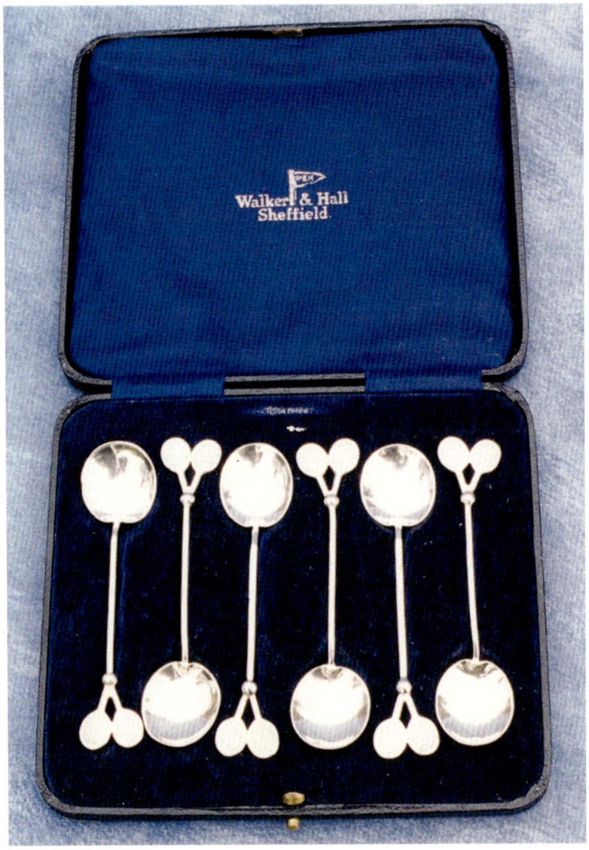

Fig. 6.174. **A Set of Six Silver Spoons**
A set of six silver coffee spoons, each with a pair of small rackets and a ball at the end of the handle. The rackets have solid stringing. The spoons are contained in the original velvet lined leather case, which was made by Walker and Hall of Sheffield. The silver is made by Sanders and McKenzie of Birmingham in 1928. Length 9.0 cms. £200-250 ($300-375)

Fig. 6.176. **A Cigarette Case**
A fine, rare, gentlemen's Art Deco cigarette-case in heavy silver metal. The front is green enamel in Faberge style with the gentleman playing a backhand, enclosed in an oval design which has a slightly darker background. The case opens with a small blue stone on the side to reveal a gold interior. (c. 1925) Height 9.0 cms. Width 7.0 cms. £600-650 ($900-1000)

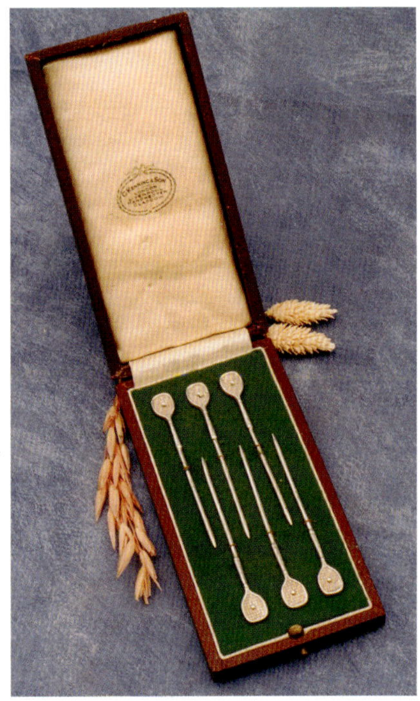

Fig. 6.177. **A Boxed Set of Cocktail Sticks**
All the rackets are marked 'Silver', and the original box is marked: 'G. Kenning and Son, Liverpool, Manchester, Glasgow.' Box Length 15.1 cms. Width 7.7 cms. Depth 2.6 cms. £75-100 ($100-150)

Fig. 6.175. **A Tie Pin**
An intriguing pin, in that it is marked as Swedish 18ct. gold. (Manufactured by J. S. M.) The letters 'K K L T' represent Kronpinsens Lawn Tennis Klubb of Stockholm, Sweden, which was certainly in existence in 1900. (c. 1910) £50-150 ($75-225)

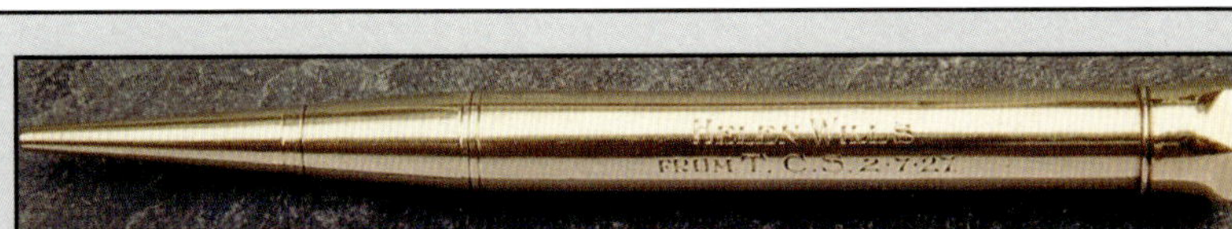

Fig. 6.178. **A Gold Propelling Pencil**
This superb 9ct. gold propelling pencil is inscribed: 'Helen Wills from C. S. 2.7.1927.' The maker is 'Bakers Perm-Point Pencil 144966'. The monogram 'H W' is moulded into the end of the pencil. It was sold at auction in a collection of items belonging to the late Helen Wills Moody Roarke. The inscription date is significant as it commemorates Helen Wills' first Wimbledon singles victory on the 2nd July 1927. Length 11.0 cms. £750-1000 ($1000-1500)

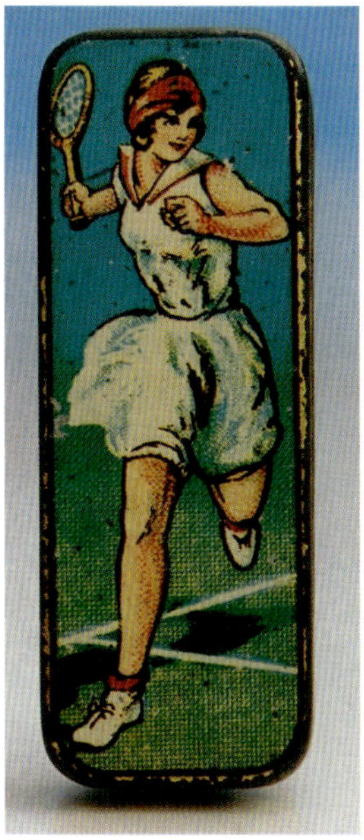

Fig. 6.179. **A Small Tin**
A very small 1930s tin. This must have been manufactured to contain either gramophone needles or cachous. I would choose the latter simply because firstly, despite my meagre knowledge of gramophone needle tins, I would have thought that a manufacturers name would have been an essential detail. Secondly, I know other versions of these tins have also featured images of a boxer and a cricketer. This seems to suggest they were made as a kind of 'collector's set' for children or adults. Length 4.6 cms. Width 1.7 cms. £30-50 (45-75)

Fig. 6.182. **A Pillbox**
A ladies gilt metal pillbox, from the 1950s. The box has a strong sprung hinge, which helps keep the contents from being lost. Length 4.0 cms. Width 3.5 cms. Height 1.3 cms. £40-60 ($60-90)

Fig. 6.180. **A Letter Rack**
A wonderful letter rack from the 1930s, designed as three parallel sets of posts and nets, mounted upon a heavy marble base. Base Length 16.7 cms. Width 9.8 cms. Height 7.2 cms. £100-150 ($150-225)

Fig. 6.181. **A Sewing Case**
A ladies felt sewing case, complete with embroidery silks, metal needle case, and press-stud fastening. The front flap shows an applied white metal figure of a 1930s lady playing tennis. Length 8.3 cms. Width 5.3 cms. £20-40 ($30-60)

Fig. 6.183. **A Selection of Four Tins**
All four tins are printed with illustrations of sporting scenes, one on each side of the tin. All three of the large tins appear to be French in origin but there are no identifying marks. The two similar tins have a panel with people playing the French game of Boule. The example in the centre shows a scene in the identical style of an artist who illustrated a set of postcards in the early 1900s. The small hexagonal tin in the centre foreground is by Taylor Brothers of London. A small panel shows an early game of lawn tennis consistent with a well known etching of Renshaw and Lawford playing for the Championship at Wimbledon in 1881. (c. 1885-1950) Ave. Height 17.0 cms. Ave. Width 12.0 cms. £50-150 ($75-225)

Fig. 6.184. **A Selection of Five Tins**
From left to right: An 'Oxbridge Biscuits' Tin (c. 1985); a 1lb. James Keiller's Toffees Tin (c. 1935); an unidentified 'Battledore & Shuttlecock' tin; a modern tin by The Silver Crane Company (© 1987) containing a facecloth, talcum powder, a headband, wristbands, and a pair of shoe laces; and a modern pencil box. The Keiller's toffee tin is particularly attractive and sought after. Illustrations of sporting equipment are printed around the circumference. Diam. 17.7 cms. £75-120 ($100-180)

Left:
Fig. 6.185. **A Keyring**
A white metal key ring, complete with two 1950s lawn tennis rackets and balls. The ring, which has a press button release, has the word 'ESPANA' as a part of the design, while on the reverse is the monogram: 'PHP' Length 8.3 cms. £40-60 ($60-90)

Right:
Fig. 6.186. **A Paper Clip**
An unusual stamped steel paper clip showing racket and net (c. 1950). Length 4.3 cms. Width 3.5 cms. £20-40 ($30-50)

Fig. 6.188. **A Lawn Tennis Bracelet**
A fine gold Italian lawn tennis bracelet with four tennis rackets included as part of the chain. The item is stamped- 9k 375 Italy. (c. 1970) Racket length 0.8 cms. £50-75 ($75-100)

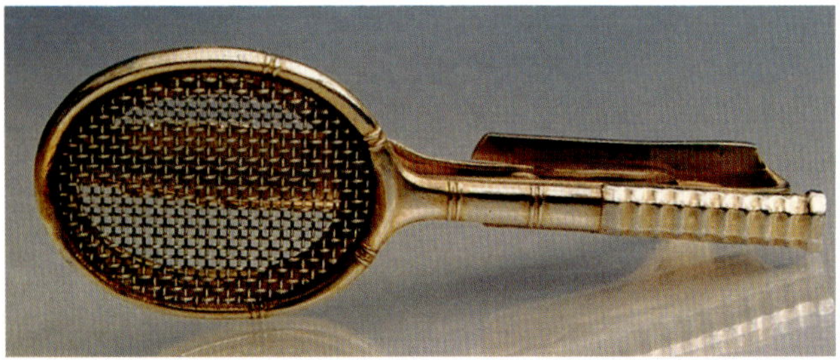

Fig. 6.187. **A Tie Clip**
A gilt metal tie clip, possibly from the 1950s. Length 5.0 cms. Width 1.7 cms. £20-30 ($30-45)

Fig. 6.189. **'Bilston and Battersea', and Crummels Enamels**
An oval Bilston & Battersea "Halcyon Days" enamel trinket box celebrating "Tennis at Wimbledon in Edwardian England," with bronze trimming. (c. 1985) Length 5.3 cms. Width 3.8 cms. Depth 2.6 cms. £50-75 ($75-100)

A Bilston made "Halcyon Days" copper enamelled trinket box trimmed in brass, celebrating "A game of tennis in the 19th. century" showing a Victorian tennis scene, with a brief historic notation (c. 1990). Diam. 5.7 cms. Depth 3.0 cms. £50-75 ($75-100)

A Crummels enamel trinket box, which was made for the All England Club Wimbledon, it shows the entrance to the Centre Court. The box was produced as a limited edition (no. 199) but there is no guide to how many were manufactured. (c. 1985) Length 4.8 cms. Width 4.5 cms. Depth 2.4 cms. £50-75 ($75-100)

Fig. 6.190. **A Money Clip**
A 9ct. gold plated money clip in the shape of a tennis racket (c. 1990). Length 5.2 cms. Width 3.5 cms. £20-30 ($30-45)

Collectors' Glossary

Art Deco: A style which derived its name from the Exposition Internationale des Arts Decoratifs et Industriels Modernes, in Paris (1925). It can be recognised by the use of geometric forms and bright metal surfaces.
Art Nouveau: An original style developed on the European Continent during the late nineteenth century. Art Nouveau takes its influence from the flowing lines of floral and natural forms.
Asymmetrical: In this case, it is usually a term to describe a racket or bat which is not symmetrical in shape. The head of the racket will appear to tilt to one side.
Ball-Tail: The very end of a wooden racket handle which has been turned to resemble a ball.
Battledore: A small wooden bat, sometimes strung, sometimes faced with vellum or parchment, which is used to hit a shuttlecock or a ball.
Binding: When applied to a racket, it refers to the support or decoration which is wound around any part of the frame.
Bisque: A white, unglazed porcelain which has been fired before being glazed.
Blade: The flat wooden part of a table tennis bat which is used to strike the ball.
Brass: An alloy of copper and zinc.
Bronze: An alloy of copper and tin.
Butt End: The very end of the handle of a racket, usually flat, with a disc of leather adhered to it.
Cabinet Card: A photograph mounted on card from the Victorian era. They were introduced in the mid-1860s and measured about four and a half inches by six and a half inches, including the card.
Carte de Visite: Originally invented as illustrated calling cards mounted on card. The approximate size is four by two and a half inches. The cards are Victorian in origin.
Centre-Mains: The vertical strings of a racket; those in the centre were often paired together, passing through the same hole in the frame.
Chromolithograph: A lithographic print made in more than two colours. The artist would supply a separate drawing for each colour, then print them one on top of the other, to effectively combine to produce other colours.
Collar: A band of leather, copper, or even silver which was added to a racket about half way up the frame, and just below the wedge. Most likely used for strengthening and decorating the racket at this point.
Concave Wedge: Usually referring to a hard wood piece which is 'wedged' into the frame of a racket where the head meets the handle. The piece is curved inwards, making a hollow or 'cave' shape.
Convex Wedge: The same as 'Concave' but this time the piece is the opposite in shape, i.e., rising in the centre.
Cut Glass: Glass which has been ground down to a required pattern by using a grindstone equipped with a stone or metal disc. As opposed to moulded or pressed glass, cut glass has very sharp edges to the engraving.
Delftware: Earthenware which has been coated with a lead-glaze, which is made opaque by adding tin ashes. Named after the town in Holland, but also made in England.
Dust Cover: Often a paper wrapping around a book which protects the hard cover from damage or dust.
Electroplate: In this case electroplated silver. A base metal, which is usually but not always copper, coated with a layer of silver by electrolysis.
Enamel: A kind of glass which can be fused to metal or glass with the application of heat.
Engraving: A print obtained by the process of an artist incising lines into a metal plate with a graver.
Fishtail: The very end of a wooden racket handle which has been modelled into a shape resembling that of the tail of a fish. An attempt to forge these handles has been made but, more often than not, a forged example is smaller in diameter than the racket handle, whereas a genuine example is usually not.
Flat-top: The head of a racket which has been deliberately shaped to form a flat or almost flat top to it.
Glaze: The application of a glassy material to porcelain or earthenware.
Halftone: A way of producing a photographic effect by converting a photograph into different sizes and shapes of dots.
Handle Pieces: Two thin pieces of hard or soft wood which are applied to either side of a wooden racket handle, which help make the shape of the handle more round in cross-section.
Head: The part of the frame of a racket which contains all the strings.
Hourglass: Refers to the shape of one of the earliest lawn tennis courts suggested by Walter Clopton Wingfield in 1874. It was narrower at the centre than at the ends and had the appearance of an hourglass.
Jet: A fine black order of lignite, which can be highly polished.
Laterals: The strings of a racket which pass from left to right through the frame.
Lop-sided: Exactly the same as Asymmetrical, when applied to the description of a racket.
Mary Gregory glass: Coloured glass decorated in opaque white enamel, depicting young children in various poses. Mary Gregory was an American glass painter; many pieces are attributed to her but this fact has never been proven. 'In the style of' Mary Gregory.
M. C. C.: Marylebone Cricket Club in London. The Club was founded in 1787 and took a major part in the formation of lawn tennis rules during the 1870s and 1880s.
Milled: Referring to coins and tokens, which have been transversely grooved on the edge.
Monochrome: Meaning anything which is represented with a single colour.
Nap: Referring to the depth or fineness of the cloth material on the surface of a lawn tennis ball.
Obverse: The side of a coin, token, or medal showing the head.
Offset: See Asymmetrical and Lop-sided.
Porcelain: A fine white earthenware first made in China.
pp.: Refers to 'printed pages' in any publication.
Reverse: The back of a coin, token, or medal; the side which doesn't show the head.
Seams, Hand-stitched: Refers to the stitches which hold together the two pieces of Melton cloth on a lawn tennis ball. The seams were eventually bonded to the ball when the process was developed during the mid-1920s.
Shoulders: The part of the frame of a racket on either side and just above the wedge piece. They are often bound to strengthen them.
Shuttlecock: A projectile (designed to be struck with a racket or bat) often in the form of a piece of cork which has been pierced with feathers. The feathers help the projectile fly smoothly through the air, and also slow it down.
Spelter: Impure zinc or base metal.
'Sphairistike': The name given by Walter Wingfield to his racket game which was played in his patented 'Portable Court'. Believed to have been derived from the Greek language, meaning 'Ball Game'.
Stevengraph: A silk picture woven in colours.
Swallow-tail: The end of the handle of a wooden racket which resembles the shape of a swallow's tail.
Trebling: A few rows of lateral strings which have been added to and woven in and out of the vertical strings at the top and bottom of the head. They add strength, and are usually the strings referred to when someone calls rough or smooth to decide who will commence a match.
Verticals: The strings in the head of the racket which pass vertically through the frame.
Woodblock Engraving: Engravings made by first removing the reverse of a required design from the surface of a piece of wood. A tradition started by Thomas Bewick. Many of the illustrations of the 1860s were reproduced by wood engraving.

Endnotes

Chapter 1

1. The chapter on Tennis begins: 'Whereby a perfon who has never feen a Tennis court, may learn in what manner this game is played, the ufual odds, and the method of betting at the fame.'

2. In Tom Todd's *The Tennis Players,* 1977, he lists the surviving copies of Major Wingfield's *'Sphairistike' or Lawn Tennis* (published by Harrisons & Sons, London.) The first five editions take us up to 1876. It appears that once the new rules for 'Lawn Tennis' had been resolved and published by the M. C. C. in May 1878, French and Co. had found themselves (as agents for the inventor) in something of a quandary. The original game (so vigorously promoted by Wingfield as his own invention) was by now so completely out of favour with the public and the tennis authorities that not a single law or specification remained. What were they to do? French and Co. continued to produce lawn tennis equipment. Their original boxed set (of 'Sphairistike') was still available from the Parkins & Gotto store 'by special license of the patentee' (advertisement on the back page) in Oxford Street, London, but had been relegated to third position in importance. French and Company employed the services of a local printer to print a new set of rules (which also served as an advertising leaflet) in accordance with those published by the M. C. C. They decided to use the services of Thomas Vickers Wood, 'bookseller, stationer, bookbinder and music seller' who was to be found just five doors away at number 34 Churton Street.

3. It is interesting to note that the rules of tennis, as they are recorded here, proposed that the winner will be the first to secure fifteen (points), and a point would only be won on one's own service. Scoring in this way was generally abandoned by 1878. One other point is that the new championships at Wimbledon (1877) are not referred to anywhere in the text, rather an unexpected omission from a book which had been published just one year later.

4. Henry Jones was a physician who later became a journalist for *The Field* gentleman's newspaper; he was an authority on the game of whist and other card games, for which he produced several editions of similarly formatted works. He also became Secretary of the All England Club, Wimbledon. He registered a pseudonym 'Cavendish' as a trademark in 1884, and it was he that introduced the game to the All-England Club, and later became the referee for the first Wimbledon Championships in 1877.

5. Thomas Henry Gem (1819 - 1881) was a very keen sportsman. The games of cricket and racquets featured highly in a list of his favourite leisure activities, and he also excelled at running, jumping, and horsemanship. Experiments with a lawn game which took place at 'Fairlight', the home of his friend Mr. J. B. Perera (a merchant), in the late 1860s eventually lead to the game of 'Lawn Tennis or Pelota' being played on the lawns of the Manor Hotel in Leamington, as early as 1872.

6. The author lists the leisure facilities offered by the town to visitors. Under the heading Rackets, Tennis, and Lawn Tennis, he tells us that these games are available at: 'The Racket Court, Middle Street, and the Tennis Court, Little Preston Street, where the Prince Consort was taught the noble game of tennis, and also where lawn tennis is played.' Another heading: 'Croquet Club and Germain's Lawn Tennis' reveals that lawn tennis had been added to the itinerary of the Sussex County Croquet Club, which held its meetings on the lawn of the Pavilion every Tuesday and Friday. This is the only time I have ever discovered evidence of Germain's Lawn Tennis being played anywhere.

7. The author (who according to one source is Captain Rawden Crawley) observed that: 'The introduction of Lawn Tennis into English society is generally, and I think correctly ascribed to Captain Wingfield. But he certainly did not invent it.' It's a pity that there are many lawn tennis authors who have never realised this point! He reminded readers that he too could stake a claim as a visionary. 'As long ago as 1862 I advocated its practice (lawn tennis) in these words: "I see no reason why a space marked off in a field or playground would not as well serve for Tennis as an elaborately furnished and covered gallery. Let players try and make a game for themselves, unencumbered by the restrictive rules which govern this ancient and scientific pastime.".' Included in the book are two rare illustrations, which show the 'hour-glass' shaped court with the very early 'serving diamond'.

8. The 'Field' Lawn Tennis Calendar was first published in 1882 as a six-month review of the early season. Apparently this was then combined with details from the second half of the year and then republished as a single volume later. All the details contained within were originally published in *The 'Field' Gentleman's Magazine* as a part of the weekly tennis report. The book continued to be published until 1891, but is extremely difficult to find. Reverend Walter Frederic Eaton (1841-1916) was educated at Trinity College, Cambridge, and was a priest at Ely, Huntingdon, Retford, Ringwood, and Bournemouth before his retirement in Kent.

9. A smaller Standard edition, with red boards, was also printed in 1885.

10. This book was also published by Wright and Ditson in the USA, with plainer grey covers. A further English edition with hard covers was printed in 1888. James Dwight was one of the earliest American 'stars'; successful at national standard tournaments, he published a further book in 1897 entitled *Practical Lawn Tennis*.

11. A limited edition (of 250 copies), larger format book was also published in 1890.

12. The remainder of the book (thirty-eight pages) gives so much information on Peck and Snyder lawn tennis equipment that it becomes a reference book on its own. Twelve different rackets, two types of tennis ball, thirteen boxed sets and all their contents, eight net and pole sets, and six line markers are just a few of the items featured. For these reasons, little books such as these are very desirable. The inside front cover features testimonials to Peck and Snyder from some of the nation's leading lawn tennis players.

13. There are some small but very interesting differences between the two volumes. In the first edition there's an article concerning an 'Iron Filings Tennis Court(s)'! It involves a description of how a surface should be made up from 'fine ground foundry hards, about one-eighth inch cubes, mixed with fine cast iron borings'. It obviously didn't catch on! It was omitted from the third edition. A fourth edition, also with red decorated boards, was published in 1910.

14. Sir Herbert William Wrangham Wilberforce (1864-1941). Wilberforce was born in Munich, Germany, and was quite an active and successful tennis player in his youth. He became doubles champion of Wimbledon in 1887 with Patrick Bowes-Lyon, was a Cambridge tennis 'blue', and at Wimbledon held the posts of Secretary (1888-91), President (1921-29) and Chairman (1929-36). A barrister by profession, he was knighted in 1931.

15. The incident is quite interesting. When Archibald Palmer was the secretary of The All England Club, it seems that he had organised a circular, signed by many of the days leading players, requesting that Ayres' lawn tennis balls should be replaced by those of Slazengers. In his book *Forty Years of Lawn Tennis* (p44), George Hillyard takes up the story: 'So far as the club was concerned, no fault was to be found with the balls hitherto used; on the contrary, it had every reason to be well satisfied with Ayres in all his dealings … I break no confidence in mentioning that a member of a firm of ball-makers, a perfect stranger, called on me to say that he was contemplating retirement from the business, but longed to put the coping-stone (as he romantically expressed it) on his career by having his goods selected for the Championship. The appeal left me cold, and the decision, had it been in my hands, would have been different.' It is no secret that in 1905, Palmer received and accepted an invitation to join (and become manager of) the firm of Slazengers. In the same year, a scandal arose involving one of the umpires at Wimbledon receiving an envelope containing £100, along with a note from Slazengers (following the umpire's declaration of his disagreement with the use of Slazenger balls). Palmer was still the club's secretary. Eventually, the dispute lead to Palmer's resignation from the AELTC.

16. A further English edition was published in 1932 (87pp.); curiously, it contained only one photograph and is more difficult to find than the original two copies. However, it retains very little of the original style or penache!

17. Beldham and Vaile also produced similarly formatted books on golf and cricket.

18. At least five editions of this book were published.

19. A book which is difficult to find, it covers the History and Science of the propulsion of all kinds of sports ball, including lawn tennis.

20. Francis Russell Burrow was born in Malvern, on January 30th. 1866. He was educated at Harrow and represented Oxford University at lawn tennis against Cambridge in 1888. His profession was that of a barrister and a journalist, later becoming the All-England Club referee from 1919 until 1936. He became well known for an incident at the 1926 Wimbledon Championships when he was the referee. The episode resulted in Suzanne Lenglen playing her last match at the Championships. (See Larry Engelman, *The Goddess and the American Girl,* 1988, p.223-234) Burrow wrote several other books on the game and was a very keen and successful Worcestershire county golfer.

21. This is volume four in a series of seven in the Lawn Tennis Library.

22. In the same year as this publication (1924) an English edition was also published, this time in green boards. Commander George Whiteside Hillyard R. N. was born on February 6th. 1864. In 1901 he beat Laurie Doherty at Wimbledon, and then lost a close match with Arthur Gore, the eventual winner. He was secretary of the All-England Club and the Championship Meeting at Wimbledon from 1907-25. He had also represented both Leicestershire and Middlesex at first class cricket, and toured North America in 1891 and 1894 with Hawke's teams. His wife (formerly Miss Bingley) won the ladies singles championship at Wimbledon six times. He died on 24th March 1943 at Pulborough, Sussex.

23. A particularly interesting chapter is devoted to 'The Development of the Tennis Racket' where the advantages of using a 'Birmal' are examined. The chapter 'Badminton' is preceded by an advertisement for Birmal badminton rackets, which are undoubtedly more difficult to find than their cousin! There's also a chapter on 'Hockey', and before you start to wonder...no, there wasn't a 'Birmal' aluminium hockey stick!

24. Myers was born in Kettering on 24th July 1878, and became a well-known journalist when a special correspondent of the *Daily Telegraph*. As a young man he was particularly successful in doubles tournaments, an experience which served him well when he was finally victorious in both the All-England (1920) and U. S. A (1923) veterans' doubles finals. He was the founder of the International (lawn tennis) Club of Great Britain in 1924, and was awarded Legion of Honour in connection with the I. C. movement in 1932.

25. I had to look up 'Rabelaisianism' and found that it referred to an admirer of the French satirical author Francois Rabelais (c.1494-1553). There you are...now you can use this phrase in everyday conversation with family and friends!

26. This Annual was also published in 1932, 1934, & 1936. I have never seen a 1935 edition, but this doesn't mean that there wasn't one published! All editions were published with dust covers and an advertising bookmark tied and fixed to the inner spine with a green ribbon.

27. E. Latham, commonly known to his friends as 'Emille', was, in fact, Frank Latham, (I suppose Emille could have been his second name) son of the great Peter

Latham. Apparently he presented this book to a friend as a keepsake of their friendship and when Frank died in 1965, his widow donated further associated photographs and press cuttings, which were also acquired by the author. 'Revelstoke' was Lord Revelstoke who was President of The Royal Tennis Court at Hampton Court Palace.

28. The photograph at the bottom right of the dust cover is of the Harrow cricket eleven for 1869. Seated in the centre of the group, with his head bowed down, is none other than Spencer Gore, first winner of the Wimbledon Singles Championship in 1877. A larger and clearer copy of this photograph is to be found inside.

29. A description of the game of Poko from the catalogue enlightens us very little: 'Poko, supplies the long-felt want of a game possessing the advantages of Lawn Tennis without requiring so much space. "Poko" can be played on a lawn half the size required for Tennis, yet the fascination of the paternal game is to be found in its offspring, and although less fatiguing, it requires considerable agility, while the skilful hand and the quick eye is as essential for the new game as for the old.' Sets were available for either two or four players. The larger 'superior quality' set, supplied in a box with rules, cost the princely sum of 40/-.

30. Editions from as early as 1877, covered topics such as the proposal to change the name of the 'All England Croquet Club' to the 'All England Croquet and Lawn Tennis Club'. In a regular column entitled 'The Exchange' readers were invited to submit (under the strictest regulations!) the details of any item they were willing to exchange with one of equal value. The typical index of items was extremely varied, for instance an issue for March 24th included: a Pulvermacher chain battery; a donkey; three Kerry cows and one Kerry Bull; and a Geneva watch. Others included, 'Five best quality (tennis balls) to exchange, double covered kid; one dozen smaller size, wash leather; all new', and a 'Jacque's full-sized set of lawn tennis, with extra net and shuttlecocks, for badminton combined, complete in polished lock box, to exchange to the value of £4.10s. in jewellery.'

Chapter 2

1. Edwin Trim set up his printing business in 1862 at 30 Homefield Road, Wimbledon. He consistently printed photographs of Wimbledon and its players from 1910-35, and copies of these cards are all keenly sought after. Early Trim cards were unnumbered with handwritten competitors names across them. Later, they were alphabetically numbered, but to date no one has been able to work out the sequence. So far there is no reference to Trim being a photographer. – Barry Ordish, *The Tennis Collector* No.32, April 1998 p14-15.

2. Positioned on three sides of the base a circular label reads: ' "Libertyland" Where "Liberty" Bodices are made MARKET HARBOROUGH ENGLAND.' Inside the base the remaining part of a paper label declares the manufacturers as being 'Models (Leicester) Ltd., Factory Street, Loughborough'. The model, which is also coloured on the remaining three sides, was designed for the centre of a display, allowing the possibility of viewing it from any angle. It is consistent with the more common (but still highly sought after) models of the day, which portray chefs or butchers, and is in perfect condition. A photograph of another model has recently come to light showing a thirties tennis lady (in plaster relief on a flat wooden background) advertising "Londonus" Sporty Shorts, and it was made by the same company. Golf collectors will be familiar with the similar figures of "Dunlop man" and "The Silver Queen".

Chapter 3

1. John G. (Gloag) Murdoch established his business in 1863 at 91-93 Farringdon Road, London. He did a prolific trade in musical novelties and photograph albums and imported thousands of movements, many of which were also marked 'Made in France' which were then stamped with his initials. Many albums have movements marked 'J. G. M. & Co., Paris.' and it is known that Murdoch traded with Thibouville - Lamy (q.v.) which bought extensively from French musical-box makers such as L'Epee. - Arthur W. J. G. Ord-Hume –*Musical Box* (1st. ed) 1980, George Allen & Unwin Ltd. London.

2. **Ernest Wool Lewis (1867-1930)**

Lewis was a tremendous first class player. He won the Wimbledon Doubles Championship with H. S. Barlow in 1892 but never quite excelled in the singles competition. He was covered court champion seven times between 1887 and 1896, and won the Irish championships on two occasions. He was a doctor by profession, but had retired before his death.

3. **Carlotte Dod** (24th September 1871 27th June 1960)

Lottie Dod was quite an accomplished all-rounder. Quite apart from winning the Wimbledon Ladies Singles title on five occasions, she also became the Irish Champion. She then turned to golf, at which she was British Women's Champion at Troon in 1904. She was capped twice for England at hockey and won a silver medal at the Olympics in London (1908) at archery. As a skater she passed both the women's and the men's test at St. Moritz and also completed the Cresta Run. She was a mountaineer, rode horses and rowed too. In later years she became a member of the London Oriana Madrigal Society and had a fine contralto voice. In her spare time (if she ever had any!) she played the piano and was quite partial to a game of bridge.

4. An obituary to Herbert Chipp was written in the *Lawn Tennis and Croquet* journal of 2nd September 1903:

'THE LATE MR. HERBERT CHIPP.

We much regret this week to have to record the sudden decease of Mr. Herbert Chipp, whose death took place at Ely on Tuesday week, Aug. 25. Some years ago, it appears, he suffered severely from pleurisy, which left a certain weakness behind, but his health has been good up to quite recently, when about three weeks ago, while staying at Reigate, he met with a serious cycle accident, which resulted in concussion of the brain, and though he had, in the main, recovered from that, it is probable that indirectly it may have paved the way to his sudden and fatal illness. He was taken ill Friday week and was ordered to bed by his medical adviser. No serious results were then anticipated, but the disease developed very rapidly, and early on Tuesday morning he died, the cause of death being laryngitis and pneumonia. Mr. Chipp, who was born in 1850, followed the profession of an artist. While at school he was at first a keen cricketer, and afterwards, in 1878, became a very enthusiastic lawn tennis player. Mr. Chipp's game was essentially one of a base liner, and having the power of playing with both hands he was most deadly in his drives and passing shots. He played his first public match in 1882, when he was defeated by A. J. Stanley in the All Comers', at Wimbledon. In 1884 he made his way into the last four at Wimbledon, beating J. Dwight and W. C. Taylor in the second and third rounds respectively. One of his best performances was his win in 1885 in the Open Singles at Chiswick Park, where he defeated, amongst others, the late H. Grove. In 1886 he was second best to E. L. Williams in the final round of the All Comers' Singles (Covered Court Championship) and won the Kentish All Comers' Championship at Beckenham the same year. He was also likewise a fine player of the double game, one of his favourite partners being E. W. Lewis. These are just a few of the successes and doings of the deceased. Of late years Mr. Chipp has acted as referee and handicapper at many of the principal tournaments throughout England, and has made himself a host of friends in so doing. The deceased gentleman contributed in no small degree to the better making known of lawn tennis, and his "Lawn Tennis Recollections" have been widely read. He acted as Editor of this paper from May 1, 1897, till July 23, 1899, and he was also responsible for a good deal of the articles on lawn tennis in the New Badminton Library. The deceased, who was a member of the Lawn Tennis Association, and likewise on the lawn tennis committee of the Queen's Club, leaves a large circle of friends by whom he will be much regretted. The funeral took place last Friday at Ely. The deceased has left a widow and two children, to whom we beg to offer our sincere sympathy and condolence.'

A further entry in *Lowe's Lawn Tennis Annual o f 1933* reveals more about this early lawn tennis player:

'CHIPP, Herbert; b. 1850, d. Ely, Aug. 25,1903. The first ambidextrous player of note has probably since been unequalled as such except by G. de Stefani. Stronger on the left-hand side, he played entirely from the baseline and the ease with which he controlled and placed his hardest drives made him a very difficult man to volley. Reached singles semi-final at Wimbledon, 1884; won Middlesex championship singles, Chiswick, 1885; second in covered court singles championship, and won Kent championship, Beckenham, 1886, achieved many successes in doubles in partnership with the late E. W. Lewis (q.v.). Was first hon. secretary of the L.T.A. and for many years a leading referee and handicapper at open tournaments. An authoritative and most able writer on the game, he contributed much of value to its literature and was editor of the lawn tennis journal for several years.'

5. Such was the prominence of many of these gentlemen that a list of names is warranted. Mr. F. B. Vanderbyl, Mr. J. F. Marshall, F. Covey, C. Baldwin, Mr. J. R. McClean, W. Webb, C. Lambert, E. Grey, A. White, A. Smith, Mr. E. B. Noel (Amateur Racquet Champion), Mr. E. Brunton, George Lambert (ex-Champion), Tom White, A. Tomkins, F. Forester, C. Feldon, Mr. Jay Gould, E. Lambert, Mr. J. M. Heathcote, Jim Harradine, A. Forester, Mr. R. D. Walker, Mr. H. A. Chapman, Mr. C. D. Rose, Peter Latham (Challenger), C. 'Punch' Fairs (Champion), Mr. Ashworth. A chapter of a book could easily be written about any one of them, and anyone who is interested in further reading should consult Noel and Clark's: *The History of Tennis,* (1924) Oxford University Press.

6. Arthur Wardle is widely recognised as probably the finest English watercolourist of animals, particularly dogs, and his work is sought world-wide by fine art collectors.

7. 'SEM' is a French native who began his career as a caricaturist. His work was published in several satirical journals of the day.

Chapter 4

1. In the British Trademark Journal (1891, p.976) an entry by William Lerro relates to the Dean Trade Mark. It shows that he was trading as Dean, Lerro & Co. Manufacturers of 99, East Street, Walworth, London, and registered the mark on 12th August 1891. Apparently, Lerro and his predecessors had used this mark on measuring tapes for about thirty-four years before 13th August 1875, taking them back to 1841.

2. A Peck and Snyder rules book of 1892 contains a small advertisement for this marker: 'This is a 'Dry Marker' and requires no mixing of material with water to get ready for use. ...put in any powdered material such as marble dust, air-slacked lime, plaster paris or ground plaster...flour &c. ...By using a sprinkler immediately after marking, or marking at eve, before the dew falls, a more permanent result will be obtained.' The original price was $2.00.

3. In the early 1880s, Lunn and Company of Horncastle, Lincolnshire, in England, was one of the premier lawn tennis manufacturers and suppliers. From their retail premises in Berners Street and Oxford Street in London, customers were offered an opportunity to purchase their new line in 'Col. Godfrey's Marking Pins - for preserving court boundaries, 5s. per set' - (*The Field Lawn Tennis Calendar 1884.*) Mr. Greenway was obviously the original patentee, but another advertisement from 1888 shows the intention of the company and the continued success of their product. 'Lunn & Co., Patentees and Sole Manufacturers of Col. Godfrey's Marking Pins' - (The *Post Office Trades Directory* 1888.) This marker is made from a single piece of cast-iron and measures 4 inches long by 4 inches wide. The width of the 'line' (when the pin is pushed into the court) is almost 1 inch, but a more accurate size would be 22.5 mm. Two prongs, which extend from each end of the centerpiece reach 2 inches into the turf.

4. The mansion of Cassiobury stood in an extensive and well-wooded park, through which the river Glade flows. The park is situated near Watford, Hertfordshire, in England. Compared with a nineteenth century coloured etching of the mansion, the artist's impression of the building is extremely accurate, even down to the perspective, which is completely at odds with that which applies to the two racket games in the foreground.

According to the *Red Book of Commerce* (1916), Dean and Son Ltd. were established in the early 1700s. There had been a series of partnership successions, and they were now in the hands of Arthur (Chairman) and Henry Dean (M. D.) Their speciality was children's picture books, but they were also the publishers of *Debrett's Peerage, Baronetage, Knightage and Companionage.*

5. This is a truly classical example of the style of racket, which was used soon after the game became popular. In his book, *Forty Years of First Class Lawn Tennis*, George Hillyard recalls his first encounter with the game of lawn tennis: 'My earliest recollections of lawn tennis are somewhere about the middle 'seventies, ... The rackets were shaped very much like those used in tennis, heads heavily 'cast off' and very small.' (p.2). The playing area presented by the strings is just 47.5 sq. ins. (compare this to the 137 sq. ins. of the Big Bubba Ti racket [Fig. 4.151] of over a century later!) and the centre vertical strings tilt over at an angle of 14° from the vertical. Originally it is quite possible that this racket had a sheepskin covering over most of the length of the handle.

6. Allegedly, this racket was found under the floorboards of a Georgian House in Eaton Square, London. The handle was originally wrapped in a broad band of black silken material, which quickly perished.

7. An English trade directory of 1892 shows that this firm was trading from both 15, Basnett Street, Liverpool and 13 Castle Street and were described as 'Fishing Tackle Manufacturers'. Henry Whitty, (a sports outfitter) was born in 1841 in Liverpool, married Kate Ramsden at Walton-on-hill in 1870, and died at Prescott aged 88 in 1929.

8. There were 'Old England Stores' situated in several of the major cities of Europe.

9. Arnold Lunn & Co. was not listed in trade directories either before 1885 or following 1901, but in between these dates they were retailing from 41 Berniers Street, in London. 'When lawn tennis boomed in the later 1870s the leather and gut workers of the small Lincolnshire town of Horncastle turned to racquet making, but their involvement had declined before the end of the century.' Wright N. R., *Lincolnshire Towns & Industry 1700-1914* (Lincoln 1982).

10. The Company was listed in an English trade directory of 1881 as 'Garden Furniture Manufacturers' of 86 Chiswell Street, Ipswich, Suffolk. By 1893 the company warranted a more substantial entry: 'WRINCH & SONS, St. Lawrence Works, Ipswich. Garden Implement & Chair, Lawn Tennis, Poultry House, Dog Kennel & Wheel & Sack Barrow Manufacturers, Horticultural Builders, & Hot Water Engineers, 57, Holborn Viaduct E. C. London.

11. Stanley Morrison, of 9 Gracechurch Street, London E. C. This racket was advertised in a copy of *Pastime Magazine* in 1888, it cost 7s. 6d. By 1890, the firm's address was listed as 17, Fenchurch Street, but after 1901 I could find no mention of the company. It remains as the only Stanley Morrison racket in existence that I've ever heard of. (I've no doubt that others will come to light soon!)

12. In English trade directories of 1890 and 1894, Henry Hutton was described as a cricket outfitter of 14, Elvet Bridge, Durham.

Chapter 5

1. 1st Baronet (Created 1909) Sir Charles Day Rose, was born 23rd August 1847 and was educated at Rugby School. After serving in the Canadian Militia he became a partner in the banking firm of Morton Rose and Company, and he had homes at 31 St. James Place - London, Hardwick House - Whitchurch, Oxon, and Suffolk House - Newmarket. In 1891 he became a member of the Jockey Club, and was well known as a breeder and owner of racehorses. He was elected Liberal MP for the Newmarket Division of Cambridge from 1903-10 and again in 1911. A keen player of (real) tennis he built his first court at Hardwick House in 1896, with Saunders, Latham, Crawley, and Lyttleton playing 'opening' matches. In 1901 a new court was designed and built (by the celebrated designer Bickley) at Suffolk House in Newmarket. This court was opened with a special challenge match between Peter Latham (who became the professional to Sir Charles) and Cecil 'Punch' Fairs. Rose opened a second court at Hardwick House in 1907, which was still in use by 1924. Other interests included motoring and sailing, and his clubs included "The Turf', 'The Reform', 'White's', and 'Brooks". Sir Charles died on 20th April 1913.

2. They are very reminiscent of the style of Osborne plaques, and a similar, but larger pair (Diam.16.8 cms. unfortunately damaged) sold at an auction in London in 1998 (factory marks – 13 747 and 10 748)

3. 'Derby Dwarfs' have been made since the mid-eighteenth century. Similar pieces to this can be commissioned direct from the factory and will be decorated completely to the wishes of the customer. Each dwarf is entirely decorated by hand, and each has a completely original 'theme'.

Chapter 6

1. In 1880 the Renshaws made their first appearance at the Fitzwilliam Club in Dublin. Willie won the singles, thus forestalling by a year his first victory in the English event at Wimbledon. The doubles, however, went to H. F. Lawford and R. J. Mulholland. The defeat of the famous Renshaw brothers was so highly regarded that the Committee presented specially designed belt buckles to the successful pair. – *Fitzwilliam's First Fifty Years.*

2. A report in *The American Cricketer* (Vol. VI. No.212 p.216) which reviewed 'THE LAWN TENNIS SEASON OF 1883' took a retrospective look at this tournament: 'Following close upon the meeting at Hoboken, a tournament took place on the Young America Cricket Club grounds, near Philadelphia, under the auspices of that club, the Merion, Germantown, and Philadelphia clubs. It was called the 'All Philadelphia' tournament, and it seemed to be generally assumed that it was to be that and nothing else, for only two outsiders appeared to represent the rest of the world. The results were 'All Clark,' the elder brother beating the younger in the final of the singles, and the pair of them carrying off the doubles.'

In a contribution to the *History of Philadelphia Tennis 1875-1995* Frank Phelps wrote an informative article concerning Clark: 'Clarence Monroe Clark (1859-1937) led pioneer players in founding the United States National Lawn Tennis Association during early 1881 and, as its first secretary and treasurer, helped guide it through its initial year. At the Newport (RI) Casino that summer he won the first U S N L T A doubles championship in partnership with Fred Taylor, his future brother-in-law, subsequently famous as 'the father of scientific management.' A year later Clark reached the final of the U S N L T A singles and, in 1883, he and his brother Joseph Sill Clark became the first Americans to play at Wimbledon where they lost two challenge matches to the English champions, the Renshaw twins, Willie and Ernest. 100 years later Clarence gained election to the International Tennis Hall of Fame, 28 years after brother Joe attained that honour.'

3. The inaugural Cheltenham Lawn Tennis Club (Open) Tournament commenced on Tuesday 7th October 1879, and saw the first public appearance of the Renshaw brothers. (For further information see *The Tennis Collector* no.30, p.8 August 1997.) The final tie was recorded in the *Pastime* magazine of 1884: 'Capt. Wood and Mr. Sweet defeated the Americans - Messrs. Sears and Dwight - (the reigning American national champions) after a five set match, by three sets to two.' Charles Lacy Sweet was born on 24th January 1861 and was twenty-three years old when he and his partner won this trophy. A member of Maida Vale and Clifton lawn tennis clubs he was listed as secretary for the latter club in 1883. He was a prominent competitor in many of the major tournaments, including those at Bath, The Fitzwilliam Club, Exmouth, The Northern, and Leamington. I've found two accounts concerning Sweet as a player. The first is from *Lowe's Annual* published in 1936:

'One of the early pioneers of the game, and a personal friend of the Renshaws, Lacy Sweet took a prominent part in some of the early Wimbledon meetings, and while on a visit to Cooch Behar one year won the Championship of Southern India. He played Association football for Gloucestershire, and lived at Clifton, Bristol. A solicitor by profession, and a partner in the firm of Sweet and Burroughs.'

In his book *Lawn Tennis Recollections*, Herbert Chipp wrote: 'C. Lacy Sweet, was another fine player. His style was a commanding one, and his game was marked by all round excellence. Possessed of a powerful and accurate overhand service, a severe groundstroke, formidable volleying and smashing powers, and great activity, he ought to have reached the very top of the tree. But from one cause or another he was never able to give that serious and unremitting attention to the game which successful tournament play exacts from its votaries.'

In 1887 Sweet reached the semi-final stage at Wimbledon, but lost in the first round in the two following years. He passed away on 2nd November 1892 at Bristol, aged only thirty-one years. Mr. Charles King Wood R. E. reached the final of the singles at Bath losing to E. de S. Browne in 1884. At Cheltenham he lost in the mixed doubles final to Wilfred Milne and Maud Watson with Miss E. Davies as his partner, this after beating both Sears and Dwight and their partners in earlier rounds. Later that year he was posted to the Sudan. In 1889-90 he saw action in the South Africa Wars including operations at Spion Kop, Pieters Hill, and in the Transvaal. Mentioned in dispatches, he was awarded the Queen's Medal and later the O. B. E., retiring as Lieutenant Colonel.

4. Early records show that the Weybridge tournament had adopted the American draw system. A report in the *"Field" Lawn Tennis Calendar for 1884* (p.10) reports that: 'It was managed on a slight modification of the American principle of all playing all; that is the nineteen players were divided into two groups, one of nine players and one of ten, each player meeting every other player of his own group, and those two players who had won the greatest number of matches in their respective groups playing a match together for the prize. So much satisfaction did this afford to all those who took part in the handicap, that probably all tournaments in the club will in future be carried out on the same plan.'

It was so pervasive that a further comment warrants inclusion. (p.115): 'A large number of spectators watched the various matches. Among the competitors were the secretary and other representatives of neighbouring clubs, who expressed their intention of adopting the Weybridge plan of conducting tournaments for their own clubs.'

Wilfred Milne and E. J. Avory were both very good standard players, if not in the very top class. For instance, quite apart from winning many provincial prizes, Milne had played in the singles competition at Wimbledon as early as 1881 and had also reached the quarter finals on two occasions, one of which was lost to Lacy Sweet, the other to Ernest Renshaw. Milne also reached the all-comers doubles semi-final in 1886 and 1891. Avory too, had reached the quarter final round in 1891, where he was defeated in four sets by the eventual champion, Wilfred Baddeley. In his *Lawn Tennis Recollections* (1899) Herbert Chipp remembered Avory from past encounters: 'Two backcourt players of note were E. J. Avory and F. A. Bowlby. In point of merit there was not much to choose between them. They were both most determined opponents—what is known as "stickers"—stoutly contesting every stroke. It would be difficult to say which was the more persistent, and in this respect I shall not attempt to draw any invidious distinction. Avory played wholly from the base-line—I cannot remember ever to have seen him attempt a volley ... Avory possessed one peculiar stroke—a sort of hooked shot from right to left. This stroke won him many an ace, for it was of a very deceptive nature, his action when making it often leading one to suppose—as in the case of H. S. Stone's somewhat similar stroke—that he was about to play the ball down his own (forehand) line. No sooner, however, had his opponent fallen into the trap than the return would be pulled right across his front, usually alighting near the angle formed by the side and base-lines. He played with a horizontal racket and a somewhat stiff arm, taking the ball near the top of the bound. He was apt to run round the backhand returns. His service was of simple underhand character, very plain and of no great pace. It therefore offered great opportunities to the attacking player of those days, and the wonder was that with such a weak opening stroke Avory was able to hold his own as he did. He possessed a racket, which was a curiosity. It was of very lob-sided shape, was supposed to be coeval with the game, and was to be seen in Tate's workshop every year or two undergoing the process of re-stringing, each time developing a more pronounced bent back and bowed head. One would remark on such occasions, "Mr. Avory's racket being made young again, I see, Tate." "Yes, Sir," would be the reply, accompanied by a smile, "he won't hear of a new one." At last, to the great sorrow of its owner, there came a time when the trusty weapon had to be laid on the shelf, and the order for a replica reluctantly given. Rumour has it that this was never held in the same affection. Avory's style—by no means a taking one—gave the casual observer or a new opponent a very misleading idea of his strength. I well remember such was the case the first time he and I met—at Richmond in 1885 in an inter-club match. My impression, judging from the style of his early returns, was that I had a much weaker player to deal with than he subsequently proved himself to be. Many a good man playing Avory for the first time caught a Tartar in the person of this stonewall exponent of the base-line game—a tough customer indeed. The year W. Baddeley won the Championship for the first time (1891), beating in successive rounds myself, the player under notice, Ernest Renshaw, and J. Pim, the only one besides Pim able to gain a set from him was E. T. Avory.'

5. This was the tournament of the Northern Championships at Manchester in 1889, in which Hillyard and Mahony won by beating the Renshaw brothers by 3 sets to 1.

6. Harold Segerson Mahony (1867-1905), an Irishman born in Edinburgh, Scotland, came to prominence at the Wimbledon Championships in 1896 when he beat the defending champion, Wilfred Baddeley, in the Challenge Round. He held the Irish singles championship in 1898 and Ireland's mixed doubles title (with Miss Charlotte Cooper) in 1895 and 1896, as well as many victories in provincial tournaments throughout his tennis career (too numerous to mention here).

A report on the tournament in *Pastime Magazine* on June 18th, 1890 (p.414) shows us that this bowl valued at £20, was indeed superseded by a 'First Prize Cup valued at £60'. The tennis correspondent observed that: 'While players in the metropolis were bemoaning the inclemency of the weather, the Cheltenham week, with the exception of the Tuesday, on which rain fell so continuously as to stop play altogether, was rendered thoroughly enjoyable by the fine weather which prevailed.' Observing the play of Mahony, he noted that: 'In the final the Irishman was in fine form, and defeated (J.) Baldwin by three sets to one.'

It's interesting to note that this bowl was bought at auction in April 2000, when at least three other prizes secured by Mahony were 'up for grabs'. At the same venue a year previously a 'Very large tray' (160oz.), inscribed: 'Irish Lawn Tennis Championships Mixed Doubles and Runner-up Singles 1895/96' was auctioned and realised £3572 ($5180).

7. The All England Mixed Doubles Championship has a very interesting early history. In his publication *Wimbledon of the North*, David Allaby describes the scene at the first tournament, and how it was established: 'There were about 3,000 spectators at Liverpool on finals day...And the galleries were given more to cheer when the tournament secretary T. C. Kay and Miss Dod were involved in a sizzling mixed final against Ernest Renshaw and Mrs Hillyard. The southern couple won this one, with the Merseyside pair reversing the verdict a year later. It was described in *The Field* as the finest mixed doubles match ever seen. Until 1912, the Northern mixed competition *was* the All-England championship — a coveted title, which produced the first major headache for the newly formed Lawn Tennis Association. The North of England tournament, Scarborough, and the Northern both claimed the right to hold the All-England mixed doubles championship. The new L. T. A. council considered the evidence and, after putting off their decision until the end of the year, found the Manchester organisers had made good their claim.'

Apparently, an unfortunate series of coincidences caused the Northern Club quite a crisis in the mid-1890s: 'Wilfred Baddeley won the men's singles trophy outright in 1896, and at the following Tournament the (Baddeley) brothers took possession of the doubles cup. The mixed doubles trophy had also been claimed outright by Mahony and Gwen Cooper (Mrs. Sterry). Valuable challenge cups had to be replaced at a time when the club owed the bank more than £200.' Tragically, there is evidence from the consignors of this plinth that the original cup may well have been melted down. In a letter from the consignors representative in Europe it was explained that: 'There were no less than three robberies in the London house in a very short space of time and the thieves left most of the plinths.'

James Ernest Renshaw was Wimbledon Singles champion in 1888, and doubles champion (with his brother William Charles) in 1884, 1885, 1886th. 1888, and 1889. He was Irish champion on four occasions and doubles champion four times, again with his brother as partner. Mrs. Hillyard, nee Bingley, was Wimbledon Ladies champion six times, German champion twice, Irish Champion three times, and Welsh champion once, along with five further major doubles successes. Charlotte Dod was victorious at Wimbledon five times, in Ireland once, and won two major doubles titles too. Wilfred Baddeley won the Wimbledon Singles Championship three times and the doubles (with his brother Herbert) four times. He was Irish champion too and he and his brother won a brace of doubles championships. Charlotte Cooper/Sterry was the most persistent and successful of them all. Five Wimbledon Singles, two doubles, two mixed doubles, two Irish singles, four mixed doubles, one Scottish singles, one Olympic Games singles, and one mixed doubles came her way during her lawn tennis career. In Mrs. Lambert Chambers' *Lawn Tennis for Ladies* (1910 p. 116) Mrs. Sterry recalled her victory in the mixed doubles championship at the Northern Championships: 'Another great game will always be imprinted on my memory, and that was in 1894, the first year that the late Mr. H. S. Mahony and I won the All England Mixed Championship. We beat Mrs. Hillyard and Mr. W. Baddeley in the final. The excitement of the onlookers was intense, and never shall I forget the overpowering sensation I felt as we walked, after our win, past the Aigburth Cricket Ground Stand, packed to its limit. How the people clapped and cheered us! It was tremendous.'

8. This trophy was won at the same tournament as the rose bowl (Fig. 6.7). However, the report in *Pastime* clearly states that Grist was the runner-up in this tournament, and not the victor! It may be, of course, that the report is mistaken. We will never know how the information reached the publication and whether or not the reporter or the typesetter was having a particularly bad day. I assume and hope that we can accept that this trophy was indeed valued at £5 as reported!

9. The Eisbahn-Verein auf der Uhlenhorst, (meaning 'owls' hurst [= coppice, wood]) lawn tennis club was formed on 26th October 1888. It was only the second year of the German Championships. The following passage is extracted from the English journal *Pastime Magazine* on September 20th, 1893, p. 184: 'Dr. A.H. Williams, T.H. Horley, and E.A. Rehder, a gentleman who played under the name of 'Reihcrob', were English visitors, but, with the exception of Horley, who obtained second prize in the Hamburg championship, success in the singles competition was not forthcoming. In both the Open and Handicap Doubles, however, Dr. Williams and Horley took the first prize, and the former, with Miss M. Holtz, was also successful in the Mixed Doubles Handicap.'

[A report on the tournament in *Erstes Deutsches Lawn Tennis-Jahrbuch* edited by Baron Robert von Fichard 1894 has Horley's initials as F.K. only]. It confirms that Horley won second prize in the Hamburg championship. Williams and Horley, winners of the doubles, are said to have played together the whole summer; (p. 117) implying that they might have lived in the same town or city.

In a final section of the book titled *L.T. Bits* "extracted from 'English Chat'," a supplement to the German, Berlin-based journal *Spiel und Sport*, there is the following paragraph: '[1893] Dr. Williams and Mr. Horley, who took away something like a round half-dozen of most handsome silver cups between them, will want to come again. Dr. Williams says it certainly is very tempting. Well, we know the Hamburgers, amongst whom they have made a host of friends, hope they will. At the same time, for the sake of progress in German play, we hope they will find the work a great deal tougher next year.'

Williams and Horley are also known for the fact that it was they who donated a prize to be played for at the national championships of Holland. A rare 1895 photograph shows the pair playing doubles at the Leimonias Club in The Hague.

10. The tournament was held under the auspices of the Turnier Club during the Whitsun holidays on May 28th and on the following days. Curt von Wessley was from Prague, Austria, and easily beat the German Schindler 6-3 6-2 6-0 in the final. Mr. Lissner (that's the best way of spelling his name), according to the Berlin directory of 1903, was a merchant, his address at the time being Augsburger Str. 34. As from 1907 he styled himself "Fabrikbesitzer," owner of a factory, and in 1909 his address changed to Augsburger Str. 25. Such remained the case until 1924 when his name disappeared from the directories. There is a photograph taken at the 1903 Pentecostal tournament showing both Eugen Lissner and Curt von Wessley amongst a host of players and officials.

11. In *Sport im Bild*, Vol.III (1897), No. 36, p.602, a writer by the pen name of 'Volley' made a complaint regarding Brooke's handicap, which he thought was far too favourable. He thought that Brooke should have played in the first class rather than the second class handicap where he was victorious. Henry Brooke became a member of the Hamberger Lawn-Tennis Gilde (founded 1900) a later annual report recorded his address as: 'The Novello Works, London W., - Hollen Street, Soho.'

Many thanks to Heiner Gillmeister, for supplying all the information concerning German trophies.

12. Carrick-on-Shannon is a town in County Leitrim, Southern Ireland.

13. The Edgbaston Archery Society was formed at the Botanical Gardens, Birmingham (England), on March 5th, 1860. Croquet made its appearance in 1870 and the Club Minutes record that Sphairistike (a name invented by Walter Wingfield the inventor of a 'portable court' on which to play tennis outdoors) — the game soon became known as lawn tennis and was played at the club as early as 1875.

Lawn tennis was such a success that in March 1877 the club changed its name to 'The Edgbaston Archery and Lawn Tennis Society'. A circular to all members of 1896, written by the secretary, J. Howard Heaton, shows that the competition for the Gentleman's Challenge Cup commenced on Saturday 4th July. This tankard could have been a prize for winning the 'Challenge Cup' but the whereabouts of the club's trophy remains a mystery. Both Heaton and Watson had become Vice-Presidents of the club by 1930.

As far as the Botanical Gardens are concerned, an interesting but bizarre piece of information can be found (under 'Bye-Laws') in an 1893 club publication. It reads: 'Each member of the said Archery and Lawn Tennis Society shall become a member of the Horticultural Society, either in his or her personal capacity, as a subscriber of ten shillings and sixpence annually to the Horticultural Society, or as one of the resident members of the family of a member or shareholder of the said Horticultural Society, in order to entitle him or her to admission to the Horticultural Gardens, and he or she shall be subject to the ordinary conditions and rules of the said Horticultural Society.'

The Edgbaston Archery and Lawn Tennis Society claims to be the oldest lawn tennis club in the world. This claim is substantiated by the earliest minute book, which still exists. Lawn tennis is still played today on six of their original courts, which are kept in magnificent condition.

14. In his book, *Wimbledon, Centre Court of the Game – Final Verdict,* (3rd edit. 1987 p. 17) Max Robertson describes this figure as Frank Hadow. (Winner of the second Wimbledon Championships in 1878.)

15. Edouard Fraisse, sculptor and engraver of medals, was born at Beaune on May 14th. 1880, and died at Paris on September 13th. 1945; he was made a Chevalier de la Legion d'Honneur in 1929. Benezit states that he was known "above all, for compositions inspired by sport." – *Christie's Traditional Sports,* Wednesday 20th August 1997.

16. The combination of bronze and ivory, with the ivory representing exposed flesh and the bronze the clothing, had been well known for generations, but it was not until the 1920s and 1930s – the Art Deco period – that this combination was exploited to the full. Johann Philipp Ferdinand Preiss (born 13th February 1882) is recognised as a leading sculptor in bronze and ivory, and the figures he produced were magnificent works. An important aspect of his work related to sport and his work in this field was based on the German ideals of youth and the so called 'master race', a fact which is particularly evident from the works he produced during the Berlin Olympics in 1936, this figure being an example. – Bryan Catley, *Art Deco and other Figures,* 1978.

17. During the seventeenth century tradesmen's tokens were issued for three of Oxford's tennis court keepers. They were Thomas Burnham, Thomas Wood, and Thomas Butler. These professional racket court keepers (traditionally known as 'paumiers') were qualified to maintain the upkeep of the courts, make balls with which the games were played, string rackets, and teach, as well as 'umpire' the racket games. In his time, Thomas Burnham kept all three of Oxford's courts and became a very prominent citizen of the city during his lifetime. He became a freeman of the city in 1650, was elected a bailiff in 1665, and was a member of the city council. He died on 20th June 1776 and his will was sealed with a circular wax design featuring a tennis racket and his initials.

Thomas Wood also had become a freeman of the city in 1646. His wine bottles were stamped with an image of two tennis players and he was also a dancing master! He died in 1663. A similar token was also issued for Thomas Butler, which had the words 'at Rackit & Ball in Oxford' as part of the design. – *Tennis and Oxford,* Jeremy Potter (1994).

18. On page 237 of Tom Todd's excellent book *The Tennis Players* (Vallancey 1979), a line drawn image shows a man about to serve a lawn tennis ball. A small caption reads: 'British Argosy Braces are Best for Lawn Tennis'. Unfortunately, Todd doesn't tell us where this advertisement came from and there is no reference to it anywhere else in the book.

19. Hendon (or The Hyde Tournament) was regarded as one of the most important English lawn tennis tournaments in the late nineteenth century.

20. The Princes Club formerly of Lennox Gardens moved to Knightsbridge, London, in 1886.

21. The Dean Lawn Tennis and Squash Club (formerly Dean Lawn Tennis Club) was founded in 1884, when six guarantors acquired the lease of ground (Dean Park Crescent) in the heart of Edinburgh. One of the guarantors, W. S. C. Shaw was the man who, in 1890, presented to the club the 'Silver Challenge Cup' for the annual Open Gentlemen's Singles Championship. The club joined the Scottish Lawn Tennis Association (formed in 1895) in 1896.

22. Philip Wyndham Cobbold was born in Hollywells, Ipswich in the county of Suffolk, England on 5th January 1875. He attended Eton school from 1888 until 1893 and during his time there he represented the cricket eleven. He won the single racquets competition in 1892 and the doubles in 1892 and 1893. He represented Cambridge University at both rackets and tennis (from Trinity College). At racquets, he played in the final of the singles matches between the Oxbridge teams in three consecutive years (1894 –96) meeting on each occasion probably the best University rackets player of all time, namely H.K. Foster. A quote from *Fifty Years of Sport – Oxford and Cambridge,* (Vol. 1) recognised his undoubted abilities: ' Mr. Foster made four appearances and won each time. On three occasions he did not lose a game; but once, the first of the three years in which he played Mr. P.W. Cobbold, who was another of those players to whom grace at ball games comes naturally, he lost two games. Mr. Cobbold was indeed unlucky to run up against so great an opponent during his university career. Players of far less class have had easy victories.' He was more successful at (Real) Tennis where he was victorious in the inter-university challenges in both the singles and doubles of 1896. He played and was captain of Suffolk County cricket team (1902-11) as a lower order right-hand batsman, leg break bowler, and fine slip fieldsman. Following his sporting career, he became Mayor of Ipswich, 1910/11, and again in 1933/34. He passed away at Tattingstone, Ipswich on 28th December 1945. His family had direct associations with development of Cobbold's famous brewery and Ipswich Town association football club.

23. Bonham Carter Eveleigh was born in Portsmouth on 6th December 1847 and became well known for his expertise as a tournament referee and handicapper for almost thirty years. As well as being a journalist and later the lawn tennis editor for the *Field*, he was also a very accomplished croquet player, winning the Wimbledon Championships on three occasions. In 1890 he was appointed as referee of the championships at Wimbledon. He died at his home at 'Woodlands', Wimbledon Common, on the morning of Monday 7th March 1910 and was buried at Wimbledon Cemetery.

24. Cyril Gladstone Eames was born at Sydenham in Kent on October 20th. 1890. He won the Junior Singles Championships of Great Britain in 1908 and represented Great Britain in the Davis Cup on five occasions. Throughout his tennis career he won many doubles titles including The Covered Courts Championships of Great Britain and the Hard Courts Championships too. In 1925 (with Crole-Rees) he reached the French Doubles semi-final round. In 1926 Eames retired after being two sets to one and four games to one down against Bunny Austin.

25. It appears that the term "Field Tennis" was first penned by William Hickey in 1767. In his diaries, edited by Peter Quennell in 1978 as *The Memoirs of William Hickey,* he described how he (a boisterous, hard living attorney) and some friends played this game in London: 'In the summer we had another club, which met at the Red House in Battersea Fields, nearly opposite Ranelagh, a retired and pretty spot...This club consisted of some very respectable persons, amongst them were Mr. Powell, of the Pay Office; Mr. Jupp, the East India Company's architect; Mr. Whitehead, a gentleman of independent fortune; King, the celebrated actor; Major Sturt of the Engineers; and others. The game we played was an invention of our own and called field tennis, which afforded noble exercise…The situation of the house, which was close upon the edge of the river, and no public carriage road near it on the land side, rendered it as private as if it had been exclusively our own…' He continued: 'Our regular meetings were two days in each week, when we assembled at one o'clock, at two sat down to dinner...At four our sport commenced, continuing until dark; during the exercise we refreshed ourselves with draughts of cool tankard, and other pleasant beverage. The field, which was of sixteen acres in extent, was kept in as high order, and smooth as a bowling green…Our club consisted of twenty and was always well attended; any member who absented himself, no matter from what cause, on a dub day forfeited half a crown, which was put through a hole made in the lid of a box, kept under lock and key, and opened only once a year, when the amount of forfeits was laid out in an extra dinner at the Red House, generally about 20th December...Besides our regular days, some of the members met every evening during the summer months to have a little field tennis'. The game was obviously very popular for some time, and did not, it seems, contain itself as a regional pastime. A passage in the *Sporting Magazine* (Vol.2 P.371, Sept. 29th, 1793) shows its vitality as an open air game: 'Field Tennis threatens ere long to bowl out cricket. The former game is now patronized by Sir Peter Burrel; the latter has for some time back been given up by Sir Horace Mann' (presumably in favour of Field Tennis) For a longer, more in depth investigation into these clocks, please see the article: 'Automated Field Tennis' by the author. (*The Tennis Collector* No.32, April 1998, p. 8)

26. Samuel Mordan & Co. artisans were widely regarded as high class silversmiths in the late 1800s, particularly as makers of small silver items (not just tennis related) and other wares, which are keenly sought today by collectors worldwide. All their items realise high prices, mainly due to the fine level of craftsmanship.

Bibliography

Many of the references in this book are drawn from the books listed in Chapter One, as often they are in themselves a very good contemporary source of information. Quite apart from any hand written correspondence which may still exist, they are often the only 'primary' source.

Barcellon, Pierre. *Rules and Principles of Tennis.* Translated by Sir Richard Hamilton, Bt. Oxford: Ronaldson Publications, 1987.

Book Building, A Guide for Authors. Atglen, Pennsylvania: Schiffer Publishing, Ltd., 1997.

Bradbury's Book of Hallmarks: Compiled by Frederick Bradbury, F. S. A. Sheffield: J. W. Northend Ltd., 1988.

Caring for Your Collections: The National Committee to save America's Cultural Collections. Edited by Harriet Welchel. New York: Harry N. Abrahams, Inc., Publishers, 1992.

Chipp, Herbert. *Lawn Tennis Recollections.* London: Merritt & Hatcher, Ltd., 1898.

Cigarette Card Values. London: Murray Cards (International) Ltd., 1996.

Connor,Chris. *Postcards, A Collector's Guide.* London: Octopus Publishing Group, 2000.

Debrett's Book of Antiques. Edited and Compiled by Patrick Macnaghten. London: Debrett's Peerage Ltd., 1980.

Fine and Rare Antique Silver from the 17th to early 20th Century. Dorset, Nicholas Shaw Antiques: The Friary Press, 1999.

Fine and Rare Antique Silver from the 17th to early 20th Century. Dorset, Nicholas Shaw Antiques: The Friary Press, 2000.

Ford, Colin and Harrison, Brian. *A Hundred Years Ago Britain in the 1880s in Words and Photographs.* London: The Godfrey Cave Group, 1994.

Holt, Richard. *Sport and The British A Modern History.* Oxford: Oxford University Press, 1992.

Hurst, Derek. *Lawn Tennis, Cigarette and Trade Cards.* 1987.

Jones, Stephen G. *Sport, politics and the working class, Organised labour and sport in interwar Britain.* Manchester: Manchester University Press, 1992.

Little, Alan and Lance Tingay. *Wimbledon Ladies A Centenary Record 1884-1984 The Singles Champions.* Wimbledon, London: The Wimbledon Lawn Tennis Museum, 1984.

Little, Alan. *Maud Watson, The First Wimbledon Lady Champion.* Wimbledon: The Kenneth Ritchie Wimbledon Library, 1983.

_____. *May Sutton, The First Overseas Wimbledon Champion.* Wimbledon: The Kenneth Ritchie Wimbledon Library, 1984.

_____. *Kathleen Godfree, Wimbledon Champion of 1924 and 1926.* Wimbledon: The Kenneth Ritchie Wimbledon Library, 1984.

_____. *St. Leger Goold, A Tale of Two Courts.* Wimbledon: The Kenneth Ritchie Wimbledon Library, 1984.

_____. *Dorothea Chambers, Wimbledon Champion Seven Times.* Wimbledon: The Kenneth Ritchie Wimbledon Library, 1985.

_____. *Lena Rice, The only Irish Wimbledon Lady Champion.* Wimbledon: The Kenneth Ritchie Wimbledon Library, 1985.

_____. *This is Wimbledon, The Official Guide to the Championships.* Wimbledon: The All England Lawn Tennis & Croquet Club, 1987.

_____. *Tennis Fashions, Over 100 Years of Costume Change.* Wimbledon: The Kenneth Ritchie Wimbledon Library, 1993.

Lowerson, John. *Sport and the English middle classes 1870-1914.* Manchester: Manchester University Press, 1993.

Mappin, George. *Electroplated Nickel Silver, Old Sheffield Plate and Close Plate Makers' Marks from 1784.* Cippenham, Berkshire: Foulsham Publishers, 1999.

McCarthy, Tony. *War Games The Story of Sport in World War Two.* London: Queen Anne Press Ltd., 1989.

Pols, Robert. *Dating Old Photographs.* Birmingham: The Federation of Family History Societies (Publications) Ltd., 1995.

Robb, Beverly. *Golfing Novelties.* Atglen, Pennsylvania: Schiffer Publishing, Ltd., 1992.

Sporting Pastimes. Edited by Dorothea Hall. London: Marshall Cavendish Books, 1990.

Strutt, Joseph. *The Sports and Pastimes of the People of England.* A New Edition edited by William Hone. London: Printed for T. T. and J. Tegg, Cheapside, 1833.

The Chicago manual of Style. The University of Chicago Press Ltd., 1993.

The Connoisseur's Handbook of Antique Collecting. Edited by Helena Hayward. London: Book Club Associates, 1969.

The Oxford Companion to Sports & Games. Edited by John Arlott. London: Oxford University Press, 1975.

The Tennis Collector. Edited by Gerald Gurney. Published in the Winter, Spring, and Summer each year, The University of Essex Print Department, December 1987-Winter 2001.

Whitehead, Winifred. *Wimbledon 1885-1965.* Wimbledon: The Shamrock Press Ltd., n.d.

Whitman, Malcolm D. *Tennis Origins and Mysteries.* New York: The Derrydale Press, 1968.

Wingfield, Mary Ann. *Sport and the Artist, Volume 1: Ball Games.* Woodbridge, Suffolk: The Antique Collectors' Club, 1988.

Wisden's Who's Who in Lawn Tennis. Edited by Herbert L. Bourke. London: John Wisden & Co. Ltd., 1917.

Vale, Marcia. *The Gentleman's Recreations, Accomplishments and pastimes of the English gentleman 1580-1630.* Cambridge: D. S. Brewer Ltd., 1977.

Index

US $69.95

9 780764 316470 56995

ISBN: 0-7643-1647-8